A.W.N. PUGIN
Master of Gothic Revival

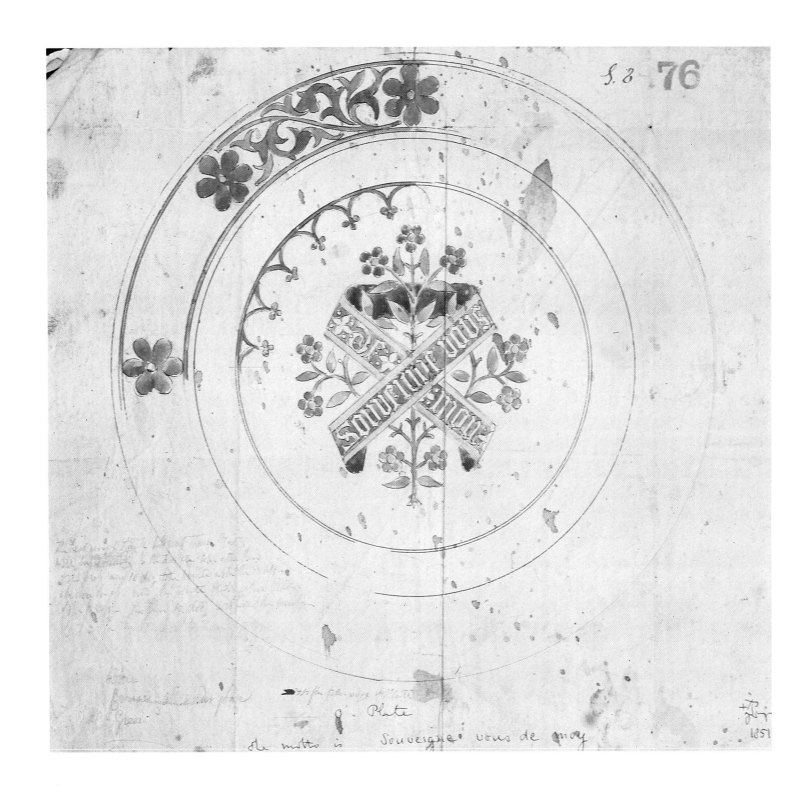

9. Plate

the motto is   Souveigne vous de moy

1851

A.W.N. PUGIN
Master of Gothic Revival

Megan Aldrich
Paul Atterbury
Barry Bergdoll
Margaret Henderson Floyd
Rosemary Hill
David Meara
Roderick O'Donnell
Andrew Saint
Clive Wainwright

Paul Atterbury, Editor

Published for The Bard Graduate Center for Studies in the Decorative Arts, New York,

by Yale University Press, New Haven and London

This catalogue is published in conjunction with the exhibition *A. W. N. Pugin: Master of Gothic Revival* held at The Bard Graduate Center for Studies in the Decorative Arts from November 9, 1995 to February 25, 1996.

Exhibition Curator: Paul Atterbury
Project Coordinator: Nina Stritzler-Levine
Project Assistants: Lisa Arcomano, New York, and Catherine Arbuthnott, London
Project Editors: Martina D'Alton, New York, and Sally Salvesen, London
Designer: Michael Shroyer

Composition by U.S. Lithograph, typographers, New York
Printed in Italy

Library of Congress Catalog number: 95-078296
ISBN: 0-300-06656-2 cloth
        0-300-06657-0 paper

On the cover: Design for Wallpaper (see cat. no. 96), by A. W. N. Pugin; green, black, and maroon body-colors on red-tinted paper. (The Board of Trustees of the Victoria and Albert Museum, London)

Frontispiece: Design for Plate (see cat. no. 114), by A. W. N. Pugin; pencil and watercolor, ca. 1851. (Minton Museum, Royal Doulton Plc)

The martlet-bird motif on the half-title page is adapted from Pugin's heraldic device as seen in tiles at Saint Augustine's, Ramsgate.

Contents

Foreword

Few figures in the history of decorative arts can compare with Augustus Welby Northmore Pugin and his prodigious output as a designer, architect, and theorist. He was singlehandedly responsible for the early nineteenth-century interpretation of medieval art and architectecture that blossomed into the Gothic Revival. His work in this idiom consumed his entire life and left a legacy that was felt internationally.

A. W. N. Pugin: Master of Gothic Revival is the first in a series of Bard Graduate Center exhibitions focusing on individual contributors to the history of decorative arts. Future exhibitions will examine the work of the architect/designers Josef Frank and E. W. Godwin and the artist Alexandre Brongniart. Pugin is indeed a noteworthy beginning. For as significant a figure as he was, he has been studied by only a small coterie of scholars and is surprisingly little known to the general public. Few among the throngs of people who visit the Houses of Parliament in London each year or walk by Saint Patrick's Cathedral in New York City realize that Pugin made important contributions, direct and indirect, to the creation of these great monuments.

Although this is not the first publication on Pugin, it differs substantially from the others

by providing a detailed analysis of 144 selected works that document the formation and flowering of the Puginian Gothic Revival. Thus the reader may glean insight into the intricacies of how, for example, a specific chair, drawing, or wallpaper fits generally into the realization of the Gothic Revival in the early nineteenth century and specifically into Pugin's unique oeuvre.

The primary objective of the exhibition is to examine Pugin's role as a designer in the Gothic Revival idiom. The catalogue picks up where the exhibition leaves off. Through a series of essays, it provides an in-depth exploration of the multifaceted nature of Pugin's career as both architect and designer, of the forces that shaped his remarkable infatuation with the Gothic realm, and of the extent of his influence on the Continent and in North America. The Pugin exhibition and its accompanying catalogue comply with the academic mission of The Bard Graduate Center to enhance scholarship and develop public awareness of the decorative arts.

* * *

I am indebted to James Joll who originally introduced me to the idea of a exhibition focusing on Pugin, a subject for which he has a contagious enthusiasm. James acquainted me with *Pugin: A*

Gothic Passion which was held at the Victoria & Albert Museum in 1994. This event served as the inspiration for The Bard Graduate Center exhibition and established important contacts for us in London that were crucial to the realization of the project. An undertaking of the magnitude of *A. W. N. Pugin: Master of Gothic Revival* could only have reached fruition with the assistance and dedication of a large group of people. Paul Atterbury's curatorial work was integral to its success, and we are thankful for his commitment.

No exhibition is possible without the generosity and commitment of the lenders, and foremost in this regard I am most grateful to Her Majesty Queen Elizabeth II. Loans were also solicited from many institutions both in Great Britain and the United States, and I would like to thank all our lenders: The Palace of Westminster, London; The Board of Trustees of the Victoria & Albert Museum, London; The Roman Catholic Archdiocese of Birmingham; Saint George's Cathedral, Southwark; Erdington Abbey, Birmingham; The Trustees of Ushaw College, Durham; Westminster Cathedral, London; The Minton Museum, Royal Doulton Plc, Stoke-on-Trent; The Lewis Walpole Library, Yale University; The Beinecke Rare Book and Manuscript Library, Yale University; The Art Institute of Chicago; The Brooklyn Museum; The Detroit Institute of Arts; The Carnegie Museum of Art, Pittsburgh; and The Philadelphia Museum of Art. The selection of works in the exhibition was greatly enhanced through the generous loan of objects from private collections as well: Dr. Clive Wainwright, James Joll, J. S. M. Scott, Michael Snodin, The Squire de Lisle, The Family of the Late Michael Pugin Purcell, Mrs. David Houle, Geoffrey Munn, Wartski & Company, Mrs. J. E. Franklin, Mrs. J. Sherliker, Mrs. Mark Guiver, Richard Dennis, James Hervey-Bathurst, Eastnor Castle, Rosemary Hill, Paul Atterbury, and Dr. Stephen Parks.

I am most appreciative of the efforts of the many individuals who undertook the burdensome but important task of contending with the administrative and logistical details of the exhibition loans. In Great Britain this includes: The Most

Reverend Maurice Couve de Murville, Archbishop of Birmingham; Reverend Canon James Pannett, Saint George's Cathedral, Southwark; Reverend T. A. Farrell, Diocesan Treasurer, Archdiocese of Birmingham; Father Patrick Daly, Saint Chads's Cathedral, Birmingham; Father David Oakley, Saint Mary's College, Oscott; Father Peter Stonier, Our Lady, Blackmore Park; Father Bede Walsh, Saint Giles's, Cheadle; Father F. J. Dickinson, Erdington Abbey, Birmingham; Father Tim Dean, Westminster Cathedral; Dr. Jan Rhodes, Librarian, Ushaw College; D. J. K. Walters, Saint Edmund's College, Ware; Mrs. Joan Jones, Curator, The Minton Museum; Ruth Gosling and staff, Archives Department, Birmingham Central Library; Malcolm A. C. Hay, Curator, Works of Art, Palace of Westminster; Sir Geoffrey de Bellaigue, Director, and Miss Caroline Paybody, Loans Officer, the Royal Collection Trust; and Michael Snodin, Susan Lambert, Ann Eatwell, Oliver Watson, Christopher Wilk, and Paul Harrison of the Victoria & Albert Museum, London. In the United States loans were prepared by Father Michael Lankford, Diocese of Trenton; Stephen Parks of the Beinecke Rare Book and Manuscript Library, Yale University Library; Billie Salter, Librarian, The Lewis Walpole Library, Yale University; Ghenetta Zelleke of the Department of European Decorative Arts and Sculpture, The Art Institute of Chicago; Kevin Stayton of The Brooklyn Museum; Alan P. Darr of The Detroit Institute of Arts; Kathryn B. Hiesinger of the Philadephia Museum of Art; and Sarah Nichols of The Carnegie Museum of Art, Pittsburgh. I want to thank British Airways for contributing to the cost of bringing the exhibition couriers to The Bard Graduate Center.

The extensive knowledge and insight of the catalogue authors Megan Aldrich, Paul Atterbury, Barry Bergdoll, Margaret Floyd, Malcolm A. C. Hay, Rosemary Hill, David Meara, Roderick O'Donnell, Andrew Saint, and Clive Wainwright have made this a major scholarly effort that contributes greatly to our understanding of Pugin. This is the first catalogue conceived by The Bard Graduate Center to be published outside the institution, and I want to thank our publisher, Yale University Press, especially John Nicoll, managing director, and Sally Salvesen, project editor, for their belief in the project and for the outstanding collaborative effort that resulted in the production of this book. They worked tirelessly and with marvelous success with our production staff: Martina D'Alton, project editor, and Michael Shroyer, designer. We are grateful to Gloria Dougherty, indexer, Roberta Fineman, proof-reader, and U.S. Lithograph, typographers. The exhibition department of The Bard Graduate Center administered this collaborative effort. Lisa Arcomano was essential to the production of the catalogue, and Nina Stritzler-Levine was responsible for overseeing the project in New York City. At the Bard Graduate Center, Derek Ostergard provided creative assistance in the conception of the catalogue and the exhibition installation. In addition each of the Center's departments played an active role in this project. I would like to thank Linda Hartley and Andrea Morgan of the Development Department; Elaine McHugh and her staff in External Affairs; Tim Mulligan in Public Relations; Lisa Podos and her staff in Public Programs; and Bobbie Xuereb and her staff in the library.

Finally, the important job of coordinating the logistics of the exhibition installation was carried out by Steven Waterman, chief preparator, and the registration of objects by Pat Courtney. Richard Domanic and his staff were responsible for the security and maintenance of the galleries during the four-month run of the exhibition. The dedication and professionalism of everyone involved in A. W. N. *Pugin: Master of Gothic Revival* have made this project not only a success but a great pleasure as well.

Susan Weber Soros
Director, The Bard Graduate Center

Introduction

In 1838 Saint Peter's Church in New York's Chelsea area was completed. It was one of the city's first Gothic Revival buildings. Planned originally by James W. Smith in a conventional Greek Revival style, the church was at the last moment Gothicized, at the instigation of its sponsor, Clement Clarke Moore. The inspiration for the exterior with its tall pinnacled tower seems to have come from the nineteenth-century English Commissioner style of Gothic church, and the model, perhaps seen on a visit to London by Moore, may have been Saint Luke's in London's Chelsea. The Gothic of Saint Peter's is essentially decorative. The external pinnacles may look like stone but were in fact made from carefully shaped and colored sheet metal and had no structural function. Inside, the roof has a dramatic pendant vault, also largely decorative, and the gallery, a fundamentally non-Gothic architectural form, is enriched with elaborate Gothic carving in a broadly late eighteenth-century style.

Two years before New York's Saint Peter's was completed Augustus Welby Northmore Pugin had published his *Contrasts* (1836), a revolutionary book whose outspoken text and polemical illustrations laid down for the first time the design principles that were to establish the genuinely structural and medievally based Gothic, as opposed to the decorative and fanciful Gothic, as the primary style of the nineteenth century. In 1838 Puginian Gothic, with its emphasis on structural integrity, honesty, and the correct use of sources and ornament, was still unknown in New York, and so the city's first Gothic buildings such as Saint Peter's reflected the decorative Gothic language developed in England in the late eighteenth and early nineteenth centuries.

This was all soon to change, in New York and the United States as a whole, and by the 1850s the characteristic style of nineteenth-century Gothic had been established by a new generation of architects and designers broadly familiar with the work of Pugin and his followers. Indeed in North America the term *Gothic Revival* is often seen as synonymous with nineteenth-century design. Despite this, Pugin is still a curiously little-known figure in any public sense, partly a result of his early death in 1852 at the age of forty and partly because so many of his ideas, while fundamental to any understanding of the development of taste and style in the nineteenth century, have been adopted and exploited by his followers. In Britain, all major architects and designers working in the latter part of the nineteenth century, up to and including C. F. A. Voysey, along with others in Europe and North America, acknowledged their debt to Pugin, but after that his name virutally disappeared. His ideas simply became part of the broad and undefined design legacy of the nineteenth century.

Pugin was a man of precocious talent and prodigious originality. His short life is a catalogue of astonishing achievement. As an architect he designed cathedrals, churches, colleges, convents, and a wide range of domestic buildings, revolutionary structures that established Gothic as the national style for Britain by linking it firmly to its medieval, and pre-classical, roots. As a designer he masterminded the interiors of the new Palace of Westminster, the most important design commission in Britain's history and in this and other buildings, laid the ground rules for modern concepts of interior design. As an industrial designer Pugin applied his skills to metalwork and jewelry, pottery and tiles, furniture and woodwork, textiles and costume, wallpapers, stonework, stained glass, and typography. He was masterful in his use of color and pattern, and the controlled use of ornament. Above all, his books, with their powerfully expressed ideas and richly engraved or color-printed illustrations, made his design principles and vision of a new Gothic world accessible to a wide audience. He was a major collector and scholar, and a pioneer in the appreciation of objects as diverse as Italian maiolica, medieval ivories and metalwork, and Flemish stained glass. In his Mediaeval Court at the Great Exhibition of the Works of Industry of All Nations, held in 1851, he worked closely with leading industrialists to make Gothic a genuinely universal style.

A. W. N. Pugin: Master of Gothic Revival, in its title and its wide-ranging display of objects designed by or associated with Pugin, places A. W. N. Pugin back in the forefront of nineteenth-century design history. It also gives him an international context, as a figure of dynamic creativity and originality who, albeit indirectly, played a vital role in the development of the Gothic Revival in North America. The inspiration was Pugin: A Gothic Passion, an exhibition held at the Victoria & Albert Museum in London in 1994 and the first major study of Pugin's ideas, work,

and influence since his death in 1852. With its 750 objects and richly colorful setting, the Victoria & Albert exhibition was able to do much to reawaken a broad awareness of Pugin's importance. From the start, The Bard Graduate Center exhibition was planned to be different, in its content and layout and in its presentation of Pugin as a figure whose ideas grow from his eighteenth-century and Regency background via a developing enthusiasm for the art and architecture of the Middle Ages. The exhibition then shows the full maturity of his work in both ecclesiastical and secular fields. The emphasis is deliberately upon Pugin the designer of products and interiors rather than Pugin the architect.

In many ways the most important and certainly the most durable part of the exhibition is its catalogue. It is not only a record of the objects in the exhibition, but through a series of essays it explores many aspects of Pugin's work and influence. Scholars from Britain and the United States have worked together to create a new understanding of the Gothic Revival in general and of Pugin in particular, underlining his role in the development of Gothic Revival as a truly international style in the nineteenth century. I am grateful to Megan Aldrich, Barry Bergdoll, Margaret Henderson Floyd, Rosemary Hill, David Meara, Roderick O'Donnell, Andrew Saint, and Clive Wainwright for their valuable contributions to this catalogue.

This project is the culmination of several years spent in the company of Augustus Welby Northmore Pugin, his ideas and achievements. During this time I have been helped, encouraged, and guided by many people who have been generous with their time and knowledge. These include the lenders to the exhibition, and the many public institutions and private individuals who have in their collections objects designed by or associated with Pugin. I am particularly indebted to the many members of the Pugin family who have always been supportive and enthusiastic. Any study of Pugin and his work is dependent upon the friendship of the Roman Catholic Church in Britain, and it has been a great pleasure for me to have enjoyed the support so freely offered by the Most Reverend Maurice Couve de Murville, Archbishop of Birmingham; Father Patrick Daly, Saint Chad's Cathedral, Birmingham; Father Tim Dean, Westminster Cathedral; Father F. J. Dickinson, Erdington Abbey, Birmingham; the Reverend T. A. Farrell, Diocesan Treasurer, Archdiocese of Birmingham; Father David Oakley, Saint Mary's College, Oscott; Canon James Pannett, Saint George's Cathedral, Southwark; Father Peter Stonier, Our Lady, Blackmore Park, and, last but not least, that great Pugin enthusiast, Father Bede Walsh, Saint Giles's, Cheadle. Particular thanks are also due to Dennis Hall; Malcolm A. C. Hay, Curator, Works of Art, Palace of Westminster; Ruth Gosling and the staff of the Archives Department, Birmingham Central Library; Mrs. Joan Jones, Curator, Minton Museum; Father Michael Lankford, Diocese of Trenton, New Jersey; Dr. Jan Rhodes, Librarian, Ushaw College; D. J. K. Walters, Saint Edmund's College, Ware; and the many members of the staff of the Victoria & Albert Museum, London, who have facilitated my exploration of Pugin's life and work.

I should like to offer my personal thanks to those fellow Pugin enthusiasts and friends who have by their help, support, and lasting enthusiasm contributed so much to this project: Rosemary Hill, Graham Miller, Roderick O'Donnell, Stephen Parks, Clive Wainwright, and, most important of all, Alexandra Wedgwood, whose work is the inspiration for and the basis of all modern Pugin studies. My final debt of gratitude is to those in New York without whose dedication neither exhibition nor catalogue could ever have existed: Susan Weber Soros, Derek E. Ostergard, Nina Stritzler-Levine, and Lisa Arcomano of The Bard Graduate Center; and Martina D'Alton, Michael Shroyer, and Steve Waterman.

Paul Atterbury

Fig. 1-1. *View of Fonthill Abbey, Wiltshire*, Charles Wild; watercolor, 1799. Wild based this view on designs exhibited by James Wyatt at the Royal Academy, London, in 1798.

1. Gothic Sensibility: The Early Years of the Gothic Revival

Megan Aldrich

The Ruins of a Monastery arrest the attention . . . . The rich Canopy and other decorations of this venerable spot are objects which cannot fail to produce the most powerful sensations in the minds of the admirers of the piety of our forefathers.

Sir John Soane, 1833[1]

During the Romantic movement, European culture underwent a profound change in terms of its relationship to the past, and in northern European countries the past was signified by Gothic architecture. Victor Hugo, in that quintessential French Romantic novel, *The Hunchback of Notre-Dame* (1830), devoted twenty-five pages to a description of the architecture of fifteenth-century Paris, decrying the destruction of this fabric in his own day. He wrote, "At the rate at which Paris moves it will be renewed every fifty years. Thus, also, the historical meaning of its architecture is daily becoming effaced."[2] At the heart of old Paris, Hugo described Notre-Dame Cathedral (fig. 1-2) as

> a vast symphony in stone . . . the prodigious result of a draught upon the whole resources of an era—in which, upon every stone, is seen displayed, in a hundred varieties, the fancy of the workman disciplined by the genius of the artist— a sort of human creation, in short, mighty and prolific like the Divine Creation, of which it seems to have caught the double character— variety and eternity.[3]

Attitudes to the past in the seventeenth and early eighteenth centuries were of a different nature, where historical monuments were viewed as interesting and worthy of respect but as empirical phenomena to be classified and examined. These attitudes were manifested in the 1707 refounding of the Society of Antiquaries of London, followed by the establishment of other quasi-scientific bodies to study historical remains. This empirical approach gradually gave way during the eighteenth century to a view that, by means of intuition and empathy, a profound understanding, if not an actual re-experiencing, of the past could be achieved. As Horace Walpole, that central figure of the early Gothic Revival, was to write, "How these antique towers and vacant courts chill the suspended soul!"[4]

Sir Walter Scott, the most influential and widely read novelist of the early nineteenth century, noted the power of physical remains from the past to call forth strong emotions. In his preface to an edition of Walpole's *Castle of Otranto* (1764), which he recognized as "the first modern attempt to found a tale of amusing fiction upon the basis of the ancient romances of chivalry," Scott wrote:

> He who, in early youth, has happened to pass a solitary night in one of the few ancient mansions which the fashion of more modern times has left undespoiled of their original furniture, has proba-

Fig. 1-2. *A Fire on the Isle St Louis*, artist unknown; oil on canvas, 1635. (Paris, Musée Carnavalet)

bly experienced, that the gigantic and preposterous figures dimly visible in the defaced tapestry, the remote clang of the distant doors which divide him from living society, the deep darkness which involves the high and fretted roof of the apartment, the dimly-seen pictures of ancient knights, renowned for their valour and perhaps for their crimes, the varied and indistinct sounds which disturb the silent desolation of a half-deserted mansion; and, to crown all, the feeling that carries us back to ages of feudal power and papal superstition, join together to excite a corresponding sensation of supernatural awe, if not of terror.[5]

Scott's own house was, like Walpole's, built in the medieval style and furnished with antique objects of different periods.[6] While sensations of supernatural awe were not the province of any one architectural style, there can be no doubt that the Romantic movement provided a context for those who turned to the medieval rather than the classical past for inspiration, and who sought to find antique objects with strong historical associations with which to furnish their "Gothic" rooms. While antiquarian publications and collecting helped to spark the Gothic Revival early in the eighteenth century, the Romantic movement gave it a context in which to flourish a century later.

The Gothic Revival stands as one of the more remarkable chapters in the history of ideas, for it was founded on the premise that medieval forms of (usually ecclesiastical) architecture could be re-used appropriately within a modern setting. The same argument could be used in defence of classical styles of architecture, with the great difference that classicism had been the established canon of design since the Renaissance, whereas the appearance of Gothic forms signified a challenge to the supremacy of classicism. The Gothic Revival began during the first half of the eighteenth century in Britain with the appearance of Gothic architectural ornaments, including fake ruins, in picturesque landscape gardens (fig. 1-3). These were used for their novelty, variety, and qualities of association with the distant past, for it was recognized at the time that the monuments of British antiquity were chiefly Gothic, rather than classical.[7] From landscape garden architecture, the use of Gothic spread to house architecture by the mid-eighteenth century. Designs for Gothic interiors and Gothic furniture began to appear shortly afterward, as is demonstrated by pattern books of the 1750s, when the revival was truly under way.

Much of the credit for establishing the Gothic as a worthy alternative to classicism can be given to Horace Walpole, the son of the great Prime Minister, Sir Robert. Walpole grew up in a Palladian mansion designed by William Kent, and he was well aware of the interest this Italian-trained architect and designer had in the medieval period. In 1730, for example, Kent had been paid by the royal household for painting three scenes from English medieval history.[8] Certainly, Kent and his contemporaries associated the Gothic style with the medieval origins of British civil liberties, a link made explicit by the construction of a Gothic Temple to Liberty in 1741 in the gardens of Stowe House, Buckinghamshire, by the architect James Gibbs.[9]

However, there was a more direct source of Gothic influence upon Kent. Because of the excellent connections of his patron, Lord Burlington, Kent received commissions for work at a number of important medieval and Tudor sites, such as Hampton Court, the cathedrals of Gloucester and York, and Westminster Hall.[10] The latter, the Great Hall of the Norman kings, was the principal structure of the rambling, medieval complex of Westminster Palace, London. Kent designed a

Fig. 1-3. Gothic "ruin" at Hagley, Worcestershire, designed by Sanderson Miller, 1748.

Gothic screen for the hall, which relied upon genuine medieval architectural elements such as ogee arches, crocketed pinnacles, and quatrefoils. Horace Walpole, who served as a Member of Parliament from 1741 to 1768, knew of this Gothic reconstruction by Kent.

Of greater interest to Walpole was the house Kent began to design around 1733 for the antiquarian, Henry Pelham, in Esher, Surrey. Pelham was the owner of a fifteenth-century tower surviving from the residence of William Waynflete, Bishop of Winchester, and he engaged Kent to design symmetrical, battlemented wings with Gothic windows to encase the Tudor structure. Esher Place, demolished in 1805, has been described as, "the first major country house of the gothic revival."[11] Walpole visited Esher Place several times in the 1740s, as it had been brought to his attention by his friend and traveling companion, the poet, Thomas Gray, who was also a knowledgeable enthusiast of medieval architecture. Both he and Gray were initially delighted with Esher, for it demonstrated the possibilities of the Gothic as a style for domestic architecture and interiors.[12]

Fig. 1-4. Strawberry Hill, Twickenham, Middlesex, designed by Horace Walpole et al., ca. 1750–90.

Late in the 1740s Walpole had turned his attention to Twickenham, on the south bank of the Thames, as a location for a residence outside London. The area was a fashionable one where many members of the aristocracy had houses, and the proximity of Esher, Hampton Court, and, most immediately, the villa of Alexander Pope, with its landscape garden, appealed to Walpole. He purchased a small house in 1748 which he decided to remodel extensively in the Gothic style. The property became known as Strawberry Hill (fig. 1-4), and it was to be the first completely Gothic house of the revival, having interiors and furnishings as well as the exterior in the Gothic style.

Walpole was well aware of the importance of Strawberry Hill, for he published *A Description of Strawberry Hill* in 1774,[13] and commissioned the architect, John Carter, draftsman to the London Society of Antiquaries, to record the interiors of

the house in a series of watercolors in 1788.[14] This was unprecedented in the history of domestic architecture and reveals Walpole's belief in his interiors as documents in their own right. The development of Walpole's ideas on interiors can be traced to the 1750s and early 1760s, when the principal rooms of Strawberry Hill were created and furnished.[15]

The two most important interiors of the early phase were the Great Parlour (1753–54), where meals were taken (jokingly referred to by Walpole as the Refectory), and the library, which housed his collection of antiquarian books. To assist him in designing his house in a style with which most professional men were unfamiliar, Walpole formed a Committee of Taste, composed of himself; his close friend, John Chute, a gentleman architect; and Richard Bentley, the talented but lazy son of a Cambridge academic. Eventually Walpole and Bentley fell out, and the third seat of the committee was given in 1761 to Thomas Pitt, a gentle-man architect who had been tutored by Thomas Gray.

The Great Parlour (see cat. fig. 4a) illustrates Richard Bentley's fairly free interpretation of Gothic features, which initially pleased Walpole, with its canopied chimneypiece encased in lacelike tracery loosely derived from late French Gothic forms. The chimneypiece was topped by slender crocketed pinnacles, amidst which were displayed ceramic pots. At the far end of the room, as seen in Carter's watercolor, was a striking pair of Gothic style pier-glasses in black and gilt, designed by Walpole; elsewhere was an ebonized side table by Bentley.[16] Opposite the chimneypiece were six ebonized beech chairs with rush seats designed by Bentley under Walpole's direction in 1754 (see cat. no. 4).[17] The high backs of these chairs took the form of a triple lancet window with tracery

of cusped quatrefoils and rosettes. This ground-breaking Gothic furniture was made for Walpole in 1755 by William Hallett, a leading London cabinetmaker, who may also have made the mid-eighteenth-century ebonized pier-glass, console table, and girandole in the Gothic style acquired by John Chute for his own seat, the Vyne, in Hampshire.[18]

It is significant that, when furnishing the Holbein Chamber at Strawberry Hill in 1758–59 (fig. 1-5), Walpole purchased real antique ebony furniture at auction instead of designing contemporary furniture, an idea also followed by Chute at the Vyne (in the ante-chapel). Walpole considered ebony, or ebonized, furniture to be Tudor in origin and hence appropriate to a Gothic style house.[19] Walpole and Gray had seen ebony chairs at Esher and had associated them with Cardinal Wolsey, who had stayed there. The Tudor associa-

Fig. 1-5. *The Holbein Chamber at Strawberry Hill*, John Carter; watercolor, 1788. The impressive three-part screen was designed by Richard Bentley based on a model in Rouen Cathedral. (The Lewis-Walpole Library, Yale University)

Fig. 1-6. *The Library at Strawberry Hill*, John Carter; watercolor, 1788. (The Lewis-Walpole Library, Yale University)

tions of the Holbein Chamber were strong, with copies of Holbein miniatures on the walls and Wolsey's hat hung beside the (contemporary) bed. As an antiquarian interior, the Holbein Chamber represented a considerable advance upon the Great Parlour.

Similarly, in the course of designing the Library (1753–54; fig. 1-6), Walpole eventually rejected the freely interpreted Gothic design by Bentley, with its doubled arcading, in favor of a design by Chute, in this case, the choir screen of the Gothic Cathedral of Saint Paul's in London (fig. 1-7), lost in the Great Fire of 1666. It was carefully adapted from one of the antiquarian volumes Walpole owned. The magnificently detailed illustrations of the cathedral by Wencelas Hollar, published in 1658 in William Dugdale's *History of St. Paul's*, were used by Chute, under the direction

of Walpole, to make highly effective Gothic-style bookcases. Increasingly, Walpole opted for the literal adoption, rather than the interpretation, of medieval sources for the architecture at Strawberry Hill; thereby he set the course for much of the Gothic Revival, where an archaeological impulse was to dominate.

If the fact that Walpole created the first complete house, interiors, and novel of the Gothic Revival were not enough to secure him a place in history, he had one more major contribution to make—namely, recognizing and promoting the talents of the architect, James Wyatt. He recommended Wyatt to his friend and fellow antiquary, Thomas Barratt, in 1783, when Barratt decided to Gothicize his house in Kent, renamed Lee Priory.[20] In addition, Walpole, who used a variety of prominent professional architects during the late work at Strawberry Hill, engaged Wyatt in 1790 to build an office block to a design of 1774 by James Essex in "a collegiate style" of Gothic.[21]

It has been suggested that through the career of James Wyatt the Gothic style was first established as "a major concern of a professional architect."[22] Wyatt, the leading architect of his day, received the important appointment of Surveyor to the Fabric of Westminster Abbey in 1776 when he was just thirty years old, followed by his appointment as Surveyor General and Comptroller of Works for the Crown in 1796. This last marked the pinnacle of his career. Wyatt had first experimented with a rather thin, linear Gothic style in designs of 1776–77 for Sheffield Park, Sussex, the seat of the first Earl Sheffield.[23] In 1785–86 he designed a battlemented seat, Shane Castle, County Meath, Ireland, for the second Lord Conyngham, which was to prove an important source of inspiration to Gothic Revival architects in Ireland. Conyngham had a strong interest in

medieval architecture and engaged the Irish architect, James Murphy, to travel to Portugal in 1788 and prepare a detailed monograph on the famous Gothic abbey at Batalha.[24] *Plans, Elevations, Sections and Views of the Church of Batalha* was published in London in 1795 and set new standards of accuracy and detail in terms of sources for the Gothic Revival.

Conyngham's interest in the architecture of Portugal was echoed by the formidable figure of William Beckford, who had visited Batalha in 1794, returning to England two years later to begin a project he had long dreamed of—the building of what was initially a large Gothic folly in the extensive grounds of his seat, Fonthill, in Wiltshire. Beckford was a great connoisseur and the wealthiest man of his era. The fact that he should engage James Wyatt as the architect for his Gothic "abbey" attests to the status Wyatt had achieved. In 1798 Wyatt exhibited his proposals for Fonthill Abbey in London at the Royal

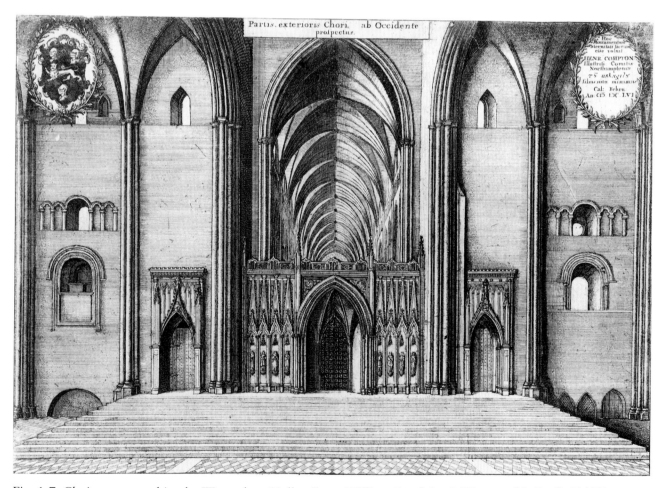

Fig. 1-7. Choir screen; etching by Wenceslaus Hollar. From William Dugdale, *A History of St Paul's* (1658).

Fig. 1-8. Saint Michael's Gallery, Fonthill Abbey. From John Rutter, *Delineations of Fonthill* (1823).

Academy, where they aroused great public interest (see fig. 1-1). Prominent in the design was an octagonal tower with a tremendously tall spire (never executed) resembling the famous medieval example at nearby Salisbury Cathedral. The octagonal tower had been used by Wyatt at Lee Priory and may have been inspired by that at Batalha.[25]

At first Beckford intended his Gothic Abbey to be a grand place of entertainment on the grounds of his father's Palladian mansion. He christened it by means of a party given in December of 1800 in honor of Admiral Nelson, which received attention in the *Gentleman's Magazine*. Nelson's mistress, Lady Hamilton, was present, as was Benjamin West, President of the Royal Academy, to sample the delights of a medieval banquet offered by servants in period dress.[26] Beckford decided to make Fonthill Abbey his principal residence and moved into it in 1807, when a great deal of building work was still in progress. As

time went on, he became more reclusive in his habits, which only served to fuel public interest in the largest and most lavishly furnished house of the Gothic Revival.[27]

Only a fragment of Beckford's legendary "Abbey" remains today, for the central Octagon collapsed during a thunderstorm in 1825, ruining the structural integrity of the building.[28] This was three years after it had been sold due to Beckford's loss of income from shrinking investments in the West Indies. However, owing to the sale of Fonthill Abbey in 1822, public access was gained by more than seven thousand people, and two of the six books published on Fonthill give detailed information concerning the interiors. Uncharacteristically, Beckford cooperated with John Rutter of Shaftesbury, who published *An Illustrated History and Description of Fonthill Abbey* (1823), subsequently retitled *Delineations of Fonthill and Its Abbey*. Rutter's work provided the greatest amount of information on the Fonthill interiors.

The most notable features of Fonthill Abbey were the sheer size of the building, inside and out, and the lavish richness of its principal interiors in terms of their coloring and contents. The central axis of Fonthill, which was asymmetric in plan (in common with Walpole's Strawberry Hill), was formed by two enormously long galleries, one dedicated to Saint Michael (fig. 1-8), pointing to the south, and the other to King Edward, pointing to the north. Like Walpole, Beckford was concerned with concocting a medieval pedigree; he claimed descent from King Edward III. The galleries were joined by means of a central octagon situated beneath the tower. In these galleries were displayed many of Beckford's famous collections of objects, books, and manuscripts.[29] Rutter described the bosses and heraldic emblems on the oak ceiling of King Edward's Gallery, the seven Gothic windows, the stained glass, and the books and antique furniture displayed here, writing, "This gallery has been designed for the purpose of commemorating the names of those individuals of Mr. Beckford's ancestry, who have been honoured with the illustrious knighthood of the Garter,"[30] which had been founded by King Edward III.

Saint Michael's Gallery had a fan-vaulted ceiling derived from the cloister of Gloucester Cathedral, and Rutter described its lavish decoration as "a specimen of the richest combinations, which the genius of gothic architecture has yet invented, beautifully contrasted with the artificial gloom of the opposite gallery, by terminating in an oriel-window of painted glass, exposed to the rays of a meridian sun."[31]

The iconography of the gallery referred to the knights of the Order of Saint Michael, while the lavish color scheme of deep crimson with purple dazzled those who saw it. The poet Samuel Rogers was shown around Fonthill by Beckford himself in 1817, and his reaction to the visit was recorded by a contemporary, Lady Bessborough. She describes Rogers entering through the thirty-foot-high front door, manned by a dwarf in livery (reflecting Beckford's rather acerbic sense of humor), and ascending the stone steps of the stair hall (fig. 1-9). This hall was designed in the Early English Gothic of Salisbury Cathedral, where Wyatt was engaged in controversial restoration work.[32] From the hall Rogers entered the "vast" Octagon with doors of "violet velvet covered over with purple and gold embroidery," leading on to "numberless apartments all fitted up most splendidly." He approached Saint Michael's Gallery, "that surpass'd all the rest from the richness and variety of its ornaments. It seem'd clos'd by a crimson drapery held by a bronze statue, but on Mr. B's stamping and saying, 'Open!' the Statue flew back, and the Gallery was seen, extending 350 feet long."[33]

While Rogers was actually referring to the length of the entire vista created by both galleries and their connecting Octagon, it is nonetheless clear that first-hand experience of the scale and rich decoration of Fonthill Abbey was an overwhelming, if not intimidating, experience for contemporary visitors to the house. Its vast proportions were far removed from the intimate scale of Strawberry Hill; or as Kenneth Clark has observed, "Not before Fonthill was architecture meant to make one's hair stand on end."[34]

Undoubtedly, one factor accounting for the

Fig. 1-9. The stair hall, Fonthill Abbey. From John Rutter, *Delineations of Fonthill and Its Abbey* (1823). James Wyatt drew upon the architecture of nearby Salisbury Cathedral for Fonthill.

intense public interest in Fonthill Abbey was the character of the owner himself. Despite his marriage and fathering two daughters, Beckford preferred his own sex, and this was not publicly accepted in his day. He had traveled abroad in the 1790s to avoid public scandal, and in later years he was known to be a recluse. Indeed, there are a number of parallels to be drawn between William Beckford, the foremost collector and house builder of the Romantic period, and Lord Byron, the foremost English poet of the period. Both men, for example, had a fascination for Islamic culture. Beckford actually published a "Gothic" novel, *Vathek*, begun in 1782, which was set in the medieval Islamic world.[35]

Byron was also fascinated by the medieval world and the clash of Islamic and Christian cultures during the period of the Crusades. Born in 1788, he had grown up in a Gothic house, Newstead Abbey, Nottinghamshire, and was edu-

Fig. 1-10. Examples of Perpendicular Gothic. From Thomas Rickman, *An Attempt to Discriminate the Styles of English Architecture* (4th ed., 1835), pl. 9.

cated in the medieval setting of Trinity College, Cambridge. His literary fame was established with the publication of the first two parts of *Childe Harold's Pilgrimage* in 1812, inspired by his recent Grand Tour.[36] While most eighteenth-century travelers returned to Britain with ideas of classical antiquity, Byron's vision was of the wandering knights of the Middle Ages, whom he considered ordinary beings with all the usual human flaws and shortcomings. "The vows of chivalry were no better kept than any other vows."[37] The profound and melancholic awareness of now-vanished cultures is one of the overriding themes of the poem.

The remainder of *Childe Harold* was not published until 1818, two years after Byron had left England for good under a cloud of scandal regarding his personal life. He traveled with Dr. John Polidori, who had translated Walpole's *Castle of Otranto* into Italian, reaching Geneva late in May 1816, where they joined Percy Shelley and his wife, Mary Godwin Shelley.[38] This party of young Romantics amused each other by recounting ghost stories. One result was Mary

Shelley's novel, *Frankenstein*, published in 1818 and retold ever since, as well as Polidori's *Vampyre* of 1819, based upon ideas of Byron's. Polidori's tale was turned into an opera by the French writer, Charles Nodier, and performed in 1820 at the English Opera House, where it caused a sensation.[39] There was even a German production of the opera.

At Geneva Byron finished *Childe Harold* and wrote *The Prisoner of Chillon* (1816–17), another poem with a medieval setting featuring descriptions of Gothic architecture. His most detailed treatment of medieval architecture was contained in *The Island*, written in Genoa in 1823, in which Byron likened Gothic features to the growth patterns of trees.[40] The following year Byron died of a fever contracted in Missolonghi while defending the cause of Greek liberty from the Turks. His body was not allowed a burial, or even a memorial monument, within the hallowed walls of Westminster Abbey owing to his reputation. However, the news of his premature death sent shock waves through the British national consciousness.[41] In 1825, the year after Byron's death

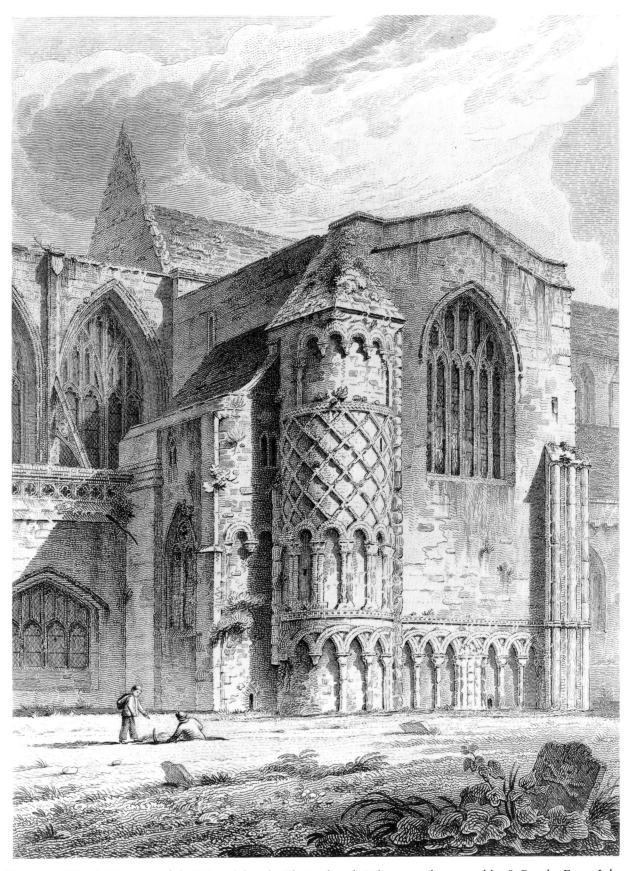

Fig. 1-11. "North Transept of the Priory Church, Christ-church," drawn and engraved by S. Rawle. From John Britton, *The Architectural Antiquities of Great Britain,* vol. 3 (1812). The illustrations give a more picturesque than precise impression of medieval architecture.

Fig. 1-12. "York Cathedral Church: View of the East End," drawn by Frederick Mackenzie, engraving by J. LeKeux. From John Britton, *The Cathedral Antiquities: York* (1819). The clarity of the plates in this series set a new standard for illustrating Gothic architecture.

and twelve years after James Wyatt's death in a carriage accident, the Octagon at Fonthill Abbey collapsed, taking with it most of the building, and the Romantic vision of the medieval world was brought to earth with a crash.

During the 1820s, the Gothic Revival was undergoing a quiet but profound change of direction. Horace Walpole, who had encouraged others, such as J. H. Müntz and James Essex, to publish a history of Gothic architecture,[42] died twenty years before an accurate chronology of medieval styles of building became available. It was formulated by a Quaker accountant in Liverpool, Thomas Rickman, who may have become interested in Gothic architecture while wandering through churchyards mourning the death of his young wife.[43] In 1817 Rickman published a compact text based upon an essay he had written in 1812. It was entitled *An Attempt to Discriminate the Styles of English Architecture* (fig. 1-10) and proved to be the first accurate account of the development of Gothic architecture.[44]

Rickman's little book went through eight editions from 1817 to 1881 and was in continuous use as the standard text on English Gothic architecture until the First World War. He described it as "a text-book for the architectural student . . . . The want of such a work, particularly as it respects the English styles, is generally acknowledged."[45] In it, Rickman suggested the terminology still in use today—namely, Norman, Early English, Decorated, and Perpendicular Gothic. Rickman regretted his lack of opportunity to study medieval buildings in France, for he correctly intuited that this might be the birthplace of Gothic architecture. However, in the fourth edition of *An Attempt* of 1835, Rickman added an appendix "On the Architecture of a part of France," chiefly Picardy and Normandy, where many of the great Gothic cathedrals are found. His visit came five years after the establishment of the Society of Antiquaries of Normandy, under the scholar Arcisse de Caumont, at a time when interest in the great monuments of the French medieval past was burgeoning.

However, if Rickman's text set a new standard in terms of providing a rational system of classification for Gothic architectural features, he himself acknowledged the criticisms of John Britton, the leading publisher of antiquarian volumes, that the book lacked detailed illustrations of real medieval buildings.[46] In his preface to the first edition of the book, Rickman wrote:

> This essay is by no means intended to supersede that more detailed view of English architecture which the subject merits and requires: an undertaking of this nature must necessarily be expensive, from the requisite number of plates, without which it is impossible to give a full view of this interesting subject . . . .[47]

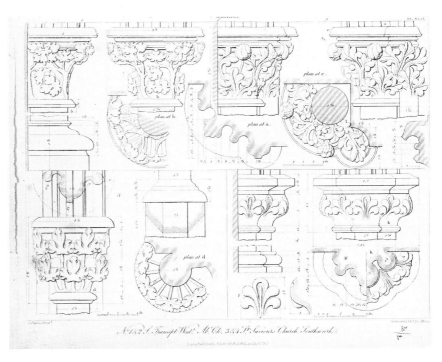

Fig. 1-13. Gothic capitals. From A. C. Pugin, *Specimens of Gothic Architecture* (1825).

In 1841, Rickman was actually preparing a deluxe, richly illustrated version of his book but he did not live to see it published. The preparatory copy contains numerous illustrations in pencil taken directly from the architectural books published by John Britton.[48] Britton was at the center of a commercial publishing operation that demonstrated the intense desire for information on medieval architecture during the first thirty years of the nineteenth century.[49] His two best-known series were *The Architectural Antiquities of Great Britain* (fig. 1-11; published in five volumes between 1807 and 1826); and *The Cathedral Antiquities* (fig. 1-12; fourteen volumes between 1814 and 1835). Britton's text, supplied by various writers, relied upon the terminology and chronology of Gothic architecture worked out by Rickman. However, the primary contribution of these volumes was their excellent illustrations by leading draftsmen such as James Wyatt's nephew Jeffrey Wyatt (who later changed his name to Wyatville), and John Adey Repton.

Other publications also attempted to answer this thirst for detailed, accurate illustrations of Gothic architecture. In 1821–23 John Britton brought out a key sourcebook, *Specimens of Gothic Architecture*, with a descriptive text and glossary by the architect E. J. Willson and meticulous illustrations of Gothic features by Auguste Charles Pugin. The significance of this volume was profound:

> The earlier books of specimens, bent chiefly on showing the sublime and picturesque effects of Gothic, had avoided too great precision of detail. Pugin's book gave sections of every cusping and geometrical measured drawings of every crocket and finial reproduced. Thenceforward Walpole's dream of correct gothic was realisable.[50]

Certainly, the combination of Rickman's accurate text on Gothic and Pugin's detailed illustrations made Walpole's dream realizable.

Auguste Charles Pugin established himself as the foremost architectural draftsman of the Gothic Revival during the 1820s and early 30s,

Fig. 1-14. Windsor Castle, Berkshire; late 19th-century photograph by Henry Taunt showing alterations made in the early 19th century by James Wyatt and Jeffrey Wyatville. These included raising the height of the Round Tower (*right*) to make its silhouette more picturesque.

until his death in 1832.[51] He had been twenty years old at the outbreak of the French Revolution and arrived in London not long afterwards, around 1792, to enroll at the School of the Royal Academy. He found a position as draftsman with the Crown architect, John Nash, during the 1790s, becoming Nash's "specialist" in the Gothic style (fig. 1-13). Pugin then established an office in London for training architectural draftsmen, described by one of his pupils, Benjamin Ferrey, as, "the best school for obtaining a knowledge of Gothic architecture . . . . Accompanied by his pupils he visited different towns for the purpose of sketching and measuring such details of medieval buildings."[52]

In 1825 A. C. Pugin took a group of his pupils to Normandy to sketch, resulting in another key architectural sourcebook, *Specimens of the Architecture of Normandy* (1827–28, published by John Britton). During this visit he met the French antiquaries, E. H. Langlois and Arcisse de Caumont. Ferrey, who was of the Pugin party, recorded the ruinous state of many French monuments they saw.[53] During the Revolution great damage had been done to church architecture, much of which was medieval, as the Church was seen as synonymous with the power of the State. During the Napoleonic period in France the Empire style, a form of Neoclassicism based upon Roman imperial forms, was developed as the Court style of the French emperor. In Continental Europe, the Gothic style became associated with those who wished to distance themselves from Napoleon. It interesting to speculate whether the Gothic had this meaning for A. C. Pugin, as well.[54]

In the same year as the visit to France, another important publication was in preparation. It was to become the first book of design devoted exclusively to furniture in the Gothic style: *Pugin's Gothic Furniture*, published in London in 1827 by Rudolph Ackermann (see cat. no. 20). Ackermann himself was an extremely interesting figure, a German coach designer who trained in Paris and settled in London in 1786. By 1795 he had business premises on the Strand as a publisher and

Fig. 1-15. Examples of "the extravagant style of Modern Gothic." From A. W. N. Pugin, *The True Principles of Pointed or Christian Architecture* (1841).

drawing school master.[55] In 1809 he began an influential monthly magazine, entitled *The Repository of the Arts*, which covered a wide range of topics besides fashion and decorative art.[56] Between 1825 and 1827 A. C. Pugin contributed a series of twenty-seven plates with designs for Gothic furniture which were brought together in one volume in 1827. It seems likely that, in this venture, he may have had assistance from his only child, Augustus Welby Northmore Pugin, who was then training in his office.

Beginning with plate 149, published in the *Repository* in June 1825, A. C. Pugin's Gothic designs demonstrate a meticulous attention to accurate architectural detail that is not found in the few early Gothic designs put forward by Ackermann. These details were culled in part from Pugin's own publications.[57] Admittedly, a number of the furniture forms used were standard Regency Neoclassical types such as the Greek *klismos* or the Roman *triclinium*. However, in terms of the 1820s, Pugin's designs broke new ground and set new standards for the design of Gothic Revival furniture.

A combination of A. C. Pugin's close relationship to the circle of Nash and the Gothic furniture designs published by Ackermann helped to secure a most important commission in 1827 for his precocious son, then fifteen years old. A. W. N. Pugin was invited to design Gothic furniture for the State Rooms at Windsor Castle (fig. 1-14), which was under refurbishment by Jeffrey Wyatville during the years 1825–40.[58] Chief among the resulting furniture is a rosewood and gilt suite of chairs, tables (see cat. fig. 10a), and sideboards with traceried designs and gilt bronze mounts in the form of Gothic rosettes. This superb furniture, which remains in the Royal Collection, was made by the top-quality London cabinetmakers Morel and Seddon for the Windsor State Dining Room and demonstrates the superiority of Pugin father and son to their contemporaries who were designing furniture and fittings in the Gothic style.[59]

His son, Augustus Welby Northmore Pugin, was without question the most important contribution made by A. C. Pugin to the Gothic Revival. In 1835 the younger Pugin offered a revised and "improved" version of Gothic design to the public,[60] followed by what was arguably the most influential book on design of the nineteenth century, *The True Principles of Pointed or Christian Architecture* in 1841.[61] In this impassioned manifesto, A. W. N. Pugin rejected his "enormities" at Windsor Castle of 1827 and, in a plate illustrating the "false principles" of design (fig. 1-15), showed objects closely resembling designs by his father published in Ackermann's *Repository*. With the death of A. C. Pugin in 1832, and the rise to prominence of his remarkable son, the Gothic Revival was about to enter a new dimension.

1. *A New Description of Sir John Soane's Museum*, 7th ed. (London, 1986), p. 31.

2. Victor Hugo, *The Hunchback of Notre-Dame*, Wordsworth Editions (London, 1993), bk. 3, p. 104.

3. Ibid., pp. 81–82.

4. As quoted by Ann Radcliffe in 1791, in Chloe Chard, *The Romance of the Forest* (Oxford, 1986), p. 15.

5. E. F. Bleiler, ed., *Three Gothic Novels* (New York, 1966), pp. 8–9.

6. See Clive Wainwright, *The Romantic Interior: The British Collector at Home, 1750–1850* (New Haven & London, 1989), chaps. 6–7 and 4, respectively.

7. Ibid., p. 5; Horace Walpole resigned from the London Society of Antiquaries in 1738 over this issue.

8. Now in the Royal Collection. See Michael I. Wilson, *William Kent: Architect, Designer, Painter, Gardener, 1688–1748* (London, 1984), p. 148.

9. See Megan Aldrich, *Gothic Revival* (London, 1994), p. 48. This idea is discussed in John Dixon Hunt, *William Kent: Landscape Garden Designer* (London, 1987), p. 57. Stowe was to become the largest Neoclassical country house in Britain, while Gibbs trained in Rome in the Baroque style and published designs that had a great impact on church design in North America in the eighteenth century.

10. The designs for Gloucester, York, and Westminster were published in John Vardy, *Some Designs of Mr Inigo Jones and Mr William Kent* (London, 1744), pls. 49, 51, and 48.

11. John Harris, "William Kent's Gothick," in The Georgian Group, *A Gothick Symposium* (London, 1983), unpag.

12. Later, as Gray's knowledge of the Gothic developed, he criticized Kent's stylistic incongruities. See Michael McCarthy, *The Origins of the Gothic Revival* (New Haven & London, 1987), pp. 66–67.

13. Horace Walpole, *A Description of Strawberry Hill*, rev. ed. (London, 1784).

14. These watercolors are now divided between the Huntington Library, San Marino, California, and the Lewis-Walpole Library, Yale University, in Farmington, Connecticut.

15. These interiors have been widely published and discussed. See, in chronological order: Wilmarth Sheldon Lewis, "The Genesis of Strawberry Hill," *Metropolitan Museum Studies 5* (1934–36), pp. 57–92; J. Mordaunt Crook, "Strawberry Hill Revisited," pt. 1, *Country Life* (June 7, 1973), pp. 1598–1602; pt. 2 (June 14, 1973), pp. 1726–30; pt. 3 (June 21, 1973), pp. 1794–97; McCarthy, *The Origins*, chap. 3; Wainwright, *The Romantic Interior*, chap. 4; and Aldrich, *The Gothic Revival*, pp. 58–69.

16. Wainwright, *The Romantic Interior*, pl. 60 and pp. 81–87.

17. One is now in the Victoria & Albert Museum, London; another is in the Lewis-Walpole Library, Yale University.

18. I am grateful to Mr. Douglas White, National Trust Administrator for The Vyne, for discussing the matter with me. Further research is needed to establish the exact origins of this furniture.

19. Clive Wainwright, "Only the True Black Blood," *Furniture History* 21 (1985), pp. 250–55.

20. See Aldrich, *The Gothic Revival*, pp. 81–82; see also Hugh Honour, "A House of the Gothic Revival," *Country Life* 151 (May 30, 1952), pp. 1665–66.

21. Crook, "Strawberry Hill Revisited," pt. 2, pp. 1729–30.

22. McCarthy, *The Origins*, p. 2.

23. John Martin Robinson, *The Wyatts: An Architectural Dynasty* (Oxford, 1979), pl. 37.

24. Count Plunkett, "James Cavanah Murphy," *The Irish Builder and Engineer* 51 (May 15, 1909), pp. 295–97.

25. Aldrich, *The Gothic Revival*, pp. 82 and 86.

26. "Nelson at Fonthill," *Country Life* 121 (February 28, 1957), correspondence, p. 389.

27. See John Wilton-Ely, "The Genesis and Evolution of Fonthill Abbey," *Architectural History* 23 (1980), pp. 40–51.

28. This was the second occasion the Octagon collapsed, having done so in 1800 due to Wyatt's careless supervision of his men. See Boyd Alexander, "Fonthill, Wiltshire," pt. 2, *Country Life* 140 (December 1, 1966), pp. 1430–34; and idem, *Life at Fonthill, 1807–1822* (London, 1957).

29. Beckford as a collector is discussed in detail in Wainwright, *The Romantic Interior*, chap. 5.

30. John Rutter, *Delineations of Fonthill and Its Abbey* (1823), p. 33.

31. Ibid., p. 20.

32. Wyatt was criticized by some for his overzealous clearing of monuments of later date than the cathedral.

33. Bleiler, *Three Gothic Novels*, p. xix.

34. Kenneth Clark, *The Gothic Revival: An Essay in the History of Taste*, 3rd ed. (London, 1962), p. 45.

35. The complicated publishing history of Beckford's novel is discussed in Bleiler, *Three Gothic Novels*, pp. xxii–xxiv.

36. *The Works of Lord Byron* (Ware, Hertfordshire, 1994), p. vi.

37. Ibid., p. 175.

38. Bleiler, *Three Gothic Novels*, p. xxxii.

39. Ibid., p. xxxviii.

40. This idea had been much discussed since the late eighteenth century, most notably by Sir James Hall, who had a willow cathedral erected in his garden in the 1790s. See Aldrich, *The Gothic Revival*, pp. 112–13, ills.

41. See Andrew Rutherford, "The Effect of Byron's Death," in Fani-Maria Tsigakou, ed., *Lord Byron in Greece* (Athens, 1987), pp. 45–46.

42. McCarthy, *The Origins*, pp. 17 and 23.

43. Howard Colvin, *A Biographical Dictionary of British Architects, 1600–1840*, rev. ed. (London, 1978), p. 688.

44. The original essay was published in James Smith, *Panorama of Science and Art* (1815); apparently Smith had urged Rickman to publish the essay in book form.

45. Thomas Rickman, *An Attempt to Discriminate the Styles of English Architecture*, 4th ed. (London, 1835), preface to the first edition, p. iv.

46. John Britton, *The Architectural Antiquities of Great Britain* 5 (London, 1827), p. 94.

47. See n. 45.

48. See Megan Aldrich, "Gothic Architecture Illustrated: The Drawings of Thomas Rickman in New York," *Antiquaries Journal* 65 (1985), pp. 427–33. The preparatory copy is now in the Avery Architectural Library, Columbia University, New York.

49. J. M. Crook, "John Britton and the Genesis of the Gothic Revival," in J. Summerson, ed., *Concerning Architecture: Essays on Architectural Writers and Writing presented to Nikolaus Pevsner* (London, 1968), pp. 98–119.

50. Clark, *The Gothic Revival*, p. 80; see Paul Bremen, *The Gothic of Gothick* (London, n.d.), cat. no. 198.

51. See Alexandra Wedgwood, "The Early Years," in Paul Atterbury and Clive Wainwright, eds., *Pugin: A Gothic Passion* (New Haven & London, 1994), pp. 23–24.

52. Clive Wainwright, Introduction to *Recollections of A. W. N. Pugin and his father Augustus Pugin*, by Benjamin Ferrey (London, 1861; reprint 1978), p. 16.

53. Ibid., pp. 17–19.

54. "Germans struggling to throw off the Napoleonic yoke were to find in Gothic architecture an emblem of national unity." Hugh Honour, *Romanticism* (Harmondsworth, 1979), pp. 17–19.

55. Stephen Jones, in *Ackermann's Regency Furniture and Interiors* (Marlborough, Wiltshire, 1984), p. 11.

56. Pauline Agius, in *Ackermann's Regency Furniture*, p. 17.

57. For example, tracery on a Gothic bookcase in plate 153, *The Repository*, strongly resembles that on an oak panel in Pugin's own collection, drawn by Benjamin Ferrey and published in *Gothic Ornaments* (London, 1831), pl. 53.

58. Geoffrey de Bellaigue and Patricia Kirkham, "George IV and the Furnishing of Windsor Castle," *Furniture History* (1972), pp. 1–34.

59. Nicholas Morel was himself a Frenchman of A. C. Pugin's generation. For further reading, see Frances Collard, *Regency Furniture* (Woodbridge, 1985), p. 332.

60. A. W. N. Pugin, *Gothic Furniture in the Style of the Fifteenth Century* (London, 1835).

61. A. W. N. Pugin, *The True Principles of Pointed or Christian Architecture* (London, 1841), based on lectures given at Saint Mary's College, Oscott.

Fig. 2-1. *Augustus Welby Northmore Pugin*, by Louis Lafitte; pencil on paper, 1814. (Trustees, Victoria & Albert Museum)

2. Augustus Welby Northmore Pugin: A Biographical Sketch

Rosemary Hill

Nothing in the work of Walter Scott is more evocatively gothic than the true account of John Hardman Powell's arrival in 1844 at Pugin's house, Saint Augustine's Grange.

The Grange stands on the cliff top at Ramsgate on the Kent coast and it was—it really was—a dark and stormy night just before Christmas when the fifteen-year-old Powell "teeth chattering . . . in an east wind" knocked at the massive oak door.[1] Many years later Powell (fig. 2-2) wrote a memoir to which we are indebted for the best first-hand account of Pugin at the height of his career. So, let "the Governor," as Powell knew him, burst upon the reader now as he appeared to his apprehensive visitor that night.

After a suitably imposing interval for "the shooting back of bolts" and "the taking down of a massive bar . . . candle in hand was seen the strongly built form of Pugin, dressed in pilot cloth, his handsome features sparkling with good humour . . . 'You will find lots of fires, and bread and cheese in the house; Compline at 8, supper at 9, bed at 10 . . . I must get back to my work.'"[2] Powell went in. He had come as a pupil, he stayed to become a friend and, in time, a son-in-law. For the next seven years, until Pugin's death, The Grange was the hub of his existence.

1845: "That extraordinary genius . . . that unrivaled man."—Henry Weedall

Pugin (fig. 2-3), at thirty-two, was a national figure. As an architect, designer, and polemicist he had changed the course of the Gothic Revival. In the religious debates of the previous ten years, as the Oxford Movement roused the Church of England from the complacency of generations, Pugin's had been a loud, outspoken voice in the Catholic cause. He attracted passionate admirers, including Gilbert Scott,[3] and implacable detractors, of whom the most damaging would be John Ruskin. The speed with which he worked was legendary; in one month the previous summer two churches and a cathedral had been completed. He was well-known enough to be satirized in *Punch* as "Pugsby," an architect able to supply "every article in the medieval line . . . . Designs for Cathedrals made in five and forty minutes" (fig. 2-4).[4]

In person, as Powell discovered, Pugin was less daunting than his reputation might suggest. He was short, about five-feet-five, clean shaven, contrary to the fashion of the day, with gray eyes, brown hair, and a loud but pleasant voice. The "pilot cloth" that Powell and others remarked on was a hard-wearing, dark blue wool, used for

Fig. 2-2. John Hardman Powell; daguerrotype, 1850s. (Private collection)

naval greatcoats. It was Pugin's usual working dress, practical if unconventional, and was one of several clues, along with the rolling walk and the methodical neatness of his house, to his love of sailing.

John Powell arrived at a time of personal and professional stress in Pugin's life. His second wife, Louisa, had died suddenly the year before, leaving him with six children, the youngest still a baby. In a situation difficult for any man, especially in an age when children's lives were so fragile, Pugin suffered more than another might. He depended on the companionship of marriage. Domestic upheaval of any kind drove his always active temperament to a restlessness bordering on distraction: "I would sooner go before the mast than live in this dismal solitude," he told his friend, John Hardman, the Birmingham metalworker, "the rooms are melancholy beyond description when everybody is going to bed & I am obliged to work late no sleep."[5]

Later the Arts and Crafts movement would advocate the integration of life and work as an ideal, but for Pugin it was a necessity. Just as he believed that Gothic architecture expressed a revealed truth, and that bad design was heresy, so it followed that there could be no distinction between work and religion, art and love. At Saint Augustine's he created a self-contained world (fig. 2-5), "not an untrue bolt or joint from foundation to flag pole."[6] Within it the true life was lived out, as complete, as secure, as the world depicted in a medieval book of hours, such as Pugin loved to look at and to buy whenever he could. As Powell told his brother William, the house was "a sort of monastery in its way"[7]; the holy offices the fixed points in the round of rest and labor; "compline . . . supper . . . bed."[8]

In 1845, in addition to loneliness and anxiety for his children, Pugin faced an enormous work load, even by his standards. His house was not yet finished, the church adjoining it was just beginning. At Cheadle, Staffordshire, another church, Saint Giles's, which was to be his "consolation" and the fullest expression yet of his artistic and religious vision, was nearing completion. But the budget, as usual, was running out. To add to which he was in constant fear of falling short of the ideal. He had started work on the interiors for the Palace of Westminster. Until now he had worked alone, dismissing the idea of a clerk: "I should kill him in a week."[9]

But John Powell was a different proposition. He was the nephew of John Hardman (fig. 2-6), Pugin's devoted friend and collaborator, and must have known Pugin since childhood. Like all the Hardmans and their employees, Powell was a Catholic. He worked hard at modeling, drawing, and turning himself into "an admirable sacristan" for the chapel.[10] He fitted happily into the Ramsgate regime, which, if it was monastic, was by no means dour. The bustling, cheerful spirit that Pugin believed had characterized the Middle Ages—"Catholic England was merry England"— could be found at Saint Augustine's even at such difficult times as these.[11]

With six children in the house it could not but

be lively. In addition there were three servants as well as the draftsmen who worked with Powell in the garden studio on cartoons for stained glass, which Hardman began manufacturing that year. There was already a *tendresse* between Powell and the thirteen-year-old Anne Pugin (fig. 2-7), who eventually became his wife. She was such a constant visitor to the studio that her governess, Miss Holmes, imposed a fine every time she was caught there. "I am getting on famously," Powell told his uncle that autumn, with the confident immodesty of youth, "as you will see by the moddles [sic] in capital spirits and working very hard."[12]

Models, along with sketches, designs, glass cartoons, and copious written instructions, issued in a torrent from Pugin's library study. This room, with its sea views and the coats of arms of his closest friends and patrons painted on the cornice, was the center of a complex network. Its main outposts were Hardman's Birmingham works; the builder, George Myers (fig. 2-8), in his Thamesside premises near Westminster; John Crace's decorating business in Wigmore Street, in the West End of London; and Herbert Minton's pottery at Stoke-on-Trent. In addition, there were patrons to be kept informed and placated, as well as workmen on site who wrote for materials, instructions, and, not infrequently, money.

Pugin traveled regularly to inspect work in progress. Between his visits drawings, samples, and furnishings for Saint Augustine's arrived by post, boat, and, after 1847, by rail at Ramsgate, to be met with Pugin's frank criticism. He was generous with praise, blunt about shortcomings. Powell, like everyone else, including at times Pugin's noble patron the Earl of Shrewsbury, got used to being "blown up." Pugin was no respecter of persons. He used very nearly the same tone to everyone and was often tactless, but he had no spite or rancor. This directness made his friends and workmen love him, his opponents dread him, and more subtle temperaments, such as John Henry Newman,[13] shudder with embarrassment.

For an intimate such as Hardman it was quite usual to receive a letter such as one Pugin wrote in October, making no concession to formality and

Fig. 2-3. A. W. N. Pugin; photograph probably made from a daguerrotype dating to the 1840s. (Private collection)

little to punctuation:

> only think in spite of my poverty I have been forced to give 60 *guineas*!!! for a small manuscript about 8 inches x 6. I was obliged to buy it. If you knew what it contained, you would start off here to see it. it is the *finest I have ever seen.* you will be delighted to hear that Miss Greaves has made her profession of faith & received the holy communion Deo gratis. send me my lock handles you vagabond.[14]

Here Pugin must be writing very much as he spoke, in the full grip of some of his great passions: medieval antiquities, the Catholic faith, and women, in this case Miss Greaves.

Pugin was highly attractive to women and very susceptible. He fell in love easily, profoundly, and often—rather more often perhaps than was strictly consistent with his religious principles.

Fig. 2-4. Page from *Punch* (vol. 9 [1845], p. 238), satirizing Pugin's style and the speed with which he worked.

Before Louisa's death he had become close to Mary Amherst, a cousin of Lord Shrewsbury. Soon after he was widowed he proposed to her. She accepted but broke off the engagement to enter a convent. After this, it seems, Pugin's attentions were directed toward Miss Greaves, a friend of Louisa, who was living at The Grange where she remained until 1846.

Miss Greaves came to help look after the children. But, whatever the nature of her relationship with Pugin, it was daring for an unmarried woman in the 1840s to move into a young widower's house. Eyebrows were no doubt raised in Ramsgate where, although Pugin had many friends, the townspeople at large were hostile. The "bigots," as they were known in The Grange, were anti-Catholic to such an extent that Pugin's plumber found it difficult to buy lead. They were also conventional, and there was much about Pugin and his household that was ungenteel.

Pugin's many visitors included artists and foreigners; visiting Catholics of all kinds, especially sailors, were encouraged to come to mass. More outrageous to local sensibilities must have been Pugin's purchase in 1849 of a lugger, *The Caroline*. These boats went out to ships in distress in order to rescue the crew and take off the cargo for salvage. The "wreckers" operated at the edge of legality. They were notorious along that part of the Kent coast for "thrusting their services on craft in minor trouble . . . demanding preposterous sums" and caring more about booty than saving lives.[15] None of this applied to Pugin's boat, but the enterprise is typical of his insensitivity to public opinion.

At Saint Augustine's, behind the knapped-flint walls, the world could be kept at bay. But there were demons within. His cheerfulness and enthusiasm masked, but never quite overcame, a nervous sensibility that could break through on very slight provocation. He was afraid of the dark, of ghost stories, even of Powell when he discovered that the boy walked in his sleep. "You should have told me," he wrote to Hardman, ". . . I had no idea of such a dreadful thing in practice . . . . I am all night on the listen . . . . I do not think he is happy in his mind I don't indeed."[16]

These terrors were as much a part of the Gothic repertoire as the traveler at the gate, and they did not belong only to the world of lurid novelettes. We may think of Shelley waking up screaming in the villa on the Bay of Lerici and running to his wife's room, where he saw his own ghost trying to strangle her; we may remember Coleridge's

Fig. 2-5. The Grange, Ramsgate, designed by A. W. N. Pugin; constructed 1843–44.

"fiendish crowd/ of Shapes and Thoughts."[17] Pugin was familiar with such states of mental anguish, the fear of madness and of dissolution of self that characterize the Romantic temperament.

Like Coleridge, Pugin was haunted by the "ache to know something *great*—something *one and indivisible*"; unlike Coleridge, he found it—in the Catholic Church.[18] But he nevertheless shared the Romantic sense of longing and regret, believing that what he searched for had been found and lost once already. His vision of the Middle Ages had something in common with the poets' sense of a lost ideal childhood. The sense of place and power of association were as important to him as to Wordsworth.

In 1845, widowed and anxious, Pugin was troubled by the past. He found visits to London, where he had spent the first twenty years of his life, almost unbearable: "I fear sometimes you will think it is affectation," he told Hardman, "but . . . I feel a loneliness & depression in London that is

quite dreadful & sometimes quite alarms me" and, in another letter, "it . . . increases on me God only knows now much l suffer in my mind every place is associated with innumerable ideas."[19]

1814: The Microcosm of London

Pugin at the age of two, as he appears in the drawing by his uncle Louis Lafitte (see fig. 2-1), is a serious child, the large, rounded forehead and direct gaze already remarkable.[20] Great hopes were vested in him. His parents had been married ten years when he was born and were both in their early forties. He was their only child, destined always to be "the pride of papa's and the anxious joy of mama's heart."[21]

Lafitte's portrait displays the polish and urbanity that might be expected of a man who had been a court painter to Napoleon. It is one of the flashes of glamour against a background of hard work and genteel poverty that characterized

Fig. 2-6. John Hardman the elder, 1838.

Pugin's childhood. When he was born his parents were living in Bloomsbury, north London. "Keppel Street" as Anthony Trollope, who was also born there, noted, "cannot be called fashionable, and Russell Square is not much affected by the nobility."[22] Yet it was a stimulating household, peculiarly suited to nurturing Pugin's tastes and talents.

His father, Auguste Charles, was French (fig. 2-9). He came to England as a young man during the Revolution and gave various interesting, if unreliable, accounts of his origins, occasionally styling himself "le comte de Pugin." In fact his family was modest, petit bourgeois. A. C. Pugin had worked in Paris as an illustrator, a line in which he continued in London, becoming a draftsman to the great architect of the Regency, John Nash. A. C. Pugin's best-known work, *The Microcosm of London* (fig. 2-10), which he illustrated with Thomas Rowlandson, had appeared four years earlier, and he had also acquired a reputation of his own as a watercolorist. In 1814 the critic of the *Repository of the Arts* singled out his view of Christ Church, Oxford, for its extraordi-

nary realism, making the viewer feel that "we are actually within the hall."[23]

Auguste was a handsome, easygoing man whose career had been enhanced when he met his wife, Catherine Welby (fig. 2-11). She was a bluestocking, clever and energetic enough to help him make the most of his talents. But despite her efforts money was always tight. It was a terrible anxiety in an age when debt meant either prison (a fate that overtook some in their circle) or ignominious flight abroad (the course Trollope's family eventually took). On the whole, however, the Pugins were sanguine. "There is not . . . a whole hat, coat or gown shoe or boot among us," Catherine wrote cheerfully to her sister Selina, "but Pugin says that is the more picturesque."[24]

One effect of the family's relative poverty was to keep them together. There could be no question of sending their son away to school; indeed, except for some private lessons in mathematics and Latin at Christ's Hospital, subjects which he neither cared for nor excelled in, he had no formal education. His mother made him write a weekly essay, which he also disliked, while his father taught him drawing, for which he instantly showed a precocious talent. "I was very fond of perspective," he later remembered, "and made a good proficiency of it," adding airily that when he was seven he "began to design buildings etc."[25]

Throughout Pugin's childhood, London, already the biggest city anyone had ever seen, was expanding. More prosperous middle-class families, such as the Pugins' friend, Rudolph Ackermann, publisher of *The Repository of the Arts*, and their neighbors, the Ruskins, moved out to villas south of the river at Camberwell and Herne Hill. Ackermann and Mr. Ruskin commuted over the new bridge to carry on business, leaving their families in secluded, semirural domesticity.

Such a villa was beyond the Pugins' means and at Keppel Street there was constant bustle. A. C. Pugin's friends and colleagues on the humbler fringes of the art world, water colorists, draftsmen, antiquaries, picture dealers, decorators, came and went in the midst of family life. In time he took on pupils, who boarded in the larger house the family took in Great Russell Street nearby. Pugin, though he was an only child, could never have been lonely. His developing talents were spurred on by competition with older boys. This was the original model of the busy, affectionate household—where work and leisure, private and public life were all one—that was later so essential to his happiness.

Of all the circumstances of this happy, if unusual upbringing, however, the most important was that it placed him from birth at the center of the Gothic Revival. In 1814 Gothic taste was on the turn. This year saw the publication of the first of Scott's "Waverly" novels, with succeeding volumes appearing annually throughout Pugin's childhood. *The Antiquary* (1815), *The Monastery* (1820), *Kenilworth* (1821), all fed the public taste for history and particularly for the details of everyday life—the food, furniture, and clothes. The world of Walpole's *Castle of Otranto* (1704) came to seem mere pasteboard scenery as a more solidly historical sense of the past developed in fiction and so, too, in architecture.

A. C. Pugin accordingly turned his talents as a draftsman to the production of books of measured details drawn from actual medieval buildings. These books, which provided patterns of such quality that they are still used today in restoration work, marked a new stage in the progress of the Gothic Revival toward archaeological accuracy. His wife and son accompanied him and his pupils on annual expeditions around England and, after 1815, to France to collect material. These tours combined work with visits to A. C. Pugin's sisters in Paris and to Catherine's relatives in Lincolnshire. Lincoln Cathedral was one of the first buildings Pugin could remember and it was always important to him. He learned it as he learned the others, by climbing over it, drawing it, touching it, spending hours in contemplation of the structure and the details.

Such detailed empirical knowledge characterized the cutting edge of the scholarly Gothic Revival. But its counterpart, the fashionable, novelty Gothic, popular for interior decoration,

Fig. 2-7. *Anne Pugin Powell*, attributed to A. W. N. Pugin; pencil on paper, ca. 1860. (Private collection)

still flourished, and this too Auguste's young son was well placed to observe in its most characteristic form. He may have been present when M. Vilmont, the royal chef, came to ask Auguste for advice about Gothic table decoration. He was certainly told, very often, of the occasion at Brighton Pavilion when his papa had the honor of having his paints knocked over by George IV. By the time he was fifteen he knew the language of popular Gothic well enough to design furniture for Windsor Castle.

Pugin was fluent too in French; he had a collection of antiquities; he was well traveled and streetwise, a precocious but in many ways naive youth. He was the center around which his parents' thoughts and hopes, especially his mother's, revolved. Inevitably he was spoiled, not indulged, but used to such constant, benign attention that he would always find opposition hard to bear and malice impossible to understand.

When this secure and self-contained existence ended, he was propelled towards the central crisis of his life.

Fig. 2-8. *George Myers*, artist unknown; oil on canvas, ca. 1850. (Private collection)

June 13, 1832: An End and a Beginning

> I frequently think how often he used (before he was fourteen years of age) to say "my dear own how happy I am! nobody can be happier than me" alas! alas! look over these years which have passed since that period and we find a whole life of woe such as is experienced by the generality of men huddled into it . . . he has already experienced a long life in a short one and when he dies he will not die without some dignity.[26]

Catherine Pugin was writing to her sister, Selina, from the house in Great Russell Street. Her husband and son had gone to Christchurch in Dorset, to bury Anne, Pugin's wife, who had died a week after the birth of their daughter. She was eighteen. They had been married for a year. To Catherine it seemed but the greatest of a series of calamities her son had suffered, for there had been a number of false starts since his promising debut at Windsor. He had set up a furniture-making business which failed financially and had nearly been drowned when his first sailing boat was wrecked.

His second attempt at a career, as a scenery designer at Covent Garden Opera House, was not succeeding as well as he hoped.

Now he was ill with grief. There was the baby to care for and, yet again, money was short. But this was not to be the last of his "heavy domestic afflictions."[27] In December his father died, after a long and painful illness. His mother then succumbed to jaundice and was herself dead within four months. "All I can now hope," Pugin wrote to his father's friend, Edward Willson, as his mother was dying, "is that the little girl which is left me will prove half as great a blessing as her mother was . . . but for this I must wait."[28]

With his mother's death the household that had been his only home, his school, the place where he had met his earliest friends and to which throughout his recent trials he had been able to return for comfort, was broken up. Catherine Pugin was a perceptive woman, but she cannot have known how truly she spoke in suggesting that her son had already lived one life. Over the next three years the fragments of that shattered first life gradually re-formed to make a new one.

1834: "The world is charged with the grandeur of God."—Gerard Manley Hopkins

In January 1834 Pugin wrote laconically to his friend William Osmond, a stone mason:

> I feel perfectly convinced the roman Catholick church is the only true one and the only one in which the grand & sublime style of church architecture can ever be restored. A very good chapel is now building in the north & when compleat I certainly think I shall recant.[29]

The belief that came to him during these years, and on which all the rest of his life and work would be premised, is set out here almost casually; the Catholic Church is the true church, Gothic architecture its revealed form, true in the sense of absolute, a divine, revealed truth.

Seven months later, writing to Edward Willson, himself a Catholic and so a more sympathetic correspondent than Osmond, Pugin is more expressive:

I have seen and learnt more in the past three
months than in the 3 past years such Glorious
buildings *perfect* no revolution, not [sic] reformation . . . at Nuremberg . . . when I first entered
the church & the grandeur of the interior burst
on me I could have repeated the song of Simeon
without profanation.[30]

The song of Simeon, the *Nunc Dimittis*, begins:
"Lord, now lettest thou thy servant depart in
peace according to thy word./ For mine eyes have
seen thy salvation."

Pugin never elaborated much on the process
by which he came to this insight. He was often
accused of having changed his religion for
aesthetic reasons, of having sold his soul for a
crocket. It was untrue, but he never went further
than to say, in various ways, that he had learned
the truth in the crypts of the old cathedrals.
He was received into the Catholic Church on
June 6, 1835.

Can we say any more than he did? Such an
experience comes as close as any to being wholly
private, interior. Yet if we consider its expression,
its profound effects on the architecture and ideas
of his contemporaries, then we may feel that it
is possible and necessary at least to see it in a
context.

The Gothic Revival grew up in dialogue with
literary Gothic. It had transformed itself from the
grand guignol of Walpole to the sturdiness of
Walter Scott. There, however, it had stuck, not
least for the prosaic reason that England was for
so long at war that there was a missing generation
in architecture: the contemporaries of Coleridge
and Wordsworth had little chance to develop.[31]
Architecture had not, of course, stood still since
the end of the Napoleonic Wars in 1815, but it
was only now in Pugin's passionate spiritual and
emotional identification with the Gothic that it
achieved the equivalent of Keats's "twilight saints
and dim emblazonings," the aesthetic intensity of
"The Eve of Saint Agnes."[32]

Like Wordsworth, Pugin gave to stones "a
moral life"; he "saw them feel or linked them to
some feeling."[33] The contingent circumstances
of a lost childhood, spent in his case not in the

Fig. 2-9. *Auguste Charles Pugin*, artist unknown; oil on
canvas. (Private collection)

Lake District but among the stones of Lincoln
Cathedral and Notre-Dame, were transfigured
into a guiding moral and artistic purpose. It is
what the Romantics called an "epiphany." The
whole nineteenth-century religious revival was
shot through with Romanticism, with the influence particularly of Coleridge. But the Romantic
poets were not, in any orthodox sense, religious,
nor was Pugin a Romantic like the writers of the
1790s. Indeed, he never saw himself as an artist in
the sense of being individually expressive. He
believed in the objective truth of his ideas.

Few people ever shared his vision fully, but
many responded to a part of it. The Gothic
Revival was transformed by his profound understanding of the structure and language of
medieval architecture. The ideas he set out in
1836 in *Contrasts* touched anxieties felt by many
of his contemporaries; the torpidity of the English
church and the moral and physical squalor of the
expanding industrial cities. From now on his
influence would grow.

Fig. 2-10. *Exhibition Room Somerset House*, aquatint by J. Bluck after A. C. Pugin and Thomas Rowlandson, *The Microcosm of London* (June 1, 1809).

Fig. 2-11. *From left*: Pugin's father Auguste Charles Pugin, mother Catherine Welby Pugin (the only known likeness of her), aunt Selina Welby, cousin Richard Earle Welby, and Augustus Welby Northmore Pugin, age seven; silhouettes, ca. 1819. (Private collection)

1851: "The heavy weight of hours"— Percy Bysshe Shelley

That autumn, as the Great Exhibition at the Crystal Palace drew to a close, there was a sense of lassitude and anticlimax at Ramsgate. "I ran up to London on Friday for a last look," Powell told his brother William. "I had scarcely seen it before our time was so short. It looks very shabby now and the people seem very careless everybody is quite tired and wishes it done."[34]

The Mediaeval Court, Pugin's contribution to the exhibition, had been well received but preparations for it had been exhausting. In an attempt to show how the "true thing" could be adapted to domestic furnishings, Pugin had designed the court as an ensemble—rather than showing chairs, china, and so forth separately as most exhibitors did. It was, as ever, the totality that mattered for him, but the creation of such an integrated display was a prodigious task. The sheer labor was immense (he was still working on the Palace of Westminster), in addition to which relations between his old collaborators, Crace, Hardman, and Myers, had been strained to the limit. Pugin had struggled to keep the peace.

There were still new projects, the production of painted panels and triptychs, a pamphlet against modern church music—"a regular BLAST" Pugin told Crace.[35] There was a "tremendous metal order"[36] for Westminster and Powell had enough glass work for a year.

There were new people too. Pugin had married Jane Knill in 1848 (fig. 2-12). Their daughter, Margaret, was born in 1849 and a boy, Peter Paul, in the summer of 1851. The same year Powell, who had married Anne Pugin in 1850, made "the Governor" a grandfather.

Both privately and professionally, however, Pugin was facing unprecedented difficulties. The illness he had fought for years was beginning to get the better of him. He suffered from painful inflammation of the eyes with periodic loss of vision and from "nervous fever." How, if at all, these symptoms were related or what diagnosis modern medicine would offer is difficult to say. The mercury that he, like many others, was given as an anti-inflammatory and sedative, can only have aggravated his condition. He was ill and exhausted to the point where even home and family were insufficient consolation. "My nights are dreadful & my days incessant work," he told Crace in November.[37]

In his practice there were also difficulties. He had had fewer commissions for churches since the mid-1840s. In part his own success was to blame. His ideas had been so influential that he had many imitators, most of them cheaper and all of them more accommodating. Intellectually too he was winded. There is some truth in Ruskin's sneering characterization of him as a clever boy, his precocity the ominous, unbalanced growth of the hothouse specimen, destined to fail early.[38] He could not go the distance with the more complex minds of Ruskin and Newman who, on the aesthetic and religious fronts respectively, now overtook him.

He fretted even more than usual about money. Powell thought that his lowness of spirit made him exaggerate financial difficulties. Funds were short, but there was a more than immediately practical anxiety in his letter to Crace that December, written after another bout of illness. It echoes uncannily the train of his mother's thoughts in 1832: "I am getting better," he wrote, ". . . but it has been dreadful . . . I have lived sixty years in forty . . . do let us get our accounts properly made out."[39]

1852: Ebb Tide

That a mind long strained by holding in tension the peculiar contradictions of Pugin's vision should finally fly apart has an apparent, metaphoric inevitability. But people do not die of paradox. It was perhaps the effects of the mercury that caused him in February to suffer a complete mental breakdown.

Unable to recognize even his wife, he was admitted to the Bethlem Hospital in London. It was opposite his own cathedral, Saint George's, where, four years earlier, he and Jane had been married. The Provost, Thomas Doyle, could see his friend wandering in the asylum grounds, a shambling figure, his head shaved. Jane hardly recognized him: she thought he looked seventy. But with great courage, in view of his restlessness and unpredictable behavior, she took him home. Sometimes he would seem to know her. Once he rallied enough to make a drawing of a weathervane (fig. 2-13). Powell seized on every small improvement to write to Birmingham that the Governor was better. "We shall value him treble after this," he promised his uncle, though he could have had little with which to reproach himself.[40]

Fig. 2-12. Jane Knill Pugin (1827–1909), *second from left*, with family members at The Grange, possibly in the 1890s. (Private collection)

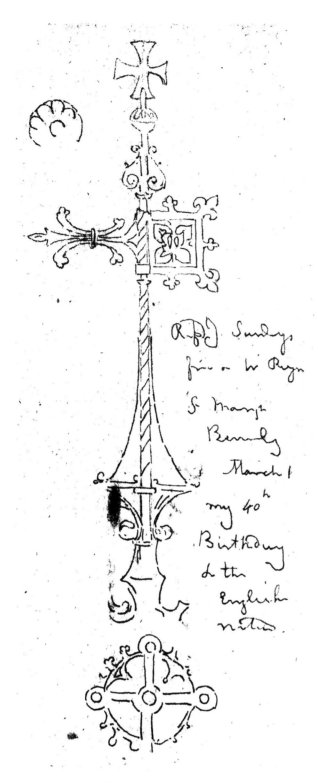

Fig. 2-14. Tomb of A. W. N. Pugin, Saint Augustine's Church, Ramsgate; design by Edward Welby Pugin, 1852. The figures along the front and sides represent members of Pugin's family. *Shown, from left*: his children Edward, Agnes, Cuthbert, Katherine, and Mary.

Pugin died on September 14, 1852. He was buried in the vault in his church (fig. 2-14). He was forty. After the funeral Powell sent his brother a penciled note, asking, as usual, for money. He concluded:

> This has been the most melancholy day I have yet known. I shall be unhappy until I get away from St. Augustine's where I have spent so many jolly hours in the old time.[41]

It was the end of a chapter in English Catholic architecture; the end, too, of Powell's own Gothic romance, that adventure which began seven years before when he stepped down from the Ashford stagecoach and knocked at the door of The Grange.

Fig. 2-13. Design for a weathervane, sketched by A. W. N. Pugin; pen and ink, 1852. This was made during his final illness; the inscription written by Pugin reads in part, ". . . St Mary's Beverley March 1 my 40th Birthday & the English nation." The design was executed and the piece installed on the corner pinnacle of Saint Mary's, Beverley. (Myers Family Trust)

I am grateful to Michael Hall for reading this essay in manuscript and discussing it with me. His comments have improved it and contributed to my understanding of Pugin's work as a whole.

1. Alexandra Wedgwood, ed., "Pugin in his Home: A Memoir by J. H. Powell," in *Architectural History* 31 (1988), p. 174.

2. Ibid.

3. Sir George Gilbert Scott (1811–1878) was one of the most prominent and prolific Gothic Revival architects. His work includes the Albert Memorial in London.

4. *Punch* 9 (London, 1845), p. 238.

5. Letter, Hardman Archive (Birmingham City Archives, Central Library, Birmingham, England), n.d. (hereafter cited as Hardman Archive).

6. Wedgwood, "Pugin in his Home," p. 175.

7. Letter, Hardman Archive, n.d.

8. Wedgwood, "Pugin in his Home," p. 174.

9. Benjamin Ferrey, *Recollections of A. W. N Pugin and his father Augustus Pugin*, reprint with introduction and index by Clive and Jane Wainwright, appendix by E. Sheridan Purcell (London, 1978), p. 187.

10. Letter, Hardman Archive, n.d.

11. A. W. N. Pugin, *The True Principles of Pointed or Christian Architecture* (London, 1841), p. 61.

12. Letter, Hardman Archive, n. d.

13. John Henry Newman (1801–1890) was one of the founders of the Oxford Movement. Newman was a shaping influence on nineteenth-century religious thought and its expression in literature, architecture, and design. He became a Roman Catholic in 1845.

14. Letter, Hardman Archive, n. d.

15. *The Journal of William Stanton: A Pilot of Deal* (Portsmouth, 1929), p. 2.

16. Letter, Hardman Archive, n. d.

17. S. T. Coleridge, "The Pains of Sleep," in *Christabel and Other Poems* (London, 1816).

18. Quoted in Rupert Christiansen, *Romantic Affinities* (London, 1988), p. 91.

19. Letters, Hardman Archive, n. d.

20. cf. Wedgwood, *Catalogues of the Architectural Drawings in the Victoria and Albert Museum: A. W. N. Pugin and the Pugin Family* (London, 1985), p. 16, which attributes this drawing to Antonia Lafitte. Antonia, Lafitte's daughter, was still a child. The drawing has been recatalogued.

21. Letter from the correspondence of A. W. N. Pugin in the Yale Center for British Art, Ms/Pugin/45, September 1824 (hereafter cited as Yale).

22. From *Lady Anna*, quoted in Victoria Glendinning, *Trollope* (London, 1992), p. 4.

23. *The Repository of Arts, Literature, Commerce* 1 (1814), p. 287.

24. Yale, Ms/Pugin/50, May 30, 1828.

25. Ms notes for an autobiography, reproduced in Wedgwood, *A. W. N. Pugin*, p. 24.

26. Yale, Ms/Pugin/52, June 13, 1832.

27. Letter in the John Work Garrett Library (The Johns Hopkins University, Baltimore, Maryland), September 13, 1834.

28. Ibid., February 26, 1833.

29. Letter in private possession, January 2, 1834.

30. Letter, John Work Garrett Library, August 22, 1834.

31. John Summerson, *Georgian London* (London, 1962), p. 135.

32. John Keats, "The Eve of Saint Agnes," in *Lamia, Isabella, The Eve of St Agnes and other Poems* (London, 1820).

33. *The Prelude*, bk. 3, ll.125-7 (1805 text), edited by Ernest de Selincourt (London, 1933).

34. Letter, Hardman Archive, n. d.

35. Pugin letters in the British Architectural Library (RIBA, Manuscripts Collection: Crace papers), London P/8/51, n. d. (hereafter cited as RIBA).

36. Letter, Hardman Archive, n. d.

37. RIBA, P/8/60, n. d.

38. Wedgwood, "Pugin in his Home," p. 183 and n. 69.

39. RIBA, P/8/64, n. d.

40. Letter, Hardman Archive, n. d.

41. Letter, Hardman Archive, n. d.

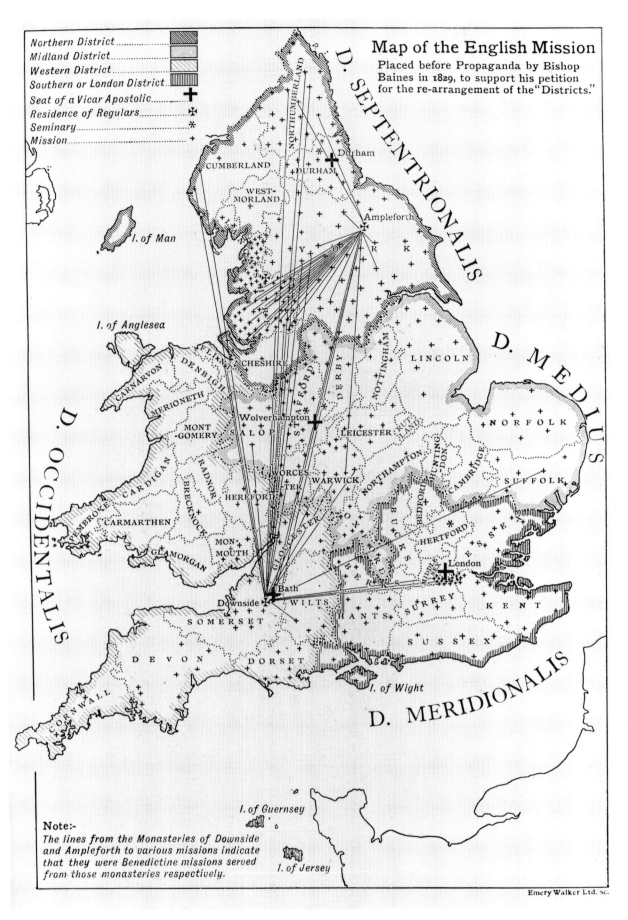

Fig. 3-1. Map of the English Mission, 1829, showing the four districts, the seats of the vicars apostolic, and the Catholic missions. (The Clifton Archives, Bristol)

3. The Catholic Context

David Meara

Pugin was born into a Regency world of jollity, excess, and outward show, tellingly exposed in the plates of Rudolph Ackermann's *Microcosm of London* (1808–10), on which Pugin's father, Auguste Charles, extensively collaborated.[1] However, this superficial world of *Vanity Fair* was played out against a background of widespread political, social, and cultural change stimulated both by a political revolution in France and an industrial one in Britain.

These events inevitably had an effect on the artistic and literary life of the country. "Old orthodoxies were shaken, old certainties were undermined."[2] New convictions began to emerge about the importance of imagination, the value of the emotions, the centrality of aesthetics, and the need for the arts to be expressive of high ideals and beliefs. These beliefs found expression in such works as the lyrical ballads of William Wordsworth, the paintings of J. M. W. Turner, and the music of Beethoven. Many artists of the period were inspired by and involved in public affairs. They tended to "extremes of view": they were not moderate but "committed" in their attitudes and beliefs.[3]

Much of the art of the period is a reaction against the bourgeois society that the Industrial Revolution had created. The poet William Blake was the earliest writer to foresee the upheaval caused by machines and factories. Essayist and historian Thomas Carlyle commented on the present condition of England in *Past and Present* (1843), and other writers contrasted the present state of society with a romanticized and well-ordered medieval age — for instance, William Cobbett in his *History of the Protestant Reformation* (1824) and Robert Southey in *Sir Thomas More* (1829). Southey's book blamed the commercial system of his day for the evils of society, contrasting the monasteries of More's day with the steam engines and cotton mills of the nineteenth century. In embryo it contained much of A. W. N. Pugin's own social criticism, and demonstrated the attractions of the hierarchical and patriarchical society of the Middle Ages.[4] The medievalism of the time has been described as "the badge of the conservative and especially the religious anti-bourgeois everywhere."[5]

Pugin accurately reflected the passions and contradictions of the period in which he grew up, moving from the Regency world of his boyhood into the more serious and earnest world of Victorian Britain. If he seemed more at home in the world of Fonthill Abbey and Ashridge, of Byron and Shelley, it was because he was essen-

Fig. 3-2. Interior view of the Church of Saint Mary, Moorfields, London. From Bernard Ward, *The Eve of Catholic Emancipation* (London, 1911).

tially a "child of Arcadia," a student of the picturesque,[6] whose "love of all things medieval was not an intellectual one, but had the passionate character of the Romantics."[7]

As Pugin grew up in the well-ordered and protected environment of his parents' home, he became aware of two things—the glories of Gothic architecture and the powerful religious beliefs of his mother. He was a precocious child, and gained most of his education among the pupils of his father's drawing office and on family visits around England and to the Continent. He developed an intense visual sense, and what he saw on his travels, particularly the relics of the past, had a great impact on him:

> What did Pugin find? Cathedrals turned into shows, Parish Churches left to rot or be defaced by galleries and pews everywhere, the Pulpit the centre of devotion, hammer-beamed roofs ceiled

over, the glass destroyed, the wallpaintings whitewashed; and all this wreck he believed firmly to be "the real work of the Renaissance."[8]

The sight of the ruined glories of the Middle Ages led the young Pugin to seek the reason why and then to set himself the task of bringing back to England "the Christian spirit and integrity in Architecture and its kindred arts."[9]

This youthful ambition, however, was at first thwarted by his mother's enthusiasm for dragging him from church to church to hear eminent preachers, especially Edward Irving. Irving was a minister of the Church of Scotland who in 1822 was appointed to the Caledonian Chapel in Hatton Garden, London, where his magnetic personality and revivalist preaching soon drew large congregations.[10] Benjamin Ferrey, Pugin's biographer, describes this experience in detail:

> Wet or dry, no matter what might be the state of

the weather, the expedition to Hatton Garden was never abandoned. Such cold and tedious services as those belonging to the Presbyterian Scotch Church were by no means suited to young Welby's taste, and the long-spun orations of the preacher . . . failed to keep his attention awake . . . . often on a fine morning, when he would have hastened with delight to Westminster Abbey his desire was overruled by his mother, who compelled him to accompany her to Hatton Garden . . . . However, such was the effect of his mother's want of judgement that it helped forward the change in his religious views which subsequently took place.[11]

There is no doubt that these early experiences drove Pugin away from Calvinism toward a richer, warmer, and more visual expression of the Christian faith. Even so, some interesting parallels have been made between Pugin and Irving, suggesting that Irving may have left a lasting impression on the young Pugin:

Like Irving, Pugin wore flamboyant cloaks and delighted in acts of the humblest charity to the poor. There is a story of Pugin carrying a seaman's chest on his back, as of Irving carrying the load of an Irish pedlar; we find Pugin founding a charity for seamen and Irving preaching gratis for one. Both died worn out in their early forties—Pugin was just forty—having in a brief life-time done the work of many ordinary men. Irving also delighted in children, was a brilliant teacher, and was known to have preached with a child high on his shoulder. In him, as in Pugin, there was a democratic approach to the common people, a deep humanity instinct with a wholly conservative politics, which bred in him, as in Pugin, otherwordliness. The Catholic Pugin and the Catholic Apostolic Irving were alike in revolt against the stifling respectability and concern for appearances which were to make up the pervasive ethos of the England of Victoria: that worship of Mammon, of the ideals of comfort and a competence, was one point of Irving's rejection of the "respectable, religious world."[12]

This period of his life was a traumatic one for Pugin. In 1829, he set up a furniture business that failed financially. His first wife died in childbirth in 1832, the year after he married her. The same year he also lost his father and in 1833, his

Fig. 3-3. *John Talbot, 16th Earl of Shrewsbury*, artist unknown. (Saint Mary's College, Oscott)

mother. It was a devastating yet also a liberating time for him; still an artistically immature but promising student, he had begun to work at what were to become two of his major adult preoccupations—the concept of satire by contrast, and the association of Roman Catholicism with the beauties of Gothic art.

The travels he took around England in 1833 and 1834, visiting cathedrals and major churches, provided a turning-point for Pugin's religious thought. Writing in 1850, he explained:

I gained my knowledge of the ancient faith beneath the vaults of a Lincoln or a Westminster and I found it indelibly marked in the venerable piles which cover the face of this land . . . . This period of my life was one of great mental happiness. I almost lived in those great churches, and revelled in the contemplation of their ancient splendour.[13]

However, Pugin's conversion to Roman Catholicism was not solely the result of aesthetic factors. Writing in 1837, he claimed that his researches into ancient liturgy and among the "old chroni-

Fig. 3-4. John Rouse Bloxam, ca. 1865. (Magdalen College, Oxford)

cles" over a three-year period led him to "surrender my own fallible judgement to the unerring decisions of the Church."[14] He took the step and was baptized into the Catholic Church on the eve of Whitsunday, June 6, 1835.

Pugin's conversion was a courageous decision and not without its painful consequences. In becoming a Catholic he denied himself the aesthetic pleasure of worship in England's medieval buildings, he sacrificed the possibility of widespread architectural work within the Church of England, and he risked being relegated to a lower stratum of society. Worst of all, he joined a church whose buildings and liturgy gave him considerable pain.

The Roman Catholic Church in Britain had endured almost two centuries of persecution. As a result of the religious settlement under Elizabeth I, the monarch had been made supreme governor of the Church in England and Papal Supremacy was denied. The Act of Uniformity (1559) abolished

the Catholic liturgy and substituted the English Prayer Book. The penalties attached to these statutes began the long series of Penal Laws that were designed to contain what was perceived as the Catholic threat. They were of enormous importance in determining subsequent Catholic self-consciousness in England. Closer to Pugin's time, the Gordon Riots (1780)[15] had been an outburst of anti-Catholic hostility in which Catholic chapels and houses were burnt and 285 people were killed.

By the early nineteenth century, however, the Catholic Church was moving into a period of toleration and gradual expansion.[16] Newman's famous word picture of the Catholic church as "a few adherents of the Old Religion, moving silently and sorrowfully about, as memorials of what had been,"[17] hardly does justice to the reality of Catholic life. Numbers were increasing, stimulated by the Irish immigrants who had begun entering the country before 1800. Between 1780 and 1840 the Catholic population rose from 70,000 to about 300,000[18] and the church was in a condition to face the future with reasonable confidence.

Catholicism, however, tended to flourish in pockets. The Catholic squire and the Catholic yeoman, with their servants and dependants, living normal but discreet lives in the countryside, centered on country-house chapels, while in the towns there was greater secrecy. In London only the chapels attached to the foreign embassies of Catholic countries were plainly open for worship; they were often of a highly ornate character. The Sardinian chapel, for example, was an impressive galleried hall with appropriate ritual furnishings for the liturgical life of the period. Pugin thought the chapel "dark and grated, like a chapel for convicts."[19] In 1820 a new church had opened in London—Saint Mary, Moorfields—larger and more richly furnished than any previously erected (fig. 3-2). Pugin was not impressed:

I once had a peep into Moorfields chapel, and came out exceedingly distressed before the service, of which I had not a very clear idea, was concluded. I saw nothing that reminded me of the ancient religion, from the fabric down to the vestments of the celebrants. Every thing seemed strange and new: the singing, after the solemn chants of Westminster, sounded execrable, and I returned perplexed and disappointed.[20]

The freedoms enjoyed by Roman Catholics were increasing all the time. The Relief Act of 1791 had abolished the double land tax on Catholics and permitted the celebration of Catholic worship in public chapels. After a number of abortive attempts, and with the constant threat of rebellion from across the Irish Sea, the Emancipation Bill was finally passed in 1829, allowing Catholics to hold government office. Cardinal Nicholas Wiseman later said: "The year 1829 was to us what the egress from the catacombs was to the early Christians."[21]

Although this was a milestone for Catholic expansion, the leadership and administration of the church was still effectively in the hands of the Catholic nobility and gentry. The country was divided into four ecclesiastical districts (see fig. 3-1), the Northern, Midland, Western (including Wales), and the London districts, each with a vicar apostolic of Episcopal rank appointed directly by Rome. While within each district the missions (or parishes) were dependent on the vicar apostolic, chapels were under lay ownership and patronage. This tension between the inherited rights of the old Catholic gentry and the desire of the bishops for greater control was a symptom of a deeper division between opposing views over the right balance between loyalty to Rome and allegiance to the Crown. The Cisalpines believed that Catholicism could and should exist without the dominance of the pope, although they did not reject his primacy and preferred government by the bishops rather than directly by Propaganda. This was a version of Continental "Gallicanism," so-called because the French church had been governed in this way between the Reformation and the Revolution.

Ultramontanism was the belief that the clergy should be subject to the Pope, the people to the clergy, and society to the church. This much

Fig. 3-5. John Henry Newman preaching at Saint Mary's Church, Oxford, artist unknown; engraving, Wyatt & Son, Oxford, 1841. (National Portrait Gallery Archive)

more clerical and centalizing movement gained ground during the mid-nineteenth century. It was favored by, for example, Frederick William Faber, an Oratorian and founder of the Brothers of the Will of God in Birmingham, and also by William George Ward, a leading Tractarian who became a Catholic in 1845 and for whom Pugin built a house, as well as by missionary priests.

Pugin, who was temperamentally more at home with the old ways, needed the patronage of wealthy landowners for his church-building work. He was fortunate to secure the interest of John Talbot, sixteenth Earl of Shrewsbury (fig. 3-3), and of Ambrose Phillipps de Lisle of Grâcedieu Manor in Leicestershire. The Earl of Shrewsbury was to give him some of his best commissions, and Ambrose Phillipps was to widen his contacts, both with Continental Catholicism and the Church of England.

Through Phillipps's good offices Pugin came into contact in 1839 with Count Charles de Montalembert,[22] an aloof aristocrat and historian who shared his passion for the Middle Ages. In 1837 he had published his aesthetic manifesto, *De l'état actuel de l'Art religieux en France*, in which he declared that the religious art of the previous century was the culmination of a period of decay which began at the Renaissance. Gothic art was to him "catholique avant tout," and he encouraged his fellow countrymen to look to Germany, where the spirit of the Middle Ages was still stronger than it was in France.

Montalembert may have introduced Pugin to the writings of Alexis François Rio who published his *De la Poésie chrêtienne* in 1836. This book was an attempt to reassess medieval and in particular Italian art in the light of "spiritual values" or what Rio called "Christian poetry." He used art history as a weapon in a moral and religious crusade. According to Pugin, Rio's book was "an admirable production, and must produce many converts to ancient art."[23]

These ideas had already been taken up in Germany by a group of young artists who had established themselves in a monastery in Rome and called themselves the Nazarenes. One of their number was Friedrich Overbeck, a German painter, whom Pugin praised as "the great Overbeck," and whose disciples "deserve the warmest eulogiums and respect for their glorious revival of Christian art and traditions."[24] By the 1830s the Nazarenes had become the champions of the art of the Middle Ages and a powerful influence on the Pre-Raphaelite movement.

Pugin's acquaintance with these French and

German artists and writers was complemented by his own extensive library, which contained many French and German works on history, liturgy, and topography. This new Continental perspective was incorporated in the second edition of Pugin's book *Contrasts* (1841). From his studies Pugin had come to feel that the Reformation was the effect of "another and more powerful agency," namely the Renaissance ideas which had swept across Europe during the fifteenth century and infected the English Church. Accordingly, the expanded 1841 edition contained material on the state of medieval buildings, religion, and taste on the Continent. In particular he included a long essay, "Account of the Destructive and Revived Pagan

Principle in France," by Montalembert. Pugin thus turns his attack upon the gradual "paganizing" of Catholic architecture on the Continent over the previous four hundred years, and he lays much of the blame for this at the door of the Catholic hierarchy. The Church was beset not only by the enemy of Protestantism from without, but also by the insidious forces of paganism within. It was a conviction that was to color much of Pugin's thought and polemical writing for the rest of his life.

Phillipps was also able to help Pugin establish contact with the leaders of the Oxford Movement, a reform movement that began in 1833 at Oxford within the Church of England. The catalyst for

Fig. 3-7. Nicholas Wiseman, Archbishop of Westminster, shown as Rector of the English College in Rome.

Fig. 3-8. Frederick William Faber (1814–1863) as an Oratorian, ca. 1848. From Bernard Ward, *The Sequel to Catholic Emancipation*, vol. 2 (London, 1915), p. 178.

this movement was the Whig Government's proposal to reduce the number of Irish bishoprics and redirect their revenues. This provoked John Keble, an Anglican theologian and one of the leaders of the movement, to deliver his Assize Sermon of July 14, 1833, in which he asked by what right an assembly composed of atheists and anticlericalists could legislate in spiritual matters. Pugin must have known of the events in Oxford, but it was not until 1839 that we have evidence of his contact with the city. In that year a proposal had been published to erect a memorial in Oxford to the martyrs of the English Reformation, largely as a test of the loyalty of the Tractarians to the Church of England. Tractarianism, so-called because of the widely circulated and influential tracts which propogated the ideas of the leaders of the Oxford Movement between 1833 and 1841, met with hostility because of its alleged tendencies toward Rome.

Pugin had published a pamphlet opposing the idea of the memorial and had made a trip to Oxford to deliver it by hand to "the University bigwigs." By 1840, through the agency of Dr. Daniel Rock, Lord Shrewsbury's chaplain, he had made contact with the Revd. J. R. Bloxam (fig. 3-4), a Fellow of Magdalen College, who shared his antiquarian interests and became a close friend and correspondent. Bloxam was Pugin's chief source of information about the Oxford Movement and introduced him to other leading Tractarians, including James B. Mozley,[25] W. G. Ward, and John Henry Newman (fig. 3-5), leader of the Oxford Movement.

Pugin met Newman on February 2l, 1841, just before the publication of Tract 90 (so his diary records). He was delighted by the stand Newman took in this tract defending a Catholic interpretation of the Thirty-nine Articles:

> A tremendous sensation had been created among the Protestants by an Oxford tract just published in which the doctrine of *Purgatory* [and] the *sacrifice of the mass for the living & dead* are fully proved to be of equal antiquity *with Christianity itself*. The invocation of saints and indulgences are also well defended. These Oxford men do more good in one week than we do in a whole year toward Catholicizing England.[26]

Pugin clearly felt that he shared a common outlook with "these Oxford men" and that Newman would influence the Church of England toward Catholicism. Over the next few months Pugin watched Newman's progress keenly. Late in March 1841 he reported to Bloxam how pleased he was to see an article in the *Tablet*, a Catholic newspaper, doing "justice to Mr. Newman & acknowledg[ing] . . . his honourable & high minded principles."[27] And he assured his friend that Dr. Wiseman, the new president of Oscott College, "speaks with great respect of Mr. Newman" and that "Tract 90 has done great good" in that place.[28] Even though he is aware of forces that might make Newman and the other Tractarians pause—the outcry and opprobrium from the Protestant quarter, for instance—he hoped that

> all *will stand fast* & not yield or *compromise*. They have high vantage ground & they *must keep it*. Pray tell me if you think the main body of Catholic-minded men will persevere through all these difficulties. Surely they will or they are not the men I believe them to be.[29]

By the middle of April 1841, Pugin was back in Oxford and probably staying with Bloxam at Magdalen, convinced that the reunion of the Anglican and Roman churches was just over the horizon. He had come from a visit to Ambrose Phillips in Leicestershire, whose wish for the union of the churches of England and Rome was, if anything, stronger than Pugin's, and Pugin lost no time in sending him a long account of developments:

> Everything here is going on as well as we could even *hope for*. The progress of Catholic affairs since my last visit is immense. The late events have been *productive of incalculable benefit* & brought over hundreds of hitherto vacillating individuals. I feel now quite satisfied Newman is right in the course he is pursuing. He has nothing but the reunion in view & is working towards it as fast as possible.[30]

Part of the evidence for Pugin's optimism lies in the fact that "new editions of 90 are now being printed"; and he is "quite satisfied that Newman has gained immensely by his submission . . . be assured, my dear friend, all is *working together for the greatest good*."[31]

As the letter draws to its close, Pugin allows himself to dream: "My dear friend, according to present appearances, you & I by the blessing of God may yet walk in some glorious procession through the ailes [sic] of Westminster." Such heady visions were destined not to come to pass. With his characteristic eagerness, Pugin had overestimated the tendency of what was happening. It was to be four and a half years before Newman, and only a relatively few others with him, turned to Rome. During that interval Pugin continued to encourage the movement toward the Gothic and the Catholic (for him, they were synonymous terms) by all the means in his power. When in June 1841 there was talk of furniture for Littlemore, the semimonastic community outside Oxford where Newman lived until 1845, Pugin, probably replying to an inquiry from Bloxam, advised against copying one of his executed designs: "I do not think the seats at Reading [in the church of St. James that he had designed there] would be quite in character for Littlemore. I will send you a better plan."[32] If this offer was transmitted to Newman, there is no evidence that it was taken up. In December of the same year Pugin inquired whether the rumor that "Mr Newman is building a monastic establishment at Littlemore"[33] was true, for if so he would like to know the style and the plan. Perhaps he wanted to make his help available again. He sent Bloxam

Fig. 3-9. Interior of the Oratory, King William Street, London. (Collection of the London Oratory)

engravings of his buildings, inviting him to show them to other "Oxford men." He made gifts of brass rubbings and casts of carvings and sculpture to the Oxford Architectural Society which Newman had helped Bloxam and others to found. He read the *British Critic*, the Tractarian journal that Newman edited till mid-1841, and did his utmost to increase its circulation among Catholics. By way of Bloxam he presented Newman with a copy of his book, *An Apology for the Revival of Christian Architecture in England*, issued in 1843. In 1844 he agreed to provide illustrations for the ill-fated series of *Lives of the English Saints* of which Newman was the nominal editor and which had incurred ecclesiastical displeasure over the Catholic tendencies of the writers, especially Faber.

Throughout Newman's long delay, as it must have seemed to him, Pugin tried hard to keep his faith in the Anglican leader's eventual destination, and also endeavored to inspire others with a comparable vision of the future. For example, late in 1842 in a letter to his friend the marine painter Clarkson Stanfield, alluding to the new respect in which medieval architecture was held, he explained that:

> men are filled with veneration for Catholic antiquity—& when we see the glorious works which are daily put forth by the Oxford men, can we doubt that God has great things in store for us? & all this will be brought about by the Anglicans & I think it is our bounden duty to aid, advise & assist them in every way.[34]

When Newman finally made the decisive change in October 1845 Pugin's notice of the fact was on the whole quiet. "Of course you have heard of Newman's reception. Deo gratias," he writes to John Hardman, his closest friend, in Birmingham.[35] Pugin's early enthusiasm for Newman waned after this, partly because Pugin had lost hope in the Oxford men, partly because of temperamental differences, and partly because the importance of proper outward forms in architecture, art, and liturgy, so important to Pugin, were lost on Newman. After his conversion Newman told Ambrose Phillipps that there were persons "more distressed at a man's disliking a chancel screen than at his being a

Fig. 3-10. Sketch of the Lowther Rooms, London, inscribed "The Narthex or Porch of a modern temple of Bacchus or Therpsichore," by A. W. N. Pugin in a letter to John Hardman, n. d. (HLRO Historical Collections, Pugin/Hardman correspondence, no. 231).

Gallican" (surely a reference to Pugin).[36] Pugin's passion for chancel screens was to be his ultimate downfall in the late 1840s.

Phillipps, like Pugin, supported the movement and wrote about it approvingly to Montalembert in 1842, but Montalembert insisted that while they had the right forms, they did not have Catholic unity: they had the frame, but not the picture.[37] Even Pugin came to believe that "the Oxford Men stand in an essentially false position," and that "patching up Protestantism with copes and candles would be no better than whitening a sepulchre."[38]

Pugin's own Catholicism was essentially unworldly, and in his politics he was close to the High Tory views of Benjamin Disraeli whose novel *Coningsby* (1844) includes thinly disguised portraits of Pugin's two patrons, Lord Shrewsbury and Ambrose Phillipps de Lisle. Pugin had a hierarchical view of society and thus of the Church, and a great fear of liberalism and revolution. His letters to John Hardman contain frequent references to the dangers of socialists and Chartists and he had an obsessive fear of brigands and highwaymen. In one letter he writes:

> Pray order for me 12 percussion lock muskets without fail with cartridge cases etc., complete pray do not neglect this there are so many blackguards about it is necessary to be prepared. Mind they are good strong muskets—fit for service— which will not burst when used. [And in another letter:] Don't forget the muskets. We shall want

them before long. What a horrible state of things in France . . . . What liberty. What scurrility. I would shoot any Chartist as I would a rat or mad dog. Send me muskets.[39]

This natural conservative High Toryism allied with his Gothic medievalism made Pugin naturally suspicious of the clergy and especially of the proletarianization of the Church which began with the influx of large numbers of Irish Catholics.

Pugin disliked the Irish and although he had met Daniel O'Connell, the Irish nationalist leader who had helped achieve Catholic emancipation, he was suspicious that under O'Connell's leadership Catholic agitation in Ireland would develop into radical, even revolutionary action. Pugin expressed his feelings in a letter to his friend Bloxam:

> The truth is that devout and sincere men of both parties should meet and instead of expending our resources against each other should turn them against the common enemy of Liberalism and infidelity. Could we but *pair* off the O'Connell agitation men and the Exeter Hall declaimers how much better things would go on. To a truly Catholic soul political influence is an object of little moment intrigue is utterly incompatible with truth. . . . If the clergy of Ireland took half the interest in the splendours of the altar which they do in a contested [?] election the Catholic churches of Ireland would not present their present miserable aspect of neglect and filth.[40]

In fact Pugin did undertake a number of commissions in Ireland, including cathedrals at Enniscorthy and Killarney, conventional buildings in Wexford, and the extension to Saint Patrick's College, Maynooth, in 1845.[41] But his links with Ireland were never particularly strong and his ideas failed to take root among the Irish clergy and Catholic peasantry.

Pugin by now had to fight his battle for the Gothic cause, not only against Protestantism and liberalism, but also increasingly with his own hierarchy. By the mid-1840s the face of English Catholicism had changed considerably from the early years of the century. The reasons for this include the exodus of rural Catholics to urban centers, the growing determination among the vicars apostolic to reassert their authority, the influx of Irish immigrants, and the growing Continental influences. These began with the influx of emigré French clergy and included the return of exiled religious orders, the arrival of foreign missionary orders, and the gradual penetration of Continental devotions.

Although the influence of French emigré clergy has been exaggerated,[42] they did have an impact on individual English men and women (such as Ambrose Phillipps, whose French teacher, Abbé Giraud, made a strong impression on him), and their more open piety undoubtedly had an effect on susceptible young minds. The return of the religious orders to England after the Revolution brought French manners and devotional customs, which were disseminated through their presence in particular localities, through their teaching in schools, through the use of public statuary and devotions such as benediction. This movement toward an increasingly ultramontane piety was not imposed by Rome but grew gradually through its appeal to popular sentiment. Although in the country the liturgy was usually celebrated simply, at embassy chapels in London High Masses were sung, vespers chanted, and benediction said.

Because of Pugin's sustained polemics and his prolific architectural practice, during the early 1840s Gothic art, architecture, and liturgy were undoubtedly in the ascendant. The Shrewsbury–Phillipps–Pugin party, supported by a majority of the bishops—Thomas Walsh (fig. 3-6), Thomas Giffiths, William Riddell, R. W. Willson, and, in these early days, Nicholas Wiseman[43]—were in a dominating position, strongly opposed only by Bishop Peter Augustine Baines in the Western District. Baines was a zealous opponent of Pugin and the Gothic Revival. He acted like a medieval prelate and waged war against Pugin's medieval vestments. On Baines's death Pugin wrote to Bloxam, "I suppose you have seen the death of Dr. Baines in the *Tablet*. He was privately a very good man but sadly mistaken in his views   he will be no loss to the church   the only really *pagan* Bishop we had . . . ."[44]

Pugin not only had a commanding position within a network of personal friends, patrons, and supporters, he also dominated the media through which religious dialogue was conducted during the mid-nineteenth century—the published treatise, the polemical tract or pamphlet, and the specialist periodical. He and his party were poised to win the battle of the styles, but various factors combined to cause their eclipse.

Pugin miscalculated the public mood, which was becoming increasingly receptive to Continental piety. The directness and warmth of the "new" devotions—the processions, hymnsinging, meditations, and benediction, among others—encouraged especially by the foreign missionaries, such as the Italians Dominic Barberi of the Passionist Order and Luigi Gentili, a Rosminian priest who preached in the industrial towns, appealed to public sentiment and romance. The increasing numbers of Irish immigrants were particularly susceptible.

Pugin also failed to make his liturgical requirements intelligible to the clergy. His liturgical ideas were so complex and demanded such detailed antiquarian knowledge that many clergy and small parishes simply would not have understood what to do. Pugin was once asked how Holy Communion could be distributed when a screen intervened between priest and people. In small parishes there would seldom be three clergymen to occupy the sedilia Pugin provided in the chancels of his churches; and many clergy would have been ignorant about the use of the piscina and Easter sepulchre. Pugin wrote, "the truth is the churches I build do little or no good for want of men who know how to use them. Dudley is a complete facsimile after an Old English parish church and nobody seems to know how to use it."[45]

He assumed seminarians and clergy were as well-read as he was, and although he tried to establish Saint Mary's College, Oscott,[46] as a place to disseminate his ideas, he failed to maintain his influence there during the 1840s, and so no systematic teaching was carried out.[47]

During the late 1840s there were a number of significant deaths among Pugin's clerical supporters: Griffiths died in August 1847; Walsh in February 1849; Riddell in 1849. Furthermore, Willson had gone to New Zealand in 1844, and Lord Shrewsbury spent much of his time abroad, having exhausted his fortune. All these events combined to undermine Pugin's power-base and sphere of influence. A sign of this is that while Pugin's opponent Bishop Baines had been unsuccessful in 1839 in attempts to ban Pugin's Gothic vestments, by 1852 he had succeeded.

Pugin's ideas also failed to take hold because there was a growing campaign within the religious periodicals against him. J. M. Capes, editor of the *Rambler*, attacked him in print on three fronts: because his ideas were anachronistic; because medievalism was an inadequate response to the conditions and problems facing Britain and the Church; and because there were inconsistencies in the church buildings he had designed, especially in relation to screens.

Frederick Lucas, founder of the *Tablet*, another Catholic periodical, "ploughed a furrow hostile to English peers, unsympathetic to Tractarians and increasingly sympathetic to Ireland."[48] Lucas preferred militant ultramontane Catholicism, and his particular target was Pugin's patron, the Earl of Shrewsbury.

The Gothic crusade was also hindered by Wiseman (fig. 3-7), who on Bishop Walsh's death had become vicar apostolic of the London District. Wiseman was never as committed to the

Fig. 3-11. "The Guy Fawkes of 1850," reflecting antipapist sentiment at the time of the "Papal Aggression" (*Punch*, vol. 29, [November 1850], p. 197).

Gothic Revival as Pugin would have liked. Pugin at first thought that Wiseman shared his own beliefs, but there were early warning signs (for example, his attempt to block the installation of the rood screen at Saint Chad's, Birmingham).[49] Wiseman lost faith both in the Oxford converts and in Pugin and while preferring the old ways was quite clear that:

> If on Gothic principles a sanctuary could not be erected where every rubric of the modern Church might be literally obeyed, then he would discard Gothic, for it is the modern Church that must save us—These externals must be reduced to what they are, a mere indifferent matter of taste, and all things must give way to the exigencies of the rubrics of the church, and to the spirit of modern devotions.[50]

This was seen as the definitive public answer to Pugin and sealed the fate of his campaign, after Newman's failure to support him in the rood screen controversy. Although the screen in question was meant for Saint Wilfrid's, the so-called screens controversy began in the *Rambler* in July

1848 in relation to Saint George's, Southwark, and became the focus for anti-Pugin criticism. The dispute centered on the fitness of Gothic churches for the Continental devotion practices, especially the Quarant'ore, a spectator-centered ritual commemorating the forty hours of Christ's entombment, which Wiseman was anxious to introduce. Pugin, however, believed passionately in the revival of the late medieval church type with cruciform plan, screen, reredos, raised altar, and side-chapels, each part clearly expressing its function. Such a plan, however, did not lend itself to the Roman rites and devotions whose performance should be readily visible to the congregation. Unfortunately for Pugin, Newman, who had confessed to a predilection for the Italian style ever since entering Trinity College Chapel, Oxford, as an undergraduate, failed to support him. He admired Pugin's work (he called Saint Giles's, Cheadle, "the most splendid building I ever saw"[51]), and was not as anti-Gothic as is sometimes thought. In his novel, *Loss and Gain* (1848), when one of the characters is asked "and which are you for, Gothic or Rome?", he answers "for both in their place."[52] That he was intellectually persuaded of the superiority of Gothic architecture is shown by this passage from *The Idea of a University* (1873):

> For myself, certainly I think that the style which, whatever be its origin, is called Gothic is endowed with a profound and a commanding beauty, such as no other style possesses with which we are acquainted and which probably the Church will not see surpassed till it attain to the Celestial City.[53]

But the externals of religion were very secondary matters for Newman, and his theory of development made him predisposed to believe that: "There could hardly be a development of doctrine without its being accompanied by a development of ritual and worship."[54]

Newman was therefore open-minded about architectural style, and he allowed himself to be identified with the line taken by Frederick Faber (fig. 3-8). Faber, who had converted to Catholicism in 1845, began a small monastic community in Birmingham near Saint Chad's Cathedral. At this stage he preferred English to Continental Catholicism and when the chapel at Colmore Terrace, where the community now lived, was being fitted out it was decorated in the Gothic style, with an altar after a design by Pugin. However, Faber visited Italy in 1846, and his liking for the Gothic gave way under the influence of Rome and his fondness for Italian devotions.

On Faber's return to England, Lord Shrewsbury gave him a mansion, Cotton Hall in Staffordshire, and Pugin designed a church there dedicated to Saint Wilfrid, so that the congregation of Saint Wilfrid could have a proper home. It was here that one of the great engagements in the war of the Gothic and Italianate theorists took place. In the spring of 1848 Ambrose Phillips and Pugin paid a visit to Faber, who was unwell. The trouble started because Phillips asked why there was no screen at Saint Wilfrid's. The ensuing row, in which Faber and Ambrose Phillips traded insults, had significant repercussions. It confirmed Newman in his rejection of Pugin's ideas, and signaled the impracticality of Gothic art and architecture for the new religious orders and popular devotions.

In 1848 Faber's community merged with the Oratorians, a community following the Rule of Saint Philip Neri, which Newman had established in Birmingham. However, differences soon developed between Newman and Faber, and Faber established a separate house, the London Oratory (fig. 3-9), in 1849. He leased and transformed the establishment known as the Lowther Rooms off the Strand as a temporary church. Pugin was horrified and felt betrayed by men whom he had expected would be sympathetic to the Gothic cause. In a letter to John Hardman he writes:

> I am exceedingly disgusted at the oratorians hiring the Lowther rooms for a chapel. They are rooms of notorious bad character let out for Masquerades & the lowest debauchery & they have *hired* them for the solemn practices of the church . . . of all the disappointing men that have ever existed these are the most . . . .[55]

He returns to this theme in numerous letters,

including a cartoon (fig. 3-10) entitled "The Narthex or Porch of a modern temple of Bacchus or Terpsichore," and reserves his most splenetic comments for the Oratorians: "Socialists, levellers of sanctuaries!"[56]

Pugin and the "Gothic party" had lost the battle of the styles, a defeat sealed when Pope Pius IX restored the Hierarchy (the collective body of archbishops and bishops governing England and Wales) in September 1850 after which Wiseman was appointed as the first Archbishop of Westminster. Pugin deeply regretted that Wiseman should occupy such a dominating position and in his writings began to adopt a more strident tone as he felt his own position undermined.

The process of petitioning for the restoration of the Hierarchy had begun in earnest in 1845 and intensified on the election of Pope Pius IX in 1846. Wiseman and James Sharples, coadjutor of the Lancastrian District, were sent to Rome in 1847 to put their case to the new pontiff and were sympathetically received. Pugin, too, was in Rome that year. His diary shows that he arrived on April 24 and stayed until May 4. Richard Simpson, a fellow Catholic, wrote an account of Pugin's visit in the Rambler,[57] describing Pugin's disgust at most of the architecture, especially Saint Peter's. Simpson arranged for Pugin to meet Friedrich Overbeck, the leader of the Nazarene school of painting in Rome. Pugin also had an audience with the Pope, at which he received the papal medal. It was "the greatest day of his life."[58]

It is interesting to speculate on the reasons for Pugin's visit to Rome. Was it just a desire to see the city's architecture or was he hoping to influence the moves toward establishing the Hierarchy and try to reassert the position of the landed gentry and the "medieval party" in English Catholic life? It is impossible to tell from Simpson's brief article, and Pugin's diary is tantalizingly vague. He may have wanted to try to provide a counterbalance to the influence of Newman, who was in Rome at the time.

On the restoration of the Hierarchy, Wiseman rashly issued his pastoral letter, "Out of the Flaminian Gate," in which he referred to "govern-ing" the English counties. This caused an anti-Catholic uproar fanned by The Times, which warned of "Papal Aggression" (fig. 3-11). The Prime Minister, Lord John Russell, denounced such pretensions to supremacy over the realm of England, and Wiseman responded by publishing "An Appeal to the Reason and Good Feeling of the English People," which presented the case for the Hierarchy.

Pugin was determined to do what he could to strengthen the Catholic movement. He composed and circulated a tract entitled An Earnest Address on the Establishment of the Catholic Heirarchy, in which he urged Catholics to support the Hierarchy by individual financial contribution so that corruption among the Catholic clergy should not again endanger the faith. To support his proposal, he explains the causes of the Reformation and the need for ecclesiastical freedom from the State. Although Pugin was merely developing conclusions that he had first reached in the 1841 edition of Contrasts, he also spoke of the essential catholicity of the Church of England and hence the implied validity of Anglican orders.

His views attracted a hail of protest from the Catholic clergy and mild censure from Wiseman. Pugin had to declare publicly that he was a loyal and orthodox Catholic while at the same time remaining firm in his charitable attitude to the Church of England. A draft manuscript exists in one of his notebooks of a further work which Ferrey entitled An Apology for the Church of England.[59] It sought to reassess the relationship between the two churches and establish a new basis for rapprochement.

But with these latest writings Pugin had effectively separated himself from the mainstream of Catholic thought and progress. It was perhaps the pain of realizing that he had failed to persuade the Catholic community of the validity of his ideas that contributed to his mental decline. His starting point had been that "the Roman Catholic Church was the only true one, and the only one in which the grand and sublime style of architecture can ever be restored."[60] His dream had been "the dream of a generation which throught it could redeem the evils of industrialism by re-living the art of the Middle Ages."[61] He had labored hard to build the dream and to persuade those who mattered that England would be converted through Gothic architecture, Gregorian chant, and medieval vestments. His final illness and subsequent death meant that he never witnessed the eclipse of his belief in the unbreakable link between Gothic art and Christian faith. As Newman put it:

> The living ritual of the nineteenth century needed the living architecture of the nineteenth century. Gothic is now like an old dress, which fitted a man well twenty years back but must be altered to fit him now—an architectural movement had become a sort of antiquarianism, a dilettante unpractical affair for Puseyites, poets and dreamers.[62]

And Pugin, as well as being a loyal Catholic, was above all a dreamer of dreams.

1. Rosemary Hill, "Bankers, Bawds and Beau Monde," *Country Life* (November 3, 1994), pp. 64–67.

2. Hugh Honour, *Romanticism* (Harmondsworth, 1981), p. 21.

3. "I have no respect of the Whigs," said Wordsworth, "but I have a great deal of the Chartist in me" (E. C. Batho, *The Later Wordsworth* [1933], p. 227).

4. R. J. Smith, *The Gothic Bequest* (Cambridge, 1987).

5. Eric Hobsbawn, *The Age of Revolution 1789–1848* (London, 1962), p. 320.

6. Interestingly, he designed a memorial brass to Uvedale Price, the student of the picturesque, now in Yazor Church, Herefordshire.

7. Clive Wainwright, "Pugin and His Influence," in Paul Atterbury and Clive Wainwright, eds., *Pugin: A Gothic Passion* (London & New Haven, 1994), p. 6.

8. John Hardman Powell quoted in Alexandra Wedgwood, ed., "Pugin in his Home," *Architectural History* 31 (1988), p. 180.

9. John Hardman Powell quoted in ibid., p. 179.

10. For an account of Irving, see Sheridan Gilley, "Edward Irving: Prophet of the Millenium," in Garnett and Matthew, eds., *Revival and Religion since 1700* (London, 1993), pp. 95–111.

11. Benjamin Ferrey, *Recollections of A. N. Welby Pugin and his father Augustus Pugin* (London, 1861), pp. 43–48.

12. Gilley, "Edward Irving," p. 97.

13. A. W. N. Pugin, *Some Remarks on the Articles which have recently appeared in the* Rambler *relative to Ecclesiastical Architecture and Decoration* (London, 1850), pp. 17–18.

14. A. W. N. Pugin, *A Reply to Observations which appeared in Frazer's Magazine for March 1837 on a work entitled Contrasts* (London, 1837), pp. 5–7.

15. The Gordon Riots were so-called after Lord George Gordon who inflamed Protestant opinion against the Catholic Relief Act of 1778.

16. Lady Jerningham of Costessy in Norfolk wrote in her gossipy letters to Lady Bedingfield about the considerable part Catholics were playing in London Society at the turn of the century. In 1786 she wrote "I think the Catholick Ladies seem to be in fashion!" and by 1819 she could say, "It is really fashionable to be a Catholic. Tempora Mutantur." See Jerningham Letters, vols. 1 and 2.

17. John Henry Newman, "The Second Spring," in *Sermons Preached on Various Occasions* (London, 1857), p. 200.

18. John Bossy, *The English Catholic Community 1570–1850* (London, 1975), p. 287. See also Philip Hughes, "The English Catholics in 1850," in G. A. Beck, ed., *The English Catholics 1850–1950* (London, 1950).

19. A. W. N. Pugin, "Lectures on Ecclesiastical Architecture," *Catholic Magazine*, new series 2, 1838, p. 332.

20. A. W. N. Pugin, *Some Remarks on . . . Architecture and Decoration.*

21. Nicholas Wiseman, *The Religious and Social Position of Catholics in England* (London, 1864), p. 9.

22. Pugin's diary for June 26, 1839 says: "Returned to London. Count Montalembert" (Alexandra Wedgwood, *Catalogues of the Architectural Drawings in the Victoria and Albert Museum: A. W. N. Pugin and the Pugin Family* [London, 1985], p. 42).

23. A. W. N. Pugin, *Contrasts* (1841), p. 18.

24. Idem, *An Apology for the Revival of Christian Architecture in England* (London, 1843), p. 44n.

25. Both James and his brother Thomas Mozley were involved in the Oxford Movement and known to Pugin. James mentions meeting Pugin in a letter to his sister, Anne, in February 1841 (*Letters of the Revd. J. B. Mozley, D. D.,* ed. Anne Mozley [London, 1885], pp. 99–100).

26. Letter to Lord Shrewsbury of March 17, 1841.

27. Magdalen College Archives, Oxford, Pugin/Bloxam correspondence, no. 528.

28. Ibid., no. 125.

29. Ibid.

30. Ibid.

31. Magdalen College Archives, Oxford, Pugin/Bloxam correspondence, no. 125. Newman had been asked by Dr. Richard Bagot, Bishop of Oxford, to cease publication of the Tracts, and had agreed (Ian Ker, *John Henry Newman: A Biography* [Oxford, 1990], p. 221).

32. Magdalen College Archives, Oxford, Pugin/Bloxam correspondence, no. 125.

33. Ibid.

34. Westminster Diocesan Archives, SEC 21/4.

35. HLRO Pugin/Hardman correspondence, no. 318.

36. Purcell, *Life of Ambrose Phillips*, vol. 2, pp. 204–205.

37. Quoted in the *Dublin Review* (1954), p. 199.

38. Pugin to Ambrose Phillips, January 12, 1842 (Purcell, *Life of Ambrose Phillips*, vol. 2, p. 226).

39. HLRO Pugin/Hardman correspondence, no. 17.

40. Magdalen College Archives, Oxford, Pugin/Bloxam correspondence, Ms. 528, No. 8.

41. For a discussion of Pugin's work in Ireland, see chap. 7.

42. Aiden Bellenger, *The French Exiled Clergy* (Downside, 1986).

43. Thomas Walsh (1779–1849) was vicar apostolic of the Midland District, then of the London District, and a loyal supporter of Pugin, who eventually designed Walsh's tomb in Saint Chad's Cathedral, Birmingham. Thomas Griffiths (1791–1847), president of Saint Edmund's College, Ware, and subsequently vicar apostolic of the London District, was conservative and cautious in his attitude toward Continental devotional practices, the reestablishment of the Hierarchy, and other new ideas. William Riddell (1807–1847), a priest at Saint Mary's, Newcastle, coadjutor to the vicar apostolic of the Northern district (from 1843), and vicar apostolic (from 1947), knew Pugin from 1842 when Pugin began work on the design of Saint Mary's. Pugin called Riddell's death from fever "an awful and distressing event" (HLRO Pugin/Hardman correspondence, no. 381) and subsequently designed a memorial brass in his honor. Robert William Willson (1794–1886) of Nottingham commissioned Pugin to design and build the church (now cathedral) of Saint Barnabas. When he left England in 1844 for assignment in New Zealand, Pugin and Hardman gave him a large collection of artifacts, designs, and cartoons to help him introduce "sound things" into the New World. Nicholas Wiseman (1802–1865), president of Oscott College from 1840, was a brilliant and ambitious man who supported Pugin at first but by the late 1840s considered him an obstacle to the work of converting England to Catholicism.

44. Magdalen College Archives, Oxford, Pugin/Bloxam correspondence, ms. 528, no. 81.

45. Purcell, *Life of Ambrose Phillips*, vol. 2, p. 213.

46. Saint Mary's College, Oscott, was founded in 1793 for the education of Catholic boys and seminarians. At first situated in Handsworth, Birmingham, it outgrew its original buildings, and a new site was found six miles north of Birmingham at Sutton Coldfield where a new college was built, designed by Joseph Potter of Lichfield and completed by A. W. N. Pugin, who became Professor of Ecclesiastical Antiquities. After Wiseman became president in 1840, the college was the center of Catholic activity in the Midlands.

47. Roderick O'Donnell points out that no handbook of the liturgy/symbolism etc. was published until the First Provincial Synod of Westminster, by which time the instructions under Wiseman's influence were hostile to Pugin's principles. By contrast, Anglicans were well served by the Ecclesiological Society's publications.

48. Sheridan Gilley, "Frederick Lucas, The *Tablet* and Ireland," in *Modern Religious Rebels*, ed. Stuart Mews (London, 1993), p. 66.

49. Purcell, *Life of Ambrose Phillips*, vol. 2, p. 213. See also Ward's anecdote about Wiseman bringing ladies into the chancel, W. G. *Ward and the Catholic Revival* (1893), p. 386.

50. *Tablet*, May 1851.

51. Charles Stephen Dessain, *Letters and Diaries of J. H. Newman* 11 (London, 1961–68), p. 210.

52. John Henry Newman, *Loss and Gain* (Longman's 1903 ed.), p. 285.

53. Idem, "Bearing of Other Branches of Knowledge on Theology," in *The Idea of a University* (1873), Discourse 4, section 7.

54. *Ecclesiologist* n.s. 7, 1850, p. 322.

55. HLRO Pugin/Hardman correspondence, no. 8.

56. HLRO Pugin/Hardman correspondence, no. 220.

57. *Rambler* 3rd series (September 5, 1861), pp. 394–402.

58. Ibid.

59. Ferrey, *Recollections*, p. 266 n. The manuscript is in the Victoria & Albert Museum Library, London, press no 86 MM 48.

60. Ferrey, *Recollections*, pp. 88–91.

61. J. Mordant Crook, *William Burges and the High Victorian Dream* (London, 1981), p.16.

62. Dessain, *Letters and Diaries* 12, pp. 460–62.

Fig. 4-1. A gallery in the Musée des Antiquités, Rouen, formerly the Convent of La Visitation Sainte-Marie.

4. A. W. N. Pugin and France

Clive Wainwright

Augustus Welby Northmore Pugin's French ancestry gave him a special affinity for France. Despite the Napoleonic Wars, his father Auguste Charles Pugin, who had moved to London around 1792, kept in touch with several members of his family both in northern France and in Paris, the city of his birth. Sadly, A. W. N. Pugin's diaries do not start until 1835, so the details of his early visits to France are not known. He was certainly there with his father and mother first in 1819, when he was seven years old, then again in 1821, and every year from 1823 to 1828. In his notes on his early life he mentions two visits:

> 1819 first visited france, and saw my French relatives, entered Paris in the midst of a thunderstorm. Spoke French a little began to draw slightly. Lodged at the Hotel Bourbon les Bains rue Jacob, and stayed at Paris about two months . . . in 1823. Visited Paris and Normandy, studied different styles of Gothic, and became fully capable of fixing dates. In this journey I saw Paris, Rouen, Caen, Bayeux. I began to collect antiquities, purchased some tiles from the Ducal Palace, Caen, and got some fragments of stained glass from the circular windows at the end of the hall. Assisted my father in his work of Normandy by making several sketches. I worked hard all the time and measured a great deal. Began to speak French fluently and could make myself under-

stood everywhere. We returned by the route of Le Havre, Honfleur and so to Calais and returned to England after an absence of about 3 months.[1]

At the age of eleven Pugin was already collecting not at random but almost certainly on the basis of published descriptions of medieval antiquities. The tiles from Caen to which he refers in the passage above may well be those now at Oscott College, Birmingham (see cat. no. 50) which are labeled "Ducal Palace Caen in Normandy Given by A. W. Pugin Esq." At the very least, they are from the same floor. The surviving tiles in the Ducal Palace were of great importance in the revival of encaustic tile-making to which Pugin was later to make such a significant contribution. The Caen tiles had been discussed as early as 1767 by Andrew Ducarel, the antiquary and expert on Normandy, in his *Anglo Norman Antiquities,* and Pugin's father certainly had a copy of this in his library.[2] It was this well-stocked library that was to do so much to nourish the young Pugin's enthusiasm for the study of antiquities, architecture, history, and collecting. Pugin was to acquire many objects for his collection while traveling in France.[3]

It is also likely that Pugin had seen *Two Letters on the Origin, Antiquity and History of Norman Tiles Tained with Armorial Bearings,* that incun-

Fig. 4-2. "Corner of the rue St. Marten, Beauvais" and "bracketing of a house near Chateaudon" by A. W. N. Pugin. Plate from Pugin, *Details of ancient timber houses of the 15th & 16th centuries . . .* (London: Ackermann & Co., 1837).

able of tile literature by John Henniker. Published in 1794, the text had been given as a paper at the Society of Antiquaries of London in February 1788, when the tiles described in it—all of which were from Caen—were presented to the society for their museum. The museum itself was in the society's rooms at Somerset House in London, and Pugin and his father could have seen the actual tiles there. One of these tiles (see cat. no. 50, *left*) is illustrated and identifed by Henniker as bearing the arms of the celebrated Norman family of Tilly.

Pugin was able to experience French life not as a tourist but as part of a French family. Antonia, one of A. C. Pugin's sisters, was married to Louis Lafitte, a history painter and designer. In 1791 Lafitte had won the Grand Prix de Rome and studied in Rome and Florence for several years,

but by 1799 he was back in France painting wall decorations in the dining room at Malmaison for Napoleon. His career survived the fall of Napoleon, and in 1817 Louis XVIII made him *Premier dessinateur du cabinet du roi*. He had come to London in 1816 to visit A. C. Pugin and was involved in designing the sets for a grand fire-work display presented by the Prince Regent at Carlton House to honor the Duke of Wellington for his victory over Napoleon. (Lafitte also de-signed a shield to be presented to the duke, but this was probably not executed.) Lafitte already had experience in this type of set design, having worked on the sets for the wedding of Napoleon and Marie-Louise. He went on to do similar work for the wedding of the duc and duchesse de Berry and for the baptism of their son, the duc de

Fig. 4-3. Details of timber construction by A. W. N. Pugin. From Pugin, *The True Principles of Pointed or Christian Architecture* (London, 1841). The two top figures may illustrate examples seen by Pugin in Rouen, France.

Bordeaux, in Notre-Dame. He also helped on the funeral of Louis XVIII at Saint-Denis, and on the entry of the duc d'Angoulême into Paris in 1823. He worked with J. I. Hittorff on the coronation of Charles X,[4] having been given the Légion d'honneur for his design work in 1823. J. I. Hittorff, who was later to design the church of Saint Vincent de Paul and the Gare du Nord, was very much the coming architect in Paris and known to the Pugins. Perhaps it was Lafitte who introduced them. Lafitte also designed ceramics for Sèvres, as well as silver, coins, and medals.

Wholly familiar with many aspects of the art and design world of Paris, Lafitte introduced the Pugin family to members of the highest circles of French society. Several very interesting letters from Pugin's mother, Catherine Welby, to her sister Selina in London survive from the 1824 visit to France,[5] and these give a clear picture of the introduction that young Pugin had to French cultural life through the Lafittes:

> They live in a highly respectable style keeping two men and four maid servants a carriage and three horses and their house is as neat and well regulated as an English one. They are altogether a thriving family in the right road to preferment. Uncle Lafitte is now a Knight and wears the scarlet ribbon. He called on me in his full court dress after the levée. It is extremely rich and the gold-handled scabbard of his sword is carved from his own design. All these things give me pleasure for this reason that hereafter when my son may visit France his family connections will be very respectable. His aunt Lafitte has promised him a drawing of the family arms having supporters

Fig. 4-4. *Self-Portrait*, E. Hyacinthe Langlois (1777–1837); pencil on paper, 1819. (Trustees, Victoria & Albert Museum)

and a certain mark indicating her father to be the younger son of a noble family of Switzerland. This delights Augustus . . . .

The letter also mentions how A. C. Pugin was collaborating with Lafitte in the design of a Gothic building for the duchesse d'Angoulême, daughter of Louis XVI. This building, probably a garden building, could have been either at the Château de Saint-Cloud, on the outskirts of Paris, or on the duchess's nearby estate of Villeneuve l'Etang. It has not been possible to establish whether it was ever built; if so, it may still exist. As far as young Pugin was concerned, however, he may well have seen at first hand his father designing a Gothic building for a royal patron. Just three years later,

A. W. N. Pugin himself, at the age of fifteen, would be designing furniture for King George IV at Windsor Castle.

Although he was not to become a Roman Catholic for another ten years, Pugin was taken by his mother to a Sunday High Mass in Paris, an event she also described in her correspondence with her sister. It was celebrated " . . . at St.-Roche by the Archbishop of Paris and we all went to see it. The church was excessively crowded but with perseverance Augustus and I made our way up to the rails of the choir, in which all the ceremonies are performed, and I must say in point of pomp, magnificence and music they far exceed any I had before witnessed." Sainte-Roche is in the rue Saint-Honoré, in the center of Paris near the Louvre.

Catherine W. Pugin and her son were invited by other relatives to visit the Château de Rosny, near Mantes and not far from Paris, which belonged to the duchesse de Berry, daughter-in-law of Charles X and sister-in-law of the duchesse d'Angoulême. The duchess was not present for the Pugin's visit, but, Catherine wrote, "after going through the apartments of the château all of which are elegant we went on the river Seine at the side of the garden in a large boat belonging to the duchess." The duchess was one of the leading figures in the cultural life of Paris and was particularly involved in promoting the Gothic Revival style and the study of the Middle Ages. In Paris she lived in the royal Palais des Tuileries. It was there in 1829 that she held her so-called Marie Stuart costume ball, to which she came dressed as Mary, Queen of Scots. In 1820 she had headed the list of subscribers to the first volume of that celebrated *vade mecum* for medievalists, Charles Nodier and Justin Séverin Taylor's *Voyages pittoresques et romantiques dans l'ancienne France*. The subscribers' list also included "Pugin architecte à Londres" and "Lafitte artiste à Paris," and the volume itself, devoted to "Ancienne Normandie," was still in Pugin's library when he died. The Pugins' association with these members of the French aristocracy came to an end in 1830 when Charles X was deposed and went into exile, along with the duchesse de Berry and duc d'Angoulême. By this time uncle Lafitte was also dead.

In August 1825 the Pugins, father and son, with some of the other pupils from the Pugin studio traveled to France to study and record Norman architecture for a later publication. They "set out for Normandy and, crossing from Brighton to Dieppe, proceeded to Rouen, where he [A. C. Pugin] commenced the execution of this design. In this ancient and interesting city he found abundant objects for his pencil. The churches of St.-Ouen, St.-Maclou, the Palais de Justice, the Convent of St.-Armand, the Hotel Bourgtheroulde and other buildings furnished excellent details, all of which were measured and rendered in a practical manner."[6] The publication referred to was *Engraved Specimens of the Antiquities of Normandy*, with plates by A. C. Pugin and his pupils and text by John Britton, published in 1827. This illustrated a number of buildings from Rouen, including those mentioned above, and some from Bayeux, Caen, and other places in Normandy such as the elaborate late medieval Château de Fontaine Henri near Caen.

It was to Rouen that Pugin was to return time and time again, and once his yearly diaries start in 1835 these visits are easy to document. (He was there, for example, in 1836, 1837, 1838, and 1840.) Nowhere else in Europe could he find such a concentration of Gothic churches, with Saint-Ouen, Saint-Maclou, and the cathedral itself all within five minutes' walk of each other. In 1838 he wrote that "the western end of Rouen Cathedral presents one of the grandest façades of pointed architecture existing."[7] There were also fine examples of secular medieval buildings, such as the Palais de Justice, but Pugin was particularly drawn to the many surviving timber-framed houses (figs. 4-2, 4-3). In 1849 John Ruskin, also an enthusiast for Rouen, having spent much time there writing *Seven Lamps of Architecture*, described the city and its timber houses:

. . . its grey and fretted towers misty in their magnificence of height, letting the sky, like blue enamel, through the foiled spaces of their crowns of open work, the walls and gates of its countless churches warded by saintly groups of solemn statuary, clasped about by wandering stems of

Fig. 4-5. "Hôtel de Cluny," by A. W. N. Pugin. From *Paris and its environs . . .* , vol. 1 (London, 1829).

Fig. 4-6. "Barrier of St. Denis, Burnt down July 29, 1830," by Joseph Nash. From *Paris and its environs . . .* , vol. 2 (London, 1830).

sculptured leafage and crowned by fretted niche and fairy pediment . . . in the midst of the throng and murmur of those shadowy streets—all grim with jutting props of ebon woodwork, lightened only here and there by a sunbeam glancing down from the scaly backs, and points, and pyramids of the Norman roofs.[8]

Pugin was a pioneer in recognizing the importance of these surviving houses to scholars. His enthusiasm for them as architects was as vernacular sources of simple Gothic Revival domestic houses. He brought these French examples to international attention in 1837 in his book, *Details of ancient timber houses of the 15th & 16th centuries selected from those existing at Rouen, Caen, Beauvais, Gisors, Abbeville, Strasbourg etc., drawn on the spot & etched by A. Welby Pugin* (see fig. 4-2). Then in *The True Principles of Pointed or Christian Architecture* in 1841, while discussing honest building methods, he illustrates another example, almost certainly from

Rouen (see fig. 4-3) and describes how: "The ancient French cities of Rouen, Beauvais, Abbeville, Lisieux and others were full of timber houses covered with carved beams and most varied ornament; but these are rapidly disappearing to make way for monotonous plaster buildings." Thus Pugin was constantly drawing his inspiration from ancient examples, but applying the medieval principles to modern purposes; he was not merely an antiquary recording what survived.

During Pugin's 1825 trip to Normandy he became acquainted with "many of the most distinguished antiquaries and artists of Normandy . . . . Two of these friendly assistants deserve a passing notice, being eminent in their particular walks. In M. Langlois, a member of the Society of Antiquaries of France, Pugin met a remarkable artist. He was the type of a class of men who rank high in French estimation. Well versed in ancient literature, an able professor in science and arts, this man of genius occupied with his family a second floor in an obscure street of Rouen . . . . To M. De Caumont, the learned antiquary, Pugin was also much indebted."[9]

Eustache Hyacinthe Langlois (fig. 4-4) was a native of Pont de l'Arche, near Rouen. He was an excellent artist who had studied with David d'Angers, the celebrated Neoclassical sculptor. He had fought under Napoleon and probably fell from favor after 1816, for in that year he moved from Paris back to Rouen where he made a living as an artist. Among the books on Norman antiquities that he wrote and illustrated, two—*Description historiques des Maisons de Rouen* (1821) and *Essai historique et descriptif sur la peinture sur verre ancienne et moderne* (1832)—were particularly appropriate for the young Pugin. These and other books by Langlois were part of the Pugin library sale in 1853. In *Essai historique* Langlois illustrates and describes the celebrated window in Rouen Cathedral dedicated to Julian the Hospitaller, and Pugin used the book when preparing lectures on stained glass. Pugin praised "the eastern window of the apse of Rouen Cathedral . . . the one [that is] situated on the Gospel side of the choir and represents the whole legend of Julian the Hospitaller."[10]

In 1828 Langlois was made Professeur de l'Ecole Gratuité de Dessin de Rouen. The school was situated in what had been the medieval convent of La Visitation Sainte-Marie in the rue Beauvoisine on a hill overlooking the cathedral. The Langlois family lived in the attics of the building, and it must have been here that the Pugins, father and son, visited them in 1825. In this same building, in 1831, the Musée des Antiquités was set up under the curatorship of Achille Deville, a friend of Langlois who immediately involved him in building and displaying the collections (see fig. 4-1). Until his death in 1837 Langlois played a key role in the creation of this remarkable museum. It had a far better collection of medieval objects for Pugin to examine than any museum at that time in England. He made many visits to the museum and certainly knew it well; he drew some of its most important medieval exhibits (see cat. no. 36). What is also interesting

is that at some time between 1831 and 1837 Pugin did a drawing of "View from the chamber of E. H. Langlois of the Musée Rouen," but sadly, this drawing is not known to have survived.[11]

A. C. Pugin was a member of the Société des Antiquaires de Normandie, which had been founded in 1824 and was one of the earliest such regional societies in France. Interestingly, neither he nor his son was ever elected to that most ancient of such societies, the Society of Antiquaries of London. When A. C. Pugin died, the society in Normandy noted: ". . . we are also sorry [to report the death of] M Pugin of London to whom science is indebted for a large number of works on religious edifices and who has already published more than 600 engravings in -4to., representing the principal monuments of this kind in France and England; M Pugin had engraved a collection of detailed drawings, admirably done, representing the most significant monuments of Rouen and Caen."[12] The close involvement of the elder Pugin with the architects, artists, and antiquaries of Rouen and Caen gave the young Pugin a great familiarity with both French medieval buildings and the individuals who were studying and restoring them. The effect upon Pugin's later architectural development was to be considerable.

Pugin's experience in the close examination of French medieval buildings was not confined to the provinces. In 1826 and 1827 he was in Paris with his parents and the other pupils, primarily to make drawings of both ancient and modern buildings. It is difficult to date the drawings, which were done over several years, but Pugin's biographer Benjamin Ferrey noted that Pugin started:

early in the year 1826, to turn his attention very closely to the study of castellated buildings. Prior to this, however, it should be stated that he went with his parents and some pupils to Paris, the elder Pugin being engaged in obtaining sketches for a work upon that city . . . . Mrs Pugin writing from Paris to her sister observes ". . . His father calls this work of Paris 'Augustus's work' and well he may, for he has done more than three parts of it, and made sketches and coloured them for the first time from Nature, and written some very good descriptions.[13]

Fig. 4-7. "Royal Academy of Music," by Joseph Nash. From *Paris and its environs . . .* , vol. 2 (London, 1830).

The drawings were published in *Paris and its environs, Displayed in a series of picturesque views. The drawings made under the direction of Mr Pugin, and engraved under the superintendence of Mr. C. Heath. The topographical and historical descriptions by L. T. Ventrouillac* (volume 1), which appeared in 1829, followed by a second volume in 1830. The drawings of many of the key buildings, including Sainte-Chapelle, Notre-Dame, and the Hôtel de Cluny (fig. 4-5), are ascribed in the captions to A. W. N. Pugin. A number of the original watercolors survive, including that by Pugin for Le Petit Trianon (see cat. no. 18). One interesting aspect of the second volume is that some of the illustrations—all by Joseph Nash, another of A. C. Pugin's pupils—show events from the revolution of 1830. For instance, the text for the engraving of the Barrier of Saint-Denis reads: "(Burnt down July 29th, 1830). The whole Faubourg St.-Denis from the Porte or Arche de

Triomphe of Louis XIV to the Barrier, was on 28th and 29th of July the scene of severe conflicts. The Porte St.-Denis was amongst the first public edifices on which the tri-colored flag was displayed . . . . Towards the close of the 28th we believe the barrier was first set on fire." The illustration (fig. 4-6) shows cannon being fired and smoke pouring out of the windows of the building.

This suggests that the Pugins and their party of pupils may actually have been in Paris during the 1830 revolution, but there are no letters for this date to substantiate this. In his autobiographical notes for 1830 Pugin recorded: "July 27. Revolution in France. In 3 days the citizens posses [sic] themselves of Paris. Charles the X obliged to abdicate and fly to England."[14] He does not give details of his own travels as he was to do later in his diaries. Provided the watercolors of the appropriate buildings had already been completed, the illustrations of them showing the revolutionaries at work could have been made from newspaper accounts.

During the time that Pugin was in Paris he became involved in the world of Parisian theater.[15] There are, however, only two tantalizing pieces of information concerning this work. His mother, in a letter of June 1832, wrote, "The manager of the French Opera House at Paris has applied to him to know his terms to go over there."[16] Pugin may well have been thinking of a career move at this time. His own furniture business had just gone bankrupt and, when the letter was written, he was actually in Hampshire burying his first wife, who had just died in childbirth. The second piece of information was given many years later by his son, Edward: "Anyone who has beheld his scenes and decorations in the operas *Kenilworth* (in London) or *La Juivre* and *Count Ory* (in Paris) will have recognized a richness of conception, powers of delineation and a knowledge of Gothic Architecture and detail perfectly wonderful."[17] The French theater that staged the two operas may be the one illustrated in *Paris and its environs* (fig. 4-7) where it is described as "Académie Royale de Musique. Such is the inappropriate name which now designates the grand French Opera House in the Rue Lepelletier. It is considered, indeed, as only a temporary Opera House, but is fitted up and supported on a scale of unrivalled magnificence." By 1850 this theater had changed from a royal to national one but was still referred to as "The ACADEMIE NATIONALE DE MUSIQUE, or FRENCH OPERA HOUSE . . . intended only for a temporary building . . . the scenic department especially has long been renowned as almost unrivalled at any other theatre in Europe."[18] Pugin would have worked in the scenic department of this theater which is known to have staged the first production of *Le Comte Ory*.[19] It has always been assumed that Pugin designed the sets for this production. It occurred, however, a year earlier than his first recorded work in the English theater in October 1829 about which Pugin himself recorded: "I had to serve as a stage carpenter all the season so that

I acquired the thorough knowledge of the practical part of the stage business which has so materially served me since."[20] I suggest, however, that the truth may be even more interesting. In May 1830 Charles X and the duchesse de Berry lavishly entertained the duchess's father, who was King of the Two Sicilys, in Paris, and on May 17 the company from the theater of the Académie Royale de Musique staged a production of *Le Comte Ory* in the state rooms of the Palais de Tuileries.[21] If Pugin did design these sets, the foundations laid for him by his uncle Lafitte had borne fruit. The project would have acquainted him with the manager of the French Opera House, an association that may then explain the offer of a job at the theater to which his mother alludes in her letter of 1832. Why Pugin did not take up the offer is a mystery.

Pugin's experience in the Paris theater would also explain why in May 1831 he designed the sets for the first English production of Victor Hugo's *Hernani*.[22] As has often been told, at the first performance in Paris on February 25, 1830, there were riots between the classicists and the Romantics, the latter led by Hugo and Théophile Gautier. Also present were Madame Récamier, Balzac, Sainte Beuve, Berlioz, Stendhal, Dumas, Delacroix, and Mérimée. There is no evidence that Pugin was there, though he must have read or heard accounts of this defining moment of the Romantic movement in Europe and it would have excited him greatly. Whether Pugin's London sets were based upon the French production is unknown. The production of *Le Juivre* is more of a puzzle, for this took place in Paris in 1835[23] by which time he had finished theatrical work in London; he was in Paris for a week in July that year.

From 1835, except for 1843 and 1846, there are Pugin's diaries giving brief details of his travels in France, the Low Countries, Germany, and Italy which he visited once, in 1847. There are also several hundred drawings and watercolors of architecture and the applied arts made by Pugin on these European journeys.[24] He was certainly in France at least once every year from 1835, except

1841, 1842, and 1848. Although there is no diary for 1843 or 1846, there are dated drawings of French subjects for 1846, and in 1841 he went to Belgium. The journeys were extremely hectic, with Pugin meeting architects and antiquaries, conducting business, doing drawings of buildings, and also buying antiquities for his own collection. As an avid collector, he visited private collections whenever possible. When he was in Paris in 1836 he sketched objects in the Sauvageot collection (fig. 4-8) and in 1847 he sketched objects in the Dugai, Henri Gerente, and Caudron collections in Paris and, most importantly, in the celebrated collection of the Russian Prince Alexis Soltikoff (fig. 4-9).

The itinerary of 1837 was fairly typical of his journeys. On June 28, 1837 he left England for Belgium and after visiting Ostende, Bruges, Ghent, Brussels, Mechlin, and Antwerp he arrived in Paris on July 9. Then on July "12 Mr Lenoir paid me 200, remains £300. 6 copies to send Furniture. 13 Left for C. 14 All day at Chartres. 15 Left Chartres for Evereux at Night. 18 Left Evereux for Rouen. 22 Left Rouen for Honfleur and Lisieux. 23 Arrived Lisieux. 25 Left Lisieux for Caen. 27 Left Caen for Bayeux and Coutances. 28 Arrived at Coutances. 29 Left Coutances for Caen. 30 Left Caen by steam for Havre. 31 Left Havre for England at night."[25] If Lenoir was a bookseller as this passage suggests, he was presumably paying Pugin for copies of his books which he had sold. The reference to furniture must refer to *Gothic Furniture in the style of the 15th century*, which had come out in 1835. Indeed, by 1837 French booksellers could have been selling *Contrasts*; Pugin's two books on precious and base metalwork; and his *Ancient Timber Houses*, all of which had been published between 1835 and 1837. Except for *Ancient Timber Houses*, Pugin's books were to be published in Paris in French editions during the later 1830s and 1840s.

The fact that there were copies of the furniture book in Paris helps to explain why illustrations from it were so quickly pirated. Although some of the French editions of Pugin's books were probably published with his permission, others were certainly copied. For instance, the Paris publisher, Emile Leconte of 37 rue Sainte-Anne, published in parts *Ornements Gothiques de toutes les époques et choix d'ornaments de la Renaissance et des différents sièclès ouvrage destinè specialment aux Fabriques de tous les genres*. Although the title page of Part Four is dated 1834, plate 29 (the only one dated) gives 1835, which explains how plate 38 came to include objects taken from four of the plates of Pugin's *Gothic Furniture*, which was published only on April 1, 1835. The images in the Leconte book are reversed when compared with the original, suggesting that, as is so often the case with copies, the French engraver drew them directly from the Pugin book so that when printed they were reversed. They have also been altered by removing the coats of arms that appear in the originals (for instance, in the center of the brattishing of the bookcase), and the lion finials that were on the right-hand armchair. Leconte's book also contains engravings of stained glass from Rouen Cathedral and from Saint-Ouen, and details from the church of Saint-Jacques in Dieppe—all copied from A. C. Pugin's book on Normandy. Several different designers are credited, that on the furniture plate being one A. Normand. Was he, perhaps, related to Charles Normand, the architect whose book[26] A. C. Pugin had translated into English in 1829? It is interest-

ing that by this date A. W. N. Pugin's designs were considered sufficiently in advance of those of French designers to be republished in Paris. Further evidence of Pugin's influence on French furniture came to light at a recent auction.[27] The elaborate carved bed (fig. 4-10) from the Château des Grandes Bourdinières, Solonge, the existence of which had been previously unknown, is very closely copied from a design published in Pugin's *Gothic Furniture* (1835). No other bed from this design is known. It would seem, however, to date to the 1850s rather than the period just after the publication of Pugin's book and demonstrates his continued influence in France.

In the late 1830s Pugin was in close touch with the new generation of French architects and antiquaries. In 1838 a new architectural and archaeological committee consisting of French architects and antiquaries was set up in Paris. It included Victor Hugo, Alexander du Sommerard, Prosper Mérimée, Montalembert, Baron Taylor, and Albert Lenoir (who may be the Lenoir mentioned by Pugin in 1837). The secretary to the committee was Adolphe-Napoléon Didron, antiquary, journalist, and stained-glass designer who was to become a close friend of Pugin's. There was a distinguished group of "Correspondans étrangers" among them the most famous European architects and medievalists of the period, including: from Germany, Leo von Klenze, Gustav Waagen, Johan Claudius von Lassaulux, and the brothers S. and M. Boisserée; from England, John Britton, Thomas Rickman, William Whewell, and "Welby Pugin professor of archaeology at Oscott College near Birmingham."[28] In a long letter to Didron written in 1843 Pugin described his recent works; his remarks were published in the committee's periodical where Didron commented, "M Pugin's letter is an excellent introduction to the work prepared. For discussion or where one wishes to recommend the gothic style, especially of the thirteenth century, in building, furnishings, and church ornament, there can be no better summary than the letter of this illustrious English architect."[29]

In May 1844 Pugin was in Paris for a week and Didron looked after him. Didron had just

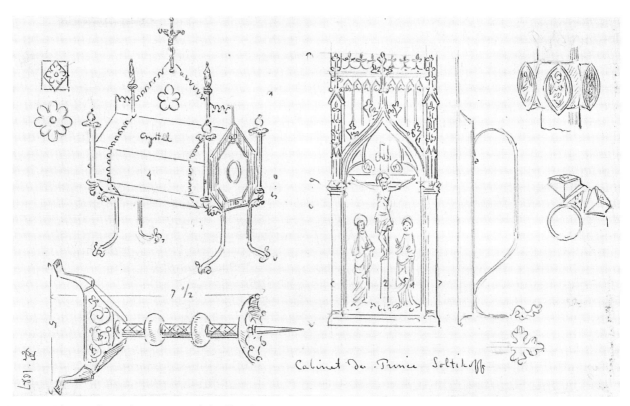

Fig. 4-9. Objects from the Prince Soltikoff collection sketched by A. W. N. Pugin; pen and ink, 1847. (Trustees of the British Museum)

established an important new periodical, *Annales Archéologiques*, which was published by his brother at his bookshop, La Libraire Achéolo-gique De Victor Didron Place et rue Saint-André des Arts 30. In it Didron reported: "M. Pugin, the young but already famous English Catholic architect, spent a few days with us in Paris. M. Pugin studied and admired the work done by our friends in St.-Germain-L'Auxerrois, St.-Germain-des-Près, and above all Ste.-Chapelle. He will take back to England happily the methods and processes for the repair and decoration of medieval monuments."[30] Pugin wrote of this visit to his patron, John Talbot, sixteenth Earl of Shrewsbury:

> I have seen most glorious things, far beyond my expectations. The restoration of the Sainte-Chapelle at Paris is worthy of the days of St.-Louis. I never saw images so exquisitely painted. I worked incessantly the whole time I was away & got most interesting sketches. I have also purchased a great many casts of the most beautiful character, which will be just the thing for the images on the spire at Cheadle & also for the reredos and chancel. They are by far the finest

sculpture I have ever seen. I have also established a regular correspondence with Paris for the execution of enamels for church ornaments which they do better and cheaper than we do.[31]

The mention of enamels is very interesting. All the extant enameled pieces of metalwork of this date by Pugin are attributed to John Hardman and no French examples have yet been identified. There is, however, no doubt that nineteenth-century French enamelers were far superior to their English counterparts. Pugin greatly admired the restoration work at La Sainte Chapelle for which Jean-Baptiste Lassus was the architect in charge. Lassus was then the most celebrated Gothic Revival architect in France. He was also working at Saint-Germain l'Auxerrois, which Pugin visited, and at Notre-Dame. Lassus certainly knew Pugin's works and designed ecclesiastical vestments closely based on the designs Pugin published in his *Glossary of Ecclesiastical Ornament*. For instance, in 1850 Monsignor Pierre Dreuze-Breze wore at a service in Notre-Dame a remarkably

74

Puginian mitre and chasuble designed by Lassus.[32] Around the same time Lassus was instructed by Monsignor Nanquette, for whom he was working at Le Mans, to provide "a mitre in the style of the fourteenth century [and] an elaborate chasuble made in the manner of Pugin."[33]

Didron was invited to England by Pugin in 1846 for the consecration of his greatest church, Saint Giles's, Cheadle,[34] and he also stayed with Lord Shrewsbury (who had paid for Cheadle) at nearby Alton Towers, which was the seat of the Earl of Shrewsbury. Didron published a long account of this event and his English visit in *Annales Archéologiques*. It is possible that Pugin met Viollet-le-Duc, the champion of Gothic Revival in France, while Pugin was in Paris or even when Viollet-le-Duc traveled to England with Prosper Mérimée in 1850 where he visited the New Palace of Westminster, though it struck him as "une affreuse monstruosité."[35] In 1844, when Pugin was in Paris, Viollet was collaborating with Lassus at both Notre-Dame and La Sainte Chapelle. In addition, uncle Lafitte was likely to have known Viollet's father, who was also in the royal household. He was superintendent of the Tuileries, a post he retained under Louis-Phillipe. Indeed, Pugin could even have met Viollet in the Tuileries in 1830, when working on the sets for *Le Comte Ory*. The Pugin diaries make no mention of their meeting, however, but neither do they mention Didron.

Pugin's works and his theories were introduced to a wide Continental audience with the publication of *Les Vrais Principes de l'architecture ogivale ou chrétienne, avec des remarques sur leur renaissance au temps actuel. Remanié et developpé après le texte Anglais de A. W. Pugin, par T. H. King, et traduit en français, par P. Lebrocquy*. This was printed and published in Bruges in 1850 and was sold not only throughout Belgium but also by Victor Didron in his Paris bookshop. Thomas Harper King, its publisher, was English, but lived in Bruges where he published books on both medieval architecture and Gothic Revival metalwork. He played an important part in the Belgian Gothic Revival and in

Fig. 4-10. Bed designed by A. W. N. Pugin; carved wood, possibly dating to the early 1850s. This elaborate work only came to light in 1995.

spreading Pugin's designs and ideas in France and Belgium.[36] He also helped Pugin's son, Edward, to find commissions in Belgium in the 1850s.

The French editions of Pugin's previous books had consisted of plates alone, but *Les Vrais Principes* had 243 pages of text and dozens of plates, including the same frontispiece that appeared in the English edition of the book. The illustrated title page (fig. 4-11) is by A. Verbeke of Bruges whose name appears in Pugin's 1851 diary. The title suggests that it is a translation of *True Principles*, but it is that and more, including text from Pugin's other works, such as *Contrasts*. The modern buildings used as illustrations are Belgian rather than English, however, and a number of other illustrations are of Belgian subjects, although there is a unique plate of furniture from the New Palace of Westminster. The book was widely known. Viollet-le-Duc, for example,

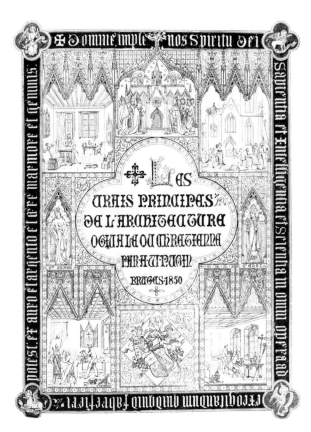

Fig. 4-11. Title page; lithograph by A. Verbeke. From Pugin, *Les Vrais principes de l'architecture . . .* (Bruges, 1850).

owned a copy of it as well as a copy of A. C. Pugin's book on Normandy.[37]

Pugin kept up his French connections to the end. He made his last visit to France in 1851, from July 16th to the 31st, and Didron came to London to review the Mediaeval Court of the Great Exhibition of 1851 for *Annales*. After Pugin's death, Didron sounded a clarion call to the Gothic Revival architects of England; it was inspired by Pugin's motto, "En Avant":

> Mr. Scott will come forward, followed by MM. Butterfield, Carpenter, Pearson, Ferrey, Cundy, Daukes, White and Salvin. The future of the [Gothic Revival] is there, in the return to the austere and beautiful forms of this primary style. We are saying that to retreat is to advance, and we remember this beautiful motto which Pugin painted on the walls of his charming home in Ramsgate where we spent three of the most enjoyable days of our life. Around his coat of arms, on the pennant flying in the wind, we read: "EN AVANT." For Pugin the "Gothic," for this retardataire, this man of the past, the motto

meant progress and the future, and perhaps we alone understood the profundity of his thought. Therefore, we will also say to the English architects, listen well to Pugin: "FORWARD."[38]

1. Alexandra Wedgwood, *Catalogues of the Architectural Drawings in the Victoria and Albert Museum: A. W. N. Pugin and the Pugin Family* (London, 1985), p. 24.

2. It was lot 140 in *A Catalogue of original drawings books of prints and an extensive architectural library . . . the property of the late Augustus Pugin . . . to be disposed of by auction by Mr Wheatley at his rooms No 91 Piccadilly on Tuesday June 4 1833 . . . .*

3. See Clive Wainwright, "The Antiquary and Collector," in Paul Atterbury and Clive Wainwright, eds., *Pugin: A Gothic Passion* (London & New Haven, 1994).

4. Françoise Waquet, *Les fêtes royales sous la restauration ou l'ancien regime retrouvé* (Paris, 1981), p. 96.

5. These are in the Beinicke Library, Yale University, New Haven; I am indebted to Rosemary Hill for bringing them to my attention. The following quotes come from the letter written on September 24, 1824 from Rouen.

6. Benjamin Ferrey, *Recollections of A. N. Welby Pugin and his father Augustus Pugin* (London, 1861), p. 18.

7. A. W. Pugin, "West Front of Rouen Cathedral," *The London and Dublin Orthodox Journal of Useful Knowledge* 6 (February 17, 1838), p. 97. I am indebted to Stanley Shepherd for bringing this article to my attention.

8. [John Ruskin] "Samuel Prout." *The Art Journal* 11, (1849), p. 77.

9. Ferrey, *Recollections*.

10. A. W. Pugin, "Lectures on Ecclesiastical Architecture, delivered to the students of St Mary's College at Oscott, by A. W. Pugin, Professor of Ecclesiastical Antiquities in that College. Lecture the Third," *Catholic Magazine* 3 (1839), p. 18. I am indebted to Stanley Shepherd for bringing this article to my attention.

11. This description is from an undated list of drawings done by Pugin in Rouen (Victoria & Albert Museum Library 86.mm.32).

12. ". . . nous avons aussi à regretter M. Pugin, architecte de Londres, auquel le science est redevable d'un grand nombre d'ouvrages sur les edifices religieux, et qui avait publiè déjà plus de 600 planches in −4to., representant les principaux monuments de ce genre, existant en France et en Angleterre; M. Pugin avait fait graver une collection particulière de dessins admirablement exécutès, et representant les monuments les plus remarkable de Rouen et de Caen" ("Membres décédés," *Mémoires de la Société des Antiquaires de Normandie Année 1835* 9 [Paris & Rouen, 1838], p. xliii).

13. Ferrey, *Recollections*, pp. 35–36.

14. Wedgwood, *Catalogues*, p. 28.

15. His career as a stage designer in London stretched from 1829 until the mid-1830s and this story has recently been fully told. See Lionel Lambourne, "Pugin and the Theatre," in Atterbury and Wainwright, eds., *Pugin*. There is certainly much more to be discovered, however, concerning Pugin and the French theater.

16. Yale University Pugin mss June 1832; I am indebted to Rosemary Hill for bringing this to my attention.

17. Edward Welby Pugin, *Who was the Architect of the Houses of Parliament?* (London, 1867), p. 3.

18. *Galignani's New Paris Guide For 1850* (Paris, 1850), pp. 486–87.

19. Announced as, "par MM***, musique de Rossini (Acad. Royale de Musique, 20 aout 1828)"; see Maurice Escoffier, *Le Mouvement Romantique 1788–1850: essai de bibliographie synchronique et méthodique* (Paris, 1934), p. 176.

20. Wedgwood, *Catalogues*, p. 28.

21. Waquet, *Les fêtes royales*, p. 20.

22. Lambourne, "Pugin and the Theatre," p. 39.

23. Escoffier, *Le Mouvement Romantique*, p. 262.

24. No analysis has ever been made of this aspect of Pugin's career, but it would be a rich and fascinating project.

25. Wedgwood (*Catalogues*, p. 38) here suggests that Lenoir was a bookseller.

26. Charles Norman, *A new Parallel of the Orders of architecture, according to the Greeks and Romans, and modern architects. With original plates drawn and engraved by Charles Normand. With the Text translated and two additional plates by Augustus Pugin* (London, 1829).

27. *En provenance de grandes demures et châteaux privés du Val de Loire a l'Orangerie du Châteaux de Cheverny . . . 14 mai 1995 . . . Philippe Rouillac Commissaire-priseur,* Lot 121. I would like to thank Philippe Rouillac for providing me with a picture of the piece.

28. "Welby Pugin professeur d'archéologie, au college d'Oscott, près Birmingham" (*Bulletin Archéologique publiè par Le Comité Historique des Arts et Monumens* 1 [1843],

pp. 6–11). This is the first volume of this periodical, but it relates to the session of 1838. Pugin had these volumes in his library.

29. "La lettre de M. Pugin comme une excellente introduction au travail que l'on préparé. Pour des discussions ou l'on voudrait recommander le style gothique, surtout le style du treizième siècle, dans la construction, l'ameublement et la décoration des églises, il n'y aurait pas de meilleure épigraphe que la lettre de illustre architecte anglais" (ibid. 2 [1842–43], p. 407).

30. "M. Pugin, le jeune et déjà illustre architecte catholique anglais, vient passer quelques jours avec nous à Paris. M. Pugin à étudié et admiré les travaux exécutés par nos amis dans St.-Germain-L'Auxerrois, dans St.-Germain-des-Près, et surtout dans la Ste.-Chapelle, il va porter en Angleterre le system et les procédés appliqués avec un certain bonheur à la reparation et à la décoration de nos monumens du moyen age" (*Annales Archéologiques* 1 [1844], p. 59).

31. Victoria & Albert Museum Library, Shrewsbury–Pugin correspondence.

32. Jean Michel Leniaud, *Jean Baptiste Lassus (1807–1857) ou le temps retrouvé des cathedrales* (Paris, 1980), p. 164 and plates 183, 184.

33. "Une mitre dans le style du XIVe siècle, une chasuble grande forme à la manière de Pugin" (ibid., p. 164).

34. For further informtion on St. Giles's, Cheadle, see chap. 5.

35. Robin Middleton, "Viollet le Duc's influence in nineteenth-century England," *Art History* 4, no. 2 (1981), p. 206. This fascinating article includes several mentions of Pugin and France.

36. Jan Van Cleven et al., *Neogotiek in Belge* (Ghent, 1994), pp. 95–96. This important book was published in conjunction with an exhibition of the same name and is the first full analysis of the Gothic Revival in Belgium.

37. Middleton, "Viollet le Duc's influence," p. 204.

38. "M. Scott avancera, suivi de MM. Butterfield, Carpenter, Pearson, Ferrey, Cundy, Daukes, White et Salvin. L'avenir de la renaissance ogivale est la, dans ce retour aux formes graves et belles du style primaire. Nous disions que reculer ainsi c'était avancer, et nous nous rappellons cette belle devise que Pugin à fait peindre sur les murs de sa charmante résidence de Ramsgate, ou nous avons passé trois des plus agréables journées de notre vie. Autour de ses armes, sur une banderole flottant au vent, nous lisons: EN AVANT. Pour Pugin le "gothique", pour ce retardataire, pour ce homme du passé, la devise appelait le progrès et l'avenir, et nous seul peut-être avons compris sa pensée profonde. Nous dirons donc aussi à messieurs les architectes anglais, dans le sens ou l'entendait Pugin: "En avant!" (*Annales Archéolgiques* 13 [1853], pp. 335–36).

Fig. 5-1. Pugin's Alton Castle, Staffordshire, with the ruins of the medieval castle.

5. Pugin's Architecture in Context

Andrew Saint

Marlow is a small, gentle town on the River Thames, some thirty miles west of London. A jumble of pretty red-brick and flint houses cluster about its high street, which leads down to Marlow's one memorable ensemble—the parish church of All Saints, overlooking a fine suspension bridge across the river.

In the early 1830s the old church had become saturated with river water, so the townsfolk rebuilt it to the design of a certain Charles Frederick Inwood, the obscure younger son of the Greek Revival architect William Inwood. What Inwood gave Marlow was a paradigm of English church architecture just before Queen Victoria took the throne in 1837. The style is Gothic, in line with England's ancient parish churches. Nothing surprising about that: great, state-aided campaigns to construct new Anglican churches over the previous few years had made revived Gothic so familiar as to become the norm for church-building. As a rule, however, it was a Gothic of efficiency and economy, and that is the main impression given by Marlow parish church as Inwood left it. It is faced with hard buff bricks, of a type and texture alien to the Thames Valley. Tall traceried windows of uniform pattern, slotted in mechanically between the buttresses, light what

in its early years was a mere galleried void, spanned by a single roof. A frontispiece with raw, overscaled carving and a quirky tower and spire offered worshipers their only moment of dignity and ornament as they entered the building.

Inwood's Gothic was not without skill. But it lacked soul or pride or imagination or local feeling, just where Marlow's parishioners might most have hoped and expected to find them. Those qualities they in fact strove to rediscover during the second half of the nineteenth century when they successively grafted on a chancel, raised the tower and spire, and replaced all the roofs and tracery to remedy the spiritual inadequacies of their church (fig. 5-2).

To understand the change of national spirit that led to these later additions, and the superior style in which they were to be made, we need look no further than a side street a few hundred yards away and a second church built only a few years later, in 1845–47. That is Saint Peter's Catholic Church, Marlow, designed by A. W. N. Pugin. Here, suddenly and on a far smaller scale, is architecture. You enter off the road through a graceful arch, set in a low flint wall (fig. 5-3). A path leads straight down the narrow churchyard, on line with the little west door. In front is the west end of the church, a thing of seeming sim-

Fig. 5-2. All Saints Church from High Street, Marlow; photograph by Henry Taunt, ca. 1875. (Buckinghamshire County Museum)

plicity. The gable end of the nave, with a tower and brief broach spire to one side of it, breaks the symmetry and masks a single, northern aisle. The walling, of rough knapped flintwork typical of the region, has a flickering, lingering texture and is drawn taut and flat across the front. The nave just dies into the tower, the tower into the nave. Breaks and projections in the main surface of the wall do not happen; the tower has a single strong setback, and a higher plinth than the nave. Openings come where they are wanted and of the size required, framed with dressed stones of uneven dimension spreading out into the flint-work. Casual though it looks, it is consummately controlled. It feels light years away from Inwood's strutting frontispiece.

Inside Saint Peter's (fig. 5-4), the visitor's awareness of compositional control gives way to a sense of emotional purpose and progression, something that is always present in Pugin's best buildings. Again, the church's small size must be stressed; less than a hundred seats were needed. It was built for what was then a tiny local Catholic community and paid for by a single donor, C. R. Scott-Murray.[1] Yet Pugin endowed this little building with every facet of the renewed Catholic architecture and symbolism to which he was so vehemently committed. There is, for a start, a firm division of parts—nave, north aisle, chancel, and sanctuary. No hint here of the bare, spatially undifferentiated box of eighteenth-century Protestant churches; the aisle is sundered from the nave by two plain arches with a single pier between them, while a high screen interrupts progress from the nave to the chancel.

Decoratively, the church gathers in force and pace as you approach the altar. Pugin puts ornament where it matters and means most. The pulpit (fig. 5-5), still in the lay portion of the church, is exquisitely simple—just three angular hunks of shaped and chamfered ashlar, with the Paschal lamb and flag carved in a quatrefoil on the long face. The chancel screen is the point of transition, pierced by tracery openings, laced with tendril and ballflower ornament, and surmounted by a rood. In the tiny chancel, the roof is boarded and painted, not open as in the nave. The floor patterning, having begun calmly with black and red tiles in the nave, intensifies and goes floral and ornamental; first yellow joins in, then in the sanctuary, blue, with the emblems of Mary and the Lamb. To one side are rich sedilia, and then up steps comes the climax of the church, the Altare Privilegiatum. On the reredos that forms a gaily painted backdrop, the evangelists scribble away with comic earnestness (even at such moments, Pugin never lacked humor). The windows glow with glass by John Hardman's firm in splashes of blue, red, and green for the figures and borders, while daintier quarries fill the ground in between. To modern architectural sensibilities, nurtured on spatial clarity, they make the church dark. Pugin would not have worried about this; he was concerned to create not openness, but mystery, mood, and enclosure.

* * *

Saint Peter's, Marlow, is a church of Pugin's maturity: serene, alive to its setting, sure in achieving the effects its creator intended. It also stands at a midpoint in the history of the Gothic Revival. Without understanding that history, it is impossible to understand Pugin's architectural revolution—a revolution that was to prove so successful in England and, indeed, beyond that it is very easy today to look upon his buildings as commonplace.

England differs from other European countries in its long and fanciful love affair with Gothic. In France, for instance, the cradle of medieval Gothic, an awareness and respect for the Gothic of the great cathedrals and the structural principles that they stood for never died. But until the nineteenth century was well advanced, this failed to burgeon into full-hearted revivalism.[2] In England, the practical survival and the revival of Gothic architecture are closely entwined. After

Fig. 5-3. View through the gates of Saint Peter's, Marlow.

Fig. 5-4. Interior, Saint Peter's, Marlow.

the Renaissance, Gothic lived on (as it did all over northern Europe) in works such as the finishing, extension, and repair of old churches, castles, and colleges. Then came the moment of self-consciousness, when Gothic gained a new lease on life in the private whims and fantasies of Georgian gentlemen. Horace Walpole is the most famous of these. Walpole's Strawberry Hill, begun just a century before the Marlow church, already displays a concern for archaeological accuracy.[3]

By the time of Pugin accuracy of Gothic detail had become an obsession. In its early stages it was a concern for accuracy of parts, for the Gothic vocabulary rather than the Gothic syntax, and for two dimensions rather than three. The ideologically dominant architecture in England between 1720 and 1820 was Neoclassicism, first in Palladian, later in Greek form. With a few exceptions, English Neoclassicism was preoccupied with surfaces rather than spaces, and this had its effect upon the way in which Gothic was relearned. Architects had first to know about old tracery patterns and moldings and vaulting before

they could learn how to knit them together. Knowledge takes time. Walpole and his many antiquarian successors, down to Pugin's father in his famous set of source books, showed architects where to look for Gothic detail.

A Gothic revival that went beyond mere Gothic motifs could not happen until the types of buildings built in the Middle Ages were again attempted in a thoroughgoing way. So, in its search for correctness, English-revived Gothic began to imply the revival of a life-style as well as an architectural style. Only extreme Romantics, however, were willing to go that far. The castles of the English picturesque movement, for instance, starting with Richard Payne Knight's sophisticated Downton Castle, Herefordshire (fig. 5-6), of the 1770s, set the trend toward the heftiness and asymmetry found in medieval originals. But such buildings remained few in number and timid in the scope which the Gothic style enjoyed once foot was set inside the portals. Whatever they wrote, Knight and his successors down to Sir Walter Scott wanted in their hearts to live like modern literary gentlemen with a taste for antiquity, not as medieval squires. Thomas Love Peacock catches the point perfectly in his satirical novel, *Melincourt* (published in 1818). When the chariot of the Honorable Mrs. Pinmoney passes the venerable battlements of Melincourt Castle, the ladies enter a court "of much more recent architecture than the exterior of the castle, and built in a style of modern Gothic, that seemed to form a happy medium between the days of feudality . . . and the nineteenth century." Ushered into the library, they find

> that the apartment was Gothic, and the furniture Grecian: whether this be an unpardonable incongruity calculated to disarrange all legitimate associations, or a judicious combination of solemnity and elegance, most happily adapted to the purposes of study, we must leave to the decision, or rather discussion, of picturesque and antiquarian disputants.[4]

In other words, by 1818 Englishmen of taste had begun to worry that the fashion for Gothic was producing nothing better than a series of eclectic shams.

* * *

That is why churches are so important. From today's overwhelmingly secular position, it is hard to comprehend a culture in which churches occupy pride of architectural place. But for the first time in Europe since the seventeenth century in Italy, such was the status that church-building held in England between about 1840 and 1870. Though new structures such as the Crystal Palace of 1851 or the railway stations might cause curiosity and excitement, the English architectural debate of these years was to be dominated by the science and practice of "ecclesiology." The difficulty today is to understand how architectural novelty and value can be buried in anything so arcane.

Fig. 5-5. The pulpit, Saint Peter's, Marlow.

83

Fig. 5-6. *A South West View of Downton Castle in the County of Hereford*, by James Sherrill; watercolor.

The background to this was the intensive English church-building campaign of the years after the Napoleonic Wars, undertaken in the hope that new churches would help to maintain the fraying social order. Anticipating the shift in attitudes when Queen Victoria took the throne, a more earnest approach toward social and religious problems gathered rapid force, in the newly industrialized and urbanized regions of England above all. Symbolic of the fresh cultural climate were the two hundred plus Anglican churches raised with state subsidy and a Church Building Commission during the 1820s.

The majority of these so-called Commissioners' Churches were built in Gothic—a fact of great significance, since the Church of England was still the official church, tied in to the powers and privilege of the State. The three-centuries-old intellectual and cultural authority of classicism had in effect come to an end in England, long before it did so in Continental Europe. Hence-

forward architects and clients would be free to choose their style. For Anglican churches, the historic associations of Gothic with the national past had become decisive. Soon afterward came the decree of 1835 that Gothic or "Elizabethan" designs alone would be allowed for rebuilding the House of Parliament. Suddenly, the immature Gothic Revival found itself blessed as the official, national style.

The Gothic of the Commissioners' Churches was low in average quality. Derided by Pugin and most of his contemporaries, it is still held in low esteem today. The churches were cheap and looked it: gaunt boxes, generally, like Inwood's All Saints, Marlow, with galleries crammed in all around and, at best, a thin tower in front. Frequently, classical or Gothic designs were offered as alternatives without any changes in planning— proof that architectural style was conceived as a two-dimensional add-on. Protestant Anglicans or their architects did not yet contemplate that layout or liturgical practice in churches ought to follow medieval precedent precisely. All the same, there were many continuities in English worship and tradition. The short step from the glorious past of Gothic to its inglorious present could be deduced from thousands of surviving old English parish churches. For the many Romantic nationalists of the 1820s and 30s, it was easier to imagine bridging that historic and archaeological gap in a building such as a church, of symbolic significance

and used only a few hours each week, than within a private residence.

In fact, many lessons of architectural value were learned from the Gothic church-building of the 1810s and 20s. In those churches where the state subsidy complemented local funds and a good architect did the job, Gothic details were competently designed and sometimes put together to make a fluent and telling composition. Saint Luke's, Chelsea (1820–24), in London, by the

Fig. 5-7. Contrasted chapels: Saint Pancras Chapel and Bishop Skirlaws Chapel, Yorkshire. From A. W. N. Pugin, *Contrasts* (1836).

Fig. 5-8. The Barn, Oxenford Farm, designed by A. W. N. Pugin, 1842.

structurally minded James Savage, for example, has a proper stone vault. Ramsgate, Pugin's home town after 1844, has another such church of some quality, Saint George's (1825–27) by Henry Hemsley and H. E. Kendall, with a convincing west tower.[5] Best of all are the clever Liverpool churches—Saint George's, Everton (1813–14) and Saint Michael's, Toxteth (1814–15) by the self-taught antiquary Thomas Rickman, who saw no reason why solidity and competence of Gothic detail should not be combined with pretty iron arcades and tracery, a practice all too soon to be anathematized by ecclesiologists. Rickman was one of the few proponents of English Gothic to have a clear philosophy of eclecticism.[6] A similar open use of the Gothic language to suit present-day needs and technologies became the point of

departure for architects such as Louis-Auguste Boileau, when revived French Gothic at last got into its stride with such fine churches as Saint Eugène in Paris (1854–55). The same kind of thing might have happened in England, had it not been for the dramatic intervention and influence of Pugin.

* * *

Pugin began as a draftsman and designer before turning architect, controversialist, and pamphleteer. Passionate though he was about Gothic architecture, he never had any formal training in the subject. But he learned with breakneck speed. When his book *Contrasts* was issued in 1836, he had yet to build a church; when *The True Principles of Pointed or Christian Architecture* came out five years later (fig. 5-7), he was only starting to build in accordance with those very principles and had his best work yet to come. So it is not surprising that his early churches are no finer architecture than those of Savage, Rickman, or the best of their successors (for instance Robert Dennis Chantrell, whose Leeds Parish Church of 1838–41 set a model for the Anglican churches of the Gothic Revival). But they begin from an altogether different social and religious standpoint.

In June 1835, at the age of twenty-three and only six years after Catholic Emancipation gave full civil rights to Catholics in Britain and Ireland, Pugin became a Roman Catholic. His conversion was both heartfelt and opportune. His training under his father and his own studies had made him expert in Gothic detail. Had he put his skills to building Anglican churches in the mid-1830s, he would have been obliged, like his predecessors, to marry archaeology with modern Protestant plan-form. As a Catholic, Pugin was now able instead to champion a complete, coherent revivalist package, in which English medieval traditions of religious worship, social hierarchy, architectural form and Gothic detail reinforced and authenticated one another. This was the program he now put forward. In *Contrasts* it took the form of a social and visual critique; Pugin then deepened and elaborated it into architectural theory in *True Principles* and all his later books. Though it informed his secular as well as his religious architecture, church-building was the central plank in the program. Catholics were now on a legal par with others in Britain, and they sorely needed churches. So Pugin had a golden opportunity to develop that program in practice.

Development, as Phoebe Stanton has shown, is the key to Pugin's church architecture.[7] Up to the time of *True Principles*, he was learning how to re-create in authentic form, with the whole kit of liturgical parts, the type of medieval-Catholic church that Rickman and others had already been paraphrasing in a loose, modern way. Usually Pugin favored the same Decorated or Second Pointed style preferred by Rickman; sometimes he used other medieval styles, straying forward into

Perpendicular, back into Early English and occasionally delving down into Romanesque. For the moment he was not averse to borrowing from the Gothic of other countries, if that seemed the right thing to do.

But by 1841, Pugin had decided that the Decorated style of around 1300 represented the acme of medieval achievement, so far as England was concerned. He saw it (as did other ecclesiologists) as the moment of maximum clarity, when the structural principles of Gothic were best understood and the different liturgical portions of a church—nave, aisles, chancel, sanctuary, tower and spire, and so on—were functionally and logically displayed, distinguished (with the "outline and breaks" which Pugin adored[8]), and ornamented. Decorated or Second Pointed offered the pedant's ideal of a medieval English church, without the ponderousness of earlier styles or the tricky, later sophistries of Perpendicular. The

Fig. 5-9. Drawing of Saint Marie's Grange inscribed, "First sketch for St. Marie's Grange—by A. W. Pugin"; pencil on paper, n.d. (The Winterthur Library: Joseph Downs Collection of Manuscripts and Printed Ephemera, no. Fol. 189)

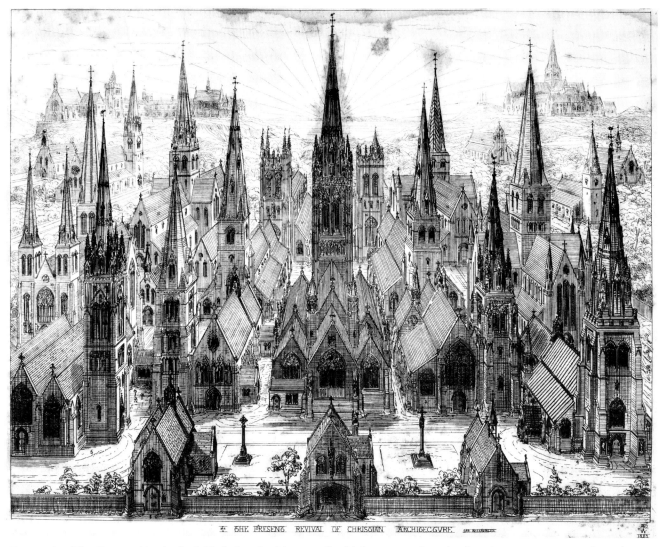

Fig. 5-10. "The Present Revival of Christian Architecture" which appeared as the frontispiece in *An Apology for the Revival of Christian Architecture in England* (1843).

Decorated style was visible in countless parish churches throughout the country, and alone furnished models that could safely be taught and disseminated. This seizing-upon a precise variant of past styles for study and development was nothing new. It had happened in England with Palladianism, and again with the Greek Revival; it now gave the Gothic cause the stylistic rallying-point that it had previously lacked.

Medieval precedent was always Pugin's church-building bible. But the sanctioning of a single style could never be enough. In order to turn the old Gothic vocabulary into a living Gothic language again and transform the two dimensions of the earlier revivalists into three, work had to be done; old building-types had to be studied and exem-

plars found. Pugin argued that there was no building problem that Gothic builders had not, at least in principle, adequately addressed. This was where his ever growing knowledge of medieval architecture (all around him as the originals of classical architecture had been for the Italians of the early Renaissance) proved invaluable. As he traveled, he sketched; at home, he amassed and ransacked books and curiosities in his thirst for practical knowledge.

The outcome was a series of typological solutions which set the next generation of Gothic Revival architects free from the stale church-building formulae of their predecessors. Pugin tackled the issue of how low-cost churches should differ in form from costly ones, how town churches should vary from country ones, and cathedrals from parish churches. For the broad auditorial urban church, he rediscovered in his competition design for Saint George's, Southwark (1839) the triple-gable roof over separate nave and aisles; for the narrower church in town or country he favored lean-to aisle roofs against the nave, with or without a clerestory. All the time, Pugin was developing in suppleness and sophistication. Towers and spires, for instance, move restlessly around his churches. They begin centrally at the west end—their invariable position in Commissioners' churches. Soon, in his important churches or cathedrals, they crown the crossing. Then in the 1840s they take asymmetrical positions, as Pugin matures, borrows a leaf from secular architecture, and groups his churches more casually and picturesquely. The science of church-planning in the mature Gothic Revival owes almost everything to Pugin. It is this more than anything which makes the better English churches in the second half of the nineteenth century stand head and shoulders above their Continental equivalents, which rarely transcend tired formulae of planning.

* * *

Pugin's reliance upon precedent and scholarship can make it hard for people to enjoy his architecture. In all stylistic revivals, there comes the moment at which designers understand their models well enough to build convincing copies: the question then arises, "What is the point?" Pugin had an answer; he wanted to revive medieval English architecture because he wanted to revive medieval English society and religion. Like many English Romantics, he disliked originality for its own sake, tied up as it was with the perilous concept of progress, which threatened to unhinge society. On the other hand he regarded Gothic as a living language, and saw no reason why it should not be developed to meet those needs of his age he agreed to be legitimate. Even so, Pugin never quite championed an absolute return to the habits of the Middle Ages. He was well aware, for instance, that he could never have built half the

Fig. 5-11. "Exterior, from the South," Saint Giles's, Cheadle; engraving.

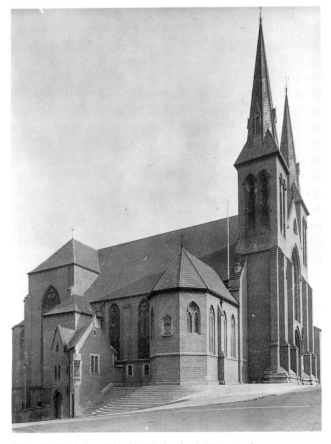

Fig. 5-12. Saint Chad's Cathedral, Birmingham.

89

Fig. 5-13. The interior of Saint Alban's, Macclesfield, designed by A. W. N. Pugin, 1839–41; lithograph by T. H. Bury. (Private collection)

medievalizing churches he did without the boon of the early railways wherewith to race the length and breadth of the country.

Even in his churches, where Gothic originals and modern equivalents corresponded most closely, he never copied exactly. No two Pugin churches are alike; they tally with each other and with their medieval models in principle alone. So in championing Second Pointed churches, there was never any need in his view to fear what Paul Waterhouse called the "corrosive effect exercised by mere imitation."[9] As for his secular buildings,

where it could plausibly be done, Pugin followed precedent just as closely. When it came to a college or a bridge, even a railway bridge, there was no dearth of models. His imposing and beautiful barn at Oxenford Farm, Surrey, too, is perfectly medieval in form (fig. 5-8). But many secular types of building were bound to differ from medieval ones. Country houses such as Charles Scarisbrick's Scarisbrick House, Lancashire, or the Earl of Shrewsbury's Alton Towers, Staffordshire, might be equipped with magnificent banqueting halls and kitchens in the pious hope that their owners would adopt the bounteous old patterns of living. But there were always comfortable rooms for modern family life; however sumptuous their Gothic detailing, there always remained something of Peacock's Melincourt about them.

From the modernist standpoint, Pugin's architecture is at its most original where there is little or no precedent to act as a guide—when, in fact, he is forced to do what Rickman had done, and find some middle path between ancient and modern. In these cases, he invents something like a new style, based upon the rational extension of Gothic principle but using only the precedent-hallowed materials of stone, brick, and timber (never iron, with its confusing proportions and hints of industrialism). The buildings in which this personal inventiveness shows up best are his range of smaller secular houses of brick, from Saint Marie's Grange (fig. 5-9), his own first home outside Salisbury (1835), to his last one, The Grange at Ramsgate (1843–44) and beyond.

Sacred or secular, precedent-bound or prophetic, Pugin's architecture possesses a strong common personality. Verticality is its most immediately striking individual quality. Gothic is a style which often (not always) aspires to height and vertical accent. In England, this was truest in its Decorated phase. Pugin often notes this in his writings; in *An Apology for the Revival of Christian Architecture in England* (1843; fig. 5-10) he abuses the "pedimented and telescopic steeples" of classicism, which he defines as a "horizontal architecture" incapable of the noble height exemplified by Gothic towers and spires (he argues that all towers should be crowned with spires and that medieval towers without them were merely unfinished), font covers, and canopies.[10] In *The Present State of Ecclesiastical Architecture in England* (also 1843) he takes the point further: "a high pitched roof is itself a great ornament to a building, and adds prodigiously to its grandeur." The lower roofs and flattened arches of later Gothic,

Fig. 5-14. The Church of Saint Lawrence, Tubney, designed by A. W. N. Pugin, 1845–47.

Fig. 5-15. Rampisham Rectory, Dorset, designed by A. W. N. Pugin, 1846–48.

he continues, mark a "departure from the vertical principle," when "the spirit of pointed architecture was on the wane."[11]

In Pugin's major buildings up to about 1845, there is a frank exaggeration of this vertical quality. In part deliberate, it may also reflect his excitable temperament. The arcades in Saint Chad's Cathedral, Birmingham, are, from the standpoint of English precedent, too tall; the spire of his "perfect" Saint Giles's, Cheadle (fig. 5-11), is implausibly, arrestingly high for a parish church of its size; the walls of many of his secular buildings, from early Saint Marie's Grange, Salisbury (1835), to the Bishop's House at Birmingham (1840) and Alton Castle (ca. 1847; see fig. 5-1) are sheer and clipped. The Palace of Westminster was the undisputed work of Charles Barry, yet the Big Ben clock tower and the other vertical accents that bristle upon that majestic fantasy would surely never have been so tight and tall without the stimulus of Pugin's example.[12] In the elements of the buildings of his middle years it is the same. Roofs are acutely angled, windows sharply pointed (Pugin's fondness for the term "pointed architecture" is telling), runs of tall arches squashed in tight together. In his domestic work, chimney breasts are slung out to external walls where the extravagant height of their stacks can

be savored; bay windows are clamped steeply upon walls, where other architects liked to let them expand easefully outwards. Only a few of Pugin's English disciples, notably William Butterfield and Henry Woodyer, copy the prickliness and occasional harshness of this verticality.[13]

Sometimes, as in the rafters of his roof structures, all this turns into an attenuation close enough to the thinness found in low-budget Commissioners' churches. Such features led to accusations that Pugin "starved his roof-tree to gild his altar."[14] Often he had difficulties finding money for his ambitious designs; many of his buildings suffer from it, as he admitted in the more self-critical days toward the end of his life. Almost by definition, his mode of Gothic was not cheap. Pugin liked to claim that it competed in economy with other styles, but his arguments on this score do not convince. Like any intelligent architect, he made conscious decisions on where to spend his clients' money; and in the "roof-tree" he seems to have been content with un-medieval thinness. Height in building costs money, and if the scantling of a rafter had to be reduced to achieve this, it was done. On buttresses, however, Pugin never stinted in his mature work; even when they do little structural work they are fat, solid and satisfying, rather than the etiolated add-ons of the Commissioners' churches. The difference between Saint Giles's, Cheadle, and All Saints, Marlow, in this respect is immediately striking.

The question of resources brings out a critical difference between the conditions under which Pugin worked and the practice of the medieval Gothic builders. In the Middle Ages churches were built slowly, perforce; Pugin was always in a hurry, in keeping with his personality and the demands of his Victorian clients. Pugin's buildings often disappoint; he took too much on. But those that do so are not so much the cheap ones as those where money was needed but not available quickly enough. A famous case was his largest London church, Saint George's Cathedral, Southwark, constructed in stages between 1841 and 1848. Pugin himself recognized it as a failure (it was never finished and has now been largely rebuilt following bomb damage during World War II).[15] Saint George's was also the ground on which John Ruskin chose to attack Pugin most bitterly, mocking his excuses about lack of money:

> Want of money! was it want of money that made you put that blunt, overloaded laborious ogee door into the side of it? Was it for lack of funds that you sank the tracery of the parapet in its clumsy zigzags? Was it in parsimony that you buried its paltry pinnacles in that eruption of diseased crockets? Or in pecuniary embarrassment that you set up the belfry fools'-caps, with the mimicry of dormer windows, which nobody can ever reach nor look out of?[16]

If Ruskin was always unfair about Pugin, he was by no means the only such aggressor. The critic and author Charles Lock Eastlake, from the perspective of the next and better-funded generation of church-builders, complained too of Pugin's miserably slight walls and "poor and wiry mouldings."[17] Pugin's predicament was certainly not easy. The grain of truth was that he lacked patience and was inclined, especially in his early work, to try and force architectural silk purses from sows' ears.

* * *

Pugin's buildings were personal and original also in their concern for context and texture. This quality, perhaps the least appreciated aspect of his architecture today, proceeded from the nature of Gothic. Classicism, though it came in many versions, was at heart an international, centralizing language of architecture which in the hands of educated designers transcended or overrode local building habits and materials. Gothic was otherwise. Not only was it native to northern climates and therefore in Pugin's eyes the right style for Britain, but it had also in medieval hands proved marvelously sensitive and adaptable to local materials and conditions. England, with its rapid shifts of scenery and geology, offered dramatic differences in the handling of Gothic from one region to another which fascinated nineteenth-century antiquarians. Alertness to vernacular and regional architecture, already a mark of the English picturesque movement, was intensifying in the years Pugin came to maturity. By the 1830s one finds in the writings of the designer-journalist John Claudius Loudon and the young John Ruskin a sharpening of the doctrine, never before explicit in European architecture, that the good architect ought to heed local traditions and conditions, wherever and whatever he builds.[18]

A scholarly Goth such as Pugin was in a far stronger position to react to this trend than a classicist. Even so, it took time for him to realize its implications. It seems obvious now that if, for instance, you build in Ireland you use an Irish style, while if you build in England you use an English style. This Pugin eventually achieved. But it first needed better understanding of the difference between English and Irish Gothic. Even in England, not until about 1840 do Pugin's buildings look purely English. His earlier works often have a tang of German or Flemish Gothic to them. Saint Chad's Cathedral, Birmingham (1839–41; fig. 5-12), in particular, with its all-embracing single roof over nave and aisles and its tight twin towers, is partially based on Munich Cathedral and on Saint Elizabeth, Marburg; it might even pass muster as the work of some emigrant Rhenish architect in a city of the American Midwest. Early on in the Birmingham project, Pugin had admitted adopting "a foreign style of pointed architecture because it is both cheap and effective and likewise because it is totally different from any *protestant* erection."[19]

Once Pugin had concluded that only English Gothic would do in England and Irish Gothic in Ireland, he stuck to his principle, although it caused him some difficulty with interior fittings. His High Victorian successors, William Butterfield, William Burges, G. E. Street, and others, on the other hand, blithely incorporated French, German, or Italian ideas in their churches when it suited their turn. Not until the late Victorian period was there a reversion to the purely national ideal of architectural style. In this respect, Pugin prefigures the Arts and Crafts movement more than his High Victorian successors do.

Contextualism in Pugin's architecture goes beyond national or regional reference. "Association," an old ideal of the picturesque movement, is always strong in his work. Where there is a specific historical cue, he never fails to pick it up. Saint James's, Reading (1837–40), his one Norman-style church in England, is so only because it stands next to the ruins of Reading's Norman abbey. The Alton Castle complex in Staffordshire (ca. 1847) likewise takes the fragment around which it is sited as the point of departure for its ultra-feudal additions. Many English castle-builders had played the same trick, right back to Sir Christopher Wren and Robert Hooke's turreted Greenwich Observatory of the 1670s, on the site of a little fortlet. But the fresh blend of scholarship, flair, and delight in sharp disjunctions and asymmetries which Pugin brought to Alton makes the castle-building of his immediate predecessors look stale and half-hearted. Alton Castle is no place to look for "true principles," but a reversion to pure romance. Among castles of the English Gothic Revival it has only one rival, Lord Tollemache's contemporary Peckforton Castle in Cheshire (1844–50) by Anthony Salvin.

Where no historical link can be made, Pugin knits his buildings to the nature of brief and locality by virtue of the materials he chooses, and adapts his detailing accordingly. The dressed ashlar of Saint Giles's, Cheadle (1840–46), the coursed rubble of his pretty little Anglican church at Tubney in Berkshire (1845–47; fig. 5-14), the rougher rubble of Rampisham Rectory, Dorset (1846–48; fig. 5-15), the Irish jumperwork of Saint Patrick's College, Maynooth (1846–53), the all-over flintwork of Saint Peter's, Marlow (1845–47), the setting-off of similar flints with chippings and stone courses at Saint Augustine's, Ramsgate (1844–50), the red brick of Birmingham Cathedral (1839–41), the yellow stock brick of Saint Peter's, Woolwich, London (1842–43), are none of them arbitrary choices. They are decisions that take local building traditions and opportunities as their point of departure and go on to guide every external detail. Just as there is a hier-

archy in Pugin's mind between the different parts of a church, so also when he designs a complex of buildings, he establishes in his mature work a hierarchy of materials. The grandest portion—the church—may be of ashlar, regularly laid and dressed but with the marks of the tool left on it to avoid a mechanical surface; the humblest portion—the school, perhaps, or cottages, or a boundary wall—will be of brick, with or without stone dressings. The method is most visible today around Saint Giles's, Cheadle, but it can also be discerned in Pugin's designs for cathedral complexes at Birmingham, Southwark, and Nottingham.

Pugin's use of brickwork is of special interest and provides the key to understanding the forward-looking element in his secular architecture. Brick was the material with which he chose to face most of his urban buildings, even his churches, as well as many humbler ones in the countryside. It was the unifying element in Victorian building construction, available everywhere. Stone-faced buildings, unless they were very costly, were lined internally with brick and then plastered; this Pugin could countenance and usually practiced. What neither he nor the later Victorian Gothic revivalists could abide was the "sham" stucco external covering that had been fashionable for houses since 1800, and trickled on (in London especially) until the 1870s.

Early on, Pugin seems to have resolved on a candid approach to external brickwork. How he arrived at his distinctive brick secular style is not quite clear. Since England has neither any Decorated Gothic churches nor any fourteenth-century houses of brick, indigenous medieval models offered no help. Instead, Pugin seems to have borrowed the red brick and diapering of the English Tudor period and improvised an earlier language out of them, with hints from Flanders and Germany. As with his churches, he by no means started in a vacuum. Architects of the 1820s and 30s had been designing amiable, informal neo-Tudor villas and almshouses, which were built in stucco or brick indifferently.[20] Pugin took this picturesque style by the scruff of the neck, shaped and sharpened it, purged it of lax or fancy

Fig. 5-16. Bishop's House, Birmingham; engraving by Pugin from his book, *The Present State of Ecclesiastical Architecture* (1843).

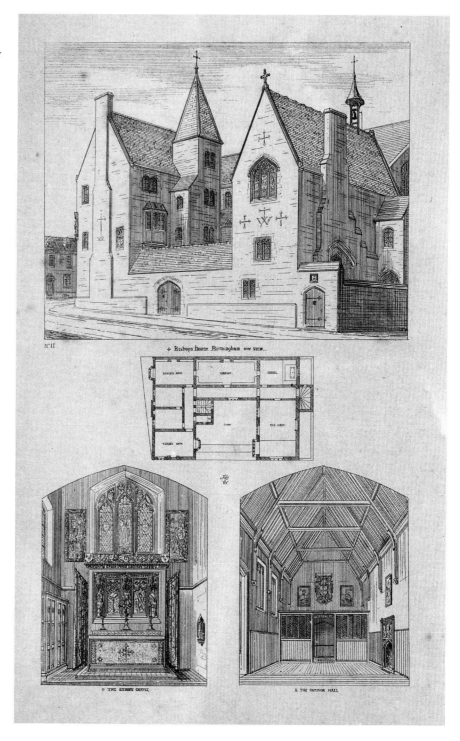

detail for economy's sake, and clad it with his new, disciplined brickwork. The outcome is the most "rational" and "progressive" part of his architectural *oeuvre*.

Pugin's brickwork begins with his very first building, Saint Marie's Grange near Salisbury, designed for himself in 1835. That Pugin, already a fervid medievalist, should have opted to start out with a house of brick is something of a puzzle. But its sheer surfaces of plain red walling, based on the ruddy brick walls of the Tudor period,

were a dramatic innovation at a time when other English architects preferred brown or off-white or yellow for their brickwork, or hid it altogether. At Birmingham, Pugin again chose red brick for Saint Chad's Cathedral and Bishop's House (1840). Bishop's House (fig. 5-16), perhaps the most influential building Pugin ever designed, was sheer, austere, and disciplined, a tight little ecclesiastical fortress devised to keep Protestants at psychological bay at a time when Catholics still feared anti-popery riots. A few stone dressings and

Fig. 5-17. The chapel at Saint Edmund's College, Ware; designed by A. W. N. Pugin, 1845–50.

square-headed windows were thrown in where they were needed. To offset the austerity, the chimney breasts and walls were peppered with crosses and the initial of Bishop Walsh in patterns. Alas, Bishop's House has gone now, but the bold and succulent texture of Pugin's brickwork can still be savored on the elevations of the cathedral next to its site. Brick building of this quality just did not exist then in England.

In his later works, Pugin clung to his rational brickwork but veered away from the strength and hotness of red. The chapel of Saint Edmund's College, Ware in Hertfordshire (1845–50; fig. 5-17), for instance, is of yellow stock brick, perhaps to match the earlier buildings of the college. Pugin's own house, The Grange at Ramsgate, too, is faced in stocks with courses of red brick, contrasting with the Kentish mixture of flint and stone on Saint Augustine's Church next door. By then a fashion for Puginian red brickwork was established. Butterfield used it for All Saints, Margaret Street (1850–59), the model London church of the ecclesiologists; hence it spread to become the common idiom for urban buildings of the Gothic Revival and later of the secular "Queen Anne" revival. The lineage of the red

brick that formed the bedrock of the best English domestic architecture at the end of the century goes back to Pugin's work at Birmingham and Saint Marie's Grange.

* * *

Ramsgate is the place to leave Pugin: specifically, The Grange of 1843–44 and Saint Augustine's of 1844–50, the juxtaposed house and church he built and paid for high on the chalk cliffs above the English Channel (figs. 5-18 and 5-19).[21] Though far from the last things he designed, they touchingly sum up the personality of the man, the state of the Gothic Revival when he died, and his own achievement in architecture. The group is forlorn today, sandwiched between a noisome road and the injury of a giant ferry terminal at the base of the cliff, ravaging the sea view Pugin once enjoyed from his towers. The one place of tranquillity is the churchyard. In front stretches the length of the church, cruciform, buttressless and sturdy, walled in flints packed together between courses of brown stonework into tight containers, like cells in a hive, with a single traceried window in the transept as enrichment. Here are a discipline, nobility, and feeling for texture that no other Gothic architect could yet match; there is even repose, something which Pugin rarely achieved. To its left ranges the house, the "substantial Catholic home, not very large but solid" of its architect's dreams[22]: bricky, irregular, quirky, restless, a little mad even (as Pugin himself was to become); a reminder of the waning Romantic movement, with a lookout tower barging upward and a tiny chapel on the end, turned reverently toward the church. Here secular and sacred come together in an epitome of Pugin's changing architectural moods.

At first sight Pugin's contribution to architecture seems imitative, archaeological, and backward-looking; on closer scrutiny, it turns out to be pregnant with future possibilities. Well before his death in 1852, his medievalizing model had swept the established Church of England and was penetrating English-speaking communities around the world. So complete was the triumph of Puginian church-building that Victorian churches of the standard, Decorated type became the norm and, indeed, something of a bore. When the town of Marlow in the late nineteenth century refashioned its Anglican Church of All Saints in the Puginian image, it was only doing what the average English community felt obliged to do after 1850. And when Nikolaus Pevsner dismissed Pugin's Saint Peter's, Marlow, as "far from distinguished," he was seeing it through the lens of countless later imitations, many of them competent enough.[23]

The stronger Victorian Gothic church-builders soon abandoned mere Puginism and pursued all sorts of Continental models, often to splendid effect. But after 1870, under the lead of George Frederick Bodley in particular, English architects reverted to Pugin's inspiration, so that Anglican churches of the late Victorian and Edwardian period are more often like Pugin's than those of the 1850s and 60s. This was deliberate; they felt that for an English context Pugin had got it right. Norman Shaw, best known as a house architect, is an example. He revisited Saint Augustine's, Ramsgate, in the early 1890s and found it "A most delightful and interesting work . . . I am afraid we have not advanced much. Such a work makes one feel small, *very* small."[24] Shaw himself lifted the plan of the Ramsgate church and its internal ashlar lining for the church he was then building at Richards Castle, Shropshire (1891–93), and its flinty texture (fig. 5-20) and central tower in his next (and last) church, All Saints, Swanscombe, Kent (1894–95; figs. 5-21 and 5-22). Unlike the earnest churches of the early ecclesiologists, these are not literal imitations; Pugin's later church-building disciples took from him what they needed and no more. They represent a reasoned homage—a tribute to someone who has created a living language and taught people how to speak it for themselves. This qualified, reasonable Puginism spread abroad too, via Bodley's pupil Henry Vaughan, via Ralph Adams Cram, via Bertram Goodhue and others, to Australasia, India, and South Africa as well as North America.

The lineage of descent for Pugin's domestic

Fig. 5-18. An aerial view of The Grange and Saint Augustine's, Ramsgate, ca. 1930.

Fig. 5-19. Interior, Saint Augustine's, Ramsgate.

were the starting point in the 1860s for Philip Webb and, to an extent, the more fanciful Norman Shaw and W. E. Nesfield, at a period when the excitement of church-building was on the wane and English architecture was turning back to its older preoccupation with houses. After them come C. F. A. Voysey (an outspoken admirer of Pugin), Edwin Lutyens, and a host of accomplished English Arts and Crafts house-builders, much admired in Germany, Austria, and America, and the influence of domestic Pugin too becomes international. With so many cross-currents in between, it is unwise to be precise about this line. Pugin and Frank Lloyd Wright would have found much to loathe in one another's sentiments and works. But Wright would not have built in quite the same spirit had Pugin never lived. The moral and missionary blood of Pugin's reforming Gothic flowed deep in his veins.

* * *

How distinguished an architect is Pugin? Cultural reputations and meanings today are expected to be internationally exchangeable; we judge buildings most often from their pictorial effect and prize them for pure originality. On terms of that kind, Pugin will remain opaque. He can boast neither the rugged inventiveness of Hawksmoor's baroque, nor the nervous eccentricity and Neoclassical experimentation of Soane (whom he

work is subtler and harder to trace. From The Grange and other lesser houses by Pugin (not the big country mansions) come first the tight, austere, minimally Gothic parsonage houses of William Butterfield, William White, and G. E. Street, beginning with Butterfield's Coalpit Heath Vicarage in Gloucestershire (1844–45). These

Fig. 5-20. The south end of Saint Augustine's, Ramsgate.

Fig. 5-21. Detail of the west end, Church of All Saints, Swanscombe.

despised), nor the budding a-historicism of C. R. Mackintosh, to name the three British architects most often admitted nowadays to lofty positions in the pantheon of design.

Pugin had a different approach to architecture from any of these men. Though gifted with a fine feeling for proportions, he had no desire to manipulate or balance form or create imposing space for its own sake. Overall grand or axial compositions were of no concern to him. For reasons of function and hierarchy, he preferred to break and divide his buildings up, to compose in the English tradition of separate, picturesque parts. At the same time, the new vitality with which Pugin endowed the language of Gothic dragged architecture away from the two-dimensional "shirt front" approach common in the 1820s to a fully three-dimensional approach to composition, allied to a new sensitivity for surfaces and textures. In his secular buildings, Bishop's House at Birmingham above all, when he found originality to be essential, he could be blindingly adventurous. These are the parts of his *oeuvre* that make today's architects sit up and take notice, because they are the first English buildings in traditional materials to foreshadow the rational construction that became an obsession of our century. But they are hardly the works that Pugin himself would have regarded most highly.

Pugin's own goal was different. Structural principle was important to him, but it was far from enough, and we err if we judge his works by that standard. He hoped to create a historicist architecture based on reason, in order to serve a higher social, moral, and religious purpose. That is why churches came top of his agenda. To be fully appreciated, neo-Gothic churches such as Pugin

Fig. 5-22. Church of All Saints, Swanscombe; designed by Norman Shaw, 1894–95.

built require sympathy with a set of hierarchical rules every bit as hard to grasp as the rules of classical architecture. There is one requirement in addition—faith. Today, if we prefer Pugin's fertility as a designer of decorative objects or his originality as a harbinger of rational construction, that means that we do not go along with his whole program. We can at least learn from it that architecture or decoration or art of any kind is impoverished without some extra, outward-looking layer of serious meaning and intention.

I am grateful to Rory O'Donnell and Sandra Wedgwood for generous help with this essay.

1. Saint Peter's, Marlow, is used here as an example of Pugin's work because it has not been much discussed in the literature. See, however, Alexandra Wedgwood, *Catalogue of the Architectural Drawings in the Victoria & Albert Museum: A. W. N. Pugin and the Pugin Family* (London, 1985), p. 196. The church was very well extended by Francis Pollen in 1969–70.

2. A satisfactory book on the French Gothic Revival is still awaited. See, however, Jean-Michel Leniaud, *Jean-Baptiste Lassus* (Geneva & Paris, 1980); Barry Bergdoll in Robin Middleton, ed., *The Beaux-Arts and Nineteenth-Century French Architecture* (London, 1982), p. 217; Frances H. Steiner, *French Iron Architecture* (Ann Arbor, Michigan, 1984); David Van Zanten, *Building Paris* (Cambridge & New York, 1994); and the copious literature on Viollet-le-Duc.

3. The best account of the early Gothic Revival in England remains Kenneth Clark, *The Gothic Revival* (London, 1928 etc.).

4. Thomas Love Peacock, *Melincourt* (1818), chap. 2.

5. It is notable that Pugin designed Catholic churches for three English towns that had newly built Gothic churches of some merit which he may have wished to outdo: first, the town of Marlow; second, Ramsgate, where Saint George's (by Henry Hemsley and H. E. Kendall, 1825–27) with its fine tower is praised by John Newman, *The Buildings of England: North East and East Kent* (Harmondsworth, 1976 ed.), pp. 421–22; third, Dudley, where William Brooks's excellent Saint Thomas's (1816–17) makes an interesting contrast with Pugin's Church of Our Lady and Saint Thomas of Canterbury (1839–40).

6. Britain's most interesting eclectic church architect after Rickman was E. B. Lamb (1806–69), a contemporary of Pugin's, whose work differs in purpose and style from that of the so-called "rogue" High Victorian architects.

7. Phoebe Stanton, *Pugin* (London, 1971), gives much the best overall account of Pugin's architecture; see also her excellent summary in *Macmillan Encyclopedia of Architects*, vol. 3, 1982, pp. 484–97.

8. Quoted by Stanton in *Encyclopedia*, p. 489.

9. Paul Waterhouse, *Architectural Review* 4, 1898, p. 67, in the course of his excellent early articles on Pugin.

10. A. W. N. Pugin, *An Apology for the Revival of Christian Architecture in England* (1843), p. 26.

11. A. W. N. Pugin, *The Present State of Ecclesiastical Architecture in England* (1843), p. 52.

12. There is no doubt that Barry designed the Palace of Westminster Clock Tower ("Big Ben" is really the clock) but equally no doubt that it was influenced by Pugin's tower at

Scarisbrick. The account by M. H. Port in his *The Houses of Parliament* (London & New Haven, 1976), pp. 157–59, equivocates.

13. Butterfield is less consistent than Woodyer in his interest in verticality; it is strongest in both men in the 1850s. See Paul Thompson, *William Butterfield* (London, 1971).

14. C. L. Eastlake, *A History of the Gothic Revival* (1872), p. 162.

15. A clear account of Saint George's and its chequered progress is given by Roderick O'Donnell and Alexandra Wedgwood in *The Buildings of England. London 2: South* (Harmondsworth, 1983), pp. 572–74.

16. John Ruskin, *The Stones of Venice,* vol. 1 (1851 ed.), pp. 372–73. The attack was suppressed in subsequent editions.

17. Eastlake, *A History,* p. 152.

18. The growing consciousness of a need for loyalty to local materials in early nineteenth-century architecture is not well explored in existing literature. See notably John Ruskin, *The Poetry of Architecture* (1839), chaps. 7 and 12; J. C. Loudon, *An Encyclopaedia of Cottage, Farm and Villa Architecture* (1833); and for the same sentiments elsewhere, Gottfried Semper, *The Four Elements of Architecture,* tr. Mallgrave and Herrmann (Cambridge, 1989), p. 48.

19. Pugin to Hardman, June 10, 1837, quoted by Alexandra Wedgwood in her essay on Pugin's domestic architecture in Atterbury and Wainwright, eds., *Pugin,* p. 51. The quotation refers to an earlier scheme than the one built.

20. The little-noticed English almshouse-building boom of the 1820s is of special interest in providing modest, disci-plined buildings, usually in the Tudor style and of plain brick. They are the kinds of buildings Pugin would have remarked, though it hardly suited his political views to note their proliferation under the gradually reforming Anglican regime. See, for instance, Blore's excellent Preachers' and Pensioners' Courts at The Charterhouse, London, 1825–30. Pugin's own Saint Anne's Bedehouse, Lincoln (1847, unsupervised), shows, however, that he was quite prepared to ornament his brick style when occasion warranted, even in almshouses.

21. The best accounts of the Ramsgate church and house are given by John Summerson in *The Architect and Building News* (December 27, 1940) and *Architectural Review* 103 (April 1948), pp. 163–66.

22. Pugin to John Bloxam, quoted in Patricia Spencer-Silver, *Pugin's Builder: The Life and Work of George Myers* (Hull, 1993), p. 13.

23. Nikolaus Pevsner, *The Buildings of England. Buckinghamshire* (Harmondsworth, 1960), p. 198. This judgment is awkwardly perpetuated in the fuller and more accurate account (by Geoffrey Brandwood) of the church in the second edition of the book by Elizabeth Williamson (Harmondsworth, 1994), p. 457.

24. R. Norman Shaw to Mrs. Johnston Foster of Richards Castle, October 18, 1892, quoted in Andrew Saint, *Richard Norman Shaw* (London & New Haven, 1976), p. 290. This letter was written when the Richards Castle church was nearing completion, but Shaw made several holiday visits to Ramsgate in this period and there can be little doubt that the plan and interior of this church were influenced by Saint Augustine's, Ramsgate.

Fig. 6-1. The interior of Cologne Cathedral, by Sulpiz Boisserée; engraving, 1823. From *Domwerk* (Cologne, 1823).

6. The Ideal of the Gothic Cathedral in 1852

Barry Bergdoll

The Pointed Arch will circle the globe.
A. N. Didron, 1853

Nurtured in the fertile soils of nationalism and the religious revival of the early nineteenth century, the Gothic Revival seemed poised, by the time of Pugin's death in 1852, to become an international affair. Revived Pointed or Christian architecture scarcely needed a renewed apology, Pugin's greatest French champion, Adolphe-Napoléon Didron, reassured the readers of his polemical *Annales Archéologiques*: "M. Pugin is dead, but he lives on in his older son and in . . . eight or ten other young architects in Great Britain who have devoted themselves to medieval architecture."[1] No other country could rival the cohort of George Gilbert Scott, William Butterfield, G. E. Street, R. C. Carpenter, William White, to name but a few "Goths" who had established respected and highly active architectural offices in London by the 1850s. But nearly everywhere the movement was gaining ground. Didron offered a field report. France was in the forefront, and the campaign there was advancing with huge strides: two hundred neo-Gothic churches were under construction and the aesthetic ministry had found adherents in nearly every region. A Gothic-style chapel was even said to be under construction in Corsica. In the politically fragmented map of German-speaking Central Europe Catholics and

Protestants alike were exploring the "national" past as essential to the forging of the "national" future. In addition to these strongholds, where Gothic antiquarianism could be traced back to the turn-of-the century, new conquests were being made each year. Medievalizing churches were planned or under way in Belgium, Switzerland, Austria, Spain, and Russia. Even Greece had given way: "The Greek style has been conquered even its last citadel, its very cradle."[2] Didron concluded in noting a neo-Gothic church under construction in Athens. Colonial Gothic was established from New Zealand to the West Indies. The next issue of the *Annales* included a report on the "mouvement archéologique" in the United States, the only independent western-style nation state with no gothic past. Even here the future was bright and Gothic: "So the pointed arch has arrived even in California and we can adopt for it the slogan we used once for Liberty: The Pointed Arch will circle the globe."[3]

By 1852, Didron had become one of the most tireless and internationally connected promoters of the Gothic cause. And he was a master at public relations. For in reality the Gothic was no more clearly triumphant at mid-century than political liberty, which had failed nearly everywhere with the collapse of the revolutionary

Fig. 6-2. Sainte Clotilde, Paris, designed by Franz Christian Gau and Théodore Ballu; constructed 1846–57.

uprisings of 1848–49. Whether the cause be the forging of a modern democratic nation state or the revival of the "national" architecture—and many were advocating that the two went hand-in-hand—it was clear in 1852 that both the stylistic and political struggles remained on the horizon. This was so even though the English, and A. W. N. Pugin in particular, had set an example. Just as Pugin's own career had taken him from ad-hoc antiquarianism to a theory of Gothic as a comprehensive system for a once and future Christian Society, so the European Gothic Revivals were evolving and facing new challenges in the 1850s.

The Gothic Cause at Mid-Century

In many ways 1852 was a signal year on the Continent. Not only was nearly every country adjust-

ing politically to the aftermath of the revolutions that had shaken the political status quo from Paris to Budapest in 1848–49, but the world of architecture was rife with conflict. Nearly everywhere key figures in the Gothic Revival took stock of their positions, and engaged, often even politically, for the fight ahead. In many cities skylines were being corrected in the spirit of Pugin's famous contrast between the industrial city of 1840 and the medieval city of 1440 (see cat. fig. 58b): Sainte Clotilde in Paris (Franz Christian Gau and Théodore Ballu, 1846–57; fig. 6-2) and the Nikolaikirche in Hamburg (G. G. Scott, 1845–63; fig. 6-3). There was also the ongoing project of completing Cologne Cathedral, where the keystone of the main arch of the west front was laid in 1852. New opportunities arose as never before; but the Gothic was anything but a *fait accompli.*

The question of style was everywhere the subject of politicized debate. In September 1852 the cornerstone was laid for a romano-byzantine style cathedral in Marseilles, the first new cathedral built in France in the nineteenth century. It was part of Louis Napoleon's campain to win over the south of France to the upcoming declaration of the French Second Empire. In the same year style was debated in the two leading German states, Prussia and Bavaria. A major polemic over the funding of architectural education arose in the Prussian parliament. In Bavaria King Maximilian II was awaiting the decision of the jury on an unusual competition to create a new style for use in a grand public building and its boulevard in Munich. In the following years major church competitions were announced for Gothic designs, in Vienna in 1853 and in Lille in 1854. The issues that loomed large in the 1850s were at once architectural and political: stylistic eclecticism versus national purity, invention versus tradition, nationalism versus cosmopolitanism, and the challenge of new building programs and new materials to the historicist logic of the Gothic Revival position.

While the battle lines of the 1830s and 40s had generally been clearly drawn between classical and Gothic camps, by the 1850s positions had evolved. Gothic Revival theorists had begun to question earlier doctrines of strict archaeological imitation, a trend announced by Pugin in his own late writings and especially apparent in the positions espoused by *The Ecclesiologist* from the early 1850s. The architectural establishment itself was changing, even if the "Goths" would not always acknowledge it in polemical exchanges. In France, Prussia, and Bavaria the academies and state schools of architecture had all been rocked by internal critiques. A younger generation challenged the absolutist aesthetics and timeless universals of doctrinaire Neoclassicism with calls for a style that obeyed the laws of historical development and responded to the relative demands of national and local conditions. The world was much changed from the polarized situation portrayed in Pugin's *Contrasts* of 1836 (2nd ed., 1841), even if this book was to have a revival in Belgium after Pugin's death.[4]

France

Throughout the early nineteenth century French Gothic Revivalists envied the advance enjoyed by the English in the historical study of medieval architecture and art, and even more the professional stature and sophistication of neo-Gothic design in Britain. Yet nowhere else did Gothic enjoy the official endorsement accorded it by the French state. Ever since the 1789 Revolution, successive regimes had drawn on the medieval past to assert the historical legitimacy of their regime, even as they came to power with a sharp rupture with the immediate past. Just such a rupture had given birth to the campaign to convert medieval monuments from symbols of a "superstitious" and "tyrannical" past, instruments of the hierarchies of church and aristocracy, into precious vessels of national identity and memory.[5] While the Revolution coined the term *vandalism*— inventing the word to kill the thing, in the Abbé Grégoire's oft-quoted words—and formulated the first legislation to place ancient buildings under government protection, it was only after the July Revolution of 1830 that a powerful set of institu-

tions was put in place, quickly becoming the model for state restoration efforts throughout Europe. This was the result of a happy conjuncture: the anxieties of the citizen king Louis Philippe (reigned 1830–48) over the shaky foundations of his regime born on the barricades combined with the entry into the government of a number of the historians. François Guizot, who was most notable among them, had already crafted an engaged practice of historical narrative

Fig. 6-3. Nikolaikirche, Hamburg, designed by G. G. Scott; constructed 1845–63.

105

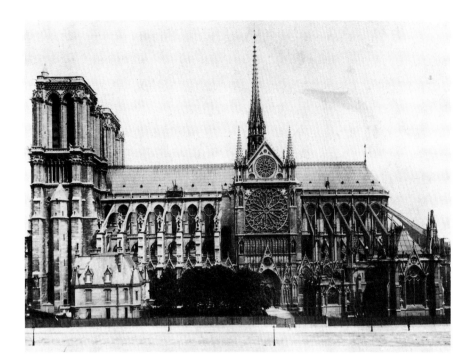

Fig. 6-4. The Cathedral of Notre Dame, Paris. This 19th-century photograph shows the sacristy added by Jean-Baptiste Lassus and E. E. Viollet-le-Duc as part of their restoration of the cathedral (1844–67). (Department of Art History, Columbia University)

and research as a powerful political tool during his days in the liberal opposition to the revived Bourbon Monarchy in the 1820s. Arguably no European government in the nineteenth century cultivated historical study more assiduously than Louis Philippe's July Monarchy. Not only was Versailles converted into a national history museum, but in the 1830s Guizot and his successor in the Ministry of Public Education, Salvandy, established commissions and committees of historians, men of letters, artists, architects, and amateur *archéologues*.[6]

Two influential committees were concerned with studying, classifying, and even conserving the nation's architectural heritage: the Comité historique des arts et monuments and the Commission des Monuments Historiques. The first, of which Didron served as secretary from 1835 to 1852, was concerned with inventorying artistic and architectural monuments throughout the country and creating a set of manuals outlining the principal styles and types of monuments likely to be encountered for the use of local historians as well as to guide any restoration efforts. They were part of Guizot's larger enterprise of writing a national history. The second had a much greater budget to undertake selective restorations on buildings of national significance. Throughout the late 1830s and 1840s these committees were sym-

pathetic breeding grounds for those architects who felt that research into the monuments of the national past and their careful restoration as "historical monuments" were preludes to the creation of an appropriate modern architecture for France. Here they mounted a challenge to the long-standing adherence of the Ecole des Beaux-Arts to an exclusive devotion to the models of classical antiquity.

This is not to say that the committees, on which architects were in the minority, had achieved a unanimous voice. There was consensus on the value of an inclusive approach to recording and even restoring the monuments of the most diverse periods of French history. But views on the implications of that historical work for contemporary design and society diverged sharply. In the showcase restoration projects launched by the commission in the 1840s two distinct camps began to emerge among the architects: one group, ever since known as the "Romantics," had already defied the academy's exclusive classicist doctrines and enjoyed the official support of the historian/ministers Guizot and Adolphe Thiers; the other, slightly younger group enjoyed especially the support of Prosper Mérimée, named Inspecteur Général des Monuments Historiques, in succession to Ludovic Vitet in 1834. Together with his protégé Viollet-le-Duc and the young renegade architect Jean-Baptiste Lassus who had strong alliances with liberal neo-Catholicism, this "Gothicist" group was to craft its own power base within the Commission des Monuments Historiques. The group saw the commission as a counterweight to the academy and as the locus for a revival of a hands-on approach to architecture that recalled the practices of the medieval cathedral mason's guilds.[7]

The Romantic architects were represented on the commission by Félix Duban, who was appointed to restore the Sainte Chapelle in 1836 and the château at Blois in 1843, and by Léon Vaudoyer. In the new world of official research and the emerging art of monumental restoration both found an enlarged scope for the historical studies they had already begun as students at the French Academy in Rome.[8] From the late 1820s they sought to challenge academic orthodoxy and the influential Neoclassical doctrine of the academy's *secrétaire-perpetuelle* A. C. Quatremère de Quincy. Their method was to expand the canon of architectural models and attempt to understand each monument historically as the relative product of its particular cultural situation rather than as an immutable embodiment of timeless ideals. Exploring the heritage of French medieval and Renaissance architecture, they saw the history of France and its institutions worked out in the stylistic evolution of its great monuments, an insight into the very nature of history which they sought to make palpable for the general public through restoration of national monuments.

For instance, the château of Blois comprised four buildings ranging in date from the early thirteenth to the seventeenth century and Duban set out to underscore the distinctive style of each building. At the same time he created transitions and continuities that revealed that the succession of styles were related to one another as links in a chain of progress, a favorite metaphor of historians taken with the notion that history could be explained as a dialectical process. For Duban the building, destined to serve as a museum in which the architecture was as much on display as the city's art works housed within, was to be celebrated as "a summary of our national architecture."[9] Along with his fellow romantics, Duban considered the stylistic diversity of monuments as more than a record of the continual dialectic between tradition and innovation that propelled stylistic change. It was testimony to the great patterns of emigration, conquest, and intermingling that had forged modern national identities and institutions out of the convulsed map of late antiquity.

In seeking lessons valuable for the architectural present, the Romantics focused increasingly on transitional styles as revealing of the very process of historical change. They examined in particular the ways in which the antique heritage of Roman Gaul had gradually been transformed, by the cata-

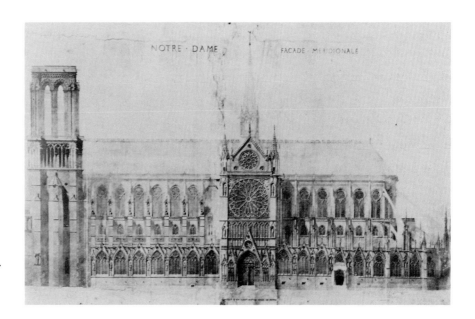

Fig. 6-5. Proposed restoration of Notre Dame in a project drawing by Viollet-le-Duc; watercolor, 1844. (Caisse Nationale des Monuments Historiques et des Sites, Paris)

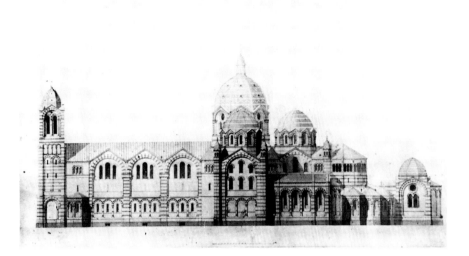

Fig. 6-6. Marseilles Cathedral, rear elevation, by Léon Vaudoyer, ca. 1855. (Collection, Musée des Beaux-Arts, Marseilles)

lyst of Byzantine influence, into the native French styles at the outset of the Middle Ages, and the critical renewal of medieval technique by the rediscovery of antique harmony at the dawn of the Renaissance. They were convinced that the imposition of rigid rules, what they labeled academicism, had gradually led to the paralysis of French art, a process that reached its high point under Louis XIV. And they saw the mission of contemporary architecture to renew the "chain of human progress," obeying the laws of historical evolution to forge a new stylistic link appropriate to the modern secular age of science still in search of an appropriate expression. They were looking for a renewal of the French classical tradition that could accommodate the accomplishments in both architecture and the enhancement of political liberties and social equalities whose gradual evolution had been traced by Augustin Thierry, Guizot, and most recently Jules Michelet.

The younger group had much the same reading list, but drew radically different conclusions. Spearheaded by the young Eugène-Emmanuel Viollet-le-Duc and the slightly older Jean-Baptiste Lassus, they sought to focus attention particularly on the last golden moment of French civilization: the early thirteenth century. Gothic architecture had then reached its perfection in the great series of urban cathedrals of the Île-de-France, and modern political freedoms and economic independence were first forged in cities freed of feudal shackles and monastic rule. For them the flourishing of

Gothic was anything but a gradual transition. It represented a veritable revolution in building, establishing a national tradition which all architects since the time of Louis XIV had dishonored and which held out the promise to serve as the catalyst for a renewal of French architecture to unrivaled rationality as well as pure national expression. Not surprisingly both Viollet-le-Duc and Lassus were virulent critics of the Ecole des Beaux-Arts, which, in their view, held a veritable monopoly on prestigious commissions and careers in architecture. And although they were sympathetic to the historical interests of the Romantics, they were wary of their conclusions and suspicious of their academic aspirations.

Like so many others, including Didron, Lassus had been deeply moved by Victor Hugo's novel *Notre Dame de Paris* (1831), with its plea for government to halt the decay and insensitive restoration under way on Paris's cathedral, which was richly portrayed in Hugo's novel as the embodiment of French genius and national identity. In restoration projects displayed at the annual *Salon*—the Sainte Chapelle in 1835 and the refectory of Saint Martin des Champs in 1836—and in his early writings for Didron's *Annales Archéologiques*, Lassus launched a full-scale attack on the summary dismissal of Gothic architecture in Quatremère de Quincy's widely respected *Dictionnaire Méthodique d'Architecture* (1832). Gothic for Quatremère was a ruleless and empirical architecture, one in which no underlying geometry or system of proportions could be found. The instinctive product of a society in decadence, it could be compared only "with the architecture produced by certain animals, notably beavers."[10] This brief comment, the final judgment of the few lines devoted to the Middle Ages in the three volumes of Quatremère's canonic work, proved a vital spur to Lassus and Viollet-le-Duc's crusade.

Beginning in the 1840s and gaining in virulence with each new conflict, they tried to demonstrate that Gothic was a highly sophisticated system, based on the most rigorously logical and rational solutions to structural problems, and that it had achieved an unimpeachable clarity and perfection in the sophisticated and daring structures of the thirteenth century in the Île-de-France. For Viollet-le-Duc the conflict was to lead to the great project of replacing Quatremère's reference work with a new *Dictionnaire Raisonné de l'Architecture* (1854–68).[11] For Lassus preservation of these monuments against the ravages of time was the sacred duty of modern Frenchmen. The cathedrals such as Notre Dame in Paris and Chartres, where he was active until his early death in 1857, were

the source of all architectural knowledge and the key to responding to the great challenge of the nineteenth century to devise a modern architectural language uniquely appropriate to the physical and social conditions of a post-Revolutionary France. Although he had been schooled under Henri Labrouste in the theories of Romantic historians, Lassus was equally influenced by the writings of the Romantic neo-Catholics, particularly those who embraced a progressive social mission for the modern clergy, including P. J. B. Buchez, H. F. R. Lamennais, and the comte de Montalembert, who was Pugin's greatest supporter in France.

Viollet-le-Duc was an avowed enemy of all academies—in 1852 he proposed that the French Academy and its Ecole des Beaux-Arts be replaced by a revival of the ancient guilds in the form of an open union of architects.[12] He considered the revival of classicism sponsored by Renaissance academies as one of the principal seeds of the decline of French architecture from its High Gothic apogee. The rationally inquiring French spirit had then been unshackled, and the work

Fig. 6-7. Marseilles Cathedral, side elevation, by Léon Vaudoyer, ca. 1856. (Collection, the Vaudoyer family, Paris)

Fig. 6-8. Marseilles Cathedral, constructed 1852–93; 19th-century photograph. (Paris, Bulloz).

of architecture had been the free expression of masons and a whole coterie of artists working in harmony. To face the challenges of a society in which scientific inquiry and free enterprise held the potential for dynamic progress Viollet-le-Duc shared Lassus's view that no better school was available than that of the national Gothic. The state-funded restoration projects were to give them high visibility in the 1840s and 1850s. Notre Dame remained one of the best funded of all the undertakings endorsed anew by Napoleon III as part of an array of projects meant to thank the church for its support in the plebiscite endorsing the declaration of the Second Empire.

In contrast to England, the French Gothic Revival was thus developing its architectural theory largely in a secular setting, with government support. Although many members of the clergy were to be won over to the Gothic cause— as recent studies of provincial architecture in nineteenth-century France are just starting to make clear[13]—the theoretical apparatus of the Gothic Revival was defined in a largely secular, and in Viollet-le-Duc's case, even anticlerical, context. In large measure this was due to the fact that since the Revolution church buildings were the

property of the state and thus—with the exception of pilgrimage or votive churches that were built by private subscription—all work, whether restoration or new construction, was reviewed by government agencies.[14] The primary stylistic battles were to take place as much over visions of the meaning of French history as over issues of theological correctness. Although a number of skirmishes occurred over parish churches in the 1840s—Sainte Clotilde in Paris, Saint Nicholas at Nantes, to name the best known—it was cathedral design that provided a series of battles with long-ranging consequences for the fate of the Gothic Revival in France. Firmly tied to French identity by Hugo's prose, the cathedral was also postulated as the great communal building characteristic of the last golden or organic period in the comte de Saint-Simon's cyclical vision of historical development.[15] It remained the vortex of the debates over style that challenged the antiquarian position in the French Gothic Revival in the 1850s.

The scene was set in the mid-1840s with the wresting of Notre Dame Cathedral (fig. 6-4) from the hands of the academically trained Etienne Godde. His austere Neoclassical church designs in

Paris and insensitive restoration work at the cathedrals of Amiens and Paris had made him the *bête noire* of the Gothic cause. Despite Hugo's stirring pleas in 1831, Godde continued his ad-hoc restoration work intermittently into the early 1840s, by which time a chorus of voices had gathered to apply pressure on the administration. In 1842 the Minister of the Interior agreed to open consultations with architects willing to present overall restoration projects, a first for what had heretofore been an entirely haphazard procedure. Lassus and Viollet-le-Duc's heavily documented report, a monument to the new standards of Guizot's historical committees, was also a manifesto for the Gothic as a system of architecture that must be restored with scrupulous attention to its own internal logic. It was accompanied by a dazzling set of watercolors envisioning Notre Dame cleansed of all post-medieval additions, its facade statuary and crossing flèche reinstated, and the building enhanced with a new sacristy on the south in a seamless extrapolation of the purest elements of the cathedral's early thirteenth-century Gothic syntax (fig. 6-5). Their appointment on March 11, 1844 was an official endorsement of this vision of the organic wholeness of Gothic construction. Even the president of the Conseil des Bâtiments Civils, reputed for its refusal to accept any neo-Gothic proposals, admitted that henceforth all restoration work required "the feeling and the science of Gothic art."[16] Ultimately the work at Notre Dame would last two decades, completed by Viollet-le-Duc alone in 1864, seven years after Lassus's death. From the Notre-Dame workshop would emerge a whole generation of committed Gothic Revivalists—in essence the school of Viollet-le-Duc—including Emile Boeswillald, Anatole de Baudot, Eugène Millet, and Edmond Duthoit, in addition to Suréda, who would emigrate to Spain where he helped establish the national historical monuments service.

As Lassus and Viollet-le-Duc began work, Didron launched the *Annales Archéologiques*; his earlier journal, *La Liberté* (1832) had folded after six issues. *Annales* was a private venture, financed by contributions from Montalembert and

Fig. 6-9. The nave of Marseilles Cathedral, constructed 1852–93; 19th-century photograph. (Paris, Bulloz).

by subscribers who included an impressive roster of foreign "Goths," from Pugin in England to August Reichensperger in Germany. It was not only an outspoken enemy of official Neoclassical taste in both the academy and the Conseil des Bâtiments Civiles, but an unforgiving critic of the more severe restorations undertaken by the Commission des Monuments Historiques, and an ardent promoter of the cause of the Gothic Revival. "Let us repeat once again that we are not involved in archaeology for our leisure, but rather as people who demand of the past all that it can offer the present and especially the future,"[17] Didron reminded his readers whenever the occasion presented itself. Although he applauded every effort to revive Gothic—and duly recorded every conversion of the clergy to the cause— Didron's own vision of the Middle Ages was strictly aligned with that of the so-called progressive "neo-Catholic" revival inspired by the writings of Joseph-Marie de Maistre, Lamennais, Buchez, and most particularly Montalembert. He was persuaded that only a revival of the Middle

Fig. 6-10. "Cathedral" by Viollet-le-Duc; from *Dictionnaire Raisonné de l'Architecture*, vol. 4 (Paris, ca. 1854).

all construction . . . its appearance is but the result of its structure." They outline the mandate of his theory for years to come, namely to describe the rapid perfecting of Gothic structure in the early thirteenth century as a triumph of the rational French spirit, and the emergence of the bourgeois urban classes from the feudal yoke, rather than a drive for spiritual expression or Christian faith. France's destiny to master the world through science and technology—the great challenge of the rivalry of nations in the mid-nineteenth century—was firmly anticipated then by this earlier flourishing of the national spirit. Interspersed with the first installments of Viollet-le-Duc's historical demonstration were the two parts of Lassus's first major polemic in favor of the neo-Gothic, "De l'art et de l'archéologie" (On art and archaeol-

Ages would bring with it a revival of the profound harmony between the civic and ecclesiastical orders that had last flourished in the thirteenth century. His vision came closer to Viollet-le-Duc's view of a secularized Middle Ages than to the Catholic nostalgia of Pugin. In addition, Didron shared Viollet-le-Duc's republican sympathies.

Lassus and Viollet-le-Duc first developed their visions of Gothic architecture's unique relevance to present-day France in the pages of Didron's magazine. In 1844 Viollet-le-Duc began to publish a series of historical articles "De la construction des édifices religieux en France depuis le commencement du christianisme jusqu'au XVIe siècle" (On the construction of religious buildings in France from the beginning of Christianity until the 16th century). These contain in seed his famous theory that "Gothic architecture is above

Fig. 6-11. Project drawing for the west facade, Notre Dame de la Treille (Lille Cathedral), by G. E. Street, 1856. (Diocesan Archives, Lille)

ogy). Lassus echoed Viollet-le-Duc's descriptions of Gothic as a logical system of design born of and uniquely appropriate to French circumstances, materials, and conditions. And although he was quick to deflect charges of flaccid copyism, he noted that the first efforts would undoubtedly be largely derivative until French architects, long burdened with the official Latin of the academy, learned once again to speak their native tongue. Copy for now he concluded, "later we'll do better, if we can."[18]

There are hints in this article, in which the evils of eclecticism were first sermonized, that Lassus was aware that the battleground was shifting. Confrontations would continue with the Conseil Général des Bâtiments Civils, dominated by older statesmen from the academy. Stalwart supporters all of Neoclassical models, they had rejected nearly every neo-Gothic design that had come before them during the 1840s. The culmination would be the battle over the design for a new parish church on a prominent site on Paris's Left Bank, near the Assemblée Nationale, to be dedicated to Sainte Clotilde (see fig. 6-2). After thrice rejecting the neo-Gothic designs by Franz Christian Gau, the Conseil des Bâtiments Civils finally consented to give their approval to his severe thirteenth-century design. This only after being threatened with an investigation into the restoration under way at the Royal Basilica of Saint Denis, where François Debret's radical restoration had so weakened the structure of the north tower that it needed to be demolished. The incident unleashed a heated debate over the question articulated by the academy: "Est-il convenable à notre epoque de construire une église dans le style dit gothique?" (Is it appropriate in our time to build a church in the so-called Gothic style?). A voluminous war of words consolidated positions. Lassus published a violent attack on the academy, and in the end the Gothic party carried the day.[19] Or so it seemed. Gau's design was a mockery of the lessons Lassus and Viollet-le-Duc had been seeking to instill. Combining elements from French and German buildings—including the rather ill-timed adoption of substantial elements from Cologne

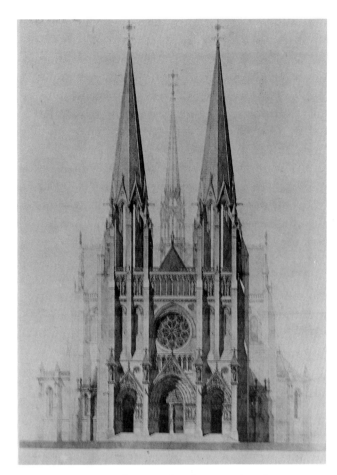

Fig. 6-12. Project drawing for the west facade, Notre Dame de la Treille (Lille Cathedral), by Jean-Baptiste Lassus, 1856. (Diocesan Archives, Lille)

Cathedral given the recent Rhine crisis which reactivated rivalries between French and German nationalism—Gau's design was anything but a fluent exercise in the language of Gothic. It was all too clearly a competent and well-intentioned exercise in translation by an architect better versed in classical design. Although Didron insisted that even an imperfect Gothic design was better than a classical one, Lassus redoubled the fight against eclecticism. The Gothic party was on the verge of splitting.[20]

While a heated exchange had been engaged with the stalwart academicians, the rising power of the younger Romantics, sympathetic to the cause of the Commission des Monuments Historiques but virulently opposed to the notion of a Gothic Revival, posed a more difficult challenge. As Viollet-le-Duc and Lassus were articulating their revivalist positions in the pages of the *Annales,* a subtly different historicist prognosis

Fig. 6-13. Project drawing for the interior of the nave, Notre Dame de la Treille (Lille Cathedral), by Jean-Baptiste Lassus, 1856. (Diocesan Archives, Lille)

for the relationship of the canon of national monuments to the problems of a modern language of architecture was being forged by the Romantics in the Saint-Simonian populist journal *Le Magasin Pittoresque*. In a serialized history of French architecture, published between 1839 and 1852, Albert Lenoir and Léon Vaudoyer set out to demonstrate that for over a thousand years French architecture had evolved as a continual dialectic between tradition and innovation. The transitions were gradual and continual, and in fact it was in the unfinished potential of the transitions from Romanesque to Gothic, and more particularly from Gothic to Renaissance, that modern architects could renew with the grand mission of French culture as the great crucible of European culture. "France," Vaudoyer explained at the peak of the Sainte-Clotilde crisis, "can be

considered as the heart of this great body we call Europe, that is to say destined to receive all foreign influences and to excercise its own universally."[21] In 1844 Vaudoyer and Lenoir interrupted their historical narrative for a direct attack on the Gothic Revival position of the new *Annales Archéologiques*:

> What! Gothic can be claimed as our national art? Should we thus renounce all the advances that have been made since! What! The limits on French genius were such that since the fifteenth century our art has lost all its originality, all its character! This we cannot accept on faith; art in general, and architecture in particular, is subject to the movement of the ideas that dominate in the era of its making. Architecture . . . is the most direct interpretation of the principles, of the morals and of the spirit of a civilized nation.[22]

Vaudoyer and Lenoir's attack clarified matters for Lassus, who now identified eclecticism as the leading danger facing the Gothic Revival cause: "Stylistic unity no matter what one does is one of those fundamental rules from which it is impossible to deviate, since without this rigorous condition there can be neither art nor artists. In architecture eclecticism is completely impossible and makes no sense whatsoever." He continued, interweaving metaphors of fashion and linguistics: "To take what is best in each time period is to transport into architecture what one does to put together one of those costumes that are indispensable for certain balls, and which are formed from the debris of twenty other costumes."[23] The linguistic analogy would remain at the center of the debate between these two conflicting views of the relationship between past and present in architecture for the next decade. In the same issue Viollet-le-Duc framed the debate even more explicitly in an article entitled "De l'Art Etranger et de l'Art National" (On Foreign and National Art): "In a country two things must be quintessentially national, the language and the architecture, for they are what best express a people's character. We haven't given up our language, we have modified it, perhaps wrongly. Why then should we give up our architecture?"[24]

Vaudoyer was quick to put forth a different image of the historical roots and future growth of French linguistic and architectural identity:

Children of Roman civilization, we have borrowed everything from antiquity; but does that mean that we don't have our own originality? Architecture follows the same rule as language, and if this analogy has been made frequently it is because no other could be as precise or as striking. Although the French language is formed of Greek, Latin, and Italian elements is it not in spite of that the most exact expression of our French spirit?[25]

At the dawn of the Second Empire, in the heated moment of church projects and restorations launched by Napoleon III aiming to consolidate the support he had found among the Catholic Clergy, and specifically from Montalembert in the pages of the liberal catholic *L'Univers,* the confrontation between linguistic and national purity and an eclectic vision of France as an historical melting pot took on a new intensity. Battle lines formed over the first newly commissioned cathedral to be built in France in nearly a century (figs. 6-6 to 6-9). In September 1852, in a bid to win over the devout, but anti-Bonapartist populations of Marseilles, Napoleon III had laid the cornerstone of a new cathedral for the country's teeming port city, with its diverse immigrant populations, during a campaign tour through the south of France. The architect chosen was none other than Vaudoyer, protégé of the newly appointed Ministre de l'Instruction Publique et des Cultes, Hippolyte Fortoul.[26] Vaudoyer had designed a romano-byzantine style building. This recently coined historical/stylistic category was based on the notion that French medieval architecture had married the traditions of the western Roman empire with the structural innovations of Byzantium—most particularly the pendentive dome—to achieve a new system of structure and decorative expression that would continue to evolve through experiment and intermingling.

In an 1853 reorganization of the administration of ecclesiastical architecture, the lines for the next skirmish between Vaudoyer's progressive eclecticism and Viollet-le-Duc's quest for stylistic unity were redrawn. Both architects were named, along with Léonce Reynaud, to serve as Inspecteurs Généraux des Edifices Diocésains, in charge of reviewing restoration and construction in all French cathedrals. Viollet-le-Duc's ongoing restoration of Notre Dame was included among Vaudoyer's assignments, while Viollet-le-Duc would keep a watchful eye on the diocese of Marseilles. Vaudoyer missed no opportunity to remind the committee that the Gothic cathedral was an historical artifact whose only lesson for modernity was a negative one, namely the expensive maintenance of its flawed system of flying buttresses and exposed structural members. Historical piety and the future of French architecture should not be confused, Vaudoyer noted. Viollet-le-Duc in turn continued to rail against the pernicious example Vaudoyer was setting as he continued to enrich his design with references to

Fig. 6-14. Design for a cathedral commemorating the Wars of Liberation, by Karl Friedrich Schinkel, 1814. (Schinkel Archive, Berlin)

an ever broader range of sources, including Byzantine, Lombardic, French Romanesque, and even Arabic elements. For Vaudoyer these were all interrelated as members of "the great Mediterranean family of architectures" which it had been the role of Marseilles throughout history to absorb into a new synthesis. Viollet-le-Duc rarely expressed his desire for linguistic purity in architecture more adamantly than his critique of Vaudoyer's revised design of 1855:

> He seems to want to prove that in the same building forms belonging to different ages and different cultures can be combined. Certainly if anyone is capable of overcoming this difficulty it is Monsieur Vaudoyer . . . who knows better than we do that architecture is not the project of chance: when one decides thus (and how can one do otherwise today) to adobt a style, why seek to compose a *macaronique* tongue when one has at hand a beautiful and simple language?[27]

What could be ruder than this accusation of the *macaronique*, a bastardized mixture of Latin and native words, a pig-Latin whose natural habitat was in the burlesque of the French theater rather than in the rational vision of structural logic Viollet-le-Duc was pursuing. Viollet-le-Duc responded in the "Cathedral" entry of his dictionary, illustrated by a bird's-eye view of an ideal French cathedral (fig. 6-10), a purified vision of the finest features of the cathedrals of Reims, Paris, Chartres, and other monuments from the best

period. In the preface to the *Dictionnaire* he had penned his program for a modern architecture:

> If all the monuments left us by the Middle Ages were above reproach then we could think of slavishly copying them in our own time, but if one erects a new building, it is but a language that one needs to learn how to use to express one's own thoughts, not to repeat what others have already said . . . .[28]

Even as he worked to bring the Middle Ages back to life in his restoration of Notre Dame, for which he now proposed to correct history by realizing the twin facade towers never completed, Viollet-le-Duc launched his own great monument: a dictionary of medieval architecture. This was to be a manual to guide the work of returning French architecture to the linguistic purity of the original gothic syntax, so rational that it could easily confront the demands of modern scientific society.

Just as Viollet-le-Duc's effort to check any possible influence of Vaudoyer's Marseilles design and the philosophy it expounded was reaching its peak, a second chance for a Gothic Revival cathedral presented itself. In Lille, the local clergy had been agitating for some time to have this booming city declared a diocese, independent of the declining capital of French Flanders, Arras. The idea had found a cool reception with Napoleon III's administration, but in late 1854 Didron seems to have been instrumental in selling the local advo-

Fig. 6-15. Southwest view of Cologne Cathedral under construction; photograph by J. F. Michiels, June 29, 1853. (Dombauarchiv, Cologne)

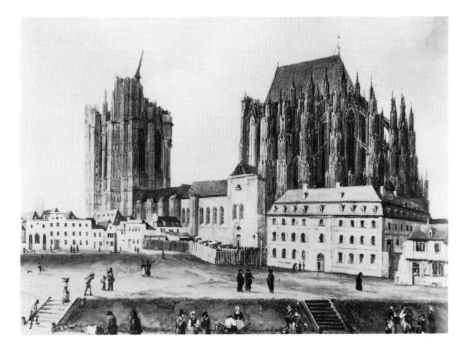

Fig. 6-16. Cologne Cathedral before completion work began; painting by J. A. Lasinsky. (Kölnisches Stadtmuseum, Cologne)

cates of the project on the idea of an international competition. It would be his most spectacular publicity gesture for the Gothic cause to date. The program called for an ambitious building and specified that only Gothic designs would be accepted. Félix Duban and Henri Labrouste refused an invitation to serve on the jury to protest publicly this exclusive stylistic demand, as they explained in the *Moniteur des Architectes* (July 15, 1856, p. 399). Thrown open to architects of all nations, the event was meant to establish what Didron had already noted in 1852 upon Pugin's death, that everywhere "people are studying, people are copying their old national monuments, still but little known not so long ago."[29] In this period where national rivalry and cooperation had been cultivated in the first Universal Expositions, Didron looked forward to a tournament of like-minded nationalists: "We await architects from every country on the battlefield at Lille that we might judge loyally if the victory will go to foreigners or to the French." The national breakdown of the entries put on display in March 1856 was a fairly accurate barometer of the relative strength of the Gothic Revival in major European states. The French and British were tied with fifteen entrants each, although the English took the lion's share of the prizes. The seven "German" entries represented the strongholds of the Gothic

Revival on the other banks of the Rhine: three came from the Prussian Rhineland, and one each from Hannover, Silesia, Karlsruhe, and Austria. In addition there were entries from Belgium, the Netherlands, Luxembourg, and Switzerland.

William Burges and Henry Clutton took first prize, and George Edmund Street (fig. 6-11), second.[30] "C'est l'Angleterre qui a triomphé" (England has triumphed), Didron admitted. Third prize went to Lassus. But even more striking is the contrast between the designs and the positions. Burges and Street had both begun to explore Continental Gothic in the early 1850s as a way of expanding the aesthetic vocabulary and historical base of their Gothic language of design. Both were leading advocates of the notion that to become a universal and modern architectural style Gothic needed to transcend national references. A cosmopolitan historical attitude was the basis for the catchword of the more progressive ecclesiology of the 1850s: *development*. By development the High Victorian Goths meant the capacity of using Gothic as a matrix, indeed a starting point, for developing a flexible style, born of historical logic but free from continual reference to precedent. This style could fill new programmatic demands, create moving effects in the modern city, and provide great scope for the individual signature of the nineteenth-century architect.

With the motto "Éclectisme est la plaie de l'art" (Eclecticism is the open sore of art)" Lassus's competition entry was scarcely anonymous (figs. 6-12, 6-13). Not only was it by far the most masterly display of fluency in pure Île-de-France thirteenth-century Gothic submitted, but the phrase itself had already peppered Lassus's polemical writings in the *Annales Archéologiques*. The text accompanying his design contained a lengthy analysis of the current situation in architecture, in addition to the required detailed description of the liturgical and iconographic specifics of his project.[31] Lassus outlined four possible positions in the quest for an appropriate style for the mid-nineteenth century: create an entirely new art; admit a melange of the forms of all past styles; copy slavishly a single past style; or take inspiration in a single past style and carry it to perfection. Needless to say the fourth was the one he argued as the only viable option. The first was immediately eliminated as in violation of the fundamental laws of history: "L'art ne s'invente pas, il s'impose" (Art can't be invented, it imposes itself), he noted briskly. The third, although it had adherents in both the Gothic and classic camps, was likewise easily discredited. The real battle was between the second proposition, eclecticism, and the fourth, the creation of a modern Gothic. For Lille, where the Gothic had made only a belated appearance historically, Lassus proposed not a revival of the Flamboyant style but rather the perfect thirteenth-century "Cathedral for the North of France" that history had failed to build.

The ensuing battle was to be fought not so much with the Establishment, which seemed to recognize that the chances of building the cathedral were remote, but with Gothic Revivalists abroad. The spirit of cooperation between the British and French soon turned to bitterness and dispute, as much doctrinal as parochial. Reviewing the projects *The Ecclesiologist* complained that Lassus's design had "the look of being too servile a copy," and that his theoretic position was inconsistent:

> The motto that the architect has chosen . . . has misled him. Unless we misinterpret altogether the conditions of the present competition, the object sought for is not a mere dead reproduction of the French style of 1200–1250, but a church in which the needs and experiences of the middle of the nineteenth century are embodied according to the architectural principles of that style. The successful competitor ought to be the man who has,

118

with a true eclecticism, laid hold of every real advantage made in construction or in taste during the last six centuries, and has assimilated it, so to say, into his design, congrously with the principles of the prescribed period.[32]

What was missing from Lassus's design were "signs of progress."

Lassus was eager to make amends. He explained at great length the danger of "a whole school" in France "who admit the possibility of creating a new art, or an entirely new philosophical doctrine, by borrowing the elements of their creation from all styles or from all philosophical systems," and suggested that his British friends had perhaps confused "eclecticism with invention, two things essentially different, we might almost say completely opposed."[33] Linguistic impurity remained the danger, lest architecture be reduced to a Tower of Babel, that oft-evoked metaphor of the period.

> I am perfectly convinced, in the state of anarchy into which art is now reduced, that there remains to us only one anchor of safety, unity of style; and as we have no art belonging to our own time . . . there is only one thing for us to do: that is to choose one from among the anterior epochs, not in order to copy it, but in order to compose, while conforming to the spirit of that art . . . but let us always preserve the unity of style, not trying to give existence to any of those hybrid and unnatural creatures analogous to the monsters who are concealed in the most obscure recesses of our cabinet of curiosities.[34]

Marseilles was not to be repeated at Lille. The event had been staged to display an international accord on nationalist art, but the level of misunderstanding between the English and French escalated when the local clergy decided to overturn the decision of the international jury in favor of a national architect, style, and religion. The idea of rallying the political and financial support for a new Gothic cathedral designed by an English Protestant seemed to raise the stakes too high, even if Burges was a profound student of French medieval architecture. In the end Lassus's design was adopted for it seemed to promise, as one promoter noted, the dream of a cathedral more perfect even than any left by the thirteenth century: ". . . this monument without equal will be national like the cathedral at Reims, beautiful like Amiens, strong like that at Chartres, as Didron put it."[35] But Lassus's was a Pyrrhic victory. He died just a few months after his last diatribe against eclecticism was published in the *Ecclesiologist*. Over the next few years his design was modified by the local Lille architect Charles Leroy, whose idea of synthesis was to copy specific parts of the major cathedrals of the Île-de-France and reassemble them in the design of Lille. The Basilica of Notre Dame de la Treille, never elevated to cathedral status, still awaits a west front. While the English Gothic Revival would create a modern Gothic cathedral at Liverpool to counter the eclectic admixture of the Catholic Westminister Cathedral, the French Gothic Revival would never produce a modern cathedral.

Fig. 6-18. The Bauakademie, Berlin, by Karl Friedrich Schinkel; constructed, 1831–35; nineteenth-century photograph. (Department of Art History, Columbia University)

Fig. 6-19. Cologne Cathedral; 19th-century photograph. (Department of Art History, Columbia University)

One year later, in 1858, Viollet-le-Duc revealed how far he had traveled from the late Lassus's position in the closing volumes of his dictionary of medieval architecture. With the dual entries "Style" and "Unity" his quest for a rational basis became even more radical, leaving behind the tutorial in Gothic design which he thought of as the prelude to a modern French architecture. In the entry "Unity" he evokes a universal rational principle for architecture which transcends historical style and rivals contemporary science in its quest for irrefutable positive grounds for experimentation:

> We are not among those who deny the usefulness of studying earlier arts, inasmuch as no one should forget, or allow to forget, the long chain of past traditions; but what every thinking mind must do when confronted with this mass of materials is to put them in order before even dreaming of using them. . . . The discoveries in the physical sciences show us every day, with increasing evidence, that if the order of created things manifests an infinite variety in her expressions, it is subject to a number of laws more and more limited . . . . It cannot be repeated too often that only by following the order that nature herself observes in her creations can one, in the arts, conceive and produce according to the law of unity, which is the essential condition of all creation . . . .[36]

At the same time he began drawing up a series

of ideal projects to illustrate his *Lectures on Architecture* in which frank use of iron and geometries based on the equilateral triangle—also found in Gothic—would generate buildings with no precedent in any of the great national cathedrals. Not the least indicative of this switch was Viollet-le-Duc's decision in 1852 to abandon the pages of Didron's *Annales Archéologiques* for those of César Daly's progressive *Révue Générale de l'Architecture*. Increasingly Viollet-le-Duc's architects, known as the *école diocésain*, would distance themselves from antiquarian and pious research into the Catholic Middle Ages. The Gothic Revival would continue to produce countless church designs, drawing on the explosion of plate books published by mid-century, but the school of architects trained in Gothic restoration were pursuing a progressive and inventive doctrine that increasingly blurred the distance between them and the progeny of the Romantics.

Germany

Although it was a late addition to the nation states of Europe, Germany was a pioneer in the ideology of nationalism in architecture. In this Gothic commanded pride of place from the start. The French were the catalysts, not only in the consciousness-raising that accompanied first the

Revolutionary armies and then Napoleon's expansionist Empire, but throughout the nineteenth century as the "other" of German national identity. As early as 1797 Friedrich Gilly, although originally enthralled like so many of his generation with the democratic and liberal ideals of the French Revolution, had made an impassioned plea for the restoration of the medieval castle of the Teutonic knights at Marienburg in East Prussia (today Poland) as the embodiment of national (German) identity.

During the wars against Napoleon, Gilly's pupil Karl Friedrich Schinkel exploited a series of Gothic dreams toward the project of rallying national sentiment against the invader. He proposed immediately after Napoleon's defeat at Leipzig that a great "Cathedral of Liberation" be constructed on Berlin's Leipziger Platz as both symbol and instrument of national regeneration (fig. 6-14). Schinkel hoped not only to revive the style that Goethe had already revalorized as "German" but with it the principle of the communal effort of building that made the Gothic the veritable symbol of a nation arising naturally from popular sentiment.[37] It was a part of a rising tide of sentiment that the Germans, divided among countless political entities, needed a national monument. Rival efforts were inaugurated by the leading states, most notably Ludwig I of Bavaria's monumental classical temple, the Walhalla near Regensberg, first proposed in 1814 and dedicated in 1842 on the anniversary of the Battle of Leipzig.

But the only project with true potential to transcend the complex political boundaries of German-speaking Europe was the completion of Cologne cathedral. This mid-thirteenth-century design cut a curious profile in the skyline of Cologne, with the twin peaks of its choir, completed in 1322, and the stump of the projected twin-towered West Front, crowned by a late medieval construction crane that had been stilled in 1560 when the project was abandoned (fig. 6-15). In the intervening years a series of modest houses had filled in the space layed out for a grand nave (fig. 6-16). By the 1820s the magnifi-

Fig. 6-20. Endplate from *Vorlesung über die Systeme des Kirchenbaues* by Franz Kugler (Berlin, 1852).

cent engravings of Sulpiz Boisserée's portfolio of the original architectural drawings (see fig. 6-1), discovered by Georg Moller, and theatrically lit visions of the completed interior provided an image of the national cathedral that history had left to modernity to complete. Many would dispute the paternity of this idea, just as the paternity —German or French—of the Gothic style would soon complicate the nationalist impulse of revived medievalism. Although both the Bavarian and Prussian kings studied the problem—in 1816 Friedrich Wilhelm III of Prussia sent Schinkel to draw up a report—and funded the project over the next sixty years, it was private interests in the Rhineland that were to remain the most tireless promoters of the project, most famously the journalist and scholar Joseph Görres and his disciple the lawyer August Reichensperger. With the

Fig. 6-21. Design for Berlin Cathedral, Friedrich August Stüler, 1849. (Brandenburgisches Landesamt für Denkmalpflege Berlin, Messbildarchiv)

Catholic Rhineland's inclusion in the redrawn map of (largely Protestant) Prussia after the Congress of Vienna in 1815 the politics of the situation grew ever more complex. The building came to serve simultaneously the symbolic needs of local pride and the campaign to foster German patriotism in anticipation of unity.[38] Cologne cathedral, where rebuilding began in 1823, was in the words of Görres the "symbol of the new empire that we are trying to build."[39]

For Reichensperger, whose career became increasingly politicized during the 1830s, the building should become the catalyst for the reform of architectural education and practice and the forging of regional identity for the Catholic Rhineland within the expansive and centralizing Prussian state. As Michael Lewis has explained,

> The same principles that motivated his political program shaped . . . his architectural program. He conceived of the Gothic Revival as an inherently regional phenomenon, based on the expression of local tradition, custom and materials. It must be free of the control of the academies, which were modeled on the French system—just as German society must rediscover its democratic roots, shunning the centralism and bureaucracy of France. It must spring instead from communal and fraternal organizations, such as the late medieval building lodge, just as the revival of these fraternal and private organizations would overturn the power monopoly of the autocratic state.[40]

When Ernst Friedrich Zwirner (fig. 6-17) was appointed head architect in 1833 Reichensperger's

hopes for a revival of the medieval mason's lodge, or Bauhütte, became a reality. Here a new generation of architects would be trained in the principles of Gothic construction. From here they would be dispersed to bring revived Gothic to parish churches throughout the German lands, or at the very least throughout the Catholic states. As he explained in his 1845 manifesto, *Die christliche-germanische Baukunst und ihr Verhältnis zur Gegenwart* (Christian-Germanic architecture and its relation to the present) Gothic would be recognized at once, in the spirit of Pugin, who remained a point of reference for Reichensperger, as the only legitimate style to express both Germany's national character and its Christian devotion.

But by 1852 Reichensperger's position had been challenged and was becoming more nuanced and accommodating. He had weathered the storm over the origins of Gothic, even conceding that Cologne's design was clearly indebted to the earlier work at Amiens cathedral. For this he expanded his notion to a "Christian-German" architecture that could include the Germanic influence all over Europe. Even as he acknowledged that Gothic had its origins in the north of France—where the influence of Germanic civilization was vital in his view—he maintained that it had been brought to mature perfection in Germany. As so often in nationalist arguments ever since, the lack of coincidence between the boundaries of the original tribes and the modern nation state based on ethnicity was quickly glossed over. In the early 1850s Reichensperger was expounding the notion that, as a universal style, the Gothic Revival must be capable of solving all building problems, even that of a modern theater, although he remained adamantly opposed to the integration of modern materials in Gothic settings.[41] Like Didron, with whom he established close contact, Reichensperger applauded all efforts even as he sought in a variety of publications and in the pages of the *Kölner Domblatt*, the official organ of the Cathedral project, to refine a purist vision of a revived Germanic Gothic from the best period.

Although the early polemicists for the Gothic Revival had framed their arguments within the spirit of the polarities between Gothic and Greek architecture first formulated by the Romantics, notably Friedrich Schlegel in his *Grundzüge der gotischen Baukunst* of 1804–1805, Germany's leading academies of architecture had evolved beyond the neoclassical doctrines of the early nineteenth century toward a synthetic historicist position.[42] Grouped under the deliberately inclusive term *Rundbogenstil*, variants of this eclectic philosophy were professed in the academies of Berlin, Munich, Karlsruhe, and Hannover. It was articulated by figures as diverse as Friedrich von Gärtner, Schinkel, and Heinrich Hübsch, who had coined the term in his 1828 manifesto, *In welchem Style sollen wir Bauen?* (In what style should we build?). The *Rundbogenstil* was based on a dynamic vision of historical evolution in

which the interaction of the material and structural demands of construction with the spiritual requirements of different cultures followed laws that could be studied and extrapolated to create modern buildings in the trajectory of historical progress.[43] It was a position with distinct parallels to that of the Romantics in France. Faced with this somewhat elusive opponent, the Gothic Revivalists articulated increasingly a position that sought to counter both the historical ideology and the formal preferences of the position they saw as eclectic, and which Reichensperger viewed with as much suspicion as his friend Lassus had in France.

In the wake of the 1848 revolutions in Prussia, Reichensperger had served in the preliminary assembly convened in Frankfurt with the aim of drafting a constitution for a united Germany. He quickly emerged as an outspoken proponent of the *Grossdeutschland* position which sought a union that would include Austria. It would associate Austria's political power with the German project and draw on its largely Catholic population to create a more evenly divided mix of Catholic and Protestant in the united state. Although the Frankfurt assembly was dissolved after one year and had few concrete results, Reichensperger continued his active political career in the Prussian Parliament, to which he was elected in 1850 (no doubt on the basis of the great local support he had for his years of labor for the cathedral cause) as a delegate from the Rhineland. Gothic architecture remained central to his vision

Fig. 6-22. Stonemasons who worked on the completion of the Cologne Cathedral prepare to participate in the historical parade for the cathedral's 1880 dedication ceremony; photograph by Fritz Schneider, Cologne, October 16, 1880. (Dombauarchiv, Cologne)

of Prussia, and a future Germany, as a state which could accommodate regional differences and religious diversity, promote private initiatives, and allow the blossoming of individual rights. Architectural reform was to serve as an opening wedge.

The building boom that accompanied Berlin's population explosion and planned expansion in the early 1850s was firmly under the control of Schinkel's pupils, who were seeking diversely to interpret the mandate of the great master's career.[44] Many of them specialized in a single aspect of the diverse solutions Schinkel had devised for domestic or public, rural or urban building programs. A core group, however, sought to adopt the progressive vision of stylistic development their master had left in his unfinished architectural textbook and made manifest in his last great public building, the Bauakademie (1831–35). The Bauakademie housed both the central building administration of Prussia, which sought to enforce standards of construction and design throughout the far-flung Prussian provinces, and the school of architecture. Its challenging architecture sought to derive a modern synthesis from the legacy of Greek and Gothic architecture, which Schinkel viewed as elements in a continual development rather than as irresolvable counter propositions. The whole was realized with the most efficient spanning forms of construction—the segmental arch and vault—and in brick and terra-cotta, materials at once with a pedigree in North German Gothic and a future in burgeoning Prussian industrialization.[45]

The implicit conflict between these two visions of the future direction of German architecture erupted in February 1852 when Reichensperger decided to oppose the normally routine annual appropriation for the Bauakademie. The Bauakademie "and all its related institutions must vanish from our budget," Reichensperger insisted on the floor of the Prussian Parliament. Only the eradication of this institution of centralization would permit the development of an independent national architectural expression. Like the Gothic, it would have its origins in the building yards and be decentralized and individualistic, even as it found unity as the natural expression of national character. "I hope that we will thereafter acquire straightforward apprentices and deft masters once more."[46] In the heat of rhetorical exchange he let fly not only at the institutions housed in the Bauakademie but at Schinkel's building itself. This he variously represented as a modern Tower of Babel in its stylistic eclecticism and as an incongruous Grecian, even foreign, intrusion on the banks of the Spree River, reflecting the conflicting legacy of Schinkel as the father both of a revived Hellenism and a progressive synthetic historicism. For a moment the Bauakademie (fig. 6-18) and Cologne Cathedral (fig. 6-19) seemed poised to become the irreconcilable poles of the debate over an appropriate national style, with each party claiming that history, nationality, and an experimental inventive artistic spirit supported their position and their position alone.

The Berlin establishment, spearheaded by the architectural press, was galvanized into action. In the *Zeitschrift für Bauwesen*, Reichensperger's speech was paraphrased and refuted line for line. Reichensperger was accused of ignorance in archi-

Fig. 6-23. The Forum on the Maximilianstrasse, Munich; late 19th-century photograph. (Stadtmuseum, Munich)

Fig. 6-24. Votivkirche, Vienna; designed by Heinrich Ferstel; constructed 1854–79; 19th-century photograph. (Department of Art History, Columbia University)

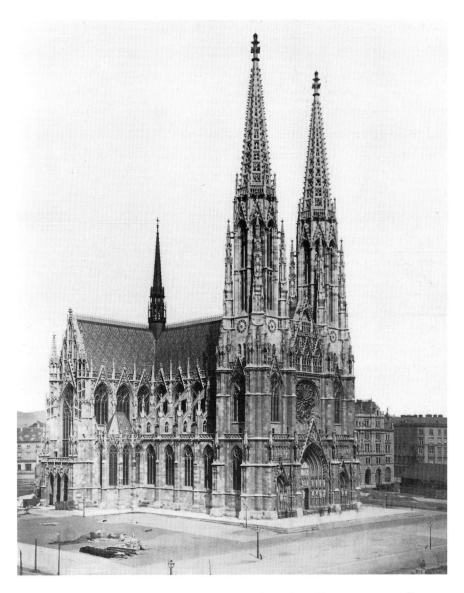

tecture (the Bauakademie was scarcely a Grecian building), of being willfully dismissive of Prussian history (the current state of Prussian architecture and public art was a fitting memorial to Prussia's glorious rise), and of being a partisan Catholic. Even more telling was the virulent refutation of his historical point of view. While the value of completing Cologne Cathedral was never called into question, the extrapolation of this act of restoration to a position of revival was seen as a mockery of the laws of history that a generation of philosophers, architects, and art historians had been seeking to elucidate in Berlin in the wake of Hegel's 1828 lectures on aesthetics. The laws of history alone argued against any return to a moment in the past. Moreover Reichensperger's critique of what he perceived as Prussia's unhealthy dependence on foreign inspiration—whether the imagery of ancient Greece of the aca-

demic institutions of modern France—was dismissed as an historically impossible position. For if Germans were to resist foreign influence, the editor of the *Zeitschrift* argued, the very mechanism of historical progress would be disabled. Gothic, just as Romanesque before it, and the German Renaissance style after it, had been born of foreign influences interacting with native talents: "Succinctly put: if the peoples that have had the greatest influence on the development of architecture, held the same narrow-minded viewpoint that Herr Reichensperger gave witness to in his speech before the Chamber, we would probably even still find ourselves among the Troglodytes and Tent-dwellers. In any case the *Christlich-Romanische* architectural style would never have developed, since this emerged from the roman-pagan styles."[47]

An even more thoroughgoing historicist argu-

125

ment was developed by Franz Kugler, Schinkel's friend and first biographer and the first director of the Altes Museum, in a revised edition of his tract on church design, *Vorlesung über die Systeme des Kirchenbaues* (Discourse on the systems of church architecture; revised edition 1852). Kugler side-stepped the pressing liturgical and denominational issues of the day to postulate church building as the leading barometer of the architectural health of a civilization. Echoing a frequent complaint of opponents of the Gothic Revival, Kugler noted that in the nineteenth century for the first time a natural relationship with the laws of history had been severed. In opposition both to the antiquarian position of the Gothic or classical revivals, and to the unrealistic notion that an entirely unprecedented new style could be created ex novo from solving modern demands by the laws of materials alone, Kugler postulated "a third way." His position was based on the new science of art history with its cardinal notion that every civilization and every phase of historical time produced, spontaneously, its own distinctive stylistic expression. He even compared this position to the middle of the road in politics, implying that it was a position that evolved from historical law rather than either hopeless nostalgia or revolutionary change. Echoing Schinkel's earlier lament that the nineteenth century was no longer graced with a naive stylistic production, Kugler argued that the modern comprehension of the laws of history offered a way out. Kugler analyzed the history of church architecture to extract a developing principle that had been carried forward by successive civilizations even as they had stamped their monuments indelibly with the particular character of their time. With intriguing parallels to Vaudoyer, who had traveled to Germany with Fortoul a few years earlier, Kugler found the solution to the dilemma of choice was not to adapt a moment in the past but rather to continue forging the chain of historical development. Follow the dictates of history he concluded: "They tell us, we should simply wait for the final goal of the movement, which imbues the spirit of modern times: the form of our architecture will generate itself."[48]

As Schinkel had sought to make evident to students and public alike in the formal language of the Bauakademie, Kugler demonstrated how a comprehensive study of history—here reduced to the development of the Christian Church type—would emerge from understanding the continual dialectic between local circumstances and a larger essence of architecture inscribed in historical progress. He sought to demonstrate how the replacement of the flat entablatures over the colonnades of Early Christian churches was but the first of a long series of integrations of daring new structural solutions into an existing tradition, which both respected and transcended the model (fig. 6-20). He concluded with Schinkel's attempts to reintegrate the dome into the organic vaulted tradition of Gothic—first proposed in his 1814 Cathedral for the Wars of Liberation—as another catalyst for a new structural and aesthetic development which would have dramatic consequences for the communal and liturgical needs of large modern Protestant churches:

> We possess a rich legacy in the long chain of ecclesiastical monuments erected over the course of fifteen centuries. To use it is not simply for us an advantage, it is an obligation. The whole secret of rendering this legacy useful, from our point of view, resides in the skill of knowing how to differentiate between general aesthetic principles and local and historical particularities, that is to say the modes of period taste in which these principles have expressed themselves in any given manifestation. . . . So if we would like to establish a firm foundation of principle for contemporary church building—to the extent that such an ideal training is in fact our goal—it would behoove us not so much to adopt one of the available systems for imitation or transformation, but rather to take possession of the sum total of our architectural heritage from which we might derive a general principle of form-making, one which would endow our modern ecclesiastical spaces with a lively dignity and an awe-inspiring rhythmic elevation. Thereby we will establish the positive bases upon which our artists can express the character of our time, of our sentiments, feelings, and thoughts.[49]

Gothic was reduced to a single manifestation of

Fig. 6-25. Linz Cathedral; designed by Vincenz Statz; constructed 1862–1925.

a longer essential history of the formal development of architecture, one of the many spiritual motors that had directed mankind's creative energies. It was not the manuals of Reichensperger's followers, with their grammars of Gothic, but a philosophical understanding of the history of architecture that would point the way to future invention.

The immediate occasion for Kugler's position paper was renewed discussion over the construction of a new Lutheran cathedral in Berlin. The eighteenth-century building, although splendidly remodeled by Schinkel to form the fourth side of the Lustgarten between the Royal Palace and the new museum, was severely overcrowded and totally out of scale with the ambitions of King Friedrich Wilhelm IV who ascended the throne in 1840 with determination to be a modern Christian monarch. His project to rebuild the cathedral

was renewed in 1849 by Friedrich August Stüler with a monumental round-arched design crowned by a huge medieval dome (fig. 6-21). It was at once a fulfillment of Kugler's program and, in the mind of the king, a worthy Protestant response to the rising symbol of Catholicism in Cologne. Work began on this new focal point for the capital in 1855 but languished as Friedrich Wilhelm IV was declared insane in 1857 and conceded power to his brother William I as regent in 1858. Although the project was revived in 1868, and Reichensperger's disciples responded with visions of the German Gothic Cathedral, a new cathedral was not in fact commissioned until 1892, long after unification. Julius Raschdorff's building, completed in 1905, is even today an out-scaled monument in the heart of Berlin. Its monumental size and bombastic classical rhetoric corresponded to an entirely different set of ambitions, namely to create a Protestant counterpart to Saint Peter's in Rome. In 1880, Cologne Cathedral was inaugurated with much fanfare and neo-medieval pageantry (fig. 6-22), but the dream of a modern Gothic cathedral was to evade Reichensperger in Germany even as it had Didron in France.

Gothic and the Rise of Nationalism in Central Europe

Frustrated in his confrontation with the Berlin establishment, Reichensperger could nonetheless find much to bolster his faith in the Gothic Revival cause as he looked across the map of Central Europe in the mid-1850s. Although in the north of Germany individual architects were to explore regional variants of the Gothic—particularly the school of Conrad Wilhelm Hase in Hannover with its revival of the northern brick or *Backsteingothik*—it was in the Catholic south that the Gothic future seemed the rosiest in 1852.

In 1850 an unusual competition had been announced by King Maximilian II of Bavaria, who had assumed the throne in the wake of the 1848 uprisings in Munich. The project centered on a grand public building to house an educational institution for future statesmen. Its site was on a prominent hill culminating a new boulevard, the Maximilianstrasse, that would span the Isar River. A long document sent to each competitor, however, also spelled out a larger mandate, namely the definition of a single appropriate nineteenth-century style.[50] The stage was set for another battle between stylistic purists and advocates of a progressive historicism, a promise made more concrete with the casting of the jury on April 15, 1852. It included two of the leading Gothicists of the German lands: Zwirner from Cologne and Karl Heideloff from Nuremberg, in addition to F. C. Gau, author of Sainte Clotilde in Paris. But the Goths were outnumbered by the Neoclassicists, led by Leo von Klenze, and a diverse group who might be called "historicists" which included Friedrich-August Stüler from Berlin, Heinrich Hübsch from Karlsruhe, and Friedrich Bürklein from Munich. Only seventeen entries were sub-

mitted, including one by King Friedrich Wilhelm IV of Prussia who proposed that Bavaria develop its own national architecture by translating the wooden houses of the Alps into a monumental urban stone style. He believed (along with Klenze) that the alpine houses were ultimately descended from the same models as the Greek temples. Already nationalist particularisms were gaining the upper hand over stylistic unity. First prize went to Wilhelm Stier of Berlin, one of the most original theorists of a hybrid style derived from an analysis of the principles of historical development, although his precise response to the central question of the period encapsulated in the Bavarian king's brief has yet to resurface.[51] But despite this defeat for the Gothic position, when work actually began on the Maximilianstrasse in the mid-1850s, now entrusted to Bürklein, who had served on the jury, a highly original vocabulary of "developed Gothic" was favored to cater to the longstanding Gothic tastes of the monarch (fig. 6-23). Dubbed overnight the "Maximilian-stil," it entered the scenographic and eclectic landscape of Munich not as a resolution to the problem of historical style but as an expansion of the representational dialectics available. The Tower of Babel had not yet been taken.

Austria, Prussia's great rival throughout the mid-nineteenth century, emerged in the 1850s as most receptive to the architectural ideology emanating from Cologne. There had been little Austrian interest in the Gothic during the first half of the nineteenth century—despite such impressive historical monuments as Saint Stephen's Cathedral in Vienna—but in 1853 the Gothic was prescribed as the requisite style for the great Votive Church (the Votivkirche) that Emperor Franz Josef determined to build (fig. 6-24). Its construction was to celebrate his 1853 escape from the bullet of a Hungarian nationalist assassin. It would be "a monument of patriotism and of devotion of the people of Austria to the Imperial House." The Votivkirche competition (open from April 2, 1854 to January 31, 1855) as well as the 1857 competition for a new Rathaus (City Hall) in Vienna—two of the most prominent monuments on Vienna's emerging Ringstrasse—were to prove major magnets for the younger generation of Gothicists rising through the ranks of the Cologne Cathedral stoneyard. Almost without rival in their expertise in Gothic design and technique, they were soon challenged to adapt their stylistic fluency to the complex issue of nationality in the Hapsburg Empire where Czechs, Hungarians, Slovenes, Italians, and others were seeking either independence or a degree of national autonomy within the empire.

Although the Votivkirche commission was awarded to a young Viennese architect, Heinrich Ferstel, otherwise untrained in the Gothic, the competition proved one of the major showcases for the formidable Gothic talent that Zwirner's training and Reichensperger's vigilance had fostered in Cologne. In addition to Georg Gottlob Ungewitter, known even in his own day as the German Pugin, Vincenz Statz and Friedrich Schmidt, both master masons at Cologne, submitted projects. They took second and third prizes respectively with designs derived from close study of Cologne as a model for future designs. As fate would have it they both won important commissions in Austria within the next two years. In 1857 Statz was appointed architect for a new cathedral at Linz (fig. 6-25), where the dream of a new Gothic cathedral was realized in Catholic Austria between 1857 and 1922. In the same year Schmidt emerged as victor in the competition for Vienna City Hall; his Gothic design established an image for the German town hall that was to have much greater progeny than Scott's widely publicized winning competition design for the new Rathaus in Hamburg. In 1857 Schmidt was also asked by the Austrians to take up a position in the academy in Milan, where he would spread the word of the revival of medieval art and of restoration in the twilight years of Austrian Lombardy. Two years later he was given a post in the academy in Vienna, the first major Gothicist to penetrate the establishment, followed by his appointment as chief architect to the restoration of Saint Stephen's cathedral in Vienna, which began in 1863 and continued for decades.[52] In

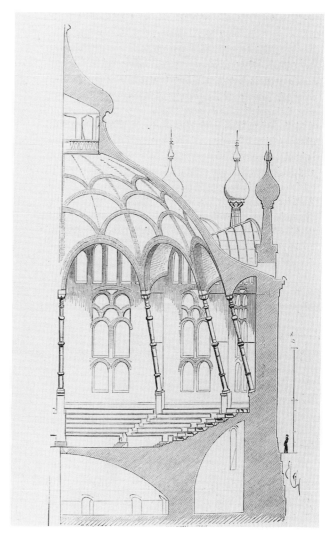

Fig. 6-26. Future Russian architecture as conceived by Viollet-le-Duc. From his book, *L'Art Russe* (Paris, 1887), fig. 77.

addition Schmidt would advise on restoration projects throughout the Austro-Hungarian Empire. From these posts, Schmidt formed more Gothic Revivalists than any other architect in Europe, men who would carry his style and ideals to the most diverse contexts. Between his office and his studio at the academy he built up an efficient Gothic machine, while remaining faithful to the humble creed of workmanship and individuality forged at Cologne. His tombstone was inscribed "Hier ruht in Gott ein deutscher Steinmetz" (Here lies in peace a German stonemason).

Even more remarkable than the selective use of the Gothic by the Imperial Austrian household and the liberal bourgeoisie of Vienna,[53] each to their own ends, is the role Schmidt's pupils played in promoting Gothic restoration and revival in the diverse non-German parts of the Hapsburg Empire. Rather than fostering the universal Gothic Revival, which Reichsensperger would continue to campaign for even after German unification in 1870, Gothic restoration and neo-Gothic went hand-in-hand as instruments of national consciousness in the Hapsburg Empire. Despite its successful squelching of the 1848–49 uprisings throughout the empire, the regime of Franz Josef II was nearly everywhere forced slowly to negotiate various degrees of local autonomy, giving in over the course of the 1850s and 1860s to the demands of the alliances of intellectuals who had formulated a vision of national identity based on ethnicity and language. The 1850s were to be repressive years in the Hapsburg lands, and architecture continued to apply the neo-Renaissance vocabulary of central authority when building was undertaken. But with the gradual granting of powers to the provinces, first to the Czech lands in the 1850s, and then to the Kingdom of Hungary in the famous "Hungarian Compromise" of 1867, Gothic architecture was poised to join the ongoing efforts at purifying the national tongue which had already fueled the great initiatives of collecting folk literatures and writing national dictionaries in the preceding decades.

Under Hapsburg Rule since the early sixteenth century, the Czechs found in the Gothic an image of the great period of the kings of Bohemia who had built the remarkable Vladislav Hall in Prague Castle and sponsored one of the grandest of Gothic workshops in Saint Vitus Cathedral. Over the course of the late 1850s and early 1860s a number of concessions were made to the increasingly vociferous demands of Czech nationalists in favor of the territorial integrity of Bohemia and Moravia, of the right to elementary school education in Czech rather than German (a full language decree would not be passed until 1880 however), and the abolition of tariffs, allowing Czech small industry to prosper. In 1859 the Cathedral Commission was established to complete Saint Vitus Cathedral within the confines of Prague Castle, a project that was to serve for decades as the

centerpiece of the search for Czech identity within the ethnically diverse Hapsburg conglomerate. Paralleling the efforts to purify the Czech language and fortify it in the battle against the German-speaking aristocracy, the cathedral was restored and completed in the principle of stylistic unity, taking inspiration at once from the writings of Viollet-le-Duc and the doctrine of Cologne. The cathedral workshop, which was later to foster a belated Gothic Revival in Czech architecture, was placed under the direction of Josef Kranner and Josef Möcker, who had trained under Schmidt in Vienna.

Even more striking is the case of Hungary, where the Magyar Nationalists had set the tone for the demands that the Czechs and Southern Slavs were making in these decades. The 1850s saw little building activity in the wake of the suppression by the Hapsburg troops of the 1848/49 Revolution in Budapest. But after the Austro-Hungarian Compromise of 1867, which granted Hungary self-determination in its internal affairs, the need for a Hungarian past became a pressing necessity. Three of Schmidt's most gifted pupils, the Hungarians Imre Steindl, Frigyes Schulek, and Ferenc Schulcz, crafted a series of medieval landmarks in the center of Budapest which were in sharp counterpoint to the prevalent Renaissance Revival of the prominent administrative buildings in the Hungarian capital, similar to those favored throughout the Empire.[54] A national church for the Hungarians was created with the restoration of the Church of Saint Mathias on the crest of Buda overlooking the Danube. Work here began under Schulek's direction shortly after the coronation there of Franz Josef and Elisabeth as king and queen of Hungary in 1867.

The nationalist ideology of the Hungarian Gothic Revival was especially stamped in the 1860s by the theories of Imre Henszlmann, who had first become interested in the "Old German" churches of Hungary in the 1840s, but soon developed notions that would lead him to envision Gothic as a way of differentiating Magyar Hungary from Germanic Austria. He spent the decade of the 1850s abroad in England and

France—the leading centers of debate over the Gothic Revival—where he developed his highly influential theory of Gothic proportions. His claim to have discovered the secret of the Gothic masons generated considerable excitement and was taken up especially by Lassus and Viollet-le-Duc, who thanked Henszlmann by name in the *Dictionnaire*. Henszlmann returned to Hungary after participating in the Lille Cathedral competition, where he was associated with two neo-Gothic architects from Rheims, and entering alone the Crimean War Chapel competition. In 1861 he collaborated on an entry in the competition for a new headquarter for the Hungarian Academy—a building with a high ideological charge as Hungary strove to craft a national identity within the empire. Associations with the great monuments crowning Buda were of importance to be sure, but Henszlmann explained neo-Gothic design with arguments reminiscent of Viollet-le-Duc's vision. He "argued that gothic had been invented in France, which was important because all things German were extremely unpopular in Hungary in those years, owing to the defeat of the Hungarians at the hands of the Austrians in the war of independence. He called gothic the style of freedom in contrast to Romanesque monastic architecture, and the style of enlightened institutions like the colleges at Oxford and Cambridge."[55] In the heat of the moment, Gothic, which no one considered indigenous to Hungary, had the great advantage of not following Austrian norms. Although the competition was won by Stüler from Berlin with a neo-Renaissance style design, the Gothic would ultimately triumph as the symbol of Hungarian national freedom with Steindl's 1883 design for the great Gothic Revival Hungarian Parliament.[56] It was completed on the banks of the Danube River, a dramatic site, in 1904. It might even be said that Viollet-le-Duc's arguments in favor of the association of the Gothic with the rise of the free bourgeoisie was to have even greater resonance in Central Europe in the second half of the nineteenth century than in France.

The history of the Gothic Revival in Bohemia, Moravia, and Hungary extends into the last third of the nineteenth century and far beyond the direct legacy of Pugin. While Pugin's utopian vision of Gothic as a beacon for the future continued to find renewed life in new arenas—notably in Flanders—direct support of the nationalist uses of Gothic restoration and revival was sought in the two continental models of nationhood: in that grandfather of national ideology, France, and in the most spectacular success of nation-making in the century, Germany. The majority of the great movements for national identity in the last third of the nineteenth century were to give renewed potency to Gothic Revival ideology and to draw heavily upon the joint legacies of Viollet-le-Duc's theories and the practices defined in the two great cathedral workshops of Paris and Cologne. By the end of the century Schmidt's pupils, for instance, could be found practicing throughout Germany, Austria, Moravia, Bohemia, Hungary, Croatia, Galicia in Poland, and Austrian Trieste, as well as in the Netherlands and Switzerland. One pupil, Josef Vancas, was serving as Cathedral Architect in Sarajevo in Bosnia-Herzegovina.[57] Viollet-le-Duc, increasingly under the spell of Count Gobineau's theories of racial purity, was consulted throughout Europe, but most particularly in the younger countries of Central and Eastern Europe, for both practical advice on medieval restoration and on the thorny issues of defining a national architectural style. Croats, Poles, Belgians, Dutch, Norwegians, Swedes, Spanish, Italians, Portuguese, and Romanians all consulted the great master either through official channels or individually in the name of the international Gothic cause.[58] But just as he admonished his own pupils in 1863 for attempting to please him by imagining a pure neo-Gothic design for the French colonies in North Africa, so Viollet-le-Duc sought to direct each of his diverse interlocutors to discovering in their own past a principle at once rational and national.

The culmination came with the invitation in 1877 by a group of Russian Slavophiles to write a book on Russian art and architecture that it might guide them in valorizing a nationalist past and defining a national future (fig. 6-26). Although he never visited Russia, relying instead on materials sent him by Viktor Butovsky and those collected by his own son-in-law, Maurice Ouradou, Viollet-le-Duc advised the Russians on the method for finding a starting point in the architecture that preceded Peter the Great's enslavement of the Russian genius to the blind imitation of western forms. But he warned them of falling into the trap of slavishly imitating any single monument, rather encouraged them to find the rational strand in the development of Slavic forms and to "choose from among these elements those most capable of improvement, those which derive from the most pure and original sources, the sources that conform most closely to the national genius."[59] Although he left the project of formal experimentation to Russian architects, he offered a vision of a progressive direction in which the tradition of Muscovite brick construction and centralized onion-domed spaces was extended to admit the modern possibilities of cast-iron construction in the form of diagonal piers and to solve the modern problem of a huge place of modern assembly. For Viollet-le-Duc this design embodied the great challenge of the age, whether it be in the older states of France and Britain or in nations just now forging their particular identity: to retain the universal rational essence of Gothic architecture while following the specific historical and regional expressions that expressed the particular genius of the diverse nation states of modern Europe. The different languages of modern Europe were to his mind perfectly compatible in the search for the higher laws of all architecture. His arguments having matured in the debates of the 1850s, Viollet-le-Duc hoped that the cause of rational architecture could take root in new soil, free of the battles of the styles that had raged in the early years of the movement in France, Germany, and Britain.

1. "M. Pugin est mort; mais il revit dans son fils aîné et dans . . . huit ou dix autres jeunes architectes que se vouent dans la Grande Bretagne, à l'architecture du moyen-âge" (A. N. Didron, "Renaissance de l'Architecture Chrétienne," *Annales Archéologiques* 13 [1853]: 314–27, here cited, p. 321).

2. "Le grec est vaincu jusque dans sa dernière citadelle, jusque dans son propre berceau" (ibid.).

3. "Voilà donc le style ogival en Californie et nous pouvons donc lui appliquer ce qu'on disait autrefois de la liberté: "L'ogive fera le tour du monde" (*Annales Archéologiques* 13 [1853], p. 270).

4. Belgian Gothic Revival was probably closer to Pugin's ideas than other national movements, thanks to A. G. B. Schayes (a frequent contributor to Didron's *Annales Archéologiques*), and to T. H. King, an Englishman living in Bruges. King published what was ostensibly a French translation of Pugin's *True Principles* under the title *Les Vrais Principes de l'Architecture Ogivale ou Chrétienne, avec des remarques sur leur renaissance au temps actuel* (Bruges, 1850). This was a compilation of elements of *True Principles* and *Contrasts* with plates relating to Belgian examples of Neoclassical work and the Belgian architectural and social situation. For further information on King and the Flemish Gothic Revival, see Jan de Maeyer, *De Sint-Lucasscholen en de neogotiek. 1862–1914* (Leuven, 1988), and Jean van Cleven, ed., *Neogotiek in Belge* (Ghent, 1994).

5. There has been considerable work recently on the new attitudes to history catalyzed by the French Revolution. See especially Anthony Vidler, "Grégoire, Lenoir et les 'monuments parlants,' in Jean-Claude Bonnet, ed., *La Carmagnole des Muses, L'homme de lettres et l'artiste dans la Révolution* (Paris, 1988), pp. 131–54; and Françoise Choay, *L'Allégoire du Patrimoine* (Paris, 1992), esp. pp. 76–95. Also see the earlier, classic sources by Paul Léon, *La Vie des Monuments Français* (Paris, 1951); and Louis Réau, *Histoire du Vandalisme* (Paris, 1958; reprint 1994).

6. For an excellent summary of this, see Laurent Thies, "Guizot et les institutions de mémoire," in Pierre Nora, ed., *Les Lieux de Mémoire: La Nation* (Paris 1986), vol. 2, pp. 569–92. For the Museum at Versailles, see Michael Marrinan, *Painting Politics for Louis Philippe* (New Haven, 1988). For the Commission des Monuments Historiques, see the works listed in note 5 and Françoise Bercé, *Les Premiers Travaux de la Commission des Monuments Historiques, 1837–1848* (Paris, 1979).

7. On Viollet-le-Duc and Lassus's activities at the Commission des Monuments Historiques, see *Viollet-le-Duc*, exhib. cat. (Paris, 1980), esp. pp. 50–59; and Jean-Michel Leniaud, *Jean-Baptiste Lassus (1807–1857), ou le temps retrouvé des cathédrales* (Paris, 1980), esp. pp. 64ff.

8. There is a growing literature on the Romantic group, but their interactions with the Gothic party has been little

discussed. For an orientation, see Barry Bergdoll, *Léon Vaudoyer: Historicism in the Age of Industry* (New York, 1994), esp. chaps. 3 and 4. Duban's key position between the two groups will be elucidated in a 1996 exhibition catalogue edited by Françoise Hamon, Bruno Foucart, and Sylvain Bellenger (Paris, forthcoming).

9. For a summary of Duban's reports and comments, see Jacques Pons, "Félix-Jacques Duban: Architecte du gouvernement 1797–1870," thesis, Ecole Nationale des Chartes, 1985; Annie Cospéric, *Blois, la forme d'une ville, étude topographique et monumentale* (Paris, 1994); and forthcoming catalogue cited in n. 8.

10. A. C. Quatremère de Quincy, "Gothique," *Encyclopédie methodique*. Paris, 1832.

11. For a summary of Viollet-le-Duc's historical views, see Martin Bressani, "Notes on Viollet-le-Duc's Philosophy of History: Dialectics and Technology," *Journal of the Society of Architectural Historians* 48 (1989), pp. 327–50; and Robin Middleton, "The Rationalist Interpretations of Léonce Reynaud and Viollet-le-Duc," *AA Files* 11 (1986), pp. 29–48. On Viollet-le-Duc's *Dictionnaire* in relationship to academic theory, and to Quatremère de Quincy in particular, see Barry Bergdoll, *The Foundations of Architecture: Selections from the Dictionnaire Raisonné of Viollet-le-Duc* (New York, 1990), introduction.

12. Viollet-le-Duc, "Un mot sur l'architecture en 1852," *Revue Générale de l'Architecture* 10 (1852), pp. 371–79.

13. For a summary of this research, see notes and bibliographical references, and the dictionary of artists, in Jean-Michel Leniaud, *Les Cathédrales au XIXe siècle* (Paris, 1993). Also see François Loyer and Hélène Guené, *L'Eglise, l'Etat et les Architects, Rennes, 1870–1940* (Paris, 1995). For a fine study on the Charente area and Bordeaux, see Claude Laroche, *Paul Abadie, architecte, 1812–1884* (Paris, 1988).

14. On the role of the state's administrations of ecclesiastical architecture, most importantly the Service des Edifices Diocésains, see Jean-Michel Leniaud, *Les Cathédrales au XIXe siècle* (Paris, 1993); idem, *L'Administration des cultes pendant la période concordataire* (Paris, 1988); and Bergdoll, *Léon Vaudoyer*, pp. 200–206.

15. For a summary of the Saint-Simonian vision of history, see Middleton, "The Rationalist Interpretations," pp. 29–48.

16. "Le sentiment et la science de l'art gothique" (quoted in Leniaud, *Les Cathédrales*, p. 284).

17. "Répétons encore que nous ne faisons pas d'archéologie en purs oisfs, mais en gens qui demandent au passé tout ce qu'il pourrait donner au présent et surtout à l'avenir" (*Annales Archéologiques* 4 [1846], 3e livraison). For a summary of the major issues raised in the magazine and its international relations, see Georg Germann, *Gothic Revival in Europe and Britain: Sources, Influences and Ideas* (Cambridge, Mass., 1972), pp. 135–50. For an excellent

discussion of Didron, see Catherine Brisac and Jean-Michel Leniaud, "Adolphe-Napoléon Didron ou les media au service de l'art chrétien," *Revue de l'Art* 77 (1987), pp. 33–42.

18. "Plus tard, à faire mieux si nous pouvons" (Jean-Baptiste Lassus, "De l'art et archéologie," *Annales Archéologiques* 2 [1845], p. 329).

19. Jean-Baptiste Lassus, *Réaction de l'Académie des Beaux-Arts contre l'art gothique* (Paris, 1846).

20. On the central role of Sainte Clotilde in the evolution of the Gothic Revival in France, see Robin Middleton and David Watkin, *Neoclassical and Nineteenth Century Architecture* (New York, 1987), vol. 2, pp. 366–68.

21. "La France peut-être considerée comme le coeur de ce grand corps qu'on appelle l'Europe, soit à la fois destinée à recevoir toutes les influences étrangères et à exercer la sienne universellement" (Léon Vaudoyer, "Histoire de l'architecture en France," in Edouard Charton, *Patria* [Paris, 1846], vol. 2).

22. "Quoi, le gothique serait notre art national! et nous devrions répudier toutes les conquêtes qui ont été faites depuis! Quoi! telles seraient les bornes imposées au génie français, et depuis le quinzième siècle notre art aurait perdu toute originalité, tout caractère! Nous ne pouvons le croire, l'art en général, et l'architecture particulièrement, sont soumis à l'impulsion des idées qui dominent à l'époque de leur production. L'architecture . . . est le plus fidèle interprète des principes, des moeurs et de l'esprit d'une nation civilisée" (Albert Lenoir and Léon Vaudoyer, "Etudes de l'Architecture en France," *Magasin Pittoresque* 12 [1844], pp. 262).

23. "L'unité de style, par exemple et quoi qu'on fasse, est une de ces règles fondamentales dont il est impossible de se départir; car, sans cette condition rigoureuse, il n'y a ni art ni artistes. En architecture, l'éclectisme est complétment impossible et ne présente aucun sens. . . . Prendre ce qu'il y a de mieux dans chaque époque, ce serait faire, en architecture, ce que l'on pratique pour composer l'un de ces costumes indispensables pour certain bals et qui sont formés des débris de vingt costumes" (Lassus, "De l'Art et Archéologie," p. 76).

24. "Dans un pays deux choses doivent être éminemment nationales, la langue et l'architecure; c'est ce qui exprime le plus nettement le caractère d'un peuple. Nous n'avons pas abandonné notre langue; nous l'avons modifiée, peut-être à tort. Pourquoi donc abanonnerions-nous notre architecture?" (E. E. Viollet-le-Duc, "De l'Art Etranger et de l'Art National," *Annales Archéologiques* 2 [1845], p. 508).

25. "Enfants de la civilisation romaine, nous avons tout emprunté de l'antiquité; est-ce donc à dire que nous ne conservions pas une originalité propre! Il en est de l'architecture comme du langage, et si cette comparaison a déjà été faite bien souvent, c'est qu'il ne saurait y en avoir de plus exacte et de plus frappante; de ce que la langue française s'est formée d'éléments grecs, latins et italiens, n'est-elle pas, malgré cela, la juste expression de notre esprit français!" (Vaudoyer, "Histoire de l'architecture," col. 2160).

26. For greater detail see Bergdoll, *Léon Vaudoyer*, esp. pp. 224–74.

27. "Il semble vouloir prouver qu'on peut allier dans un même édifice des formes appartenant à des âges et à des peuples différents. Certes, si quelqu'un est en étage de surmonter cette difficulté c'est M. Vaudoyer. . . . [il] sait mieux que nous qu'une architecture n'est pas le produit du hasard: quand donc, on se décide (et comment faire autrement aujourd'hui) à adopter un style, pourquoi chercher à composer une langue macaronique quand on a sur la main un beau et simple langage" (Viollet-le-Duc, ms. report of 1855, Service des Edifices Diocésains, Archives Nationales, Paris, F-19-7741; fuller citation in Bergdoll, *Léon Vaudoyer,* p. 254).

28. "Tous les monuments enfantés par le moyen âge seraient-ils irréprochables, qu'ils ne devaient donc pas être aujourd'hui servilement copiés, si l'on élève un édifice neuf, ce n'est qu'un langage dont il faut apprendre à se servir pour exprimer sa pensée, mais non pour répéter ce que d'autres ont dit. . ." (E.E. Viollet-le-Duc, *Dictionnaire Raisonné de l'Architecture* [Paris, 1854], vol. 1, pp xv–xvi).

29. "On étudie, on copier les vieux monuments nationaux, naguère encore si méconnus"; and "Nous attendons sur le champ de bataille de Lille les architectes de tous les pays, pour juger loyalement la victoire soit aux étrangers, soit aux français" (A. N. Didron, "Une cathédrale au concours," *Annales Archéologiques* 16 [1856], p. 115).

30. Although the competition and its role in the French Gothic Revival await proper study, the importance of this competition for the development of English High Victorian Gothic has been underscored; see especially Stefan Muthesius, *The High Victorian Movement in Architecture, 1850–1870* (London, 1972), esp. pp. 117ff. See also J. M. Crook, *William Burges and the High Victorian Dream* (Chicago, 1981).

31. The report is reproduced in full in Leniaud, *Jean-Baptiste Lassus*, pp. 243–55.

32. "The Competition for the Proposed Cathedral at Lille," *The Ecclesiologist* 17 (1856), p. 91.

33. "M. Lassus on Eclecticism in Art," *The Ecclesiologist* 17 (1857), p. 285.

34. Ibid., p. 286.

35. ". . . ce monument sans pareil que sera national comme la cathédrale de Reims, beau comme celle d'Amiens, solide comme celle de Chartres selon l'expression de Didron" (Louis Cloquet, quoted in Chanoine H. Vandame, *Iconographie de la Basilique Notre-Dame de la Treille à Lille* [Lille, 1906], p. 1).

36. E. E. Viollet-le-Duc, "Unité," *Dictionnaire Raisonné de l'Architecture,* vol. 9, p. 345, quoted in Bergdoll, *The Foundations*, p. 28.

37. On Schinkel's interest in Gothic see Georg Friedrich Koch, "Karl Friedrich Schinkel und die Architektur des Mittelalters," *Zeitschrift für Kunstgeschichte* 29 (1966), pp. 177–222; idem, "Schinkels architektonische Entwürfe im gotischen Stil 1810–1815," *Zeitschrift für Kunstgeschichte* 32 (1969), pp. 262–316; and Barry Bergdoll, *Karl Friedrich Schinkel: An Architecture for Prussia* (New York, 1994).

38. This story has been well studied: see Germann, *Gothic Revival*; Hugo Borger, ed., *Der Kölner Dom im Jahrhundert seiner Vollendung*, exhib. cat. 2 vols. (Cologne, 1980); Michael Lewis, *The Politics of the German Gothic Revival: August Reichensperger* (New York, 1993).

39. Quoted in Germann, *Gothic Revival*, p. 94.

40. Lewis, *The Politics*, p. 24.

41. Germann, *Gothic Revival*, p. 160.

42. See W. D. Robson-Scott, *The Literary Background of the Gothic Revival in Germany* (Oxford, 1965), esp. pp. 129–45.

43. On the debates over the *Rundbogenstil* in the 1830s and 40s, see *In what style should we build?: the German debate on architectural style*. Intro. / trans. by Wolfgang Hermann (Santa Monica, 1992).

44. Eva Börsch-Supan, *Berliner Baukunst nach Schinkel, 1840–1870*. Munich, 1977.

45. On the Bauakademie see Bergdoll, *Karl Friedrich Schinkel*, pp. 195–208, with older bibliography.

46. Translated and quoted in Lewis, *The Politics*, p. 155.

47. "Mit einem Wörte: Wenn die Völker, die auf die Entwicklung der Architektur vornämlich von Einfluss gewesen sind, in ähnlichen engherzigen Anschauungen befangen gewesen wäre, wie Herr Reichensperger sie in seiner Kammerrede kund gibt, so würden wir vermuthlich noch jetzt zu den Troglodyten und Zeltenbewohnern gehören; jedenfalls aber würde sich niemals der christlich-romanische Baustyl entwickelt haben, da derselbe ja durchaus vom römische-heidnischen Stile ausging" ("Der Abgeordnete Reichensperger und die Baukunst," *Zeitschrift für Bauwesen* 2 [1852], p. 234).

48. "Sie sagt uns, wir sollten nur das endliche Ziel der Bewegungen, welche die Geister der neueren Zeit erfüllen, abwarten: die Form würde sich dann schon von selber finden" (Franz Kugler, *Vorlesung über die Systeme des Kirchenbaues, gehalten am 4. März 1843 im wissenschaftlichen Verein zu Berlin von F. Kugler*, 2nd ed. [Berlin, 1852], p. 3). Written in 1843, it was republished in 1852 during the debates over the Bauakademie.

49. "Es liegt uns in der langen Folgenreihe der kirchlichen Monumente, die im Laufe von 15 Jahrhunderten entstanden sind, ein reiches Erbtheil vor, dessen Benutzung nicht bloß unser Vortheil, sonder auch unsre Pflicht ist. Das ganze Geheimniß, wie wir dasselbe der Benutzung von unsrer Seite zugänglich zu machen haben, berught eben nur darin, daß wir die allgemeinen ästhetischen Principien von den lokalen

und historischen Besonderheiten der Erscheinung, von der
Weise des Zeitgeschmackes, in der sie sich ausgeprägt haben,
zu unterscheiden wissen. . . . Wollen wir demnach für die
Zwecke des heutigen Kirchenbaues—sofern dabei überhaupt
eine ideale Durchbildung erstrebt wird—zu einer festen
Grundlage, zu einem klaren Urtheil gelangen, so scheint es
nöthig, nich sowhol ein einzelnes der vorhandenen Systeme
zur Nachbildung oder Umbildung vorzunehmen, als vielmehr
aus der ganzen Summe unsrer Erfahurungen jene allgemeinen
Gesetze der Formenbildung, durch welche der kirchliche
Raum lebenvolle Würde und fierliche rhythmische Erhebung
gewinnt, uns zu eigen zu machen. . . . Dadurch gewinnen wir
den positiven Inhalt, dem der schaffender Künstler das
Gepräge unsrer Zeit, unsrers Sinnens, Fühlens und Denkens,
aufzudrücken vermag" (ibid., pp. 22–23).

50. For studies of this event, see Eberhard Drüeke, *Der Maximilianstil, Zum Stilbergriff der Architektur im 19. Jahrhundert* (Mittenwald, 1981) and August Hahn, *Der Maximilianstil in München, Programm und Verwirklichung* (Munich, 1982).

51. On Stier, see Börsch-Supan, *Berliner Baukunst.*

52. On the participation of Cologne architects in Austrian competitions, particularly the Linz Cathedral commission, see Lewis, *The Politics*, pp. 175–82, 195–99. On Friedrich Schmidt, see Historisches Museum, *Friedrich von Schmidt (1825–1891), Ein gothischer Rationalist* (Vienna, 1991).

53. For an excellent discussion of the relationship of style to the politics of the Imperial Household and the enfranchised bourgeoisie of Vienna in this period, see Carl E. Schorske, *Fin-de-Siècle Vienna, Politics and Culture* (New York, 1981), pp. 24ff.

54. For this summary of Hungarian Gothic Revival I am most indebted to the advice and publications of József Sisa, whose forthcoming contributions to the history of Hungarian architecture, which Dora Wiebenson is editing for the MIT Press, will greatly expand our understanding of this complex issue. In the interim, see József Sisa, "Steindl, Schulek und Schulcz—Drei ungarische Schüler des Wiener Dombaumeisters Friedrich von Schmidt," *Mitteilungen der Gesellschaft für Vergleichende Kunstforschung in Wien* 37 (Sept. 1985), pp. 1–8.

55. József Sisa, "Imre Steindl and Neo-Gothic in Hungary in the Late Nineteenth Century," in Rossana Bossaglia, ed., *Il Neogotico nel XIX e XX secolo* (Milan, 1989), vol. 1., p. 142.

56. László Csorba, József Sisa, and Zoltán Szalay, *The Hungarian Parliament* (Budapest, 1993).

57. See "Verzeichnis jener Schmidtschüler, welche an der k.k. Akademie der bildenden Künste in Wien inskribiert waren," (1905) reprinted in Historische Museum *Friedrich von Schmidt*, pp. 231–38.

58. A synthetic study of Viollet-le-Duc's influence, in particular in relationship to nationalist ideologies, has yet to be undertaken; in the interim, see Pierre-Marie Auzas, *Eugène Viollet-le-Duc, 1814–1879* (Paris, 1979; first published 1965), pp. 219–51; *Actes du Colloque International Viollet-le-Duc, Paris 1980* (Paris, 1982), pp. 223–24.

59. E. E. Viollet-le-Duc, *L'Art russe: ses origines, ses éléments constitutifs, son apogée, son avenir* (Paris, 1877). For an analysis of this text see Robin Middleton, "Viollet-le-Ducksy?", *Architectural Design* 49 (1970), pp. 67–68; and, with impressive detail on the Slavophile context in Russia in the 1870s, Lauren M. O'Connell, "A Rational, National Architecture: Viollet-le-Duc's Modest Proposal for Russia," *Journal of the Society of Architectural Historians* 52 (1993), pp. 436–52.

Fig. 7-2. Saint Mary's Cathedral, Killarney, County Kerry, photographed ca. 1900 (labeled "RC Chapel, Killarney"). The interior furnishings are by Pugin's son (1853–56) and by J. J. McCarthy and Ashlin and Coleman (1908–12). (Lawrence Collection, National Library of Ireland)

pletely ruined. The new bishop has blocked up the choir, stuck an altar under the tower!! and the whole building is in the most painful state of filth: the sacrarium [sic] is full of rubbish, and it could hardly have been treated worse if it had fallen into the hands of the Hottentots. I see no progress of ecclesiastical ideas in Ireland . . . . It is quite useless to attempt to build true churches, for the clergy have not the least idea of using them properly.[3]

Many of Pugin's churches were left unfinished, and he was therefore unable to indulge either his genius for decoration or his enthusiasm for the revival of medieval church arrangements and furnishings—such as rood screens—by which he set such store. When his design for Maynooth was cut back to exclude the chapel, he resigned his appointment and only with difficulty was persuaded to continue. In England Pugin preferred to rely on a group of trusted executants of his designs such as the builder, George Myers; by contrast in Ireland he encountered great difficulty in supervising work. He seems to have allowed himself to hand over his designs first to a local

Member of Parliament, then to other architects, and finally to a clerk of works, one Richard Pierce of Wexford. None of these practices did he countenance in England. His Irish career, even more than his English, is one of early hopes, midway frustrations, and final disillusion, to which he gave vent in the Catholic press.

Yet some of Pugin's best churches and convents are in Ireland. In beautifully contrasting local building stone, they illustrate his teachings on a rationalist, picturesque Gothic far more convincingly than his often skimped English work.[4] Almost every Catholic Gothic Revival church in Ireland is popularly said to be by Pugin, but his buildings have suffered badly at the hands of radical interpreters of the liturgical norms following the Second Vatican Council (1962–66), and many (most notoriously, the cathedral at Killarney) have lost their original plans and furnishings. The Great Famine (1846–49) and Pugin's unexpected death in 1852 at the age of forty held up the development of a Puginian Catholic Gothic Revival in Ireland, with the result that some of the most impressive "Pugin" churches in Ireland are in fact those of his son Edward and of J. J. McCarthy, "the Irish Pugin."

Armed with a missionary zeal to re-educate the Catholic clergy and rehouse, or rather rechurch, the Catholic laity, even so cosmopolitan an Englishman as Pugin must have found Ireland a confusing and foreign land. The pre-Famine Ireland that Pugin first visited in 1838 had a population of over 8 million; Great Britain's was about 18 million. Outside Dublin and the largely Protestant northeast, this figure was made up of an overwhelmingly Catholic population of perhaps 6.5 million, with an underclass of landless peasants living in a poverty otherwise unknown in Western Europe. The landlord class was Protestant and for the most part belonged to the established Church of Ireland (at least four landlords—two Protestant and two Catholic— were associated with Pugin's churches). In Ireland the Reformation had failed by 1600 and the surviving Catholic Church was then put on an organized footing throughout the country. Payment for clergy, churches, and schools came from the people: there was none of the State subvention common elsewhere in both Catholic and Protestant Europe. The power of the clergy, their ability to raise money even from the poverty-stricken peasantry, and the scale and ambition of Catholic church-building in Ireland were much remarked upon throughout the nineteenth century. However, the second-class status of the Catholic Church is reflected in the fact that its places of worship were known as "chapels," while "church" was used only in reference to Protestant buildings: a photograph of the interior of the enormous Killarney Cathedral (fig. 7-2), taken around 1900, is labeled "RC chapel Killarney." As the novelist William Makepeace Thackeray concluded in his *Irish Sketchbook of 1842*, ". . . about Ireland . . . There are two truths, the Catholic truth and the Protestant truth. The two parties do not see things with the same eyes."[5]

Pugin's often hostile comments on Irish politics were balanced by an admiration for the piety and sufferings of the Catholic Irish. Nowhere is this clearer than in the response to the Great Famine of 1846–49 in which a million Irish died: the small Catholic congregation that worshiped in the church Pugin was building at Ramsgate sent the large sum of £27. 17s. 0d one January Sunday in 1847.[6] However, neither the niggardly government intervention nor private charity could avert the veritable holocaust, the effects of which were mirrored in the emigration of a million people and are still felt in Ireland today. Ironically, this contraction of the population allowed the Church to reorganize its clergy and church-building, so that the second half of the nineteenth century became the great era of Gothic Revival church-building. Its soaring spires still characterize the Irish countryside.[7]

Many Catholic chapels were built or rebuilt after Catholics were granted freedom of worship in 1793. It was noted that whereas Protestants built in the Gothic style, Catholics tended to adopt the Neoclassical. Churches in major towns

Fig. 7-3. Catholic Chapel, Bree, County Wexford; possibly designed by A. W. N. Pugin, constructed 1838–39.

Fig. 7-4. The chapel at Saint Peter's College, Wexford, designed by A. W. N. Pugin, constructed 1838–41. Above the painted gilt-wood altar, the finest of its kind in Ireland, in the triptych is a painting of Our Lady Seat of Wisdom. Interior work to Pugin's design also included choir stalls, a wooden rood screen, side altars, and the stained-glass rose window with the Shrewsbury arms.

such as Dublin or Cork were the work of church-building committees that were partly lay-controlled. None of these were to Pugin's taste:

> There is no country in Europe where the externals of religion present so distressing an aspect as Ireland; in the rural districts, the extremes of poverty, dirt and neglect, while in the large towns, a lavish display of the vilest trash about the altars, and burlesques of classical or pointed designs for churches, most costly and offensive.[8]

Although a church to Pugin's design was announced in Waterford in 1839, the commission was given to the Dublin architect, J. B. Keane. In fact, it is indicative of Pugin's narrow patronage base that he did not build in the towns. Chapels in the countryside tended to follow the established plan of a large nave and transepts forming a "T"; the chapel and the priest's house were often the only slated buildings. Commentators such as Thackeray remarked on their scale, and on the habit of leaving them unfinished, often for a generation.

Other places of worship were rudely built vernacular structures, often the successors to the bogs and so-called mass-rocks where Mass was said in the open before huge crowds. The *Catholic Directory* (Dublin) published a fascinating series of replies from individual clergy to accusations of the Revd. Mr. Leahy in his "Wants of Religion in Ireland,"[9] and these explain the conditions Pugin would have found in rural Ireland. To his specific accusation that "In some parts of Kerry and Mayo chapels of mud walls and thatched roofs which frequently admit the snow or the rain are by no means uncommon,"[10] came the reply, "There are no mud wall chapels in Kerry . . . . there are I believe about 10 chapels covered with straw,"[11] and from Tuam, "I don't know any thatched chapel in Co. Mayo but one . . . ."[12] The reply from the small and poor Achonry diocese, partly in County Mayo, was that "the entire number of chapels is thirty four; of these twenty eight are handsome slated ones, and only six are thatched"[13]—probably an underestimate given the congratulations afforded to a bishop who died in 1874 during whose episcopate all thatched chapels had been replaced. Even in the Dublin diocese the last thatched church was not replaced until 1870.[14]

A "popular" church, led in the towns by middle-class church-building committees and in the countryside by a politicized rather than a cultured clergy, did not appeal to Pugin's Romantic ideas of pious *grand seigneurs* and antiquarian clergy. He appealed to "the clergy and gentry of Ireland [to] revive and restore those solemn piles of buildings which formerly covered that island of saints" and to build churches "rude and simple,

Fig. 7-5. Saint Michael the Archangel, Gorey, County Wexford, designed by A. W. N. Pugin, constructed 1839–42.

but massive and solemn . . . harmonized most perfectly with the wild and rocky localities in which they were erected."[15] Pugin responded both as an antiquarian and an architect with a strong sense of the picturesque to such sites—for example, Muckross Abbey at Killarney—and the settings of his churches were often dramatic.[16] But even in the countryside the patronage he secured did not reflect the unbalanced social structure of Catholic Ireland. Lay benefactors included the few Catholic landowners of the southeast, particularly in County Wexford: the M.P. John Hyacinth Talbot, the Esmonde family at Gorey, and the Earl of Kenmare at Killarney. A small number of minor commissions came from members of the Catholic official class, including one for Sir Thomas Wyse and another for the Fitzpatrick chantry at Clough, County Leix.[17] A few clergymen stand out as being more than the agents of this lay patronage: in particular, Bishop Keating of Ferns, the diocese covering County Wexford (where most of Pugin's churches are to be found), Bishop Cornelius Egan of Kerry, and Canon Synott at Gorey. Only the Sisters of the Institute of the Blessed Virgin Mary (Loreto) at Rathfarnham and at Gorey, the Sisters

of Mercy at Birr, and the Presentation Sisters at Waterford could be said to have commissioned Pugin independently of lay patrons. Pugin's largest commission, the rebuilding of Maynooth College, although warmly supported by the students and staff, was paid for by the British government.

Surviving documentation of Pugin's Irish career is even scarcer than for his work in England: some references in his diary, some letters from patrons and collaborators, the important 1846 contract set of plans for Maynooth, and a few other drawings; there is also a late manuscript list of payments in a book recording expenses of Pugin's own church at Ramsgate.[18]

The difficulty of the attribution of two country churches to Pugin in 1838 is less mysterious than at first appears, considering the problems Pugin had supervising his work in Ireland. According to the *Catholic Directory*, "J. (Hyacinth) Talbot Esq., MP, had the kindness to procure from Mr. Pugin a plan of the church at Bree which is now in a state of forwardness and will be completed next summer"[19] and "to him the Revd. George Murphy and his parishioners are indebted for the plan of the church of St. James at Ramsgrange."[20] Talbot,

Fig. 7-6. The Catholic parish church at Tagoat, County Wexford, designed by A. W. N. Pugin, constructed 1843/45–48.

of Talbot Hall, New Ross, County Wexford, was a Catholic Member of Parliament and uncle of Lady Shrewsbury. He was clearly the vital link in Pugin's introduction to Ireland, as Pugin's meeting with him at Alton Towers, the seat of the Earl of Shrewsbury, in July 1839 was to show.[21] The attribution of both churches has been questioned and Pugin did not acknowledge them (but this would not be out of character—he certainly applied such censorship to some more firmly attributable early work in England). It is, however, their discontinuity with contemporary Irish country

chapel-building practice which sets them apart.

Bree Catholic Chapel (fig. 7-3) has a five-bay nave with a distinct five-sided apse, both under separate roofs. This arrangement clearly distinguishes it from contemporary barnlike Catholic "chapels." Even more characteristic of Pugin is its simple wall post and exposed truss roof. The Church of Saint James, Ramsgrange, is a much larger building, with lancets divided by prominently displayed buttressing. Internally, the nave and sanctuary are under the part-boarded, part-plastered barrel vault, with wall-posts and ribs, all elaborated over the sanctuary. The west tower and south porch are probably later. Its form and scale are quite unlike anything local; perhaps Pugin handed a drawing to a local builder.

The chapel at Saint Peter's College, Wexford (1838–41), is assuredly by Pugin. The foundation stone was laid by Pugin on June 18, 1838, on his first visit to Ireland.[22] J. H. Talbot was also singled out as the main lay benefactor and, according to the reference in the *Catholic Directory*, "the plan was furnished by the celebrated Mr. Pugin" (rather than "procured").[23] It is of a similar scale to Ramsgrange. Once again, the use of the lancet style, prominent buttresses, and a single-cell plan under a steep pitched roof are distinct from contemporary practice. Internally, the roof is built of exposed wood (an Irish architect would have put up a plaster ceiling) with a wide span of arched, braced principal trusses with long wall brackets. The pairing of the windows and the elaborate, plate-tracery rose window are even more personal than Ramsgrange. From Saint Peter's, Wexford, onward, aspects of Pugin's work in Ireland were supervised by Richard Pierce, of the Wexford ironmaster and builder family.[24]

The Earl of Shrewsbury, whose heraldry is prominent in the rose window above the altar, was also a benefactor of the Wexford college chapel, although only Talbot is named as such in the *Catholic Directory*. The altar, with its painted and gilt wood mensa and a triptych reredos, is an important example of a type favored by Pugin around this time (1838–41). It is also his most important surviving church furnishing in Ireland and, like his examples for Oscott College and Alton Towers in England, incorporates medieval fragments probably bought from a London antique dealer.[25] Unusually for a Pugin Irish church, the Wexford building campaign was short: begun in 1838, dedicated in 1840, and consecrated (that is, free from debt and furnished with the Pugin altar) in 1841.[26] The rood screen has been removed, but the glass, stenciling, and the altar and triptych make this Pugin's most important surviving church interior in Ireland (fig. 7-4).

One of Pugin's earliest documented works in Ireland was the Loreto Abbey at Rathfarnham, County Dublin, for which he designed a chapel in 1839, incorporating alternative altars and reredoses, all in the Perpendicular style. The diary for 1839 lists both visits and the completion of drawings—"finished Rathfarnham drawings" (May 28, 1839).[27] These were probably taken with him to Dublin on June 1–2. As built, the details are simplified, probably reflecting a collaboration which Pugin failed to supervise to his satisfaction. However, the elaborate plan of the nuns' retrochoir, divided from the public church by an altar-cum-reredos-cum-screen placed under the equally individual octagonal crossing (a miniature version of that in Ely Cathedral in England), follows Pugin. On the floor level above the chapel, windows within the octagon opened internally so that nuns in the infirmary could gaze at the altar below, a charming tradition that Pugin knew from the arrangement of medieval monastic houses. Here, it is a direct quotation of the similar arrangement at the eighteenth-century Bar Convent Chapel in York, which the foundress Mother Mary Ball knew. The Rathfarnham chapel (1839–40) was built by the architects, Patrick Byrne and J. B. Keane; the present screen and detached altar are of later nineteenth-century date.[28]

Pugin visited Ireland possibly ten times in all.[29] References to Irish commissions, patrons, and political and clerical leaders continue in Pugin's diary until his death. The visits were short, the longest being in 1845, for twelve days. He was prepared to send drawings, before he had seen or measured sites, against dimensions supplied by others, and to design against his own cost estimate; he tried, however, to visit the site to set out the foundations and at least once again during construction, but otherwise he directed the building work by correspondence, with reference to his specifications and to explanatory sketches. Pugin described his working methods in 1843 in a letter to J. H. Talbot: "I send . . . you the first plans for the church . . . at Enniscorthy . . . when I come over I will set out the tracery windows with Pierce as it is better I should do so with him than send them over. But there is nothing to hinder the foun-

Fig. 7-7. Saint Mary's Cathedral, Killarney, County Kerry, designed by A. W. N. Pugin, constructed 1842–1912; photographed ca. 1900, showing the church as it was from 1853 to 1908. (Lawrence Collection, National Library of Ireland)

dations of the new church being commenced as Pierce will perfectly understand the plans."[30]

Irish building conditions were primitive, so that competitive bidding was not an issue and construction was undertaken by day laborers, sometimes as famine relief. Pugin's designs in metalwork and stained glass were also in demand as early as July 1839, after Pugin met J. H. Talbot at Alton Towers. From the charges to his account, it appears that Pugin acted as something of a representative in Ireland for Hardman and Company, the Birmingham church decorators and metalworkers for whom he was the chief designer. A by-product of Pugin's involvement in Ireland was the establishment in 1853 of a Dublin branch of Hardman and Company. Under the direction of Thomas Early and Henry Powell, the Irish branch became an independent firm in 1862; it closed only in the 1970s.[31]

Saint Michael the Archangel, Gorey, County Wexford, of 1839–42 (fig. 7-5), built for Canon Synott and Sir Thomas Esmonde, is the most important Romanesque-style building of Pugin's career. His diary entry for June 22, 1839 notes that he "sent off drawings to Gorey."[32] The foundation stone was laid on August 26, 1839, Pugin visited again in 1842, and the consecration took place on May 1, 1843.[33] Pugin used the Romanesque style early in his career; though he preferred to suppress references to such early work, the Gorey church was published in a pirated drawing as late as 1845.[34] The church was based on the cruciform plan of the ruined twelfth-century Dunbrody Abbey, Wexford, with specific Irish references such as the round-tower type transept tourelle, and the stairs attached to the crossing tower, with its "Irish" battlements, and the apse. The church is built of granite with limestone dressings, the primitive local materials. The roof trusses are open, and the interior is dramatically lit from the crossing. The granite piers support not cut stone but plastered round arches. However, the use of plaster capitals to the crossing, and the plaster ceiling to the apse, as well as the marble altar made in Dublin suggest that someone other than Pugin was involved; Pugin's builder had been Richard Pierce. Some of the original parclose screens, but not the polychrome decoration, survive. Pugin designed the adjacent Loreto Convent (1842–44), also sponsored by Sir Thomas and Lady Esmonde who donated the land and money (estimated by 1846 to be £1,000).[35]

Two further parish churches in County Wexford, one at Barntown and the other at Tagoat, are also in the Ferns diocese. Saint Alphonsus, Barntown (1844–51), is the only complete expression in Ireland of one of Pugin's favorite building types, the small village parish church (see fig. 7-1). It is simple in form, the gable at the east end of the nave having a bellcote, and its lean-to aisles having a porch and sacristy projecting on either side. It was lit from paired windows, those in the gable ends being elaborate. The east window, made to Pugin's design by Hardman's, was given by J. H. Talbot.[36] There is no distinction between the nave and the chancel on the plan (which Pugin would have divided with a screen). Pugin here reiterates the formula of the medieval Long Stanton Church, outside Cambridge, one of the "model" medieval churches published by the *Ecclesiologist* and used by Pugin himself for his own small Catholic church in Cambridge. Once again, Pugin uses at least four types of local stone in a delicate constructive polychromy. (The interior of the church has been completely stripped of any original decorations by Pugin.)

The date of the Catholic parish church of Tagoat (1843/45–48; fig. 7-6) is unclear: J. H. Talbot told Pugin in July 1839 that "Fr. Rowe [is] to pay for the plans" and it was in hand by 1843. Pugin visited the site on May 24, 1845; the first Mass was celebrated on June 18, 1848.[37] It is a cruciform-plan, lancet-style church, its large scale being more typical of those built by Pugin's Irish followers. The interior has roughly dressed limestone piers and an open trussed roof elaborately wind-braced. The nave and aisles join a transept with three arches opening into the sanctuary and two side chapels. This curious layout is related partly to the traditional "T"-plan rural chapel and even to the bema transept of early Eastern Christian churches. The confident handling of the long lancets of the transept gables and the dramatic lighting still suggest Pugin's hand. There is a memorial brass to Fr. Rowe who died in 1846, given by Sir Thomas Esmonde, and a pair of Hardman candlesticks given by Pugin.[38]

Pugin built two cathedrals: Saint Mary's, Killarney (1842–1912), for the diocese of Kerry in the southwest of the country; and Saint Aidan's, Enniscorthy (1843–73), for the diocese of Ferns. Both are cruciform in plan with central towers. Killarney, designed in 1842 and visited by Pugin at least twice,[39] is truly of cathedral scale. The site, outside the gates of Kenmare House, was probably given by Lord Kenmare; he was certainly a major benefactor. The style is thirteenth-century lancet, with some plate tracery and the same rose window design that was used at Saint Peter's, Wexford. Pugin built massively and plainly here (fig. 7-7), with simplified Early English moldings, deeply embrasured openings, and flat buttresses. The gable elevations are related to those of Saint Brendan's Cathedral, Ardfert, a ruined medieval cathedral of the early thirteenth century and the historic site of the see of Kerry. The cathedral was unfinished until the early twentieth century when its sublime character was compromised by work done by the Irish architectural firm of Ashlin and Coleman (1908–12; fig. 7-8). Their 300-foot-high spire differs from that sketched in by Pugin in the frontispiece to *An Apology for the Revival of Christian Architecture in England* (1843) and also from that of the wooden model on the cathedral's font cover.[40]

The Great Famine saw many church buildings abandoned until well into the 1850s. Killarney, for example, was reported to be used as a temporary workhouse for Famine relief in 1850. The abandoned state of both Pugin's cathedrals was the object of sly comments by the Anglican journal the *Ecclesiologist* in 1850, and by way of a reply Pugin claimed in a letter to the *Tablet* that only £1,000 was needed to open Killarney.[41] Work restarted in 1853, with fundraising throughout the decade in America.[42] Although J. J. McCarthy was in charge, E. W. Pugin supplied designs for the high altar, reredos, and tabernacle.[43] The 1856 opening of the cathedral was presided over by

Fig. 7-8. Saint Mary's Cathedral, Killarney, County Kerry, initial design by A. W. N. Pugin, constructed 1842–1912; photograph showing additions made in 1908–12. The church was lengthened and the tower and spire were added by G. C. Ashlin and Coleman of Dublin.

Bishop Egan from his invalid chair.[44] The elaborate furnishings by E. W. Pugin, McCarthy, and Ashlin and Coleman were destroyed in a brutal renovation in 1972–73 (figs. 7- 2, 7-9). The most misguided decision was to strip the internal walls of their plaster.[45] Although the simple lancet style of Killarney, following that of Pugin's Saint Barnabas, Nottingham (1842–44), was felt to be appropriate for "primitive" sites, such primitivism was regulated both by his sense of rationalism and by architectural propriety. Killarney today represents not Pugin but a profoundly anti- or "post"-historical coalescence of the Modern movement and liturgical minimalism.

Pugin's intentions are far better represented by Saint Aidan's Cathedral, Enniscorthy (1843-73; fig. 7-10), a commission that resulted from Bishop Keating's involvement with Saint Peter's College, Wexford, but once again the intermediary was the M.P., J. H. Talbot, and the builder Richard Pierce. The cathedral was built in two major phases: the east parts from July 1843 to June 1846, and the nave and aisles from 1846 to 1848. The crossing was roofed in 1850, the tower and broach spire was completed only in 1873, at the second attempt.[46] Pugin possibly visited the site in 1843, and certainly in 1845.[47] Saint Aidan's is impressive from a distance, although its immediate surroundings are more urban than Killarney's. The style is Geometric or Early Decorated and therefore it is more generously lit, with richer traceried windows, than Killarney. It is partly inspired by Tintern Abbey in Wales. Once again, walling and dressings are in contrasted colors, reusing stone rubble from the ruined medieval Franciscan friary which had been donated, like the tiny so-called peppercorn rent for the site, by the landlord, the Earl of Portsmouth.[48] The church was furnished by McCarthy (1857–60); his high altar has survived later renovation and its restoration has just been completed.

Pugin built a convent at Waterford (1842–48; fig. 7-11) for the Presentation Sisters. The drawings were dispatched on December 31, 1841, and Pugin visited the site to lay the first stone on June 10, 1842[49]; he was also in Waterford in 1845, for a longer stay. It is one of Pugin's most satisfying buildings, once isolated on a small hilltop, now surrounded by housing. The complete quadrangle is related to the south and west ranges of Mount Saint Bernards Abbey as seen in the bird's-eye view published in Pugin's *Present State of Ecclesiastical Architecture in England* (1843). The distinct functions of the plan are emphasized, with the entrance and reception rooms on the west front, and the chapel on the north. The longest range is that on the south, which includes the refectory, kitchen and service areas beyond, and the cells, reached through a tower with spiral stairs. There is an internal cloister of charming, diminutive proportions, which Pugin first used at the Convent of Mercy, Handsworth, Birmingham. It is a perfect and complete example both of "picturesque utility"[50] and of Pugin's teachings as expounded in his *True Principles of Pointed or Christian Architecture* (1841). The convent was completed by E. W. Pugin, and the chapel furnishings he designed, including the stalls and rood screen, survive as the most intact Puginian church interior in Ireland.[51] Another convent, for the Sisters of Mercy at Birr (1846–56), illustrated by an elevation and a bird's-eye view in the *Catholic Directory* (1848), was also completed by E. W. Pugin, with slightly different massing.[52] The

Fig. 7-9. Saint Mary's Cathedral, Killarney, County Kerry; photographed 1994. The interior was stripped of the original plasterwork, flooring, and furnishings in 1972–73.

Presentation Brothers' monastery at Killarney (1846–62) may have been begun by A. W. N. Pugin and has been attributed to him.[53]

Pugin had just a handful of medieval churches to restore in England, and only one in Ireland. The Trinitarian Abbey, Adare, given to the Catholics in 1811 by the first Earl of Dunraven, was rebuilt as the Catholic parish church by the second Earl—at least until work was halted by

Fig. 7-10. Saint Aidan's Cathedral, Enniscorthy, County Wexford, designed by A. W. N. Pugin, constructed 1843–73.

the Famine—and the *Tablet* attributed the repair and reroofing to Pugin. He probably visited Adare Manor, for which he made designs (dated 1846–47), in 1845.[54] The completion of the church by the third Earl in 1854 was under the architect, P. C. Hardwick.[55]

Pugin's largest commission in Ireland was the rebuilding of Saint Patrick's College, Maynooth (fig. 7-12), the premier national seminary outside Dublin. It involved him in much church and government politics, and he attended meetings with the bishops who were trustees of the college, the Commissioner of Public Works, and even the Lord Lieutenant of Ireland.[56] Obviously Pugin's reputation stood him in good stead, and it is significant that the commission, unlike the three contemporary government-funded university colleges, did not go out to competition. Maynooth,

founded in 1795, was unique among Catholic institutions in the British Isles since it was partly government-funded by what was known as the Maynooth Grant. In 1845 a separate fund was voted for its rebuilding,[57] and the same year Pugin's first scheme was supported by a building committee.[58] However, the Irish Board of Works estimated from Pugin's drawings a cost of £57,400, not the £30,000 agreed,[59] and Pugin therefore resigned in January 1846.[60] However, in July 1847 he was reappointed for a reduced scheme.[61] Because of the difficulties of supervision, Pugin appointed Richard Pierce, as his clerk of works.[62] Thereafter Pugin visited the site in 1848 and twice in 1849, and certified the contract as complete in June 1850.[63] The painstakingly slow completion of the building meant that it was not occupied until the autumn of 1853.[64]

Pugin held seminary commissions to be vital to the spread of his Gothic teachings and he was no doubt heartened by the Maynooth student and staff protest at his resignation.[65] As the *Catholic Directory* noted in commenting on the progress of the Gothic Revival in Ireland: "the most encouraging sign is the erection of the new quadrangle at Maynooth after Mr Pugin's designs. We are all aware of the influence of the place of education on the young ecclesiastic."[66] The style, details, and plan of Maynooth were to have more influence on the Irish clergy, and its professors and alumni were prominent apologists for the Gothic Revival. As Pugin wrote to Lord Shrewsbury: ". . . The Buildings at Maynooth look grand from their great height & extent. They seem to give great satisfaction in Ireland which is a good thing, both for me & for the Gothic cause."[67] Maynooth is one of Pugin's most significant later buildings, as well as a testimony to the vigor of the mid-nineteenth-century Catholic Church in Ireland.

The three sides of Saint Patrick's Court, with a detached kitchen and offices, were built in local rubble with Ardbraccan limestone dressings and slate roofs. Pugin used "early" sources, thirteenth-rather than fourteenth-century Gothic, and the austerity of Maynooth anticipates something of the High Victorian style of G. E. Street. Pugin is here at his most "rational," building in a severely economical style with a minimum of external detail—such as the irregularly laid limestone quoins. Internally, the planning is institutional, with wide internal corridors under lean-to roofs. The most unexpected details are the four louvers which provide top-lighting to the corridors dividing the attics; built of timber and glass and slate-roofed, they are a far cry from Pugin's delight in the picturesque. However, the three-story elevation, double-depth plan, and endless internal cloisters have the scale, if not the escapism, of a Gothic fantasy. Pugin's plan is markedly institutional, collegiate rather than monastic, and notably different from the additive planning and elevations which he recommended in *True Principles*: it is certainly one of the "factories of learning."[68] Moreover, Pugin had to omit just the sort of service accommodation that he was often accused of skimping on for the sake of church decoration, such as a detached infirmary, covered cloisters connecting it, a stable court, and even a gas works.

The only work to be started before Pugin's death was the second court (1846–53), omitting the hall and chapel which were published in 1855

Fig. 7-11. The Presentation Convent, Waterford, County Wexford, designed by A. W. N. Pugin, constructed 1842–48.

Fig. 7-12. Saint Patrick's Seminary, Maynooth, initial design by A. W. N. Pugin, constructed 1846–53. The chapel on the right was added by J. J. McCarthy (1875–80); it was left unfinished in 1880 but lavishingly furnished in 1890–91. The tower and spire by William Hague (1895) were built by J. L. Robinson (1902–1903).

in a bird's-eye view (fig. 7-13) after Pugin had died.[69] The comparison between intention and achievement is instructive. The most important omission was that of the church. Pugin, with his strict understanding of different types of church plan, designed a college chapel arranged like a choir. Nine massively expressed flying buttresses support further flat buttresses on the eleven-bay church, under which Pugin threaded the cloister on the court side. Pugin's single vessel building was generously lit by ten two-light, apparently plate tracery windows with a single bay deep sanctuary lit from side windows. The general disposition, including the off-axis west end tower, is related to the brick-built seminary chapel at Saint Edmund's College, Ware, Hertfordshire (1845–53). Here, in consciously moving away from the

more elaborate Decorated style and the subdivided plans of his parish churches, Pugin seems to anticipate the scale and plans of his son's churches and even of his later Anglican imitators, the architects G. F. Bodley and T. Garner at Saint Augustine's Pendlebury, Lancashire (1871–74). The Maynooth chapel, built by J. J. McCarthy (1875–80), follows the plan of the Pugin scheme with the addition of a full chevet east end.[70] The free-standing tower and spire of 1895, by William Hague, were built in 1902–03 under the supervision of J. L. Robinson.

Because of the involvement of the Board of Works, Pugin's scheme for Saint Patrick's Court did go out for bids and the contract was awarded to W. H. Beardwood, a Dublin builder.[71] Seven of Pugin's fourteen contract drawings survive; they are an important document of Pugin's later style and further evidence of the economy of his drawing and working methods.[72] The 1846 drawing, "Saint Patrick's College, Maynooth, No. 7. Great Refectory etc" (fig. 7-14), shows the end gable and sections through the refectory with two floors of chambers above, the library with its hammer-beam and central king-post trusses, and the professors' dining room with the board room beyond. An elevation is provided of the three complicated bays where library, stair tower, and refectory join, with three sections. Drawing number eight (fig. 7-15) is the section and elevation of the single bay of the main entrance, with its generous internal corridor. The centrally pivoted wooden casement and the matter-of-fact timber-and-glass louvers lighting the central corridor in the attics are also shown. Number twelve (fig. 7-16) and number thirteen (fig. 7-17) are of stonework details, including a section through the entrance arch and oriel. Another sheet shows ironwork, roof truss, and privy details.

* * *

Pugin's closest Irish collaborator was the architect, Richard Pierce, who emerged from Pugin's involvement in Wexford to act as his clerk of works at Maynooth.[73] By 1843 Pugin was content for Pierce to begin Enniscorthy Cathedral from his drawings. Pierce also received scaled drawings from Pugin via his English builder George Myers, possibly for the church at Tagoat; he was also clerk of works for Lord Midleton, another of Pugin's Irish patrons.[74] Pierce began work independently on two highly Puginian churches at Wexford in 1851,[75] and completed a convent

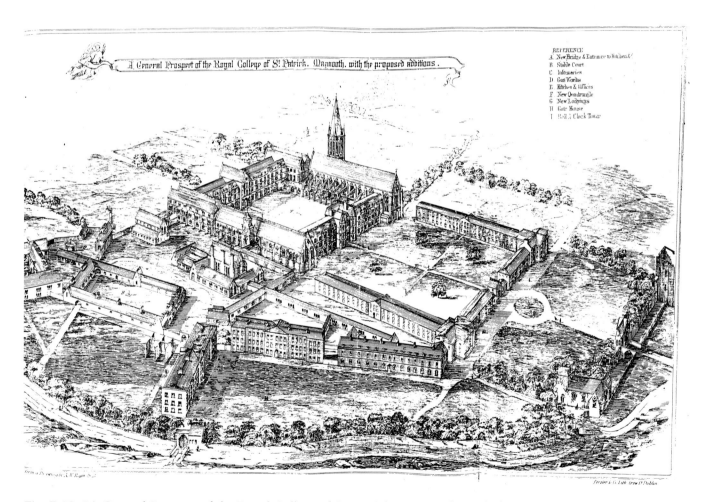

Fig. 7-13. "A General Prospect of the Royal College of St. Patrick. Maynooth. With the proposed additions"; lithograph based on a drawing by A. W. N. Pugin. From *The Maynooth Commission Report* (Dublin, 1855).

Fig. 7-14. "St. Patrick's College, Maynooth, No. 7. Great Refectory etc." by A. W. N. Pugin; pen and pencil on paper, 1846. Inscribed, "William H. Beardwood with the Commissioners of Public Works / Referred to in the agreement dated 10th day of October 1846"; signed "W H. Beardwood" and "W B Hogan." The same inscriptions are found on other contract drawings associated with this project (see figs. 7-15, 7-16, 7-17). (Irish Architectural Archive)

chapel which involved correspondence with Hardman[76]; he took over Enniscorthy Cathedral, before dying at the age of forty-three in 1854.[77] The title "Irish Pugin" went, therefore, not to Pierce but to J. J. McCarthy, Pugin's most significant Irish imitator.

One of the most influential sources of Puginesque propaganda was the *Catholic Directory*, although it did occasionally censure Pugin's extreme positions. The *Directory* reported all church-building as evidence of a Catholic and specifically "national" progress. Pugin, however, objected to the publication of the scheme for the Neoclassical Cathedral of Ardagh at Longford, which he described as a "wretched compound of pagan and protestant architecture . . . as if there was anything *national* in these importations of English and continental abortions."[78] As in England, such journalism was vital to the spread of Pugin's message, but the question of whether the *Directory* would recognize a Puginian church when it saw one is raised by the publication in 1845 of designs by Patrick Byrne for Saint John the Baptist, Blackrock, County Dublin, a markedly pre-Puginian building. "The drawings and writings of Mr. Pugin in the *Dublin Review* which

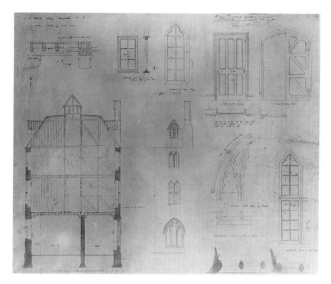

Fig. 7-15. "St. Patrick's College, Maynooth, No. 8. Section and Details of East pane" by A. W. N. Pugin; pen and pencil on paper, 1846. (Irish Architectural Archive)

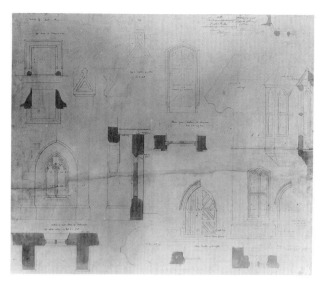

Fig. 7-16. "St. Patrick's College, Maynooth, No. 12. Details of West Pane" by A. W. N. Pugin; pen and pencil on paper, 1846. (Irish Architectural Archive)

we noticed in the Registry [are] worthy of the attention of the clergy engaged in church or chapel building and . . . their adaptation and fulfilment seems to have been most successfully carried out—perhaps even improved on—by the clever and experienced architect . . . Patrick Byrne Esq of . . . Dublin . . . . The plans and drawings were suggested by the drawings and writings of Mr. Pugin . . . in the *Dublin Review* [and] the principal outline . . . copied from Stanton Saint John's Church in Oxfordshire, the model selected by Mr. Bloxam in his *Principles of Gothic ecclesiastical architecture.*"[79] Byrne himself, despite a connection with Pugin at the building of the chapel at the Loreto Abbey in 1839, was not clearly amenable to his message; the detail of his Saint James's, Dublin, was still being finished internally, in plaster, as late as 1859.[80]

By 1853 Pugin was already claimed as a "great master and friend" and "friend and fellow labourer"[81] of J. J. McCarthy, who took over the churches not only of Pugin but also of Pierce. McCarthy, in work as early as 1846 at Glendalough and later in Dublin and County Meath, was able to achieve Puginian "correctness."[82] Descriptions of fully Puginian churches appeared in the *Catholic Directory* for 1849, with

Fig. 7-17. "St. Patrick's College, Maynooth, No. 13. Details of East Pane" by A. W. N. Pugin; pen and pencil on paper, 1846. (Irish Architectural Archive)

details of McCarthy's churches or chapels at Glendalough (with its furnishings as intended but never achieved),[83] at All Hallows College, Dublin,[84] and at Saint Skyre, Kilskyre, County Meath, which was said "to be no *barn* of overgrown dimensions and hideous aspect but a *church* of the true and ancient Catholic type . . . rood screen . . . sedilia, sepulchre and other

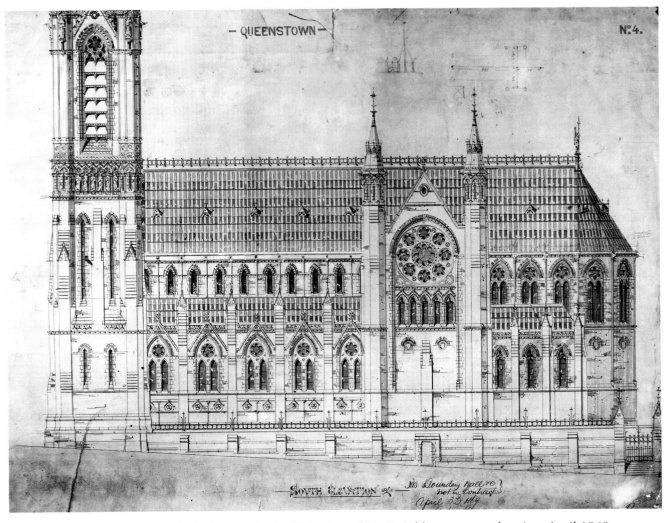

Fig. 7-18. Saint Colman's Cathedral, Cove, by E. W. Pugin and G. C. Ashlin, contract drawing, April 1869. (Ashlin and Coleman Collection, Irish Architectural Archive)

appropriate furniture and decoration".[85]

Early in 1852 McCarthy was discussing his own projects with Pugin, as well as agreeing to undertake for half the fee and all the traveling expenses the management of Pugin's commission for the small Fitzpatrick mortuary chapel at Clough, County Leix. Surviving correspondence shows the difficulties of a collaboration cut short by Pugin's illness and death, but McCarthy persevered, with J. Hardman and E. W. Pugin.[86] The chantry was completed with Beardwood as builder and was furnished with Hardman glass and a Myers altar.[87] McCarthy also asked for Pugin's advice on the design of Saint Saviour's, the Dublin Dominican church. Pugin's unexpected response on the chancel arrangements reads like a defence of his Maynooth chapel plan: "Let everybody see and hear by the chancels . . . down the

nave. Keep the churches bright with good windows . . . you will see that if you honour[?] the chancel we will make your church a chancel."[88] McCarthy's Saint Saviour's (1852–61) is something of a response to this advice, and he later had to counter the rumor that Pugin was its real architect.[89]

McCarthy requested foliage details from E. W. Pugin for the Fitzpatrick chantry,[90] and in 1854 E. W. Pugin designed the high altar at Killarney, which McCarthy was completing.[91] From what we know of E. W. Pugin's claim to be his father's successor, in practice there must have been some rivalry here. By 1856 E. W. Pugin was visiting Ireland to complete his father's buildings on his own account,[92] and in 1859 he set up a Dublin practice with his brother-in-law and former pupil, George Coppinger Ashlin, on the strength of their success in the competition for Saints Peter and Paul, Cork.[93]

The Church of Saints Peter and Paul, Cork (1859–66), was to be one of E. W. Pugin's most exciting and richly furnished interiors, as well as the first vigorous statement of High Victorian architecture in Catholic Ireland. The style is in complete contrast to his father's. The exterior is hemmed in by its city-center site like a medieval building, and the plan is ingenious.[94] Pugin's use of color is particularly important: it is built in rich, mulberry red Cork sandstone, relieved in bands and dressed with local ash white limestone and slate roofs. The polychromy is continued inside, with shafts of polished red Cork marble on black marble plinths, supporting rich, molded Caen stone capitals and arches, with the "Pugin roof" of elaborate double-backed trusses and painted panels.[95] In contrast, there is much striking dark wooden furniture from Belgium (where Pugin had important connections), such as the angels guarding the confessionals and the angel lamp-holders. Once again, the lighting is dramatic, with a massive west window, four-light clerestory windows, and long two-light apse windows, all with geometric tracery. Rhythm and scale are unusual, the arcade and clerestory continued as an open-work screen across the transepts, with massive figures of the Apostles against the spandrils. The Hardman glass was designed by Pugin, the apse glass by Barnett Brothers of Leith.[96] Sanctuary furnishings of 1874 are by G. C. Ashlin and the side altars are to E. W. Pugin's design.[97] E. W. Pugin's arrival on the Irish church-building scene in this fashion was much criticized in the newly founded *Dublin Builder*, particularly as the commissioning priest was a relative of Ashlin's.[98]

Saints Peter and Paul was to be followed by the Dublin Augustinian church (1862–93)[99] and the crowning achievement of Saint Colman's Cathedral, Cove (1859–1916).[100] The first scheme (1858) was for a modest parish church design in Cove, but two cathedral schemes followed; the second, of 1869, from E. W. Pugin's designs (fig. 7-18), was evidently handed over by him to

Ashlin, who was certainly the executant architect of the many contracts. Bishop Keane's ambition was much regretted by his successor in 1877, who complained of an unfinished church "commenced on too magnificent and costly a scale for the resources of the Diocese, but it was so advanced when it fell into my hands that I could make no change without spoiling it."[101] The original estimate of £25,000 was about one tenth the final cost of £235,000, which included deep foundations and ramped arcaded embankments, Dalkey granite and Mallow limestone dressings, and a Bath stone-faced vaulted interior. The furnishing of the church and the completion of the spire in 1916 was achieved by Bishop Browne, a former president of the Maynooth college. Contemporary commentators of broadly Unionist persuasion saw it as an example of ruinous clerical rapacity, those on the Catholic Nationalist side as an example of religious and national revival. For many, the building of Cove Cathedral must have been their last sight of Ireland as they left on the emigrant ships for America. This had always been the route not of the poorest but of the ambitious: one of these was Patrick Charles Keely (1816–96), who was born in Kilkenny and left Ireland in 1842. Keely was to be the most important Catholic architect in nineteenth-century America.[102]

The other great symbol of the resurgence of the Catholic Church was, of course, Saint Patrick's College, Maynooth. The completion of McCarthy's chapel (1875–80), which was also the work of Bishop Browne, marks the apogee of Catholic High Victorian architecture in Ireland. Six architects were invited to compete in 1890, only one of whom was an Englishman. The award went to William Hague, an Irish architect. Among those decorating the church was just one English decorator, N. H. J. Westlake, and the stained-glass makers, Cox and Buckley.[103] The inference is that English Catholic architects such as the Pugins were no longer required to design or decorate churches in Ireland. By 1890 many people in Ireland were thinking not merely of Home Rule but even of secession from Britain; dreaming of a Celtic Revival and of Ourselves Alone.

I wish to thank Alexandra Wedgwood for her comments, and Anthony Symondson, SJ, for alerting me to recent Irish publications.

1. Bishop Griffith's estimate, 1837. See W. Mazière Brady, *Annals of the Catholic Hierarchy* (1883), p. 201. There were about 250,000 Catholics in Great Britain by 1829, 350,000 by 1840, and 846,000 by 1850.

2. Pugin's Diary (July 21, 1838), in Alexandra Wedgwood, *Catalogue of the Victoria and Albert Museum Drawings Collection: A. W. N. Pugin and The Pugin Family* (London, 1985), pp. 80–81, n. 30. The First Catholic Relief Act (1778) granted Catholics inheritance, education, and property rights; the Second (1791 in England, 1793 in Ireland) granted toleration to Catholic worship and the right to build churches. The 1829 Act granted the right to vote and sit in Parliament. Daniel O'Connell (1775–1847) was known as the Liberator even during his lifetime.

3. Undated letter ca. 1850, quoted in Benjamin Ferrey, *Recollections of A. N. Welby Pugin and his father Augustus Pugin* (London, 1861), p. 125.

4. Phoebe Stanton first established the importance of Pugin's Irish churches, following the similar analysis of his English work by H.-R. Hitchcock. See Phoebe Stanton, *Pugin* (London, 1971); H.-R. Hitchcock, *Early Victorian Architecture in Britain*, 2 vols. (New Haven, 1954), especially chap. 3, pp. 56–96. See also Douglas Scott Richardson, *Gothic Revival Architecture in Ireland*, 2 vols. (New York, 1983); and Roderick O'Donnell, "Catholic church architecture in Great Britain and Ireland," Ph.D. thesis (Cambridge, 1983).

5. William Makepeace Thackeray, *The Irish Sketchbook of 1842* (1873 ed.), p. 558.

6. Pugin's Diary (January 10, 1847), in Wedgwood, *Catalogue*, p. 61.

7. R. F. Foster, *Modern Ireland 1600–1972* (London, 1988), pp. 318–72. Jeanne Sheehy, "Irish Church-building: Popery, Puginism and the Protestant Ascendancy," in Chris Brooks and Andrew Saint, eds., *The Victorian Church Architecture and Society* (Manchester and New York, 1995).

8. A. W. N. Pugin, *An Apology for the Revival of Christian Architecture* (1843), p. 23.

9. Revd. Mr. Leahy, "Wants of Religion in Ireland" (n. p., ca. 1841).

10. The *Catholic Directory* (1842), pp. 307–308. The *Irish Catholic Directory* (1870–present) began life as *A Complete Catholic Registry, Directory and Almanack* (1836–43), continued as *Battersby's Registry for the Catholic World* (1846–57), as *Battersby's Catholic Directory* (1858–64), and as *Catholic Directory of Ireland* (1865–69). For the sake of simplicity, this essay refers to all editions of the directory as *Catholic Directory*.

11. Ibid., pp. 307–308.

12. Ibid., p. 317.

13. Ibid., p. 320.

14. For a reference to Balheany, see *Dublin* [later *Irish*] *Builder* (1870), p. 123.

15. Pugin, *An Apology*, p. 23.

16. Pugin to the Earl of Shrewsbury (June 1843), in Wedgwood, *Catalogue*, p. 106, n. 29. Pugin also refers to the sites of Muckross and Dunbrody Abbeys and Ardfert Cathedral in the Diary.

17. Saint John's Manor, Waterford, for Sir Thomas Wyse, M.P., is a thin red-brick house with a two-story stone porch. Pugin's proposals to rebuild it are discussed in an undated letter in an Irish private collection (brought to my attention by Mr. Nicholas Sheaff). The private chapel at Edermine House, Co. Wexford, for Sir John and Lady Power, the owners of the firm of John Power & Sons, Distillers, is sometimes attributed to Pugin, but with as yet no primary evidence. The Bellevue chapel, Co. Wexford, sometimes attributed to A. W. N. Pugin, was by E. W. Pugin and built in 1859.

18. Wedgwood, *Catalogue*, p. 121, n. 96.

19. *Catholic Directory* (1839), p. 236.

20. Ibid., pp. 235–36. The *Catholic Directory* repeats the Pugin attribution referring to Dunbrody Abbey as the source (ibid. [1841], p. 234).

21. J. H. Talbot to A. W. Pugin (July 9, 1839), in the Hardman and Co. Archive, Birmingham City Public Reference Library (hereafter cited as Hardman Archive, Birmingham); Pugin's Diary (July 6, 1839), in Wedgwood, *Catalogue*, p. 82, n. 28.

22. Pugin's Diary (June 18, 1838), in Wedgwood, *Catalogue*, p. 80, n. 22.

23. *Catholic Directory* (1839), p. 235.

24. *Tablet* (1843), p. 198, quoting the *Wexford Independent*, cited in Margaret Belcher, *A W N Pugin: An annotated critical bibliography* (London & New York, 1987), p. 213; Pugin's Diary (1847), in Wedgwood, *Catalogue*, p. 94, n. 3. He was the brother of James Pierce, the Wexford ironmaster, and should not be confused with Richard Pierce, the builder/architect whose career continued into the 1860s. See nn. 30 and 73, below.

25. "Hull for Wexford altar £101.5.0" (Pugin's Diary [1839], in Wedgwood, *Catalogue*, p. 83, n. 83). See also Roderick O'Donnell, "Pugin as a Church Architect," in Paul Atterbury and Clive Wainwright, eds., *Pugin: A Gothic Passion* (London & New Haven, 1994).

26. *Catholic Directory* (1840), p. 235, pp. 291–92.

27. Pugin's Diary (May 28, 1839), in Wedgwood, *Catalogue*, p. 82, n. 21.

28. Stanton, *Pugin,* pp. 57–58, 119; Alexandra Wedgwood, *A W N Pugin and The Pugin Family (Catalogue of the RIBAD)* (1977), [61] 1–2, p. 73. The church was by the Dublin architect, Patrick Byrne. The Loreto Abbey, Rathfarnham, County Dublin, was founded 1822 and the church opened 1840. Lady Wedgwood makes the point that Pugin's octagon was an intervention "so sophisticated and difficult to accomplish, and the result is so good and *different* from the rest of the chapel. Was *this* his contribution to fulfill Mother Ball's request, and only this?" (personal communication).

29. These visits occurred in 1838, 1839, 1842, probably in 1843, 1845, probably in 1846, and in 1847, 1848, 1849, and 1850. See Pugin's Diary (June 15–22, 1838), in Wedgwood, *Catalogue*, p. 40, p. 80 nn. 22–23; (May 15–16, 1839), ibid., p. 42, p. 82 nn. 19-21; (June 1–2, 1839), ibid., p. 42; (June 4–12, 1842), ibid., p. 52, p. 87 nn. 22–25; (May 21–31, 1845), p. 59, pp. 92–93 nn. 15–20; (July 12–17), ibid., p. 59, p. 93 nn. 24–27; (September 10–11), ibid., p. 60, p. 93 n. 32; (July 6–8, 1847), ibid., p. 62; (July 6–8, 1848), ibid., p. 64, p. 96 n. 19; (May 29–31, 1849), ibid., p. 66; (August 16–18), ibid., p. 66, p. 97 n. 17; (June 21–26, 1850), ibid., p. 68; (June 10-12, 1851), ibid., p. 71. The Diary also noted addresses and payments such as "Wexford £36 00," and "Ireland £100."

30. Pugin to J. H. Talbot (April 1843), Bishop's House, Enniscorthy. I am grateful to the Rev. Seamus du Val for kindly providing me with a transcript.

31. *Dublin Builder* (1865), p. 145; advertisement by Early and Powell, *Tablet* (1862), p. 332.

32. Pugin's Diary (June 22, 1839), in Wedgwood, *Catalogue*, p. 42 and p. 82, n. 24.

33. *Catholic Directory* (1840), pp. 291–92; ibid. (1844), p. 395; Pugin's Diary (June 11, 1842), in Wedgwood, *Catalogue*, p. 52, p. 87, n. 25. See also W. H. Grattan Flood, *History of the Diocese of Ferns* (Waterford, 1916), p. 59.

34. *Catholic Directory* (1846), frontispiece with spire after A. W. Pugin.

35. Ibid., pp. 299-301. Sir Thomas Esmonde later built the poor school and helped with the convent.

36. *Tablet* (1851), p. 644. It was ordered from Hardman in 1848. See *The Builder* (London, 1851), p. 594; *Catholic Directory* (1851), p. 269.

37. Talbot to Pugin (see n. 21, above). *Tablet* (April 1, 1843) already refers to Pierce's role here (see n. 24, above). Pugin's Diary, in Wedgwood, *Catalogue*, p. 59, n. 16

38. Hardman Archive, Birmingham; Jeremy Williams, *A Companion Guide to Architecture in Ireland, 1837–1921* (Dublin, 1994), pp. 381–82.

39. He notes that he: "sent drawings" (Pugin's Diary [April 16, 1842], in Wedgwood, *Catalogue*, p. 51, n. 10), and "set out church" ([June 7, 1842], ibid., p. 52, n. 22). See also Pugin's Diary (May 31–June 2, 1845), ibid., p. 59; and *Tablet* (1843), p. 24.

40. Drawings for its completion are in the Ashlin and Coleman collection, the Irish Architectural Archive, Dublin.

41. *Ecclesiologist* 11 (1850), p. 271; *Tablet* (1850), pp. 170, 178 (letter), 539.

42. *Tablet* (1853), pp. 409–12; *Dublin Builder* (1853), p. 484.

43. E. W. Pugin's Office Diary (January 1–December 31, 1854), entries for January 10–14, in the Yale Center for British Art, New Haven, CT, Rare Books MS/Pugin/59; for a reference to "tabernacle Killarney . . . Nov 1854," see the "Metal Book" (1854–58), in the Hardman Archives, Birmingham.

44. Killarney was dedicated on August 19, 1856 (*Catholic Directory* [1857], p. 218). For an obituary of Bishop Cornelius Egan (1780–1856), mentioning that he "gave nearly £8000 towards the cathedral now nearly completed [and is] buried in front the Lady altar," see ibid., pp. 244-45. For descriptions of the furnishings, see *Dublin Builder* (1858), p. 280.

45. This work was commissioned by the then bishop, Eamon Casey, the influential liturgical artist, Ray Carroll, and the local architect, Denis Kennedy. Earlier floor levels were also removed. See Tomas O'Caoimh, "Killarney Cathedral," *Irish Heritage Series* 66 (Dublin, 1990).

46. Enniscorthy Cathedral was dedicated May 2, 1860 (*Dublin Builder* [1860], p. 282). McCarthy furnished the church between May 1857 and 1860 (W. H. Grattan Flood, *History of Enniscorthy and its vicinity* [Enniscorthy, 1889], pp. 197–207). The tower and broach spire are probably by McCarthy, but the *Irish Builder*, in a posthumous reference to the builder, James T. Ryan, does not mention McCarthy ([1882], p. 275).

47. Pugin's Diary (May 15, 1845), in Wedgwood, *Catalogue*, p. 59, n. 15.

48. Flood, *History of Enniscorthy.*

49. Pugin's Diary (December 31, 1841), in Wedgwood, *Catalogue*, p. 50, p. 86, n. 42, and (June 10, 1842), in ibid., p. 52, p. 87, n. 24.

50. Stefan Muthesius, *The High Victorian Movement in Architecture, 1850–1870* (London, 1972), p. 4.

51. For an advertisement by Early and Powell, see *Catholic Directory* (1855); for attribution of the chapel furniture to G. C. Ashlin, see *Tablet* (1862), p. 332; also see Wedgwood, *A W N Pugin (RIBAD)*, [15], p. 116.

52. For the drawings, see *Catholic Directory* (1848), between pp. 320 and 321; *Tablet* (1846), pp. 170, 698; ibid., (1851), p. 544. The drawings labeled "Pugin architect" and "Morrison, lith, Dublin" are not his. The chapel range was completed by E. W. Pugin in 1856 (E. W. Pugin's diary, 1856). See also *Dublin Builder* (1861), p. 603; and ibid., (1866), p. 80. There are further ranges by Ashlin. The chapel has been stripped of its furniture.

53. *Catholic Directory* (1860).

54. *Tablet* (1850), p. 613.

55. *Tablet* (1854), p. 270; *The Builder* (1852), pp. 300, 359, 599. For mention of "Mr. Hardwick," see ibid., (1854), p. 236. The Mercy Convent and Christian Brothers' school and monastery were also by the 3rd Earl, who became a Catholic in 1855; P. C. Hardwick was named as the architect for these and for the restoration of the Augustinian abbey as the Protestant church (see the Countess of Dunraven, *Memorials of Adare* [1865], pp. 65–67). For further comments on Pugin and Hardwick at Adare, see *The Builder* (October 15, 1887), pp. 283–84.

56. Pugin's Diary (July 13–17, 1845), in Wedgwood, *Catalogue*, p. 59 and p. 93, nn. 24–27; and (September 10 and 11, 1845), in ibid., p. 60, p. 93, n. 32. Copies of Pugin's letters to Lord Shrewsbury on Maynooth are in the House of Lords Record Office, Historical Collection.

57. For the most recent analysis of the story, see Patrick J. Corish, *Maynooth College 1795–1995* (Dublin, 1995), pp. 128–33.

58. He noted in his diary, "began the Maynooth drawings" ([May 2, 1845], in Wedgwood, *Catalogue*, p. 59 and p. 93, n. 31).

59. *The Builder* (1845), p. 585; Corish, *Maynooth*, p. 129.

60. His letter of resignation (January 15, 1845) to the Board of Works is cited in Corish, *Maynooth*, p. 508, n. 3.

61. *The Sixteenth Annual Report of the Board of Public Works in Ireland* (London, 1848); Corish, *Maynooth*, pp. 129–30.

62. *The Sixteenth Annual Report*; *The Builder* (1853), pp. 60, 94; *Detailed Account of the Expenditure of the Sum of £30,000 granted in 1845 for the putting of Maynooth College in repair: total amount of the grant 1846–1850* (House of Commons, London, 1851).

63. Pugin's Diary (June 6–8, 1848), in Wedgwood, *Catalogue*, p. 64, p. 96, n. 19; (May 30), in ibid., p. 66; (August 17, 1849), in ibid., p. 66 and p. 97, n. 17; (June 21–26, 1850), in ibid., p. 68. See also Ferrey, *Recollections*, pp. 131–32.

64. *The Builder* (1853), p. 60, 94; Corish, *Maynooth*, pp. 130–32.

65. For a copy of the student protest dated March 2, 1846, see Archives of the Archbishop of Dublin, Clonliffe College,

pp. 125/1, 125/2. For quotations from the protest by the staff, see Ferrey, *Recollections*, pp. 133–34. For Fr. Gaffney's letter to Pugin, see ibid., pp. 135–36; Corish, *Maynooth*, p. 129 and p. 508, n. 4.

66. *Catholic Directory* (1849), p. 191.

67. Pugin to the Earl of Shrewsbury (June 3, 1849), in Wedgwood, *Catalogue*, p. 113, n. 64.

68. Pugin, *True Principles of Pointed or Christian Architecture* (London, 1841), pp. 60–63, quotation p. 63.

69. *The Maynooth Commission Report* (Dublin, 1855), between parts 1 and 2.

70. For McCarthy's appointment as college chapel architect, see *Irish Builder* (1875), p. 43; ibid., (1879), p. 344; Corish, *Maynooth*, pp. 191–95. E. W. Pugin unsuccessfully tried to press his claims to build his father's chapel.

71. W. H. Beardwood (died 1860; *Dublin Builder* [1860], p. 251) and his son James Patrick (died 1865, *Dublin Builder* [1865], p. 253) both worked for A. W. N. Pugin at Maynooth.

72. The drawings are in the uncatalogued collection of architectural drawings at Maynooth College Library (photograph copies at the Irish Architectural Archive, Dublin). Corish, *Maynooth*, refers to tracings of the full collection in the National Archives, Dublin (37325/57), not seen by this author. In July 1978 in the building officer's room there was a block plan of the new building showing the drains, signed "R. Pierce for A. W. Pugin 28 August 1850." Other Maynooth drawings (including the 1845 bird's-eye perspective) are referred to in Wedgwood, *A W N Pugin (RIBAD)*, p. 71 [53] and pp. 104–105 [111], 72, 72v, 73.

73. Richard Pierce of Wexford (1801–54), see n. 24 above.

74. See Patricia Spencer Silver, *Pugin's builder: the life and work of George Myers* (Hull, 1993), p 24. and fig. 18, where the sketch is misidentified as a detail for Saint Peter's College, Wexford.

75. The "twin churches," Our Lady of the Immaculate Conception (1851–59) and Our Lady of the Assumption (1851–58), Wexford, were begun to the same design and at the same time in 1851 so as to minimize rivalry between the two parishes. J. J. McCarthy took over their completion in 1858.

76. Pierce wrote to Hardman on April 16, 1852 about two Pugin window designs (Hardman Archives, Birmingham).

77. "He was also engaged as architect to Enniscorthy cathedral" (*Wexford Guardian* [August 5, 1854]).

78. Pugin, *An Apology*, p. 23.

79. *Catholic Directory* (1845), p. 240.

80. Patrick Byrne (died 1864) was architect of the chapel at Loreto Abbey; Saint John the Baptist, Blackrock (1842–46); and many Neoclassical churches in Dublin.

81. *Tablet* (June 1853), pp. 410-12.

82. For McCarthy's wider career, see Jeanne Sheehy, *J. J. McCarthy and the Irish Gothic Revival* (Belfast, 1977).

83. *Catholic Directory* (1849), pp. 356–57.

84. For reference to All Hallows College Chapel, Dublin, see ibid., pp. 357–58.

85. For Saint Skyre, Kilskrye, County Meath, see ibid., pp. 322–23.

86. For six letters written between March 18, 1852 and December 22, 1852, see "1852 26 bundles," in the Hardman Archives, Birmingham. See also the "Glass Book" (1845–53), entry no. 34 (November 23, 1852), in the Hardman Archive, Birmingham; and E. W. Pugin's Diary (1854), passim. (see n. 43 above).

87. It has now been demolished except for a tomb and ledger slab brass commemorating Richard Wilson Fitzpatrick (1811–50); information Jeanne Sheehey.

88. Letter from Pugin to McCarthy (January 15, 1852) in a private collection.

89. *Dublin Builder* (1863), pp. 14–16, 79; and *Freemans Journal* (April 25, 1863). For a letter of Fr. R. White, the Dominican prior, see ibid. (April 26, 1863).

90. For the letter from McCarthy to Hardman (December 22, 1852), see "1852 26 bundles," in the Hardman Archives, Birmingham.

91. E. W. Pugin's Office Diary (see n. 43, above) records four days designing the "alter [sic] and reredos kilarney"(January 10–14, 1854) with another day's work by "J W"; letters to McCarthy are also noted. From the context it is clear that McCarthy was the commissioning architect.

92. E. W. Pugin's personal diary (1856) is in MS copy at the House of Lords Record Office, Historical Collection: see Roderick O'Donnell, "The Later Pugins," in Atterbury and Wainwright, *Pugin*, pp. 258–71, 299–301.

93. George Coppinger Ashlin (1837–1921), born in County Cork, educated at Oscott, pupil ca. 1856–59 and partner 1859–69 of E. W. Pugin in Ireland, and of P. P. and C. W. Pugin in England 1875–80; and of Coleman in Ireland ca. 1902–21. The practice continued into the 1960s, and its drawings are now deposited at the Irish Architectural Archive, Dublin. Ashlin married Mary Pugin, E. W. Pugin's sister (see O'Donnell, "The Later Pugins").

94. For Saints Peter and Paul (1859–66), Cork, see *The Builder* (1859), pp. 241, 258, 322; ibid. (1860), pp. 253, 464; ibid. (1861), p. 129; ibid. (1862), p. 512; *Building News* (1859), pp. 534, 538; ibid, 456, 477; ibid. (1860), pp. 284, 388; ibid., vol. 13 (1866), pp. 533–34; ibid., vol. 14 (1867),

pp. 205, 208; *Catholic Directory* (1860), p. 226; *Civil Engineers and Architect's Journal* (1981), p. 90; *Dublin Builder* (1859), pp. 2, 5, 59, 115, 296, 310; ibid. (1869), pp. 296, 310 (illustration); ibid. (1866), p. 15; *Tablet* (1860), pp. 187–88; ibid. (1863), pp. 358–59, 749; ibid. (1866), pp. 475–76; Wedgwood, *A W N Pugin (RIBAD)*, p. 113 [4].

95. O'Donnell, "The Later Pugins," pp. 265, 300.

96. For a notation reading "Cork . . . 10 light east window . . . E. W. Pugin (sic, for west window)" see the "Glass Book" (1855–1863), entry for March 27, 1861, in the Hardman Archives, Birmingham; for reference to the apse windows, see *The Builder* (1870), p. 591.

97. Drawings for sanctuary furniture, 1874, by G. C. Ashlin are in the Ashlin and Coleman collection, Irish Architectural Archive, Dublin.

98. For citations in the *Dublin Builder*, see n. 92 above; also see A. J. Reilly, *Fr. John Murphy Famine Priest*, (Dublin, n. d. [ca. 1960]).

99. For Saints Augustine and John, Dublin (1862–93), see *Dublin Builder* (1861), p. 557; ibid. (1861), pp. 514/5, 563, 565, 577; ibid. (1866), pp. 270, 295; ibid. (1868) p. 252; ibid. (1869), p. 150; ibid. (1875), pp. 248, 377; ibid. (1878), p. 199. For the original design, see *The Builder* (1860), p. 328; ibid. (1863), p. 849. Also see *Account Book John's Lane*, in the Augustinian Archives, Ballyboden, Co. Dublin; and Wedgwood, *A W N Pugin (RIBAD)*, p. 119 [2].

100. *The Builder* (1868), p. 901; *Catholic Directory* (1857), p. 247; ibid. (1859), p. 219; ibid. (1868), pp. 371–72; *Building News* 14 (1867), pp. 710, 746; ibid. 33 (1877), p. 614; *Irish Builder* (1867), pp. 184, 188, 282; ibid. (1868), pp. 182, 247; ibid. (1869), p. 30; ibid. (1870), p. 4; ibid. (1889), p. 27; ibid. (1890), p. 282; *St Coleman's Cathedral Queenstown: A Guide* (1916). Drawings are at the RIBA and at the Irish Architectural Archive, Dublin; also see Wedgwood, *A W N Pugin (RIBAD)*, pp. 118–19 [1].

101. Bishop James McCarthy, quoted in Emmet Larkin, "Economic Growth, Capital Investment and the Roman Catholic Church in Nineteenth-century Ireland," *American Historical Review* 72 (1967), pp. 852–84, quote p. 864.

102. The *Dublin Builder* reported that "Mr Keile [sic] has built . . . 197 churches in the USA" ([July 1, 1860], p. 291); despite the eminence of Keely in America, his career was, oddly, not otherwise reported in Ireland.

103. The chapel (1875–90) by J. J. McCarthy was furnished by William Hague and others (1890). It is filled with the woodwork, stained glass, and marble altars typical of the most elaborate Irish Catholic High Victorian taste (Corish, *Maynooth*, pp. 195–205).

Fig. 8-1. Watercolor sketch for A. W. N. Pugin's *Floriated Ornament* (1849). (Private collection)

8. A. W. N. Pugin and the Progress of Design as Applied to Manufacture

Clive Wainwright

Augustus Welby Northmore Pugin, whose ideas may seem at first glance to be rooted in the Middle Ages, was actually a child of the Industrial Revolution, sharing his generation's enthusiasm for innovation and progress. By 1812, the year of his birth, every aspect of Britain's manufacturing industry was undergoing a rapid transformation through the introduction of steam and water power, the sophisticated use of the principles of division of labor, and the development of new materials and processes. The products of the factories and workshops were being transported throughout Britain over an extensive network of canals, and by the time Pugin was established as a designer, trains and steamships were taking British products all over the world.

Britain was also benefiting, as so often in its history, from an influx of European emigrés fleeing from political persecution. As Napoleon's armies overran mainland Europe, artists, craftsmen, and inventors flocked to Britain. Pugin's father, Auguste Charles Pugin, was among those who left Paris to settle in London, arriving by 1792. Continental inventors were to play an important part in the innovations taking place in industry. Marc Isambard Brunel, for instance, another Frenchman and a friend of A. C. Pugin,

arrived in England in 1799 and revolutionized the shipyards with his rigging-block manufacturing machine. Brunel also made the boring of the first Thames tunnel. In the 1840s, his son, Isambard Kingdom Brunel, with his own improvements to steamships and railways, played as great a role in revolutionizing transport as A. W. N. Pugin was to do in the fields of architecture and design. Similarly, in the fields of illustration, printing, and publishing, a German emigré, Rudolph Ackermann, was introducing Continental innovations to Britain and using them in collaboration with the two Pugins, father and son.

Far from opposing the railways as a modern invention, A. W. N. Pugin, as his diaries show, used them constantly. Indeed, he could not have produced the volume of work he did without traveling thousands of miles a year by rail. His friend and fellow architect, Benjamin Ferrey, who was also his biographer, described how Pugin found amusement in his fellow passengers:

> He was in the habit of wearing a sailor's jacket, loose pilot trousers, jack-boots, and a wide awake hat. In such a costume landing on one occasion from the Calais boat, he entered, as was his custom, a first class carriage, and was accosted with a "Halloa, my man you have mistaken I think your carriage." "By Jove," was his

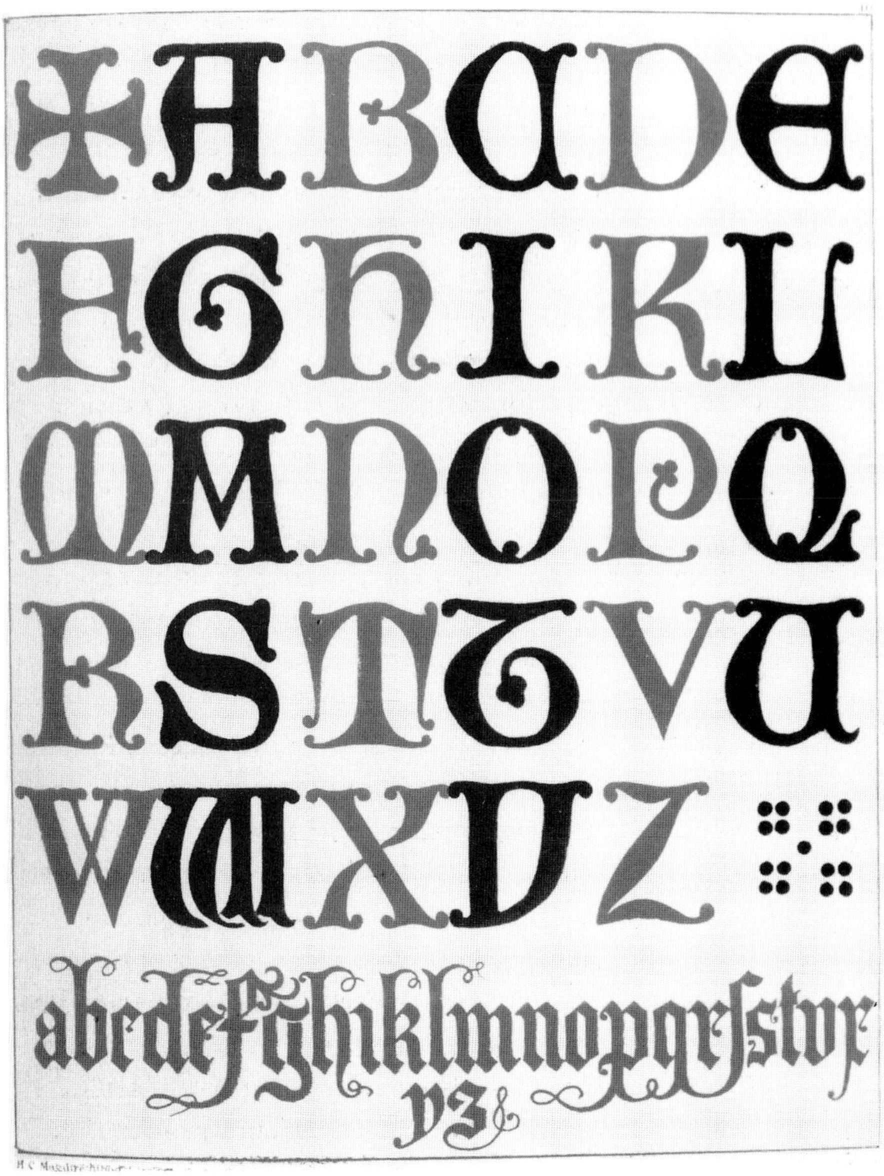

Fig. 8-2. The alphabet designed by A. W. N. Pugin. From Pugin, *Glossary of Ecclesiastical Ornament* (1844).

reply, "I think your [sic] right; I thought I was in the company of gentlemen." This cutting repartée at once called forth an apology. The remainder of his journey was most agreeably passed in examining his portfolio filled with sketches just taken in Normandy.[1]

Though Pugin never had the opportunity to design a railway station, he applied his pragmatic mind to determining the form of architecture—that of medieval military buildings—which would be most appropriate to the railways. In 1843 he illustrated a "railway bridge on the ancient principles," stating that:

> The Railways, had they been naturally treated, afforded a fine scope for grand massive architecture. Little more was required than buttresses, weathering, and segmental arches, resistance to *lateral* and *perpendicular pressure*. I do not hesitate to say that, by merely following out the work that was required to its natural conclusion, building exactly what was wanted in the simplest and most substantial manner—mere construction, as the old men weathered the flanking walls of their defences—tens of thousands of pounds could have been saved on every line and grand and durable masses of building been produced.[2]

In his book, *An Apology for the Revival of Christian Architecture in England*, Pugin took a similarly progressive view of the use of machinery and new technologies in manufacture and building:

> There is no reason why noble cities, combining all possible convenience of drainage, water-course and conveyance of gas may not be erected . . . . In matters purely mechanical, the Christian architect

162

should gladly avail himself of those improvements and increased facilities that are suggested from time to time. The steam engine is a most valuable power for sawing, raising, and cleansing stone, timber, and other materials . . . . It is only when mechanical invention intrudes on the confines of art, and tends to subvert the principles which it would advance, that it becomes objectionable.[3]

Although the title of the book naturally leads one to assume that it is deeply conservative, praising the architecture of the Middle Ages, Pugin had a far more positive and pragmatic attitude toward the use of machines than would theorists of the next generation, such as John Ruskin and William Morris. Pugin's books and letters reveal that he had no particular regard for handcraftsmanship or, indeed, for the happiness and well-being of the craftsmen. For him it was the character and appearance of the finished object that was crucial. If it possessed what he habitually called "the true thing" in quality of design and execution, then he had achieved his end. The means were of little importance.

Pugin had a thorough understanding of the nature of craftsmanship, of what might be achieved and how. In the late 1820s, while still in his teens, he had spent a great deal of time in the workshops of the celebrated London cabinetmak-ers, Morel and Seddon, overseeing the manufacture of furniture he was designing for Windsor Castle.[4] In 1829 he set up his own workshop in Covent Garden: "determined to have all carved work, whenever it was possible, executed under his own eye . . . and having secured the assistance of one or two clever carvers whom he had himself already taught, he made it known generally amongst his friends that he would undertake to supply all the ornamental portions of a building which could be executed apart from the structure and be fixed afterwards."[5] This small firm also made furniture, although only two pieces, stamped "A. PUGIN," have been discovered. A number of designs by Pugin survive, but none of the actual pieces relating to these designs have yet been discovered.[6]

Pugin's close observation of craftsmen at work and his constant examination of medieval architecture and the applied arts gave him a clear idea of the standards that might be achieved. He collected medieval works of fine and applied art and built up a remarkable library of ancient books and manuscripts, giving him an even greater depth of knowledge. It was his determined application of this expertise to the improvement of architecture and design that makes him a pioneer of the design reform movement. He set forth his major

Fig. 8-3. Designs for ornamental borders. From A. W. N. Pugin, *The Glossary of Ecclesiastical Ornament* (1844).

Fig. 8-4. One of a pair of firedogs designed by A. W. N. Pugin for Bilton Grange, near Rugby; cast iron and brass, ca. 1850. (Bilton Grange School)

Fig. 8-5. One of a pair of firedogs designed by A. W. N. Pugin for Bilton Grange, near Rugby, and probably made by John Hardman & Company; cast iron, ca. 1850. (Bilton Grange School)

tenets as early as 1841 in *The True Principles of Pointed or Christian Architecture*, one of the most influential treatises in English on architecture and design of the nineteenth century along with John Ruskin's *Seven Lamps of Architecture*.[7] Ruskin's book may be more wide-ranging in scope, but it was not published until 1849 and owes a great deal to *True Principles*. Pugin wrote:

> The two great rules for design are these: 1st, that there should be no features about a building which are not necessary for convenience, construction, or propriety; 2nd, that all ornament should consist of enrichment of the essential construction of the building. The neglect of these two rules is the cause of all the bad architecture of the present time . . . the smallest detail should have a meaning or serve a purpose; and even the construction itself should vary with the material employed, and the designs should be adapted to the material in which they are executed.[8]

These arguments are about the appropriate use of ornament and truth to materials, not about hand-craftsmanship versus the machine, and the principles adumbrated here were intended by Pugin to apply to the whole of architecture and design. Following the publication of *True Principles* and *An Apology*, and needing skilled craftsmen and efficient manufacturing techniques for the fixtures, fittings, and decorative details that he was then designing for the New Palace of Westminster, Pugin turned to the pupils at the new Government School of Design at Somerset House. He found, however, that the pupils there were not properly trained for his needs, and in 1845 he wrote to *The Builder*, the leading architectural periodical:

> I have almost given up hope of seeing any real good effected by the School of Design which ought and which (I feel assured) might be made the most powerful and effective way of creating a school of *national artists*, not mere imitators of any style, but men imbued with a thorough knowledge of the history, wants, climate, and customs of our country; who would combine all the spirit of the mediaeval architects and the beauties of the old Christian artists, with the practical improvements of our times.[9]

Here Pugin is arguing for effective design educa-

Fig. 8-6. Table designed by A. W. N. Pugin for the chamber of the House of Lords; oak, ca. 1847. (Trustees, Victoria & Albert Museum)

tion combined with modern manufacturing methods. Indeed, he was using steam-driven carving machines at Westminster. As a result of the campaign in which Pugin's letter played an important part, his friend Henry Cole, the design theorist and reformer who was later to be the first director of the South Kensington Museum, was eventually brought in to reform the school and its provincial branches. In a paper entitled "Recent Progress in Design as Applied to Manufacture" which was read to the Society of Arts in London on March 12, 1856, George Wallis, Headmaster of the Government School of Design in Birmingham, was to pay tribute to Pugin's influence on manufactures:

> . . . the influence that one mind alone undoubtedly exercised not only upon the particular department of art to which he specially devoted his attention, but indeed upon all of a kindred character, in which other minds were engaged who could appreciate his arguments and apply the principles he enunciated . . . his special views of the mission of art, and the application of modern scientific and mechanical means to the reproduction of works of excellence, his earnest and fearless denunciation of all "shams"—his expo-

sure of false systems of ornamentation—his thoroughly zealous working out "in season and out of season" of his own views in his own way must ever command the respect of every true and earnest lover of art, since it is to the influence of his example in one direction that we owe so much to the progress to be recorded in other departments of art—manufacture.[10]

Wallis was an expert on contemporary manufactures and manufacturing techniques and thus an important commentator. He had been one of the commissioners of the Great Exhibition of the Works of Industry of All Nations, held in 1851 at London's Crystal Palace, and also of another exhibition at New York's Crystal Palace held in 1853. While in America he had looked closely at machine production. Not only did he deplore the fact that in 1853 the "ordinary class of useful and cheap furniture, so largely manufactured in the western states, was not represented in the exhibition," but he even brought back to England a piece of American machine-made furniture. In 1857 Wallis became a keeper at the South Kensington Museum which was to become the Victoria & Albert Museum.[11]

Fig. 8-7. Structural chair designed by A. W. N. Pugin; oak, ca. 1838. (Saint Mary's College, Oscott)

Pugin worked on designs in several media. Early in his career, in 1826 or the beginning of 1827, he was involved in the manufacture of precious metalwork, a valuable experience:

> His first employment, independent of his father, seems to have been given to young Pugin by the celebrated goldsmiths, Messrs Rundell and Bridge. One of the firm, while engaged in an examination of some ancient designs for plate in the Print Room of the British Museum, chanced to notice that he [Pugin] was employed in copying the prints of Albert Dürer and Israel Silvester. Struck by his skill in drawing the goldsmith accosted him, and soon found that he possessed the genius his firm had been seeking. His complete knowledge of mediaeval art fitted him admirably for designing plate in the old manner.[12]

Rundell Bridge & Rundell were the royal goldsmiths, and from them Pugin learned first-hand how one of the highest quality workshops in England operated. His association with the firm dates for certain to March 19, 1827, for he recorded that on that day he "Attended with Mr. J. Bridge the sale of the Duke of York's plate at Christie's Rooms."[13] Several designs for plate by Pugin, probably for the king himself, exist from this period, but only one object of this date can be attributed to him with any certainty. This is the so-called Coronation Cup (see cat. no. 13), a silver-gilt standing cup set with enamels, diamonds, and other precious stones. It bears the mark of John Bridge and the date letter for 1826–27. In the Gothic Revival style, with a stem in the form of a twisted tree trunk, it was inspired by a Dürer drawing of a cup with a similar stem that was in the British Museum Print Room where Pugin was seen copying. The cup, which is still in the Royal Collection, is the most spectacular piece of late Georgian Gothic metalwork extant.[14] The techniques habitually used by Rundells and their contemporaries—those that were used for the royal cup—were soon to disgust Pugin. He found them dishonest compared to the techniques used by the medieval and Renaissance goldsmiths. He particularly disliked cast ornaments in any material, whether precious or base metals or plaster:

> Putty pressing, plaster and iron casting for ornaments, wood burning &c., are not to be rejected because such methods were unknown to our ancestors, but on account of their being opposed in their very nature to the true principles of art and design—by substituting monotonous repetitions for beautiful variety, flatness of execution for bold relief, encouraging cheap and false magnificence, and reducing the varied principles of ornamental design . . . . But while on the other hand, we should utterly reject the use of casting as substitutes for ornamental sculpture, we should eagerly avail ourselves of the great improvements in working metals for constructive purposes.[15]

It is important to read Pugin's arguments in the context of the metalwork that he actually commissioned to be made from his designs for his many clients. A key phrase is "monotonous repetition," by which he means repeating the design by mass producing a casting many times. If one looks at the immense surviving corpus of his precious metalwork and jewelry, the same forms and motifs turn up over and over again but are rarely used in precisely the same combination or material. There is great variety, yet all the objects relate in style and technique to each other, like the medieval pieces that inspired them.

Workshops such as Rundell, Bridge & Rundell were organized with a very sophisticated division of labor in which groups of craftsmen specialized in different techniques such as enameling or chasing and passed a particular piece from one specialist to another as it moved toward completion. By this means, mass production is achieved in terms of numbers of objects produced each day, but variation in appearance, material, and construction between one object and another is easily achieved within profit constraints. It is important to differentiate between the form of mass production and machine production. In the latter, every object produced is identical and variety is impossible. The question of how to achieve variety at acceptable cost in order to supply the new mass market was a vital issue throughout Europe and America in the 1840s and 1850s. Wallis in his 1856 lecture, four years after Pugin's death, argued:

> If modern art, whether applied to industry or the higher illustrations of the power of the beautiful, is ever to make a distinct place for itself in the coming time, it will be out of the wise and perfect use of those mechanical means and appliances with which an All-wise Providence has seen fit to furnish mankind for their use in this age; and it is fearlessly asserted, that he is a negligent worker in the present, and a betrayer of the interests of the future, who does not avail himself of every means which modern invention and discovery affords him to reproduce, in suitable form and material, such beautiful objects of art-manufacture as shall tend to the refinement and instruction of his fellow-men.[16]

Not everyone in his audience agreed, and in the discussion which followed the lecture Ruskin aired those misgivings about industry that were to lead to the handcraftsmanship ethos of that design

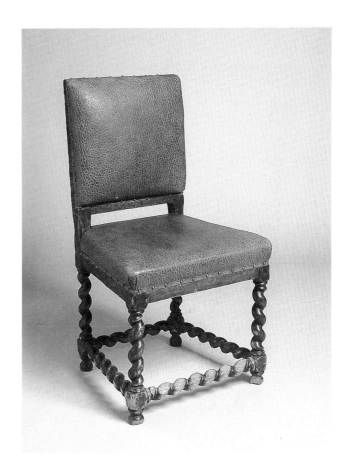

Fig. 8-8. Jacobean-style chair designed by A. W. N. Pugin; oak, ca. 1838. (Saint Mary's College, Oscott)

cul-de-sac, the Arts and Crafts movement. "In no way, therefore could good art ever become cheap in production . . . . The paper seemed to dwell wholly upon the advantage of art to the consumer, or only to the producer as a mercantile matter. He was sorry it did not show the effect of the production of art on the workman; surely the happiness of the workman was a thing which ought to be considered."[17]

Pugin knew full well (as his letters amply demonstrate) the reality of having to run a business to make a profit while also making a product to a high standard. The open-minded approach taken by Pugin and John Hardman, his metalworker, close friend, and collaborator as well as fellow Catholic, is clearly stated in a letter that Hardman wrote in 1840 or 1841 to a client in London:

> My general working method is this, either parties come to see the articles I have by me and pur-

Fig. 8-9. Structural table designed by A. W. N. Pugin; oak, ca. 1838. (Saint Mary's College, Oscott)

Fig. 8-10. Structural table designed by A. W. N. Pugin; oak, ca. 1838. (Saint Mary's College, Oscott)

chase from *them* or otherwise they say what they want and how much they can afford to give and trust Mr Pugin or me to send them as much as can possibly be done for the money—it is possible to make so much difference in all these articles by adding engraving and chasing or leaving it out as the case may be, adding or taking away other work.[18]

In *True Principles* Pugin might almost have been describing the elaborately decorated work of Rundells themselves when he compared the techniques of the ancient craftsmen with those of his own period. He began by praising the early techniques:

> Their construction and execution is decidedly of a metallic character. The ornament is produced by piercing, chasing, engraving and enamel; many of the parts were first formed of thin plates of metal, and then shaped by the pliers . . . . Silversmiths are no longer artists; they manufacture fiddle headed spoons, punchy racing cups, cumbersome tureens and wine-coolers; their vulgar salvers are covered with sprawling rococo, edged with a confused pattern of such universal use that it may be called with propriety Sheffield eternal. Cruet-stand, tea-pot, candlestick, butter-boat, tray, waiter, tea-urn, are all bordered with this in and out shell-and-leaf pattern, which, being struck with a die, does not even possess the merit of relief.[19]

Almost all of Pugin's metalwork, both precious and base, was made by John Hardman's firm. Pugin had first met Hardman in 1837, by which time Hardman was already well established in Birmingham as a button manufacturer. Until his association with Pugin, however, his products fitted into a category that Pugin was to attack in *True Principles* as "Brumagen" Gothic[20] from "those inexhaustible mines of bad taste, Birmingham." Under Pugin's artistic control Hardman's firm was transformed and moved from metalwork into stained glass, producing large numbers of remarkable windows to Pugin's design. By 1847 the Council of the Government School of Design reported that: "There is an establishment in Birmingham in which art is really cultivated—Hardman's, for the manufacture of Church ornaments and plate; but the designs are supplied by

Fig. 8-11. Panel of encaustic tiles designed by A. W. N. Pugin for Saint Winefred's Church, Shepshed; made by Minton & Company, 1842.

Fig. 8-13. Wallpaper fragment, designed by A. W. N. Pugin for the Palace of Westminster. (Trustees, Victoria & Albert Museum)

Fig. 8-12. Assortment of encaustic tiles designed by A. W. N. Pugin; made by Minton & Company, 1845–52. (Private collection)

Fig. 8-14. Outline drawings for encaustic tiles designed by A. W. N. Pugin for Saint Cuthbert's College, Ushaw; pen on paper, 1846. (Myers Family Trust)

Mr. Pugin. It is not to be expected that manufacturers who supply the ordinary market can elaborate their works like Mr. Hardman; but whatever is done, may be done well *in its degree*."[21]

Hardman's manufacturing extended far beyond church work—though this was a sizable market, given the dozens of churches built to Pugin's design as well as the metalwork and glass ordered for other churches throughout Britain and in countries as far afield as Australia. The firm made splendid examples of domestic metalwork, such as a silver cream jug with saw-pierced and engraved work[22] made in July 1852 (see cat. no. 128). It bears the crest of Charles Lygon Cocks, who was later to employ William Burges to build Treverbyn Vean, a splendid Gothic Revival house in Cornwall. (His relations, the Somers Cocks, had employed Pugin to design several interiors at Eastnor Castle in Herefordshire.) The enameled silver candlestick (see cat. no. 123), which dates from 1842, was made for Henry Bagshawe and bears his initial. This is an early example of Hardman's use of the newly perfected technique of electroplating pioneered in Birmingham by Elkington and Co. to whom Hardman contracted

Fig. 8-15. The Crystal Palace, lithograph from Dickinson's *Comprehensive Pictures of the Great Exhibition of 1851* (London, 1854), vol. 2, unpag.

Fig. 8-16. The Mediaeval Court, engraving in *The Illustrated Exhibitor*.

out work. Hardman and Pugin were to make frequent use of electroplating.

Hardman manufactured light fittings in the form of candlesticks, candle chandeliers, gasoliers, and oil fittings in brass and iron. The firm also made the whole range of hinges and door and fireplace furniture such as splendid firedogs made for Bilton Grange around 1841 (figs. 8-4, 8-5).

The same principles that Pugin used in the manufacture of metalwork and adumbrated in *True Principles* also apply to the manufacture of objects in other media, notably textiles, wallpaper, tiles, stained glass, and woodwork. His ability to combine simplicity, honest construction, and modern production methods, resulting in objects of great beauty, is nowhere more fully realized than in his designs for tables (fig. 8-6 and figs. 8-9 and 8-10). In 1849 Pugin wrote to John G. Crace, who was to make these tables, "the great sale will

be to the middling class . . . . You ought to frame a dozen of each to make them pay & keep them ready seasoned for putting together at a days notice, keeping one of a sort always on show . . . I am anxious to induce a sensible style of furniture of good oak & constructively put together that shall compete with the vile trash made and sold." As his celebrated follower, the architect G. E. Street, observed the year after Pugin's death, his furniture was:

> not Gothic certainly in the ordinary cabinet-makers sense: that is to say, his chairs were constructed without the assistance of pointed arches, and his tables did not depend upon crockets, finials and flying buttresses for all their character, but they were real, simple, and properly constructional provisions for certain wants, with no more material consumed in their construction than was necessary for their solidity, and no sham or incongruous ornaments.[23]

Fig. 8-17. Armoire designed by A. W. N. Pugin; made by J. G. Crace and shown at the Great Exhibition of 1851.

Pugin's unerring eye for pattern and color enabled him to adapt natural forms appropriately to produce brilliantly innovative flat pattern which would lay the foundations on which designers of the next generation such as Christopher Dresser, Owen Jones, and William Morris were to build so successfully. Pugin's pattern was immediately applicable to mass-produced artifacts such as wallpapers, textiles, and wall and floor tiles (figs. 8-11, 8-12). Not only did he design in all these media, but in 1849 he published *Floriated Ornament*, the seminal work on the subject. As an innovator in the field of mass book production he also produced the illustrations (see fig. 8-1) and designed its machine-stamped binding.[24] In the introduction he wrote that "nature supplied the mediaeval artists with all their forms and ideas; the same inexhaustible source is open to us. If we go to the fountainhead, we shall produce a multitude of beautiful designs treated in the same spirit as the old, but new in form. We have the advantage of many important botanical discoveries which were unknown to our ancestors; and surely it is in accordance with the true principles of art to avail ourselves of all that is beautiful for the composition of our designs."[25] Here again Pugin is enthusiastically embracing modern discoveries when he could well have confined his designs to the plant ornament known in the Middle Ages. His wallpapers (fig. 8-13), tiles (fig. 8-14), and textiles bear ample witness to how effectively he applied this theory to his own designs.

In 1851 came the culmination of Pugin's progress in promoting the manufacture of objects in all media for domestic and ecclesiastical use, by firms he had encouraged and trained. He was already a friend of Henry Cole, the principal mover of the Great Exhibition of 1851 (fig. 8-15, and was able to persuade Cole to arrange for him to be allotted a prime area in the Crystal Palace. This was the Mediaeval Court (fig. 8-16), and the objects displayed in it were designed by Pugin and made by his favorite firms—Herbert Minton for tiles, John Hardman for stained glass and metalwork, and George Myers and John Crace for furniture. The objects ranged from expensive and elaborate "one-off" pieces of furniture to mass-produced ceramics sold at the exhibition in large numbers. The exhibit was very popular with visitors: "While studying architecture Pugin was equally zealous and successful in his cultivation of the arts subordinate to it. To painted glass and

medieval metalwork he devoted particular attention, and under his directing care Mr. Hardman, of Birmingham, established his beautiful ateliers in these two branches of art. Among the numerous courts of the Crystal Palace few attracted more attention and gave more delight than Pugin's 'Mediaeval Court' rich in these departments."[26]

Before the Great Exhibition was over Cole knew that he was soon to become the director of a new museum, The Museum of Manufactures—ancestor of the Victoria & Albert Museum—which was also to include the Government School of Design. This was excellent news for Pugin who, as we have seen, was critical of the teaching at the school. He was also particularly delighted that the government had voted £5,000 to purchase modern manufactures for the museum from the Great Exhibition.[27] A committee was set up, consisting of Cole, Richard Redgrave (his colleague at the museum), Owen Jones, and Pugin. They spent £865 11s. 5d. on British objects, £1276 1s. on Indian ones, and £2075 9s. on objects from other

Fig. 8-18. Plate with molded and painted decoration, designed by A. W. N. Pugin; made by Minton & Co.; bone china, 1849. (Trustees, Victoria & Albert Museum)

countries, buying 244 objects in all. These were all modern, manufactured objects especially chosen to inspire the pupils of the School of Design. Several objects were designed by Pugin. An armoire made by Crace to Pugin's design (fig. 8-17) cost the considerable sum of £154 and, like all the objects acquired, was published in an interesting report by the committee explaining their reason for purchase. The cabinet was described as: "Remarkable as a piece of furniture in which the construction has been carefully considered, and the decoration confined to the enrichment of the necessary spaces and framing in the true style of the old work, where all ornament was strictly subordinate to the construction of the article; and the locks, hinges and other metalwork were made ornamental portions of the whole design."[28]

A number of the objects shown in the Mediaeval Court were manufactured by new techniques pioneered by Pugin and his manufacturers. For example, Pugin was very knowledgeable about chromolithographic book illustration and in 1848 encouraged two lithographers, F. W. M. Collins and Alfred Reynolds, from Clerkenwell in London, to experiment with the application of lithography to ceramic tiles and tableware.[29] The resulting patent for the process was bought by Pugin's close friend, Herbert Minton, who showed examples in the Mediaeval Court (figs. 8-18, 8-19 and see cat. no. 140): "The process is likely to come into extensive use, and has been already applied to decoration of pottery in general; tiles thus ornamented have been ordered for the smoking-room of the House of Commons and have been much used for the fireplaces in other parts of the new Palace. Specimens of them were exhibited as forming flower-pots, the gilt iron frames of which were furnished by Messrs. Hardman."[30] Two of these pots were bought for the museum, a small one and a larger one. They perfectly represent the type of manufactured domestic product design thought to be instructive to the students at the Government School of Design. Earlier, in 1844, the school had acquired its first objects, which were similar in character, at

the L'Exposition des Produits de l'Industrie de 1844, held in Paris.

Thus the Pugin objects shown in the Mediaeval Court were not only seen and bought by some of the millions of visitors to the exhibition, but they inspired and were copied by manufacturers and designers throughout the world. Those acquired by the new museum went on display in 1852 for the instruction of generations of students at the School of Design and other visitors; they are still on display in the Victoria & Albert Museum today. Pugin died in 1852, and the firms he had encouraged such as Minton's, Crace's, and Hardman's, retained many of his original designs. They were to profit greatly from marketing their Pugin products for much of the rest of the century. In fact, some of these designs, such as wallpapers and tiles, are still in production today.

1. Benjamin Ferrey, *Recollections of A. N. Welby Pugin and his father Augustus Pugin* (London, 1861), p. 98.

2. A. W. N. Pugin, *An Apology for the Revival of Christian Architecture in England* (London, 1843), p. 10.

3. Ibid. p. 40.

4. For further reading, see G. de Bellaigue and P. Kirkham, "George IV and the Furnishings of Windsor Castle," *Furniture History* 8 (1972), pp. 1–32.

5. Ferrey, *Recollections,* p. 65.

6. For further reading on the history of this firm and illustrations of a surviving piece of furniture and some of the designs, see Clive Wainwright, "A. W. N. Pugin's Early Furniture," *The Connoisseur* 191 (1976), pp. 3–11.

7. Andrew Saint, "The Fate of Pugin's True Principles," in Paul Atterbury and Clive Wainwright, eds., *Pugin: A Gothic Passion* (London & New Haven, 1994).

8. A. W. N. Pugin, *The True Principles of Pointed or Christian Architecture: set forth in two lectures delivered at St Marie's Oscott* (London, 1841), p. 1.

9. "Mr. Pugin on Christian Art," *The Builder* 3 (1845), p. 367.

10. G. Wallis, *Recent Progress in Design as applied to Manufacture* (London, 1856), p. 6.

11. Wainwright, "Some Nineteenth Century American Furniture in the Collection of the Victoria & Albert Museum," *Nineteenth Century* 11, nos. 1, 2 (1992), p. 9, fig. 2.

12. Ferrey, *Recollections,* pp. 51–52.

13. Alexandra Wedgwood, *Catalogues of the Architectural Drawings in the Victoria & Albert Museum: A. W. N. Pugin and the Pugin Family* (London, 1985), p. 26.

14. Atterbury and Wainwright, eds., *Pugin,* pl. 328.

15. Pugin, *Apology,* p. 40.

16. Wallis, "Recent Progress," p. 2.

17. Ibid., p. 9.

18. Ann Eatwell and Anthony North, "Metalwork," in Atterbury and Wainwright, eds., *Pugin.*

19. Pugin, *True Principles,* pp. 31–32.

20. "Brumagen" is a slang term for "Birmingham."

21. *Minutes of the Council of the Government School of Design from May 1846 to October 1847* (London, 1849), vol. 3, p. 170.

22. I would like to thank Martin Levy for bringing this piece to my attention and discovering the entry for it in the Hardman Records.

23. G. E. Street, "On the revival of the ancient style of domestic architecture," *The Ecclesiologist* 14 (1853), p. 76.

24. Clive Wainwright, "Book Design and Production," in Atterbury and Wainwright, eds., *Pugin.*

25. A. W. N. Pugin, *Floriated Ornament* (London, 1849), p. 4.

26. "The Late Mr Pugin," *The Ecclesiologist* 13 (1852), p. 357.

27. Clive Wainwright, "Principles true and false: Pugin and the foundation of the Museum of Manufactures," *The Burlington Magazine* 136, no. 1095 (1994), pp. 357–64.

28. Henry Cole, Richard Redgrave, and Owen Jones, *Department of Practical Art: A Catalogue of the Ornamental Art Selected from the Exhibition of the Works of Industry of all Nations in 1851 and Purchased by the Government* (London, 1852), p. 48. Pugin was mortally ill while this book was being written so could have played no part in it. It is, however, packed with terms which he habitually used. While no minutes of the committee that selected these objects have yet been discovered, notes must have been taken and justifications for the acquisition written for such a large expenditure of public money. Pugin played an active part in this process in 1851 and such notes would have been used in the compilation of this catalogue.

29. John S. Reynolds, "Alfred Reynolds and the Block Process," *Journal of the Tiles & Architectural Ceramics Society* 5 (1994), pp. 20–26. See also Paul Atterbury, "Ceramics," in Atterbury and Wainwright, eds., *Pugin.*

30. Dickinson, *Dickinson's Comprehensive Pictures of the Great Exhibition of 1851* (London, 1854), vol. 2, p. 40.

Fig. 9-1. "Fac Simile of Autograph Drawing by Augustus Welby Northmore Pugin 1832"; lithograph, late 19th century. Pugin depicts an idealized Gothic interior: an architect (Pugin?) presents his scheme for a cathedral before the full panoply of Church and State. The details—structural table, throne canopy, vestments, and floor tiles—reveal the development of Pugin's integrated approach to design. Pugin's original drawing is now lost. (Private collection)

9. Pugin and Interior Design

Paul Atterbury

Saint Marie's Grange, A. W. N. Pugin's first essay in practical architecture, was built at Alderbury in 1835. It stands among woods on the steep slope of the valley of the river Nadder, a few miles from Salisbury in Wiltshire. The distinct shape, now so characteristic of Victorian domestic architecture as a whole, stands above the surrounding trees. These trees and the changes made to the building in the latter part of the nineteenth century separate the house, now softened by time, from the one Pugin would have known. As a result, it is quite hard today to appreciate the building's truly revolutionary quality, a quality that leaps from the series of watercolors painted by Pugin in the 1830s (fig. 9-2). Saint Marie's Grange was, quite simply, the first example of genuine Gothic domestic architecture to have been built in Britain since the Middle Ages. Its form, integrity, and sophisticated simplicity set it apart from all earlier exercises in decorative or fantasy Gothic.

Brick-built, with no attempt at conscious archaism, the house draws upon a number of sources, including French domestic architecture and British vernacular traditions, largely of the Tudor and Jacobean periods, to create a new interpretation of Gothic as a unified structural form (see fig. 9-1). In his diary for November 8, 1835 Pugin wrote: "The present state of architec-ture is deplorable. Truth reduced to the position of an interesting but rare and curious relic."[1] His house, breaking away forever from the decorative facading of earlier Gothic revivalists, was the first shot in his long campaign to rebuild a proper appreciation of medieval art and architecture and to restore to Britain an honest style of building.

The architectural principles expressed so firmly by Pugin at Saint Marie's Grange anticipate those that he went on to publish in his various books, notably *The True Principles of Pointed or Christian Architecture* (1841) and *An Apology for the Revival of Christian Architecture* (1843). These include:

> 1st, That there should be no features about a building which are not necessary for convenience, construction or propriety. 2nd, That all ornament should consist of enrichment of the essential construction of the building.[2]

> That the external and internal appearance of an edifice should be illustrative of, and in accordance with, the purpose for which it is designed.[3]

> The picturesque effect of the ancient buildings results from the ingenious methods by which the old builders overcame local and constructive difficulties.[4]

> Every building that is treated naturally, without disguise or concealment, cannot fail to look well.[5]

Fig. 9-2. Views of Saint Marie's Grange, attributed to A. W. N. Pugin; watercolor on paper, mid-1830s. The spire of Salisbury Cathedral rises in the distance in the lower picture. (Irish Architectural Archive)

With these and similar statements as background, it is not hard to see how Saint Marie's Grange marked the start of a major change in attitudes to Gothic and the emergence of a style that was to become the most popular domestic building type of the nineteenth century, in Britain and elsewhere.

Having fired the first shot, so to speak, Pugin continued the fight in the front line. Subsequent houses—his own, The Grange, at Ramsgate (1843–44); the Bishop's House, Birmingham (1841); the parsonages at Lanteglos in Cornwall (1848) and Rampisham in Dorset (1846); a whole generation of small presbyteries, for example at Warwick Bridge (1840–41), Fulham (1848), Kenilworth (1841–42), Brewood (1843–44); and lodges for Bilton Grange (1846–48) and Alton Towers (1844–48)—maintained his position as the pioneering revivalist of a genuine Gothic-based domestic architecture. Others followed, notably William Butterfield who designed Milton Earnest Hall, Bedfordshire (1853–58), Philip Webb whose Red House (1859) for William Morris is an entirely post-Puginian creation, and various architects of the Arts and Crafts movement in Britain and the United States whose work reflected essential concerns about truth to materials, integrity of design, vernacular awareness, and control of ornament. These concerns were first expressed by Pugin in the late 1830s and early 1840s.

While Saint Marie's Grange survives today, albeit in an altered state, it is hard to establish with certainty the look of its interior in Pugin's time. There was a chapel complete with belfry, something Pugin saw as a necessary part of any house, even before his conversion to the Roman Catholic faith. A drawbridge, thick external walls pierced by small windows, an awkwardly placed external spiral staircase, and a series of interconnecting rooms with no corridors were other elements of the design. Pugin was very pleased with it, describing it in a letter to his friend and mentor, the antiquary E. J. Willson as "every part a compleat building of the 15th cent" whose style and details "have astonished the people about here beyond measure."[6] A few watercolors and drawings give tantalizing hints of the interior and recently the original plan of the three floors has been established.[7] There were carved stone doorways and fireplaces, some stained glass, massive exposed timbers, and decorative wall painting that expressed Pugin's enthusiasm for heraldry. From this time he often referred to himself as "Augustus de Pugin" and began to make extensive use of both the martlet bird emblem and the "En Avant" motto.[8]

Some furniture from the house survives, and this indicates that for Pugin in the 1830s, Gothic was a style that in its essential Englishness included elements that would now be called Tudor

Fig. 9-3. Model of a stage set designed by Pugin for the courtroom scene in Henry VIII, as it was performed at Covent Garden, London, on October 24, 1831. (The Theatre Museum, Trustees of the Victoria & Albert Museum)

Fig. 9-4. The Grange, Ramsgate, drawing room and library beyond, in a sketch by Peter Paul Pugin (Pugin's youngest son); pen and wash on paper, ca. 1868. (Private collection)

or Jacobean.[9] This broad definition of Gothic was not new, and it is interesting that Pugin inherited and maintained the belief, held by both Horace Walpole and William Beckford, that dark chairs with turned and spirally twisted legs were an important component of English Gothic. Chairs of this type were made in oak for Saint Marie's Grange, along with other pieces that underlined Pugin's Regency upbringing. He was, above all else, a child of the Regency, and it is from that period, as much as the medieval world, that he drew his enduring love of color, his skill with pattern and ornament, and his theatricality.

Pugin's early architecture, both secular and ecclesiastical, and his interiors in particular carry the stamp of his theatrical experience (fig. 9-3), as a stagehand and a set and costume designer.

For much of his life his architecture retained this debt to the theater, in the massing of his buildings, in his use of color and of space and perspective. Furthermore his work for the theater—with its echoes of Walter Scott, early nineteenth-century Gothic, and the colorful panorama of Regency London—remained, with medieval art, the primary inspiration for his work as an interior designer, even though much of it was at odds with his *True Principles*.

It was his experience of the theater and its particularly decorative vision of English history that led Pugin directly to his first experiments with architecture and design. These took the form of a series of "Ideal Schemes" that he drew between 1832 and 1835, richly detailed studies of imaginary medieval buildings and other structures, complete with all their fittings and contents. These include the Chapel of Saint Margaret, Le Chasteau (fig. 9-4), the Deanery, and Saint Marie's College. There are European sources for these, such as the château at Chambord, but their importance lies more in the way they reveal Pugin's developing ideas about architecture and design. The designs, drawn with great fluidity and skill, are full of references to the Renaissance and the Baroque, as well as to the medieval world, and their detailed presentation has much in common with a fully developed stage set for an historical drama.

By comparison with these complex works of the imagination, Pugin's clearer architectural vision beginning in the mid-1830s is shown in the early sketches for his own houses. Some of these drawings, unfortunately undated, give a good idea of Pugin's intentions at Saint Marie's Grange (see fig. 5-9).[10] They also show him making the classic

error of the inexperienced architect, namely designing a building from the outside in and producing, as a result, a house that was woefully impractical in its internal planning.

More remarkable is the first sketch for The Grange, Ramsgate, included in a letter written to his friend the Reverend John Rouse Bloxam, Fellow of Magdalen College, Oxford, and a fervent Pugin supporter.[11] This sketch shows the broad form of the house, as well as many of its characteristic details such as the random fenestration and the tower and flagpole. And there is plenty of evidence to suggest the internal appearance of The Grange—from diaries and journals, from drawings, designs, and watercolors by Pugin and others (fig. 9-5), from early photographs (fig. 9-6),[12] and from the house itself, which survives largely unaltered in its major rooms and its staircase hall, the latter a favorite and often

Fig. 9-5. Drawing room and library from the same perspective as in fig. 9-5; late 19th-century photograph. (Private collection)

Fig. 9-6. Fireplace sketch from an "Ideal Scheme" for Le Chasteau, by Pugin; pen and ink, 1833. (Trustees of the Victoria & Albert Museum, London)

Cheminé dans le grand salon

repeated Pugin element. Furniture, metalwork, and ceramics designed by Pugin and made for The Grange survive in public and private collections,[13] along with objects and paintings from his own huge collection of antiques,[14] while in the house fireplaces, woodwork, stained glass, doors and door furniture, wall painting, and encaustic tiles give a sense of the style he created for his own use.

In the primary rooms this was composed of strong colors and powerful patterns—on wallpapers, stained glass, and textiles—creating a richly textured and formally decorative background for dark furniture, colorful ceramics, and glittering metalwork. Pictures were densely hung on the generously patterned walls. Antiques, as well as objects designed by Pugin, were displayed

around the house. The Grange was, at the same time, a center for family life and work. The comforts it offered, combined with the regularity of Pugin's domestic and professional life there, must have given him some welcome respite from the all-encompassing pressures that were the natural by-product of his personality and way of life. The Grange also brings to life Pugin's work as a practical designer. There are drawings by him for practical things such as kitchen tables, bedroom furniture, picture frames, and bell pulls, things that emphasize his commitment to the creation of a single, unified style. In a letter discussing the ironwork for The Grange he wrote: "Everything must be done with the greatest possible simplicity combined with strength."[15]

It is this practical approach that sets Pugin

apart from his contemporaries and his predecessors and establishes him as a significant figure in the development of modern concepts of both industrial and interior design. For him, design theories and principles were universal; they applied as much to a small domestic interior as to a major national commission such as the Palace of Westminster.

There is, inevitably, another side to Pugin the designer, and one that places him even more firmly as a transitional figure between the Regency and the High Victorian period. This side is underlined by his work in Scotland with the architect James Gillespie Graham and by his early involvement in two major projects—Scarisbrick Hall, Lancashire, and Saint Mary's College, Oscott—both of which were to keep him busy for many years. The origins of Pugin's Scottish connections are hard to establish with any certainty. His biographer, Benjamin Ferrey, suggests that he met Gillespie Graham as a result of his dramatic shipwreck on the east coast of Scotland in about 1830 but this may not be correct.[16] Certainly, for the rest of his life, Pugin seems to have used a pair of drawing compasses engraved with Gillespie Graham's name and the date 1830. According to Pugin the first meeting took place on September 19, 1829, probably in London.[17] Whatever the

circumstances, the meeting marked the start of a long and, for Pugin, very influential association that lasted well into the 1840s.

At the time of their meeting, Pugin was still deeply involved in the theater, and it may be that Gillespie Graham helped and encouraged him to make the transition from stage designer to architect. Certainly, they shared an enthusiasm for a theatrical approach to design. Jacobean-style furniture (ca. 1831–35), a plan for the redevelopment of Glasgow cathedral (1836–37), some designs for the chapel at Heriot's Hospital, Edinburgh (1835), and the drawing of Gillespie Graham's entry for the Palace of Westminster competition (1835) were among the fruits of this partnership. More relevant in the development of Pugin's own style as a designer was his involvement in two of Gillespie Graham's grand schemes for large country houses. The first of these was Murthly New Castle, the Perthshire house of Sir John Stewart. Pugin's involvement is not well documented but he supplied fittings in the Jacobean style between 1829 and 1831.[18] The New Castle was never completed, but many of the fittings, for example fireplaces and grates, were incorporated into the Great Hall and the French drawing room (fig. 9-7) of the Old Castle following a fire in 1850. Photographs of Murthly taken in the 1870s

Fig. 9-7. Fireplace grate for Murthley Castle, Perthshire; design attributed to Pugin; cast iron, early 1830s. This was reinstalled in the French drawing room in about 1850; the printed tiles may also be by Pugin.

Fig. 9-8. The Library at Taymouth Castle, Perthshire, at the time of Queen Victoria's visit in 1843. From Sir Thomas Dick Lauder, *The Memorial of the Royal Progress in Scotland* (1843).

show an interesting blend of Jacobean and contemporary French styles that perhaps give a hint of the young Pugin's attitude to design at this time.[19]

Certainly the Jacobean idiom was very much in Pugin's mind, as can be seen from the furniture designs he drew for Mrs. Gough of Perry Hall, Birmingham, for the London antique dealer Edward Hull, and the designs for his own furniture making business at Hart Street.[20] It is tempting to think that Pugin may also have had a hand in the decoration of the restored chapel at Murthly, a rich explosion of colorful seventeenth-century–style designs whose fanciful lavishness contains a more substantial Romanesque or Early Gothic core. As a whole, Murthly hints at Pugin's early infatuation with the Baroque, perhaps

another legacy of his theatrical experiences, and one that also appears from time to time in his topographical watercolors.

A much more significant and far better documented example of Pugin's youthful exuberance was Taymouth Castle, the massive early nineteenth-century Gothic Revival seat of Lord Breadalbane.[21] Pugin's association with the project started in 1837 and continued until 1842, during which period he supplied designs and drawings for fittings and furniture for the library (figs. 9-8, 9-9) and the Great Hall, renamed the Banner Hall after Queen Victoria's visit in 1843. This was an immense undertaking, with the alterations and additions costing over £13,000. Although it was carried out in Gillespie Graham's name there is a clear Puginian input in the magnificent richness and complexity of the paneling, doors and screens, fireplaces, and decorated ceilings. Another feature that was typical of Pugin was the incorporation into the design of architectural antiques, notably sections of early wood carving.

Taymouth represents the full flowering of Pugin's Gothic vision of his early years, in which theatricality and historicism go hand in hand. It also demonstrates his ability to come to terms with the challenge posed by working within an existing structure, something that was to occur again and again in his professional life. Creating from scratch a unity of architecture, interior design, and fittings may have been his dream but the reality, as far as his domestic work was con-

cerned, was usually very different; most of his major secular commissions from the late 1830s onward were concerned more with interior design than architecture.

Despite this, he was able to develop a distinctive, highly unified and influential style that drew increasingly from the expertise of his professional supporters, such as the potter Herbert Minton and the decorator John Gregory Crace, both of whom came into his life in about 1840. Indeed, Crace was working at Taymouth in 1842, both independently and as an interpreter of Pugin's designs.

A later example of cooperation between Pugin and Gillespie Graham can be seen in a series of

Fig. 9-9. The Library at Taymouth Castle, Perthshire, Scotland, part of the decorative scheme introduced by James Gillespie Graham with the assistance of Pugin; photographed in 1963.

Scarisbrick Hall, Lancashire.

AUGUSTUS W. PUGIN, ARCH.T

Fig. 9-10. Scarisbrick Hall, Lancashire, in its final stage, with additions by Pugin's son Edward, the most important of which was the overly elaborate tower that replaced Pugin's original structure. From *The Building News* (April 24, 1868).

designs prepared in 1846 for the redecoration of Brodick Castle, on the Isle of Arran, for the son of the Duke of Hamilton.[22] These drawings, in Pugin's typically lively free-flowing style, are a classic example of him working purely as an interior designer, in partnership with Crace, preparing a scheme for a building he may never even have seen. Once again, the designs are Jacobean, showing his continuing interest in a style that by that date must have rested somewhat uneasily with the stricter forms of real medieval structural Gothic.

The greatest commission of Pugin's early years and the one that even more clearly than Taymouth gave him the opportunity to make his mark as an architect and designer was Scarisbrick Hall (fig. 9-10). His work for Charles Scarisbrick started in March 1837 and continued until 1845.

The link was then maintained by Pugin's son Edward who worked on the house for Anne Scarisbrick long after his father's death. As a commission, it is particularly well documented.[23] Many important drawings survive that show how well Pugin was able to create his idea of a modern Old English Catholic mansion out of a rather run-down sixteenth-century manor that had been Gothicized by Thomas Rickman early in the nineteenth century.

In Charles Scarisbrick, Pugin had the ideal client. They shared an interest in antiques, and Pugin was able to incorporate into his interiors much of the early Flemish woodwork that Scarisbrick and he had collected, creating a setting that was splendidly rich in its blend of old and new. The style of the interior, as at Taymouth, spanned several centuries, but there is a strong

Fig. 9-11. The chapel at Saint Mary's College, Oscott; as completed by Pugin, 1838; etching also by Pugin, 1839.

Fig. 9-12. The original screen and chancel at Saint Chad's Cathedral, Birmingham; designed by Pugin, completed in 1841, and photographed a century later. This glorious Pugin interior has since been extensively altered.

remodeling of the house was extensive, both inside and out, and included additions such as a two-story porch, octagonal corner towers, and a grand clock tower generally believed to have been a model for Big Ben. His internal architecture was practical and helped to make sense of a rather confused layout. He created a new staircase and added excitement to the Great Hall by lighting it from above, with daylight passing through a second-story screened corridor, and by adding color in the form of a richly decorative mosaic floor in a strong Gothic pattern.

While Pugin was subsequently very dismissive of his early work as a furniture designer for Windsor Castle,[24] he seems never to have turned his back on his early architectural and interior design work. He continued to visit Scarisbrick regularly and went on working there until 1845, by which time his involvement in the Palace of

sense of the Jacobean combined with northern European Gothic. The result is dramatic. Its originality sets it apart from the style of medieval pastiche that had characterized the Gothic Revival interior to this point. The style was echoed by the furniture Pugin designed for Scarisbrick, some of which survives, such as an armchair (see cat. no. 30). Here, he put aside the decorative Gothic forms of his youth, creating instead furniture that he based on examples he found illustrated in medieval manuscripts. It was at this point that he was formulating his design principles and his belief in the correct use of sources, and the Scarisbrick armchair is a reflection of this crucial change of direction.

At Scarisbrick, thanks to the support and enthusiasm of his client, Pugin was also able to develop his architectural ideas. His structural

Fig. 9-13. Chapel at the Convent of Mercy, Handsworth, Birmingham, a typically rich Pugin interior (destroyed in World War II).

Fig. 9-14. Frontispiece, illustrating Pugin's integrated modern Gothic style. From Pugin, *The Glossary of Ecclesiastical Ornament* (London, 1844).

Westminster had taken up all his time. He seems never to have wanted to change anything and as late as 1844 wrote to Charles Scarisbrick, "I have my heart and soul in the thing."[25] This was probably true, for it was at Scarisbrick, and to a lesser extent at Taymouth, that Pugin was able not only to develop his highly individual style of interior design—rich, sumptuous, theatrical, yet fully integrated—but also to try out for the first time those ideas that he then developed so successfully at the Palace of Westminster.

In 1837 Pugin also started to work on the other major commission of his early years, Saint Mary's College, Oscott, near Birmingham (fig. 9-11). This school and seminary had been established in 1794 and moved to a new site in 1834, to new buildings designed in a broadly Tudor revival style by Joseph Potter. Pugin quickly established himself at Oscott which for some years would be a major element in his spiritual and creative life. He gradually took over from Potter and masterminded the decoration and fittings of the chapel (1838), his first essay on a grand scale in this type of ecclesiastical architecture. Once again, his personal vision of the medieval world came to the fore, and the result was a dramatic and richly colored building beneath a soaring roof, decorated in the familiar blend of old and new. Into the chapel Pugin inserted an extravagantly Baroque set of altar rails dating to the seventeenth century, some fine old Limoges enamel plaques from the sixteenth century, and a magnificent Flemish medieval brass lectern,[26] objects which, by their presence, must have underlined for Pugin the continuity of

Fig. 9-15. Alton Castle (ca. 1847), Pugin's most picturesque secular building.

medievalism and the Catholic style. The chapel is, by its nature and style, distinctly theatrical. He also created a museum for the students, filled with a rich variety of the kind of medieval and later objects that he was continuously acquiring on his frequent visits to Europe, and, in his role as Professor of Ecclesiastical Architecture and Antiquities at Oscott, he gave lectures designed to underline the vital link between the arts of the medieval past and the arts of the present.[27] These lectures formed the basis for his book, *True Principles*, published in 1841.

At Oscott, even more than at Scarisbrick, Pugin was able to pursue his vision of an integrated medieval world, designing vestments, metalwork, and above all else a remarkable range of furniture.

It was here that what has come to be known as his structural approach to furniture design first developed, and his legacy is a range of tables, chairs, and other items whose simple functionalism marks the final break with the decorative Gothic tradition of the eighteenth century. Durability, simplicity, and cost were all important factors at Oscott, but Pugin seems to have enjoyed the challenge imposed by such conditions. For the first time he put aside his fascination with Jacobean and Flemish detail and took inspiration instead from the powerful simplicity of medieval structural woodwork.

In the late 1830s Pugin emerged as an architect and designer increasingly noted for the originality of his often outspoken ideas, and the demand for his services rapidly increased. He was widely seen as the rising star of the new Roman Catholicism, a position helped by his fervent belief in the integrated unity of faith and design, and by friends such as Bishop Thomas Walsh, Vicar Apostolic of the Midland District, and Ambrose Phillipps de Lisle, an important Pugin patron who shared his hopes for a Catholic England and his enthusiasm for Christian art and architecture. Phillipps had built Grâce Dieu in 1833–34, a Tudor-style house designed by William Railton. Pugin altered and considerably extended this, beginning in 1842.

By 1838 Pugin had met John Talbot, the sixteenth Earl of Shrewsbury, who was to become his major patron, George Myers who became his principal builder, and John Hardman whose Birmingham company was to become the major manufacturer of Pugin's ecclesiastical and secular metalwork, jewelry, and stained glass. Within a year or so he had also met Herbert Minton and John Gregory Crace. Myers, Hardman, Minton, and Crace—all skilled craftsmen, enlightened manufacturers, and practical designers—were to be Pugin's greatest supporters and friends. Through his long association with them, their families, and their employees he was able to develop fully his burgeoning skills as an interior designer.

Pugin had the ideas, but he needed these men and their support, with their craft and manufacturing skills, to launch the revived medieval style that he saw as essential to Britain's future. He now had a much bigger stage for his performance and he rose to the challenge. The last years of the 1830s saw the completion of his first major church, Saint Marie's, Derby, and the start of his first two cathedrals, Saint Chad's, Birmingham, and Saint George's, Southwark, London, along with a number of smaller churches. He could now design ambitious buildings, confident in his knowledge of medieval architecture and Myers' technical skills, and he could equip these buildings with colorful and well-integrated wallpapers, textiles, tiles, and ceramics, metalwork, furniture and woodwork, and stained glass (fig. 9-13). Through these men he could also expand his knowledge of and enthusiasm for new technology, something he saw as integral to the creation of a modern Gothic world. With Minton, Pugin was directly involved in the development of the encaustic tile process, the mechanization of tile production, and the application of a new process for color printing on

ceramics, first patented by Collins & Reynolds in 1848.[28] With Hardman and his son, he adapted traditional handcraft techniques of metalworking for modern machine production and worked to develop a new range of rich, medieval-inspired colors for stained glass. His firm ideas on the correct use of flat pattern, expounded in *True Principles* and in his *Glossary of Ecclesiastical Ornament*, published in 1844 (fig. 9-14), brought into being a new enthusiasm for wallpapers and decorative textiles, and his interest in chromolithography, the new technology of color printing, ensured that books such as his *Glossary*, and later, *Floriated Ornament* (1849) enjoyed a major and long-lasting influence upon the subsequent development of design in Britain.

The impact of the Earl of Shrewsbury upon Pugin's life was considerable, as both friend and patron. Pugin became a regular visitor to Alton Towers, the Shrewsbury seat in Staffordshire, and began to impose his design ideas upon the large and rambling house, which was built in an early

Fig. 9-16. Altar in the Lady Chapel (detail), Saint Giles's, Cheadle. Pugin's polychromatic wall painting provides a background for the 15th-century Flemish altarpiece, an example of original medieval work incorporated by Pugin into a Gothic Revival interior.

Fig. 9-17. Staircase with heraldic newel post, Bilton Grange, Warwickshire, designed by Pugin, 1840s.

nineteenth-century Gothic Revival style. Pugin's contribution was much less than at Scarisbrick, and little survives to be seen today in a house that is largely a ruin.[29] More important were other Shrewsbury commissions, such as the Hospital of Saint John at Alton, where Pugin developed his ideas for modern monastic buildings, and Alton Castle (fig. 9-15), a towering monument to his ambitions as a creative Gothic Revival architect. This castle, with its echoes of Burgundy, the Rhinelands, Normandy, and local vernacular traditions, forms a dramatic skyline high above the wooded valley of the river Churnet (see fig. 5-1). Its position and its architecture reflect Pugin's confidence and maturity, but the interior was never satisfactorily completed and gives little clue to his developing interest in interior design.

The greatest creation of the Shrewsbury–Pugin connection was undoubtedly Saint Giles's church in nearby Cheadle. Completed in 1846 at an enormous cost, this church represents Pugin's integrated style at its best. In architectural terms it is a dramatic and impressive building, with a soaring spire that dominates the landscape for miles around, establishing nineteenth-century Gothic as a powerful and highly original style that had grown naturally out of its medieval roots. However, the exterior is really no preparation for the interior, a stunning display of design virtuosity. In its richness of color, pattern, and controlled ornament Saint Giles's has no equal. Every surface is decorated with painted and stenciled patterns that reveal not only Pugin's total familiarity with his concept of the medieval world, but also his masterful use of complementary colors and the contrasting effects of day and artificial light. Fully equipped by Pugin down to the smallest detail, the church is a wonderful example of his all-encompassing view of modern Gothic. Wood-work, metalwork, stained glass, textiles, tiles on walls and floors, sculpture, carving, and wall painting (fig. 9-16), all combine to spectacular effect.

There is no other building like Saint Giles's, but at least Pugin was able to fulfill his dream on this one occasion, almost regardless of cost. In 1841, when the church was still in its early stages, he was sufficiently confident to write to his patron in very optimistic terms, "I feel truly grateful to your lordship for had it not been for you I should never have had the opportunity of doing a really good thing. Cheadle is my great comfort, at length one good building. I am sure your lordship will be delighted: it is the real thing."[30] It is hardly surprising that Saint Giles's was to remain close to Pugin's heart for the rest of his life. In 1850, when ill, exhausted, and depressed, he wrote, "Everything looks plain after Cheadle."[31]

A typical architect and designer, Pugin often had difficulties with budgets and costs, and he frequently complained about what he perceived to be the meanness of his clients and patrons. Even his friend the Earl of Shrewsbury was not spared, for

Fig. 9-18. Fireplace with stone carvings and cast-iron firedogs in the drawing room at Bilton Grange, designed by Pugin, 1840s.

Fig. 9-19. The Banqueting Hall at Lismore Castle, Ireland, with fittings designed by Pugin, ca. 1850; lithograph, ca. 1897. This project represents the final development of Pugin's interior design style. (The Irish Architectural Archive)

193

Fig. 9-20. Floor tiles in the Great Hall, Leighton Hall, Wales; designed by Pugin, ca. 1850.

Pugin took any attempt at economy as a personal insult. During one dispute about Alton Castle he wrote, ". . . as regards the hall, I have nailed my colours to the mast—a bay window, high open roof, lantern, 2 good fireplaces, a great sideboard, screen, minstrel gallery—all or none. I will not sell myself to do a wretched thing."[32] Pugin's belief in the correctness of his style was absolute, along with the need for a total commitment on the part of the client, and he had no time for compromise. Luckily, many of his clients had both sufficient faith and money to let him do what he wanted.

Typical was John Allcard, the owner of Burton Closes, a Gothic Revival house in Derbyshire, built from 1845 to the designs of Joseph Paxton and John Robertson. Pugin was called in to complete the interior of the house in 1847, and he set to work to introduce his colorfully integrated style, adding fireplaces, woodwork, stained glass, decorative painted ceilings, furniture, and much else beside. In 1848 Allcard wrote, "I do not think the word economy ever entered his (Pugin's) mind . . . . It has been my desire to let his fine and correct tastes prevail, yet I must confess I am not a little astonished at the Beauty and grandeur of our doing."[33]

Less accommodating was Captain John Hubert Washington Hibbert, the owner of Bilton Grange

in Warwickshire, one of the other great domestic schemes of Pugin's mature years. The work started in 1841 and then continued for ten years, during which time there were frequent disputes between architect and client.[34] Here, Pugin greatly expanded a small eighteenth-century house, adding a new wing that completely dominated the existing structure, and creating a sequence of new rooms that included a galleried Great Hall with stained-glass windows. There was a dramatic staircase, with carved newel posts (fig. 9-17) in the form of heraldic beasts and birds, some fine carved stone fireplaces (fig. 9-18) with heraldic andirons or firedogs, a rich array of carved and painted paneling, elaborate chandeliers, and decorative metalwork including some finely wrought keys, a Pugin specialty. A range of specially designed tiles and wallpapers featured the Hibbert initials and coat of arms. In its diversity, Bilton Grange represented a typically extravagant and completely coordinated Pugin interior, in his modern medieval style.

The secular design schemes of Pugin's maturity, such as Bilton Grange, Burton Closes, Albury Park in Surrey, The Grange at Ramsgate, Chirk Castle in Wales, Adare Manor in Ireland, and, above all else, the Palace of Westminster, reflect the increasing importance of his relationship with John Gregory Crace.[35] As the head of one of London's major interior design companies of the nineteenth century, Crace enjoyed a considerable reputation and a wide range of clients. The business was one in which the dictates of fashion were all important, and so Crace & Company was able to offer its clients a wide range of interior design schemes, with an emphasis on those that reflected the lasting popularity of Renaissance and French-inspired styles. The Gothic Revival, always an acquired taste, was by no means the core of the business, but the fact that it had considerable commercial potential must have been due to Pugin's efforts. The relationship between Pugin and Crace was based more on friendship than on commercial convenience, and both sides were able to benefit. Pugin relied on Crace for the successful development of his hastily drawn sketches into practical and commercially viable wallpapers, textiles, woodwork, and furniture. For Crace, Pugin was a dynamic mine of design ideas and a useful link to a wide range of predominantly Catholic clients. The most tangible result of the partnership was the creation in about 1849 of a Gothic showroom at Crace's premises at 14 Wigmore Street, London. This, an addition to the French-inspired showrooms that Crace & Company had developed in the late 1830s, was not only an important way of promoting Pugin's work to Crace clients, but was also a workshop where furniture and woodwork could be manufactured to Pugin's designs.

Inevitably, there were disagreements, often provoked by Crace's occasionally cavalier treatment of Pugin's designs and his reluctance to respond sympathetically to Pugin's enthusiasm for simple furniture. In October 1849, Pugin wrote, somewhat plaintively, "I do not think we make enough plain furniture. I shall send you a lot of designs for plain things, and furniture for bedrooms which could come moderate and suit Gothic houses."[36] For Pugin the fulfillment of his dreams of a modern medieval world were dependent upon the ready availability to a wide market of a range of simple Gothic designs. Crace, however, had other ideas, knowing that there was far more money to be made by satisfying the more extravagant tastes of the wealthy. The result was an inevitable compromise. For Crace's clients Pugin designed walnut furniture with lavish marquetry, extravagant paneling, richly decorative metalwork, and complex multicolored wallpapers with expensive flock finishes, while thinking about what he called a "sensible style of furniture of good oak and constructively put together."[37]

There is no doubt that for a certain type of commission, Crace turned to Pugin. They were friends, but the basis of the friendship from Crace's point of view was probably the knowledge that, for all his complaints, Pugin worked at great speed, producing complete schemes for contemporary Gothic interiors. During his last years, when he had few architectural commissions of his own, Pugin came to rely increasingly on Crace, becom-

Fig. 9-21. Staircase with heraldic newel posts and carved panels, Horsted Place, Sussex; designed by Pugin, 1850–51, and exhibited by Myers at the Great Exhibition of 1851, along with one of the carved stone fireplaces.

ing in the process more interior designer than architect. Absorbed though he was at this time in the final stages of the Palace of Westminster and the creation of the Mediaeval Court for the Great Exhibition of 1851, Pugin had no real architectural work. Furthermore, the effects of exhaustion, illness, and depression were having their toll, and he was feeling increasingly that his life had been a failure. His disillusion and despair are apparent in letters and other writings of the period: "I believe, as regards architecture, few men have been so unfortunate as myself. I have passed my life in thinking of fine things, studying fine things, designing fine things, and realising very poor ones."[38]

Despite his pessimism, Pugin's last years were actually marked by a great outburst of creativity, the direct result of his relationship with Crace. It was Crace who gave Pugin the opportunity, through a series of major country house commissions—all well documented by the Crace letters (in the RIBA) and the Crace drawings (in the Victoria & Albert Museum)—to fulfill his potential as an interior designer. The first and probably the greatest of these was Eastnor Castle in Herefordshire, a massive early nineteenth-century Gothic Revival structure designed by Robert Smirke, the architect of the British Museum.

In about 1849 Lord Somers had invited Crace to redesign parts of Eastnor Castle, and Crace turned to Pugin, who proceeded to create a magnificent drawing room (see cat. no. 102 and 112). Color and pattern were added to Smirke's Strawberry Hill–style vaulted ceiling from which was hung a splendid Hardman chandelier, one of the best of the series that, since the Palace of Westminster, had become a kind of Pugin trademark. Walls were paneled and painted, with liberal use of heraldic decoration and the initials of Lord Somers. Doors were enriched with glorious pierced brass fittings. The focal point of the room was a great carved and painted stone fireplace, surmounted by a richly ornamental family tree and equipped with Minton tiles and andirons in the form of gilded brass lions. To complete the scheme, Pugin designed a suite of richly inlaid walnut furniture, matched by a set of chairs upholstered in red velvet, and a carpet. This style of furniture was modern and structural, obeying Pugin's rules about truth to sources and control of ornament, yet full of seventeenth-century splendor. It represents in some ways his full maturity as a designer.

Pugin's drawing room at Eastnor survives virtually intact, offering a rare opportunity to appreciate his consummate skill as an interior designer in its most flamboyant, confident, and fully developed form. There is the sense that, freed from the pressures and constraints of being an architect, Pugin was able to relax into the pleasures of pure design and attain a new level of creativity. He may

have visited the house only once, when he admired the chandelier and criticized Crace's workmanship, but this is not important.[39] A detailed briefing and Crace's complete confidence in his abilities were sufficient for Pugin to work independently and develop his own vision of the interior design scheme. Lord Somers was, after all, Crace's client and not Pugin's.

The other houses of this late period have been extensively altered but in every case enough survives to indicate that each, in its own way, was probably as splendid as Eastnor. One or two may have been even more so. A partial survivor, for example, is Lismore Castle in Ireland, a house extensively altered and redecorated by Crace for its owner, the sixth Duke of Devonshire, from 1850. The castle had been Gothicized by William Atkinson from 1811, leaving a legacy of architectural decoration and plasterwork dating from that period. Once again Crace called in Pugin. While he objected strongly to having to work within the constraints imposed by the budget and Atkinson's theatrical Gothic, he nonetheless designed doors, a range of domestic furniture for both formal and private rooms, wallpapers, carpets, metalwork, and much else besides.

The glory of the castle is the great galleried banqueting hall (fig. 9-19), which became a splendid Pugin room, enriched by paneling, heraldic painting on ceiling and walls, bold wallpapers, another magnificent chandelier, and the carved stone fireplace that had been displayed in the Mediaeval Court at the Great Exhibition in 1851. Pugin also designed the small drawing room. He never saw Lismore and the work continued after his death, with Crace sometimes following his designs and sometimes adapting them to suit the needs of the moment, a characteristic feature of their working relationship.

Much more altered are the other two great design schemes of this final period, Leighton Hall, near Welshpool in Wales,[40] and Abney Hall in Cheshire. Leighton Hall was a Crace commission, begun in 1850, to create the interiors for the new house built for John Naylor, a Liverpool banker, to the designs of W. H. Gee. Crace seems to have supplied Pugin with the dimensions of the rooms and other necessary information,[41] and Pugin in return supplied a series of sketchily drawn but highly detailed exploded schemes and elevations for the Great Hall and other rooms (see cat. no. 101). These show doors and doorcases, fireplaces and overmantels, paneling, painted ceilings, and wall decoration. Some of these schemes were carried out much as Pugin had drawn them, while others were altered by Crace, but enough survives today to give an indication of the scheme's original richness and quality (figs. 9-20). The painted ceiling panels, the metalwork, the doors and door fittings, and the Minton wall and floor tiles are particularly characteristic of Pugin. They give a sense of the style of interior he was fully capable of creating from a distance.

Abney Hall, in many ways a similar story, was to be Pugin's last major commission. There were, of course, many other ones throughout the long years of the Pugin and Crace relationship, such as the alterations to Chirk Castle in Wales, carried out between 1846 and 1848, designs for Lee Castle in Scotland for Lady Lockhart in 1848, and for Horsted Place in Sussex in 1850–51. Horsted Place was designed for Francis Barchard by Samuel Dawkes. George Myers was the builder, and it may actually have been through Myers that Pugin came to design some of the internal fittings (fig. 9-21).

Abney Hall was built in 1847 for Alfred Orrell, a cotton mill owner who died in 1849. It was then bought by James Watts, a Manchester businessman, who, perhaps inspired by a visit to the Mediaeval Court at the Great Exhibition, asked Crace to develop an entirely new interior design scheme. Pugin, with the support of the familiar team of Hardman, Myers, and Minton, began to work on the designs toward the end of 1851. He was already terminally ill, his condition revealed in letters to Crace from both Pugin and his wife Jane.[42] However, he seems to have enjoyed the work, and entered into it with his usual spirit, lambasting Crace for the poverty of his ideas. In one letter he wrote, "It is the true thing that I have ever done and yours was the worst . . . I ever saw since Wyatts time (pray forgive me) but my dear friend you are worn out with imitation and cannot design other things."[43]

The designs for both Abney and Leighton continued to pour from Pugin until his final collapse in February 1852. In one of his last letters to Crace, accompanying seventeen drawings for Abney, he wrote, "I have done my best and am nearly done myself."[44] Crace, who continued to work at Abney until 1857, ignored his friend's views and assumed much of the responsibility for the design of the scheme, freely adapting Pugin's drawings, using artificial and dishonest materials such as plaster and papier-mâché, and generally creating an interior that reflected Pugin's style but lacked his remarkably consistent eye for detail and his overriding concern for the integrity and absoluteness of his modern Gothic vision. This became the pattern for the future and, while the Gothic style of interior design was to remain fashionable for some time to come in the hands of Crace and other decorators, it was a weaker thing without the guiding hand of its creator.

1. A. W. N. Pugin, Diary for 1835, quoted in Alexandra Wedgwood, *Catalogue of the Victoria and Albert Museum Drawings Collection: A. W. N. Pugin and the Pugin Family* (London, 1985), hereafter cited as Wedgwood, *Catalogue/V&A*. This is one of fifteen pocket diaries, covering the years 1835–42, 1844–45, 1847–51, which are in the Victoria & Albert Museum, London (inv. no. L5156-1969).

2. A. W. N. Pugin, *True Principles of Pointed or Christian Architecture* (London, 1841; 1853 ed.), p. 1.

3. Ibid., p. 35

4. Ibid., p. 52

5. A. W. N. Pugin, *An Apology for the Revival of Christian Architecture* (London, 1843), p. 39.

6. Letter to E. J. Willson (July 17, 1835), in Wedgwood, *Catalogue/V&A*. The original of this letter is at John Hopkins University, Baltimore.

7. Alexandra Wedgwood, with the help of the current architect/owner of Saint Marie's Grange, has established the house's original floor plan. See Wedgwood, "Domestic Architecture," in Paul Atterbury and Clive Wainwright, eds., *Pugin: A Gothic Passion* (London and New Haven, 1994), p. 44.

8. The martlet is a mythical bird, frequently used in heraldry. It has no feet, so never rests, a quality that must have appealed to Pugin. His motto, *En Avant*, means "Forward."

9. Surviving furniture includes a set of upholstered dining room chairs, now in the Speaker's House, Palace of Westminster, London, and some hall chairs and a work table in private collections.

10. These drawings can by found in William Osmond Drawings, Joseph Downs Collection of Manuscripts and Printed Ephemera, fol. 189, The Henry Francis du Pont Winterthur Museum, Delaware.

11. The letter, written in 1843 (undated), is in the Macfarlane Library, Magdalen College, Oxford.

12. See, e.g., diaries, designs, and watercolors in the Victoria & Albert Museum, London, catalogued in Wedgwood, *Catalogue/V&A*; and material in the Royal Institute of British Architects (RIBA), Drawings Collection, catalogued and indexed in Alexandra Wedgwood, *Catalogues of the Drawings of the Royal Institute of British Architects: The Pugin Family* (London, 1977). A great deal of material is also preserved in private collections.

13. Examples of furniture, ceramics, and metalwork from The Grange may be found in the Victoria & Albert Museum, London: e.g., dessert dish (inv. no. L32-1952); cabinet (loan); candlesticks (in. no. M35xA-1972); saltcellars and spoons (inv. no. M26-c-1976), and in several private collections.

14. Much of Pugin's collection was dispersed in a sale in 1853. Other parts of the collection were dispersed among the Pugin family and then sold in later sales.

15. From a letter in a private collection; for a microfilm copy, see the House of Lords Record Office (HLRO), Palace of Westminster, HLRO/128.

16. Benjamin Ferrey, *Recollections of A. N. Welby Pugin and his father, Augustus Pugin* (London, 1861), pp. 62–63.

17. "Septr 19 [1829] was introduced to Mr. Gillespie Graham, architect of Edinburgh and began to design for him" (Pugin, manuscript notes for an uncompleted autobiography, transcribed in Wedgwood, *Catalogue/V&A*, Victoria & Albert inv. no. L5204-1969). Subsequent notations (September 21 and October 5) also refer to Graham.

18. See Wedgwood, *Catalogue/V&A*.

19. For photographs of Murthley taken in the 1870s, see the Magnus Jackson Collection, Royal Commission for the Ancient and Historic Monuments of Scotland.

20. For the Perry Hall and Hull designs, see the volume of designs for furniture (1834), Victoria & Albert Museum, London, inv. no. E2588-2600.1910. For designs for Pugin's Hart Street business, see Drawings Collection, RIBA, London.

21. For references to Taymouth Castle and Gillespie Graham, see Pugin's diaries (1837–42) in Wedgwood, *Catalogue/V&A*.

22. The drawings are in the Victoria & Albert Museum (inv. no. E1512–1516.1912).

23. Drawings and designs for Scarisbrick may be found in the Victoria & Albert Museum; the Drawings Collection, RIBA, London; references are in Pugin diaries (1837–45) and the Scarisbrick family papers.

24. Pugin, *True Principles*, p. 35.

25. Letter (March 1, 1844) in Wedgwood, *Catalogue/V&A*; the original of this letter is in the Lancashire Record Office.

26. The Oscott Lectern, which originally came from a church in Louvain, Belgium, is now in The Cloisters, Metropolitan Museum of Art, New York. The other items are still at Oscott, along with a substantial part of the collection of antiquities assembled there by Pugin.

27. Dr. Henry Weedall (1788–1859) was president of Oscott until 1840 and appointed Pugin professor of Ecclesiastical Architecture and Antiquities in 1837. Pugin lectured regularly at Oscott for a few years beginning in 1838 until pressure of work made his visits there less frequent. Some of his lectures were published, for example, in the *Catholic Magazine* and elsewhere.

28. Encaustic tilework, the medieval process of inlaying patterns of colored clay into base clay, was revived by Minton, Chamberlain, and others during the 1830s. The process was simplified by the availability of the mechanical tile press, in widespread use by the mid-1830s. Encaustic tiles were initially used for restoration projects, but Pugin and others soon injected new designs.

29. Alton Towers passed out of Shrewsbury family hands in 1924. The gardens continued to flourish, but the house had a rather checkered career until the early 1950s when, already virtually a ruin, its interiors were stripped and its roofs removed. Today, as part of the Alton Towers Theme Park, it is a splendid ruin; Pugin's chapel and his banqueting hall have been restored and are open to the public.

30. The letter was written while Pugin was at Alton Towers and Shrewsbury was in Italy (September 29, 1841; in Wedgwood, *Catalogue/V&A*, inv. no. L525-1965).

31. The letter is undated but written from London, probably around November 1850, in ibid.

32. Letter refers to plans for Alton Towers, written from Homby Castle (July 30, 1847), in ibid.

33. Quoted in Phoebe Stanton, *Pugin* (London, 1971).

34. The tenor of their relationship is captured in a letter from Pugin to his wife Jane (April 20, 1850; Victoria & Albert Museum, inv. no. L226-1965): "I have been all day at Bilton

so you may imagine what I have endured. I am sure I don't know how it is all to end but it is terrible work. He [Hibbert] is certainly the most aggravating man in existence."

35. The Crace/Pugin relationship is particularly well documented. The Victoria & Albert Museum, London, has an extensive holding of Pugin designs and drawings donated by the Crace family in 1908 and 1912, many of which are working drawings for particular commissions. More than 350 letters from Pugin to Crace, written between 1844 and 1852, are preserved in the Library, RIBA, London. Other relevant sources include the HLRO, Palace of Westminster.

36. Crace letters, Library, RIBA, London.

37. Ibid.

38. A. W. N. Pugin, *Remarks . . .* (London, 1850). Quoted in Ferrey, *Recollections*, p. 164.

39. Pugin's only visit to Eastnor was on July 30, 1850; for the letter he wrote after this visit, see the Crace letters, Library, RIBA, London, Crace mss. Pug 7/46.

40. Among the drawings by Pugin donated to the Victoria & Albert Museum by the Crace family, there is a group relating to Leighton Hall which are very revealing of his working method and his relationship with Crace (see V&A inv. nos. D895–901.1908, D1038.1908, E1519–1526.1912, E77[108].1970).

41. Ibid.

42. Crace letters, Library, RIBA, London.

43. Ibid., Crace mss. Pug 8/68; also quoted in Wedgwood, *Catalogue/V&A*.

44. Ibid.

Fig. 10-1. Tabernacle doors (*detail*), Church of the Sacred Heart; designed by Peter Paul Pugin, made by Hardman & Co.; brass and quartz, 1882.

10. A. W. N. Pugin and the Gothic Movement in North America

Margaret Henderson Floyd

The influence of A. W. N. Pugin in America was profound, but indirect, for he never designed an American building. After his death, two still mysterious trips to America made by his sons, E. W. Pugin (in 1873–74) and Peter Paul Pugin (around 1880), are said to have generated thirty commissions for churches, but most of this work is still unidentified and could have ranged from decorative art projects to full buildings.[1] It was rather A. W. N. Pugin's writings and cogent articulation of his principles of design that supplied a generative force in all three phases of the American Gothic Revival: the ecclesiological Gothic Revival (1830–60); the polychromatic Ruskinian or High Victorian Gothic (ca. 1865–90); and the Neo-Gothic (1890 onward), now archaeologically correct. Scarcely would it have been believed by Pugin, dying broken and disappointed in Ramsgate in 1852, that the Gothic movement would sweep through North America on the scale and with the breadth that it did.

By the year of Pugin's death, the Gothic Revival was already being established in New York by the ecclesiologists, and within a few years Saint Patrick's Cathedral (1856–78) in New York City would be designed by James Renwick for the Roman Catholic Church.[2] Inspired by Cologne Cathedral, a Continental source that had been lauded by Pugin, Saint Patrick's brought the Gothic style in North America to a monumental scale.[3] Three decades later, the first competition for Saint John the Divine (1889), also in New York City, would initiate construction of a cathedral for the American Episcopal Church that Ralph Adams Cram of Boston would redesign in 1911 in the Neo-Gothic style. Within a half century of Pugin's death, the Gothic style would be accepted interdenominationally for countless churches and college campuses, and for George F. Bodley and Henry Vaughan's National Cathedral (1904) in Washington, D.C.[4] In America, where no tradition of monumental Gothic architecture existed, its audacious nineteenth-century appearance seems matched in intensity only by the whirlwind development of the modern movement in the twentieth century. But in trans-Atlantic passage to the New World, A. W. N. Pugin's "pointed or Christian architecture" and its attendant "true principles" passed through a prism that changed them in curious ways. The agents for the trans-Atlantic migration of Pugin's Gothic vision were initially concentrated in an Anglican network that ultimately expanded during the late nineteenth and early twentieth century to encompass America's diverse ecclesiastical structures and college campuses. In Pugin's third typology, civil and secular design, the organic signifiers of his Gothic principles, as opposed to his liturgical imperatives, aligned with the larger landscape movement and the tradition of the picturesque, also having roots in England.[5] Pugin's "true principles" were reapplied and translated into wood with the inventive techniques that distinguish American building design.

Pugin had an immediate effect on the ecclesiological Gothic Revival of the 1840s and 1850s in the mid-Atlantic region,[6] but his long-term visual and spiritual impact on the church-building programs that emerged in America well after the short trips to America by his sons is less well documented.[7] In the latter decades of the nineteenth century the generative core of the Gothic Revival shifted from New York to New England. Concurrent with the heyday of Ruskinian polychromy in the 1870s and centered at the Anglican Church of the Advent in Boston, a corridor was opened in this region through which the escalating influence

of Pugin's *True Principles of Pointed or Christian Architecture* was promulgated. Beginning in the 1890s Boston Gothicist architects Henry Vaughan, Ralph Adams Cram, and Bertram Grosvenor Goodhue would carry their Gothic Quest across America in the third or Neo-Gothic phase of the revival.[8]

A lingering medieval memory governed vernacular building of the colonial seventeenth century, but origins of the Gothic Revival per se emerged in late eighteenth- and early nineteenth-century America, as in England.[9] During A. W. N. Pugin's lifetime, the Oxford Movement and the Tractarian forces of reform in England[10] that generated new architectural standards within the Anglican Church led in 1844 to the foundation of the first Anglican parish in America, the Church of the Advent in Boston. They also brought the ecclesiological movement to New York in the 1840s, to produce Episcopal churches with separately articulated chancels, aisles, and broach spires. The earliest architects sanctioned by the church were

Fig. 10-2. "Section of the Hon. Rich. Bateman's Octagonal Room at old Windsor," by Johann Heinrich Müntz; ink and wash, 1761. (Lewis Walpole Library, Yale University)

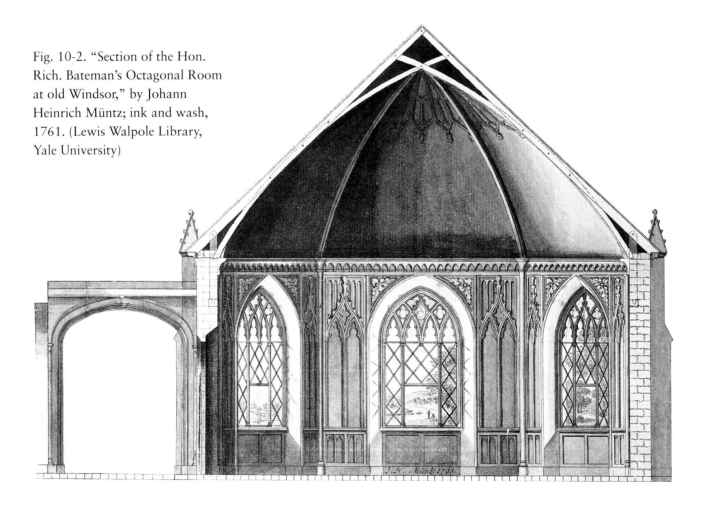

English.[11] Richard Upjohn, whose Trinity Church (1839–46) in New York City became the primary monument of the American Gothic Revival, emigrated to America in 1829, just before Pugin's books and prominent designs for the Houses of Parliament (1835–60) began to be widely known.[12] However, earlier English publications, particularly those of Pugin's father, Auguste Charles Pugin, made available drawings of actual Gothic buildings which began to be emulated in American structures.[13] The explicit reliance on A. W. N. Pugin's drawings of "pointed or Christian" architecture by Upjohn in his refinement of Trinity Church and by James Renwick at Grace Church, New York (1847), set the stage for the phenomenal spread of the Gothic style from Trinity throughout the middle-Atlantic region in the 1840s and the subsequent decade.[14] Upjohn designed fine parish churches in stone and constructionally innovative wooden ones, such as Saint John Chrysostom (1851) in Delafield, Wisconsin. His *Rural Architecture* (1852) was an American pattern book for smaller parishes that carried Puginian principles well beyond the Northeast.[15] The American demand for churches was such that the architect Frank Wills came from England via Canada to New York to work with the ecclesiologists.[16]

Upjohn's first house, Kingscote (1839), in Newport, Rhode Island, was a notable Gothic cottage, but his King Villa (1847), illustrated and described in 1850 by landscape architect A. J. Downing in *The Architecture of Country Houses*, was both round-arched and picturesque.[17] This Italianate manner, alternatively known as the *Rundbogenstil*, was easily produced in either masonry or a wooden construction, and spread to serve the expanding population of the Hudson River Valley in structures such as Frank Wills's Italian villa, Steen Valetje (1848), for Franklin H. Delano at Barrytown.[18] This round-arched, Romanesque style became a popular alternative to the Gothic throughout the East, its best-known civic example being James Renwick's Smithsonian Institution (1844) in Washington, D.C. Richard Upjohn's chapel and library for Bowdoin College

Fig. 10-3. The octagonal library at Rokeby, the William Backhouse Astor Estate, Red Hook, New York; interior design, ca. 1850.

(1845–55) in Brunswick, Maine, under construction concurrently with Trinity Church in New York, illustrates an important academic application of the Romanesque. Austere stone walls at Bowdoin underscore the sophistication of Upjohn's Gothic ornament and the comparative lack of resources available for architectural sculpture in New England until the late 1860s. This lingering technical condition stimulated the popularity of the *Rundbogenstil*, the ornamental elements of which could be more readily generated by machine than could those of the Gothic style, except in its most provincial forms.[19] Ironically, such extrinsic considerations dictated that the Romanesque style would be combined with Puginian Gothic details in Boston at the Basilica of Our Lady of Perpetual Help (1873–78), by E. W. Pugin, one direct familial infusion of his father's influence in America (see fig. 10-7).[20]

Front Elevation.

Fig. 10-4. Cottage Farm, the Amos Lawrence House, Brookline, Massachusetts, by George Minot Dexter; pen and ink, 1850. (Boston Athenaeum, Dexter Drawings Collection)

Meanwhile, the largely secular practice of American architect A. J. Davis likewise encompassed both Gothic and round-arched design.[21] His Gothic Knoll (1838) for William Paulding, enlarged in 1865 as Lyndhurst for George Merritt in Tarrytown on the Hudson, was constructed of castellated masonry, but other works were of wood construction and either round-arched or Gothic in style.[22] A. W. N. Pugin's functional principles of revealed construction were well adapted to the board-and-batten villas and cottages of the Hudson River Valley, envisioned in a picturesque and organic relationship with the landscape. This relationship would generate the most formidable secular expression of medievalism in America of the 1840s and 1850s. Ninety years before, in

Horace Walpole's Gothic Revival circle in England, Johann Heinrich Müntz's octagonal room designed for Mr. Bateman at Old Windsor (1761) originated in a similar landscape ethos.[23] Müntz's drawing (fig. 10-2) shares several levels of signifiers with the spectacular octagonal library designed in the 1850s for Rokeby, the Barrytown, New York, estate of William Backhouse Astor (fig. 10-3).[24] Although the library is still unattributed, both Davis and Upjohn may be considered likely architects by virtue of its quality, their documented designs for octagonal buildings in the Barrytown/Red Hook area of the Hudson, and their concurrent related commissions for W. B. Astor.[25] As in Müntz's eighteenth-century drawing, the Astors enjoyed a spectacular view to the river, in this case west toward the Hudson. A three-stage tower above the Rokeby library united the pursuit of knowledge and the landscape as the philosophical thrust of the secular Gothic style in America.[26] While Davis anticipated the signifiers or bonds between the Gothic style and knowledge, his vision expanded and matured primarily in domestic design in the 1850s under the influence of his friend, A. J. Downing, reaching a crescendo with his gate lodge and houses in Llewellyn Park, New Jersey (1857). Llewellyn Park was one of America's earliest garden suburbs, where a program of largely Gothic, picturesque buildings in the landscape was implemented on an unprecedented scale.[27]

During this period when Pugin's *True Principles* were applied to an ecclesiological building program in the mid-Atlantic region of New York and New Jersey, with an affiliated, more provincial infusion of the Gothic style into both domestic and educational design, the situation was quite different in New England. Indeed, the Tractarian controversies regarding liturgical changes and thereby church design within the Episcopal Church, and the virtual absence of a widespread Roman Catholic presence until the 1840s, delayed the manifestation of Pugin's direct influence through church architecture in that region. Before Davis's Gothic cottages rose in Llewellyn Park, Boston architects such as Arthur Gilman and the horticultural intelligentsia had been in direct contact with landscape architect A. J. Downing.[28] Amos Lawrence commissioned the Boston architect George M. Dexter to design a Gothic house, Cottage Farm, in 1850, poised just beyond the western edge of Boston in the town of Brookline. This rare masonry design (fig. 10-4) was a spare, utilitarian structure, more asymmetrical than Davis's cottages and with a purity of line and proportion that can be identified with most of Dexter's work.[29] Dexter's work by 1850 suggests familiarity with Pugin's published principles, well beyond the Romantic reinterpretations of Davis, and reveals the austere character of local masonry.

Where little capability was available for carving stone, and the native granite was of an intractable

hardness, the typical Boston church before the 1850s, if Gothic, might be surfaced in quarry-faced ashlar, with an axial, square tower on the center of the facade. The granite Congregational church (fig. 10-5) on Bowdoin Street (1831), Beacon Hill, by Solomon Willard, illustrates the characteristics of the pointed style in New England before Puginian principles made inroads.[30] It was here that the Anglican Church of the Advent moved in 1864, and here that its alliance with the Cowley Fathers, an English religious order, would

Fig. 10-5. Saint John the Evangelist, Bowdoin Street, Boston; designed by Solomon Willard, 1831.

205

Fig. 10-6. Saint Peter's Church, Meetinghouse Hill, Dorchester; designed by Patrick Keely, 1873. From William Byrne et al., *History of the Catholic Church in the New England States* (Boston, 1899).

be established in 1872. While ecclesiological sponsorship of church-building programs in New York supplied that area abundantly with Gothic Revival buildings, such was not the case in Boston, where the Episcopal Church was threatened by generic Calvinism after the American Revolution so that problems of the ordination of bishops emerged at the beginning of the nineteenth century, with only two extant parishes in the city to face the sweeping rise of Unitarianism.[31] Meanwhile, the Greek Revival governed civic and ecclesiastical design. Moving into a breach during the first, or ecclesiological, phase of the Gothic Revival in American architectural design was the Romanesque or *Rundbogenstil*, which was widely exploited and conjoined with popular Italianate design.[32]

The work of the architect Arthur Gilman, who practiced in both New York and Boston in the 1840s, exerted great influence on church design.[33] Traveling in the 1840s, he met architect Charles

Barry, Pugin's collaborator on the Houses of Parliament, in London and through him was exposed to the work and ideas of A. W. N. Pugin. An acerbic and sophisticated critic, Gilman experienced the rise of ecclesiology in New York. His spirited and brilliant essay, "Architecture in the United States," revealed his techniques of analysis and disapproval of the Greek Revival to have been heavily influenced by Pugin's publications and principles.[34] In a letter to Upjohn, he also commented negatively on the debased Gothic style of American Greek Revival architects such as Minard Lafever.[35] Returning to Boston, Gilman designed several Gothic churches in the late 1840s, the best-known being Saint Paul's, Dedham. Increasingly influenced by the work of Charles Barry, he designed an Italianate country house in Wellesley for Hollis Hunnewell in 1852. It was published with its elaborate landscaping in the 1859 edition of Downing's *Treatise on the Theory and Practice of Landscape Gardening*.[36] Gilman then emerged as the dominant influence in Boston architecture, forming with Gridley J. F. Bryant, Jr. (to whom he gave a copy of Pugin's *Contrasts*) a partnership that became the largest architectural practice in the city.[37] Another European trip, this time to Italy and to Paris, had a further impact on Gilman's work in the late 1850s and, with it, the direction of Boston architecture, as he turned fully toward the French neo-Baroque and away from the Gothic style that had increasingly absorbed Ruskinian polychromy. Two subsequent churches by Gilman in the Boston area were of round-arched derivation. The Romanesque Sears Chapel at Longwood (1858–63) was picturesquely sited near George M. Dexter's Gothic Cottage Farm in Brookline. The high, square tower and heavy, well-proportioned moldings reveal Gilman's debt to Barry's Italianate style, while expensive stone sculpture that was still rare in New England was avoided.

Having laid out the plan for Boston's Back Bay in 1856 on the model of Second Empire Paris, Gilman designed its first public building. For the Arlington Street Church (1859–61), Gilman drew inspiration from Santa Annunziata in Genoa, Italy (with allusion to Christopher Columbus), from the illustrations in English architect James Gibbs's pattern books, and from Peter Harrison's Kings Chapel, Boston (1749), to produce the largest church interior in Boston up to that time.[38] This spectacular design exploited monumental Corinthian columns rising to a coffered barrel vault to subdivide the rectangular basilica without either transept or apse. On three sides, a gallery ran behind the colonnade to define the central space. Yet, save for its giant order, heavy moldings, and details of the architecture, the Arlington Street Church interior remained sparse in liturgical art, as was customary in Puritan New England. While designing the Arlington Street Church, Gilman is thought to have collaborated with Patrick C. Keely, virtually the house architect for the Roman Catholic Church, on the interior of the Church of the Immaculate Conception (1858) for the Jesuit order in the South End; the barrel-vaulted design of the two basilicas bears this out. The Immaculate Conception equaled the Arlington Street Church in interior scale, having a sham coffered barrel vault and groin-vaulted aisles in plaster behind its giant Ionic colonnade. However, by way of contrast, here there was an elaborate sculptural program of plaster statuary and mural painting. These decorations established a new Roman baroque standard for the Catholic Church and, with plaster vaults, lengthened the odds against New England's producing the new champions of Pugin's *True Principles*.[39]

The Roman Catholic Church was relatively isolated from the mainstream of the American architectural profession when Patrick C. Keely, the son of a builder from Thurles, Ireland, emigrated to New York in 1842, just at the point when an enormous demand for church-building for the expanding Catholic constituency arose.[40] From this point onward, Keely effectively became the architect of choice for the Roman Catholic Church in North America, designing more than six hundred churches from Charleston to Nova Scotia, plus institutionally associated buildings, including twenty cathedrals throughout the Northeast.[41] Effectively ignored by the *American*

Fig. 10-7. Our Lady of Perpetual Help, Roxbury, Boston; designed by Edward Welby Pugin, Schickel & Ditmars; constructed 1873–78; photographed in 1910.

Architect and Building News (the primary journal of the American architectural profession that commenced publication in Boston in 1875), Keely was nonetheless thought to be the busiest architect in the United States at the height of his career, with as many as fifty projects in his New York office at once.[42] With such a practice, he necessarily relied on standard plans, often with a simple, hall-church arrangement, allowing for large congregations and using local builders for erection. Although Keely favored a diluted Puginian Gothic style, drawn largely from publications, he produced a less substantial, more fragile sort of design, with tall square or octagonal nave piers carrying thin attached shafts up to a plaster ceiling, rather than retaining the short heavy piers, low chamfered nave arcade and timber roof favored by the Pugins. Keely was also required to design Roman basilicas.[43] Fifteen years after completion of the Church of the Immaculate

Fig. 10-8. Church of the Sacred Heart, East Cambridge, MA; designed by Patrick W. Ford; constructed 1873–83. (Society for the Preservation of New England Antiquities)

The well-publicized demand for churches and church furnishings in America must have stimulated E. W. Pugin's decision to leave for America in 1873, after he had been forced into bankruptcy through his speculation on the failed Granville Hotel at Ramsgate.[46] He stayed but a year in America, returning to die at Ramsgate on June 10, 1875, and his objectives in setting up an office at Brevort House, 5th Avenue, in New York, with J. W. Walter are still unclear. Noted in his obituary are orders for thirty American churches in Washington, Chicago, and elsewhere, some of which may have been for altarpieces or decorative programs that the busy Patrick Keely had little time to design, and others possibly for entire buildings. Like the spectacular altar at the Church of the Sacred Heart of Jesus (1873–82) in East Cambridge, Massachusetts, many would have been implemented by E. W.'s brother Peter Paul Pugin whose sketchbook records some tantalizing information. He arranged a series of appointments in Boston with key individuals, including Archbishop John J. Williams.[47] Although his work in New England and elsewhere in America

Conception, Keely's Gothic Cathedral of the Holy Cross (1861–73) in Boston was dedicated with great ceremony, the same year that E. W. Pugin evidently came to New York.[44] With Gothic details drawn from Puginian precedents of twenty years before, Keely's design for the cathedral reflected little of the High Victorian Gothic of the 1860s.[45]

Fig. 10-9. Sectional drawing of the chancel, Church of the Sacred Heart, by Peter Paul Pugin; pen and ink, 1882. (Sacred Heart Archives)

Fig. 10-10. Altar, Church of the Sacred Heart, by Peter Paul Pugin, 1882. (Sacred Heart Archives)

Fig. 10-11. Stone carving (detail), Church of the Sacred Heart; designed by Peter Paul Pugin; executed by R. L. Boulton, Cheltenham, England.

remains to be fully researched, we know that Peter Paul met Revd. Peter Rownan, rector at Saint Peter's Church, Meetinghouse Hill, in Dorchester (fig. 10-6). The cornerstone for this Keely-designed church was laid on August 24, 1873, so that Pugin's role is unclear.[48] Pugin consulted with Father Boniface Bragadini of the Franciscan Order, pastor of the Italian congregation, regarding Saint Leonard's of Port Maurice, a small chapel on Prince Street in Boston's North End. P. P. Pugin may also have received a commission through Father Boniface for a Franciscan friary in the North End, also now destroyed.

Two Boston commissions are of particular interest. While the marble altar for the Church of the Sacred Heart is by far the Pugins' finest work in the Boston area, E. W. Pugin apparently furnished the first designs for the Redemptorist mission, Our Lady of Perpetual Help, a stone basilica in Roxbury, one of the largest and most impressive Roman Catholic churches in Boston

Fig. 10-12. Church of the Advent, Brimmer Street, Boston; designed by John Hubbard Sturgis; constructed 1874–88. (Archives, Church of the Advent)

Fig. 10-13. West Door, Church of the Advent, Boston; designed by John Hubbard Sturgis.

(fig. 10-7).[49] The Romanesque Basilica of Our Lady of Perpetual Help featured an octagonal lantern and dome, 110 feet high at the crossing, combining round-arched openings with Puginian Gothic detail.[50] The exterior trim reflects a lack of architectural stone sculptors in Boston, with the Norman moldings and rose window having flat machine-made surfaces. An easily executed round-arched corbel table accents the eaves, dome, and the tower base, and simple Romanesque capitals without carving appear on the arcade above the entrance portal and the drum of the dome. The entrance is more Puginian, with Norman moldings, good hinges, doors with revealed construction, and round arches beneath the central gable that have a slightly pointed profile defining the flat face of the voussoirs.[51] The round-arched basilican plan, with semicircular apse and central crossing dome, combines a nave colonnade of red and gray polished marble shafts, 21 feet high with foliate capitals and Puginian stenciling of the groin-vaulted aisles. Corbeled pilasters run from the colonnade past the round-arched triforium, meeting the Gothic ribs of a plaster vault above. The same dual style distinguishes the dome, where the ribs spring from foliate corbels.[52]

Meanwhile, in 1866, architect Patrick W. Ford emigrated from Ireland, having completed his university studies at Queen's College at Cork earlier that year. He settled in New York, perhaps working with Keely, then moved to establish offices at 3 School Street in Boston in 1873, following a short period in Worcester, Massachusetts, working with E. Boyden, its most prominent local architect.[53] From this time onward until his death in 1900, Patrick Ford would effectively assume the role of architect for the Roman Catholic Church in Boston that had been handled by Keely from New York between the time of his first church in 1851 and the completion of the Cathedral of the Holy Cross (1861–73), on which Ford may have assisted. Ford's first independent commission appears to have been for the Church of the Sacred Heart of Jesus in East Cambridge (1873–83), the oldest Catholic parish in the city. Ford's church (fig. 10-8) was Puginian in inspiration, incorporating a single roof with an unarticulated chancel, as in E. W. Pugin's designs. With his residency in Cork, Ford may have known E. W. Pugin's Saints Peter and Paul (1859–66), completed in the year in which he finished at Queen's College.

The asymmetrical, 170-foot tower with its broach spire and pinnacles is perhaps the finest feature of the design, with double-doorway variations on the Puginian theme, and with the aisles articulated to either side by separate doors in the tower and facade. With walls of Somerville blue slate and Milford granite trim, the exterior of the church is restrained if not awkward. The gables above the entrance are thin and linear in comparison to the robust designs of A. W. N. Pugin. The interior deviates from Puginian standards in the manner of P. C. Keely, with tall thin clustered nave piers. Describing the church at the time of dedication, Ford pointed out that galleries had not originally been planned, but pressure imposed by the growing size of the congregation led to their introduction behind the slender nave piers before construction was completed. The roof was subdivided by six exposed walnut trusses with ribs coupled to each pier and the spandrels of the trusses filled with Gothic tracery. The plaster was elaborately stenciled and decorated in gold leaf and buff on a Puginian scheme, and large plaster statues from Paris were introduced above the nave piers at the springing of the vaults. The placement of the Sacred Heart altar in the square-ended chancel of Ford's building appears in a plan and sectional drawing by Peter Paul Pugin (fig. 10-9) showing the large stained-glass window by Hardman, which was installed behind the altar by the time of the dedication in 1883. The chancel decorations in gold and brilliant colors were executed as projected by Ford and the Pugins.

The thirty-eight-foot-high altar, by far the most magnificent in Boston at that time, was designed by P. P. Pugin and carved by Boulton at Cheltenham, England (fig. 10-10). With its central jeweled tabernacle and crucifix, twelve alabaster pinnacles, and polished marble columns, it was fully the equal of those being produced for contemporaneous English ecclesiastical interiors.[54]

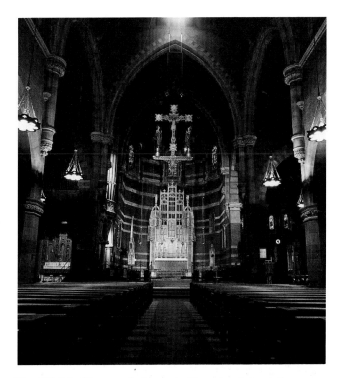

Fig. 10-14. Nave and chancel, Church of the Advent, Boston; designed by John Hubbard Sturgis; reredos by George & Peto, 1890; rood crucifix by Ralph Adams Cram, 1924.

Fig. 10-15. Rood screen, Church of the Advent; designed by John Hubbard Sturgis, 1883; drawing by Harold E. Kebbon, 1911. (Archives, Church of the Advent)

Fig. 10-16. Lady Chapel, Church of the Advent; designed by John Hubbard Sturgis; constructed 1874–76; altar and furnishings designed by Ralph Adams Cram, 1892, and executed by sculptors Kirchmayer and Lualdi.

The throne of the monstrance on the reredos above is located centrally in the altarpiece, and is of Devonshire alabaster. The foliate ornament of the throne is specifically botanical in character, rather than being stylized as the Puginian canopy above. The characteristic undercutting and accompanying naturalism appear in the "sanctus" and tympanum (fig. 10-11). The equation of preciousness of materials with liturgical significance is even more apparent in the brass repoussé door (see fig. 10-1) of the tabernacle inset with quartz gems, executed by Hardman and Company. Few altars of such elaboration were installed in America by 1883. In 1877, the English architect, Frederick C. Withers, designed an altar in memory of William Backhouse Astor (owner of the Rokeby library) for Trinity Church in New York City, noted later as the only altar more elaborate than that at Sacred Heart.[55]

In 1883, Henry Vaughan, another English architect, took a first step toward integrating English decorative arts with American resources in a spectacular altarpiece for Richard Upjohn's Saint Stephen's Church in Providence, Rhode Island. Here, the carving was by John Evans and Toombs, who were preeminent in Boston, and the assembly of the altarpiece was through Irving and Casson, another Boston firm, who were emerging as a new woodwork and carving resource for the ecclesiastical field. Twenty feet high and in seventeen compartments, the paintings in Vaughan's altarpiece were executed by Roger Watts, an artist associated with Pugin's John Hardman firm in England.[56]

The round-arched inner spaces of H. H. Richardson's Trinity Church, Copley Square (1872–77), Boston, expressed the non-Tractarian direction of the American Episcopal Church toward an expanded *Rundbogenstil*. For a while thereafter, ecclesiastical design for all denominations followed this liturgical directive. Meanwhile, at the Anglican Church of the Advent, the flame of Puginian principles burned brightly with plans for a new church (fig. 10-12). The timing of these events was fortuitous, for the communicant selected as architect for the new building, John Hubbard Sturgis, was at that time guiding the erection of his Museum of Fine Arts on Copley Square (1870–76).[57] It was the first public art museum in America, the design, collections, and program of which embodied the decorative arts spirit of the South Kensington museum in London (forerunner of the Victoria & Albert). Sturgis took frequent trips to England, where he had spent five years prior to winning the museum commission in 1870, and he, perhaps better than any other American architect, knew the work of Pugin's followers, G. E. Street, William Butterfield, James Brooks, John L. Pearson, and others whose work was illustrated in Charles Eastlake's new book, *The Gothic Revival* (1872). Educated in London in the 1850s, Sturgis was intimately familiar with Puginian dogma and ecclesiology, although he embraced the advances of Pugin's successors. He was never as liturgically bound as Pugin, yet he envisioned a mission to express an Anglican liturgical program in the building, through both its form and decorative arts. Thus the Church of the Advent was established as a junction point for bringing together the highest-quality liturgical arts in Boston.

The most impressive aspect of Sturgis's finest design is his creativity in synthesizing the latest architectural ideas from London to produce a distinguished, in several respects unique, and eminently English structure on an extremely small and awkward site, within a limited budget for a small congregation. While the Advent is not based on any individual English church, Sturgis's trip in the late summer and fall of 1875, after his appointment by the parish as architect, involved detailed examination of the best recent ecclesiastical architecture in England. The astonishing success of his solution derives from his application of Puginian principles, the organic plan and the audacious use of ornament against the bare walls. The finely laid red brick of the sheer exterior is drawn largely from the new London churches of James Brooks, particularly Saint Saviour's, Hoxton (1864), being far less ornamental than the exteriors of buildings by William Butterfield or G. E.

Street.[58] Brooks's inexpensive wooden vaulting at Saint Chad's, Hagerstown, and Saint Andrew's, Plaistow, were models for the Advent church interior, where stone vaulting was likewise eschewed, thereby eliminating any need of buttressing.

The challenge of the Church of the Advent site produced a plan like that of no other church, reflecting sophisticated ingenuity. The exterior of the church is of banded brick, closely laid up, and the sheer octagonal form of the apse and the low rounded Lady Chapel with the south porch and projecting library create a unique triangular plan that fully exploits its restricted site. Sturgis's design shares much of Pugin's vision; the irregularity and simplicity of the plan create an "accumulation of masses" on Mount Vernon Street.[59] His design methodology was likewise Puginian. The west porch of the Advent was inspired by the north porch at Wells Cathedral, a photograph of which was in Sturgis's collection, but in execution it was never surmounted by the huge crucifix that Sturgis projected in his initial sketches to encom-

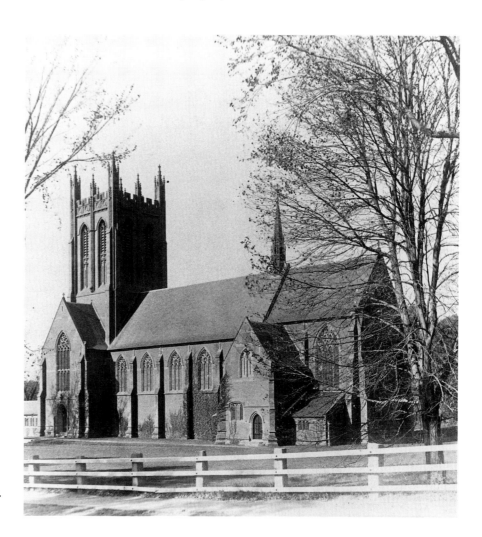

Fig. 10-17. Chapel of Saints Peter and Paul, Saint Paul's School, Concord, New Hampshire; designed by Henry Vaughan, 1890. (Archives, Saint Paul's School)

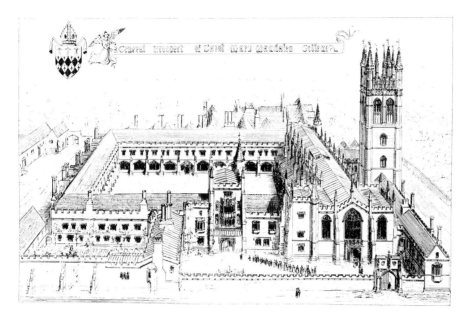

Fig. 10-18. "A General Prospect of Saint Mary Magdalen College," by A. W. N. Pugin. From Pugin, *The True Principles of Pointed or Christian Architecture* (London, 1941), pl. 9.

pass the entire west gable.[60] The metalwork of the great hinges and the wooden doors of the Church of the Advent (fig. 10-13) confirm Sturgis's Puginian proclivities, yet the design is unique in combining a bold Norman zigzag molding with intense foliate ornament personal to Sturgis.[61]

On the interior, an illusion of great length was created by canted walls at the crossing (fig. 10-14), devices employed by G. E. Street at the Church of Saints Phillip and James, Oxford (1862). The extraordinary richness and muscular nature of the crashing corbeled columns at the crossing derive from Street's work, particularly at Saint Mary Magdalen, Paddington (1867), and Saint James the Less, Westminster (1859). The brilliantly colored voussoirs, low heavy piers, and sheer pointed nave arcade create an effect that is startlingly similar to E. W. Pugin's All Saints, Barton-upon-Irwell, Manchester (1865). The intensity of ornament reaches a climax at the apse, where huge polygonal walls rise to high stained-glass windows, smaller than any designed by Brooks, and are banded in flush-laid limestone to achieve brilliant polychromy.[62] Flanked by a Lady Chapel to the south and the Chapel of All Saints to the north, the arched east end of the Advent church was made more spectacular by the introduction of Ruskinian polychromy in the chancel, striped in limestone and finely laid red brick, the first church in Boston to be so exposed on the interior.

Polychromatic and spectacular as it is, the sheer brick walls of the Advent interior serve as a foil for the decorative arts that complete the chancel. The interior and exterior carving of the Advent was completed by the Scottish sculptor, John Evans, by 1883, when the first services were held in the completed church.[63] Evans may also have carved the lower section of the Advent altar, which Sturgis designed. This was augmented in 1890 by a huge reredos carved in England after the designs of Harold Peto of George & Peto as a gift from Isabella Stewart Gardner.[64] By 1883, the Advent interior was largely completed when Sturgis designed a wrought-iron Puginian rood screen (fig. 10-15) that spanned the Minton-tiled floor below the chancel arch. With a central Crucifixion, the screen is detailed directly from Pugin's *True Principles*.

The Lady Chapel at the Advent (fig. 10-16) is a multifaceted symbol. The apsidial space with its timber half dome was finished during the second Ruskinian phase of the Gothic Revival at the time of John Sturgis's death in 1888; by 1894 it had been transformed by Ralph Adams Cram into an intimate space filled with liturgical art.[65] Cram worked at the Advent with another communicant, Henry Vaughan, who had practiced in England with George Bodley, coming to Boston in 1881 to design the Chapel for the Sisters of Saint Margaret and, by 1883, his great altarpiece in Providence.[66]

Vaughan brought the experience of a top-level English practice, which he applied to the guidance and development of young Cram who, during the furnishing of the chapel at the Advent, designed his first and one of his greatest churches, All Saints, Ashmont (1892), a return to Puginian ideals. All Saints would initiate the third, Neo-Gothic stage of the American Gothic Revival. For Sturgis, Cram, and Vaughan, the Gothic style provided spiritual means to creative design. Following Sturgis's pioneering work of the 1870s and 1880s, his successors Vaughan and Cram redefined the Gothic presence significantly by the turn of the century. The Puginian principles of control of ornament and concern for organic form that highlighted Sturgis's emphasis on decorative arts work completed a bridge to the new Society of Arts and Crafts that was established in Boston by 1897. The influence of the Anglican constituency grew from here, stimulated by Cram, an author, lecturer, and polemicist as well as architect, whose Gothic objectives were comparable to Pugin's.[67]

Meanwhile, the effect of H. H. Richardson's Romanesque masterpiece, Trinity Church, Copley Square, would dissipate surprisingly quickly in the late 1880s. The competitions for the Cathedral of Saint John the Divine, New York City, to which Vaughan was invited (but politely declined), provide a measure of American architecture in 1889, a few years after the death of Richardson.[68] Oddly enough, both Cram's entry and the design submitted by Cram's future partner, Bertram Grosvenor Goodhue, who had been practicing in the office of Renwick, Aspinwall and Russell in New York, were Romanesque.[69] Writing in 1937, Cram recalled the competition, labeling his own youthful design as "a brazen echo of H. H. Richardson" and noting that ecclesiastical architecture at that time was at its lowest ebb since the early nineteenth century.[70] Cram also recalled the subsequent triumph of Gothic ecclesiastical and college work for a generation that he, more than any other, had implemented. With his personality and his multiple accomplishments, but particularly his attitude, Cram's profile was amazingly Puginian. In America, this later phase of the Gothic Revival bypassed the Roman Catholic Church, springing instead from the Anglican Church of the Advent.

Yet Cram's Gothic mission aimed far beyond, in all denominational directions, with academic as well as ecclesiastical ambitions.[71] By 1904, the specter of the Romanesque would die and, while classicism ushered in by the 1893 World's Columbian Exposition in Chicago would continue to thrive in public building and domestic design, the Gothic would triumph in both academic and ecclesiastical venues. By 1904, Vaughan and Bodley, with a re-instituted partnership, won the competition for Washington's National Cathedral, the nation's great ecclesiastical symbol, which would be executed over the next eight decades by Robb, Frohman and Little. Its recent dedication serves as a reminder of the triumph of Pugin's Gothic principles recast for an American architectural mission. Then in 1911, Cram, Goodhue and Ferguson would take over the Cathedral of Saint John the Divine and redesign it in Gothic form.[72]

Fig. 10-19. Chapel of Saints Peter and Paul, Saint Paul's School, Concord; designed by Henry Vaughan, 1890; reredos by Vaughan, 1894; paintings by Clayton & Bell; carving by Kirchmayer, Irving & Casson, Boston. (Archives, Saint Paul's School)

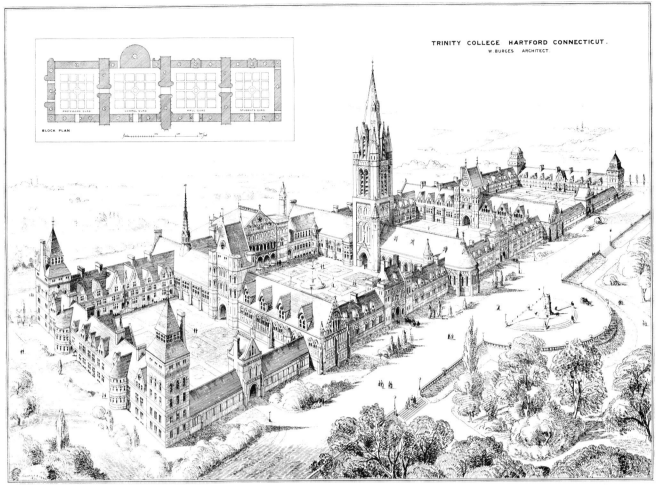

Fig. 10-20. Trinity College, Hartford, Connecticut; designed by William Burges, 1873. From *The Building News* (April 17, 1874).

The American boarding school began to be established in the later nineteenth century, with English public schools as models and usually with an ecclesiastical directive.[73] Although many new campuses were classical in style, the association of the Gothic style with rural sites for the new school and university campuses fostered yet another Puginian inspiration for America.[74] That John Ruskin felt obliged to overlook Pugin's earlier innovation only enhances Pugin's stature as a seminal artist and, more importantly, renders more astute Pugin's grasp of underlying principles that invigorate the design of communities with combinations of buildings planned together.[75] Throughout his work, the use of eighteenth-century landscape views, which he collected in large numbers, produced a concept of architecture which, unlike Ruskin's, did not focus on isolated details or on portions of a building, but rather on buildings in groups.[76] Pugin's Catholic Town of

1440, illustrated in *Contrasts*, and the frontispiece to his *Apology for Christian Architecture*, and even his own home and buildings at Ramsgate were envisioned as complexes, rather than as isolated structures. Even in his ecclesiastical commissions, the auxiliary buildings were part of a larger design concept. Thus, when the problem of the American boarding school arose, it was to Pugin's drawings, readily available through his publications, that architects turned, rather than the artistic expressions of John Ruskin, whose day was ending by the late 1880s.

When Henry Vaughan designed the Chapel of Saints Peter and Paul (fig. 10-17) for Saint Paul's School in Concord, New Hampshire, in 1890, he clearly had Pugin's magnificent depiction of Magdalen College (fig. 10-18) at Oxford and his *True Principles* in mind. On the interior of Saint Paul's School chapel (fig. 10-19), later to be enlarged by Cram, the model of the British colleges re-emerges with Vaughan's hand guided by Pugin's vision that was rooted in his study of colleges with his father.[77] The high choir seats, timber roof, and stained-glass window provide an appropriate setting for Vaughan's carved reredos, one of the most notable altars in America, fully equal to comparable designs in Britain.[78]

In college and university architecture, Pugin's bird's-eye perspective drawings of medieval complexes achieved more widespread realization in America than in England. Pugin and Barry's planning for the Houses of Parliament in London in the 1830s had an impact on many large-scale projects, such as the Law Courts in London. William Burges, a disciple of Pugin admired by H. H. Richardson, reapplied Pugin's collegiate principles at Trinity College, Hartford (1873), which, though incomplete, was America's earliest Puginian Gothic campus (fig. 10-20).[79] In America, no medieval university had ever existed and the remaining academic architecture was classical until the nineteenth century. Notwithstanding the stimulation of classicism provided by the World's Columbian Exposition of 1893 and the rising new interest in Thomas Jefferson's campus for the University of Virginia (1816–26), the long-standing association of the Gothic style with learning, with British education, and with nature that had been in place in the 1840s, re-emerged in a series of medieval quadrangled campuses throughout America.[80] Cram's designs for the United States Military Academy (1900) at West Point seem to grow organically from the landscape. The compound of attached Gothic buildings with their high buttressed walls of stone re-create the urban vision of Pugin drawings. On scores of American campuses, other architects adapted the Gothic quadrangle. In 1911, the chapel at West Point was being completed, as Saint Thomas's Church in New York City opened, and as Cram, Goodhue and Ferguson took over responsibility for the Cathedral of Saint John the Divine. That same year the Graduate School at Princeton was designed by Cram, Goodhue and Ferguson as from a Puginian bird's-eye perspective. Inspired by *True Principles*, the famous

Magdalen Tower at Oxford rises again at one corner of a quadrangle. The relationships of parts, of scale, and of proportion combine to implement Pugin's vision of an "accumulation of masses" that creates the illusion of a hallowed enclave.

1. For an undated sketchbook by Peter Paul Pugin recording numerous addresses in America, see Alexandra Wedgwood, "Pugin Family" in *Catalogues of the Architectural Drawings in the Victoria and Albert Museum: A. W. N. Pugin and the Pugin Family* (London, 1985), no. 1098, p. 316, and pl. 94, illustrating the sketch plan and elevation of the altar for the Roman Catholic Church of the Sacred Heart in East Cambridge, MA. Clive Wainwright discovered the sketchbook and made it available to the author with insightful comment drawn from his exhaustive study of the Pugins.

2. William H. Pierson, *American Buildings and Their Architects* (Garden City, NY, 1978), vol. 2, pp. 231–42.

3. A. W. N. Pugin, *The True Principles of Pointed or Christian Architecture* (1841), reprint (New York, 1973), pp. 72–73.

4. William Morgan, *The Almighty Wall: The Architecture of Henry Vaughan* (New York and Cambridge, MA, 1983), pp. 73–88, 176–177 nn. 42–45.

5. See "The Picturesque and the Gothic Revival," in Henry Russell Hitchcock, *Architecture: 19th and 20th Centuries* (Baltimore, 1958), pp. 93–114.

6. Phoebe B. Stanton, *The Gothic Revival & American Church Architecture* (Baltimore, 1968), passim.

7. Roderick O'Donnell, "The Later Pugins" in Paul Atterbury and Clive Wainwright, eds., *Pugin: A Gothic Passion* (London and New Haven, 1994), p. 300, nn. 57–58. For a description of E. W. Pugin's trip and allusions to some as yet unlocated commissions, see the *Irish Builder* (June 15, 1875), quoting from the *Kent Argus*. See also *Financial Ledger: 1 June 1873–1 January 1890* (archives, Church of the Sacred Heart, Cambridge, MA), pp. 111–13. Peter Paul Pugin's trip to America is undated, but probably occurred in 1880 or 1881 because payment to Pugin & Pugin for shipping of the completed altar for the Church of the Sacred Heart in East Cambridge took place in the fall of 1882.

8. Douglass Shand-Tucci, *Church Building in Boston* (Boston, 1974), pp. 48–114.

9. Michael McCarthy, *The Origins of the Gothic Revival* (New Haven and London, 1987), passim.

10. For a further discussion of the Oxford Movement, see chapter 3.

11. Stanton, *The Gothic Revival*, p. 185. Richard Upjohn arrived in 1829, followed by Frank Wills in 1848, Calvert Vaux in 1850, Henry Dudley in 1851, and John Notman.

12. Everard M. Upjohn, *Richard Upjohn: Architect and Churchman* (New York, 1968), passim.

13. Howard Colvin, "Augustus Charles Pugin (1769–1832)," in *A Biographical Dictionary of British Architects 1600–1840* (New York, 1978), pp. 667–68; Augustus Charles Pugin, *Gothische Ornamente. Einzelheiten der Berühmtesten Baudenkmäler Des Mittelalters in Frankreich und England*, Aufgenommen und gezeichnet von A. Pugin, Architekt (Berlin & New York, ca. 1897), passim.

14. Stanton, *The Gothic Revival*, passim.

15. Pierson, *American Buildings*, vol. 2, pp. 149–205.

16. Stanton, *The Gothic Revival*, pp. 133–53. Wills, an architect who worked with William Butterfield, went first to Canada to design St. Anne's Chapel, Fredericton (1846).

17. A. J. Downing, *The Architecture of Country Houses*, (New York, 1969), p. 484.

18. "Papers of Franklin Hughes Delano," Franklin D. Roosevelt Library (Hyde Park, NY). For definition and discussion of the *Rundbogenstil*, the round-arched romanesque style popular in German, in the 1830s and 1840s, see Hitchcock, *Architecture*, pp. 27–28.

19. William H. Pierson, "Richard Upjohn and the American Rundbogenstil," *Winterthur Portfolio* 21 (Winter 1986), pp. 223–42.

20. O'Donnell, "The Later Pugins," pp. 259–71; John F. Byrne, *The Glories of Mary in Boston, A Memorial History of the Church of Our Lady of Perpetual Help, 1871–1921* (Roxbury, MA, 1921), pp. 82–97, 100–103.

21. Amelia Peck, ed., *Alexander Jackson Davis, American Architect 1803–1892* (New York, 1992), passim.

22. Pierson, *American Buildings*, vol. 2, pp. 300–48.

23. McCarthy, *Origins*, pp. 105–15.

24. Lately Thomas, *A Pride of Lions: The Astor Orphans, The Chanler Chronicle* (New York, 1971), pp. 7–10. J. Winthrop Aldrich has kindly shared much information on Rokeby with me.

25. Peck, *Alexander Jackson Downing*, pp. 109–15; Upjohn, *Richard Upjohn*, pp. 215, 224. Davis made several designs for W. B. Astor, including Colorplate 21, The Astor Library, New York City (1830); Colorplate 33, Study for Astor Library (1843). In 1853, Davis designed additions for Robert Donaldson in Rhinebeck, NY, and an octagonal cottage. Upjohn designed Christ Church in Red Hook, NY, in 1854, for which W. B. Astor paid the construction cost; and Ellerslie (1846–47) for William Kelly in Rhinebeck, NY.

26. Thomas, *Pride of Lions*, p. 9. The house at Rokeby, originally named La Bergerie (1812–15), had been designed in Paris for Astor's father-in-law, John Armstrong, a United States emissary, and was erected after his return to New York in 1811. The Neoclassical symmetry and rationalism of this structure contrasts with the Romantic Gothic detailing of the later library interior, which embodies the essence of the American Gothic style. Margaret Armstrong Astor renamed La Bergerie, fancying a resemblance between the terrain along the Hudson and a glen described in Sir Walter Scott's poem, "Rokeby."

27. Pierson, *American Buildings*, vol. 2, pp. 49–50, 422–31. In his chapel for New York University (1837), A. J. Davis had aligned the Gothic style with academic architecture twenty years earlier, with vaulting seemingly drawn from Walpole's flamboyant Strawberry Hill interiors, Saint George's Chapel, Windsor, and other published sources that had been models for A. W. N. Pugin's earlier Gothic designs. Pugin would disavow the flamboyant period in "Illustration of the extravagant style of modern Gothic furniture and decoration," in *True Principles* (1841) as his understanding of the Gothic matured (ibid., p. 49). But Davis, who never went to England, would still re-apply the eighteenth-century Strawberry Hill cardboard Gothic style at the Wadsworth Atheneum (1844) in Hartford, CT. See Carrie Rebora, "Alexander Jackson Davis and the Arts of Design," in Peck, ed., *Alexander Jackson Davis*, pp. 36–38.

28. The 1856 edition of Downing, *Architecture of Country Houses*, was dedicated to Downing's friend and neighbor, Henry Winthrop Sargent, of Wodenethe on the Hudson; see Cynthia Zaitzevsky, *Frederick Law Olmsted and the Boston Park System* (Cambridge, MA, 1982), p. 58. Charles Sprague Sargent, Director of Harvard's Arnold Arboretum, was deeply involved in New York landscape developments.

29. Jonathan N. Pearlman, "The Architecture of George Minot Dexter: Link from Bulfinch to the Back Bay," honors thesis (Medford, MA, 1980); idem, "George M. Dexter (1802–1872): Porch for David Sears House (Red Cross Cottage), Red Cross Street, Newport, 1843–44," in William H. Jordy and Christopher P. Monkhouse, eds., *Buildings on Paper: Rhode Island Architectural Drawings 1825–1945* (Providence, 1982), p. 59; idem, "George M. Dexter: Project for a House, Newport, Ca. 1845," in *Buildings on Paper*, pp. 59–60. Trained in Germany as an engineer, Dexter emerged in the 1840s, a period of comparatively little construction in Boston, as one of its most prominent architects. The sophisticated restraint manifested in the Gothic forms of Cottage Farm reflects Dexter's wide knowledge of architectural publications, many of which he had been commissioned to purchase for the Boston Athenaeum before his return from Europe in 1831.

30. Arthur J. Krim, "Francis Peabody and Gothic Salem," *Peabody Essex Museum Collections* 130, no. 1 (January 1994), figs. 4, 5; Phillips Brooks, "The Episcopal Church," in Justin Winsor, ed., *Memorial History of Boston*, 4 vols. (Boston, 1881), vol. 3, pp. 447–66. The comparative uniformity and repetitive character of the early New England Gothic church in stone and its lack of ecclesiological accuracy is pronounced. St. John's on Bowdoin Street is a near cousin

of both Salem churches and the old Trinity Church on Washington Street that burned in the Boston fire of 1872. Exterior stone carving was extremely rare.

31. William Stevens Perry, *The History of the American Episcopal Church, 1587–1883*, 2 vols. (Boston, 1885), pp. 176–87.

32. Bainbridge Bunting and Margaret Henderson Floyd, *Harvard: An Architectural History* (Cambridge, MA, 1985), pp. 43–49. Richard Upjohn's Chapel at Bowdoin College (1845–55) was contemporary with Paul Shultze's Appleton Chapel (1844) at Harvard University. The easy interface between the Gothic and *Rundbogenstil* is demonstrated in Harvard Yard, where Richard Bond's granite Gore Library (1838–41), like A. J. Davis's Wadsworth Atheneum (1842–44) in Hartford, aligned the mission of education with the Gothic style. Across Harvard Square, Isaiah Rogers' contemporary First Parish Church, Cambridge (1833–34), was a charming wooden version of the Gothic style. All of these stray far from the high Puginian standards of the mid-Atlantic region at mid-century; they serve to underscore the long odds against New England's ever assuming the role of progenitor for Pugin's spiritual rebirth and ultimate triumph.

33. Margaret Henderson Floyd, "Gilman, Arthur Delavan," in Adolf K. Placzek, ed., *Macmillan Encyclopedia of Architects* (New York, 1982), vol. 2, pp. 208–10.

34. Arthur Delavan Gilman, "Architecture in the United States," *North American Review*, 58 (April 1844), pp. 436–80.

35. Minard Lafever, *The Modern Builder's Guide* (1833), reprint (New York, 1969); "Arthur D. Gilman to Richard Upjohn," Upjohn Papers, Box 1 (Boston, Thursday, April 10, 1845), New York Public Library Manuscripts and Archives Division. Professor William H. Pierson kindly drew this letter to my attention. Gilman's Puginian churches were: Saint Paul's, Dedham; a church in Bath, Maine; and the Romanesque Harrison Avenue Congregational Church, Boston.

36. Henry Winthrop Sargent, supplement to sixth ed., A. J. Downing, *A Treatise on the Theory and Practice of Landscape Gardening* (New York, 1859), pp. 442–47.

37. Bainbridge Bunting, *Houses of Boston's Back Bay* (Cambridge, MA, 1967), pp. 162–63. Earle Shettleworth owns Bryant's copy of *Contrasts* and kindly drew this information to my attention.

38. For a discussion of Gibbs and Peter Harrison, see Pierson, *American Buildings*, vol. 1, pp. 111–56.

39. Leslie Larson, "Boston Churches Designed by Patrick Charles Keely (1816–1896)," Tour Notes, National Trust for Historic Preservation (Boston, October 26, 1994), pp. 19–23. Gilman's involvement with Keely is still lacking in documentation but is strongly supported by the grandiose design of the interior of the Immaculate Conception that is so closely related to the Arlington Street Church in style, unlike either Keely's earlier designs or the work of others in Boston. Bryant and Gilman likewise designed the pavilioned and mansarded Boston City Hospital adjacent to the site in 1862–66, and Gilman was particularly concerned with issues of urban design, so that his involvement with the Immaculate Conception as part of a larger plan seems highly likely. The mural painting featured the Crucifixion by Garialdi of Rome and paintings of Saint Joseph and Saint Aloysius by Constantine Brumidi, who was then doing the United States Capitol interior decorations.

40. Leslie Larson has kindly shared his research on Keely with me. Although Keely apparently had little architectural training in Ireland, he completed his first American church by 1846 and in 1849 was asked by Archbishop McClusky to design a cathedral at Albany, New York.

41. "Obituary: P. C. Keely," *Boston Evening Transcript* (August 13, 1896).

42. "Obituary: P. C. Keely," *American Architect and Building News* (August 22, 1896).

43. This non-ecclesiological approach may well explain the involvement of Arthur Gilman as designer of the high baroque interior of the Jesuit's Immaculate Conception in 1858, for Keely did little interior design.

44. Winsor, ed., *Memorial History of Boston*, vol. 3, p. 544.

45. Charles Eastlake, *A History of the Gothic Revival* (1872), reprint (Deposit, NY, 1975). Busy with his American practice, Keely apparently did little to keep up with successors to A. W. N. Pugin in England and Ireland, as did E. W. Pugin. Rather, it was the Anglican Episcopal constituency in America that absorbed new ideas, including those of John Ruskin.

46. O'Donnell, "The Later Pugins," pp. 259–71.

47. James S. Sullivan, ed., *A Graphic, Historical, and Pictorial Account of the Catholic Church of New England Archdiocese of Boston* (Boston and Portland, 1895), pp. 130–32, 158–59. Although the pace of construction of Catholic churches in America was escalating in the early 1870s, it seems certain that E. W.'s stay was too brief to have widespread impact. The severe economic depression of the mid-1870s may have curtailed some projects, and no identifiable body of work has yet been brought together. Peter Paul's undated later trip to America remains a mystery.

48. Leslie Larson informs me that Saint Peter's is the only one of Keely's Boston churches to have a heavy hammerbeam trussed roof, a true Puginian detail.

49. Byrne, *Glories of Mary*, p. 48. Our Lady of Perpetual Help was founded by the Order of Christ the Redeemer (the Redemptorists), being thus a monastic foundation rather than a diocesan church. Shand-Tucci, *Church Building*, p. 38; Sullivan, ed., *Graphic, Historical, and Pictorial Account*,

pp. 155–56. The Basilica was attributed to Schickel & Ditmars of New York, who may well have been the architects executing E. W. Pugin's earlier designs. The German training of this firm could account for some of the anomalies of the Gothic-cum-Romanesque detail.

50. O'Donnell, "The Later Pugins," p. 268; For mention of a "church . . . for the Redemptorists at Brookline Boston with a central lantern 40′ square with an octagon above," see "Obituary: E. W. Pugin," *Irish Builder* (June 15, 1875). Since this Basilica is so well described, the placing of it in nearby Brookline, where no such structure has been identified, is presumed to be due to rearrangement of town boundaries in the nineteenth century. Pugin is also credited with the high altar, but church records suggest that the current altar is not original. See William Byrne et al., *History of the Catholic Church in the New England States* (Boston, 1899), pp. 147–49. The cornerstone was laid in 1873 and the building completed, save the towers, and opened in 1878. Its paired granite towers and an elaborate new rectory were added by Untersee in 1910, along with mission buildings and a school.

51. The tympana are defined by ribbon moldings and punctured by mixtelinear, baroque windows, suggesting the intervention of Schickel & Ditmars. Remaining in the doors and many of the upper windows is plain geometrical colored glass that apparently was original to the building, while the lower windows and most of the interior detailing have been replaced or elaborately modified.

52. Byrne et al., *History of the Catholic Church*, pp. 100–103, 166–80. Although later painted mural decoration has been introduced, fragments of the original stenciled patterns remain in the narthex, and on the staircase revealed construction that must have been part of the original design is exposed. The secondary altars have likewise been changed but the American-made pews, with Gothic quatrefoils, and the confessionals seem to be original from the 1870s. While details of the design are still undocumented, the Basilica demonstrates that the Gothic style was still alternating with the Romanesque in Boston, apparently appropriately for a parish that was Irish and German. See Kathleen Curran, "The German Rundbogenstil and Reflections on the American Round-arched Style," *Journal of the Society of Architectural Historians* 47 (December 1988), pp. 351–73.

53. "Architect P. W. Ford, 33 School Street," in *Leading Manufacturers and Merchants of the City of Boston* (Boston, 1885).

54. John Wright, *Some Notable Altars in the Church of England and the American Episcopal Church* (New York, 1908), passim; "A Beautiful Church," *Boston Post* (January 29, 1883); "Dedication of the Church of the Sacred Heart," *Cambridge Chronicle* (January 27, 1883) 1, col. 3; "Magnificent New Church: Dedication in East Cambridge, Mass.," *Pilot* (January 29, 1883).

55. Wright, *Some Notable Altars*, p. 247. The mosaic and statues were executed in London, the altar by Ellin & Kitson, New York.

56. Ibid., p. 335.

57. Margaret Henderson Floyd, "A Terra-Cotta Cornerstone for Copley Square: Museum of Fine Arts, Boston, by Sturgis and Brigham (1870–1876)," *Journal of the Society of Architectural Historians* 34 (December 1973), pp. 83–103.

58. Eastlake, *History of the Gothic Revival*, pp. 363–67. Brooks's work for the densely populated, poor London parishes often eliminated the stone vaulting that appeared regularly in more lavish English ecclesiastical design, and this aligned well with Boston.

59. Phoebe Stanton, *Pugin* (New York, 1971), pp. 160–61. The densely centripetal parts of the exterior of Sturgis's design create on Brimmer Street an environment not unlike that of Pugin's frontispiece for A. W. N. Pugin, *An Apology for a Work Entitled Contrasts: Being a Defence of the Assertions Advanced in That Publication Against the Various Attacks Lately Made Upon It* (Birmingham, England, 1837).

60. For Sturgis's sketch of the Advent, see *American Architect and Building News* I (May 27, 1876). See also Stanton, Pugin, p. 173 ill. The resulting door, while more ornamental, shares much of the feel of the Springhouse (1841–48), which Pugin designed at Oxenford Farm, Peper Harrow, for Lord Midleton.

61. During the 1850s, Sturgis had practiced in England with J. K. Colling, author of *Art Foliage* (1865), who indeed later worked for Sturgis on the Boston Museum. The Advent was begun in 1876 and was almost complete at Sturgis's death in 1888, but it was the building's function as a foil for the decorative arts that was so remarkable, because during that interval a remarkable group of sculptors and decorative artists would be assembled in Boston and, by 1890, liturgical decorative art of the highest level was being produced in America. No longer would it be necessary to order from Cheltenham an altar such as that at Sacred Heart.

62. Eastlake, *History of the Gothic Revival*, pp. 251–63. This treatment is clearly drawn from the exterior of William Butterfield's Keble College (1867) at Oxford, which was completed while Sturgis was living in England.

63. Ann Clifford, "John Evans (1847–1923) and Architectural Sculpture in Boston," masters thesis (Medford, MA, 1992). Evans had arrived in New York in the early 1870s and had been sent to Boston first by Ellin & Kitson of New York to execute the carving on the New Old South Church (1874) on Copley Square. This firm, a primary architectural sculpture provider, employed carvers in the more advanced New York area, and Evans's work at the New Old South Church would introduce the most important architectural sculptor of the later nineteenth century to Boston. Shortly, Evans also carved the facade of H. H. Richardson's Trinity Church.

64. A moving spirit in the heightened intensity of the decorative arts environment, Sturgis had designed and enlarged Mrs. Gardner's own house at 152 Beacon Street, in which were introduced numerous decorative and art display concepts, which were then re-applied by Mrs. Gardner at Fenway Court in 1900 (now the Isabella Stewart Gardner Museum). The focus of Sturgis in the decorative arts seems to have governed the establishment of a new generation of Gothic design that would be generated from the Advent.

65. *The Parish of the Advent in the City of Boston. A History of One Hundred Years, 1844–1944* (Boston, 1944), passim. The Baptistry, with Frank Wills's Gothic font (1850), and All Saints Chapel at the Advent were completed after Sturgis's death. Included in the All Saints Chapel were Wills's altar of 1850 with its notorious cross against a new reredos designed by Ralph Adams Cram, who also designed the altar, furnishings, and reredos for the southeastern Lady Chapel by 1894.

66. Morgan, *The Almighty Wall*, pp. 6–9. The Sisters of Saint Margaret was an order from East Grinstead in Sussex, who were invited to establish a convent in Boston by the Church of the Advent.

67. Shand-Tucci, *Church Building*, pp. 48–114. At the Advent itself, Vaughan designed a handsome carved pulpit and Clipston Sturgis the lectern, while the stained-glass windows were all made by Clayton and Bell in England under a program defined by John Sturgis, except those in the clerestory which were installed in 1910 after the designs of another English glass artist, Christopher Whall. The stained-glass school of Charles Connick in Boston sprang from Cram and his work at the Advent (much inspired by the glass there, and in a sense repeating the earlier relationship of Pugin with John Hardman and his company) and the sculpture of Boulton at Cheltenham that had produced the altar at the Church of the Sacred Heart in East Cambridge in 1882.

68. Florence Wood, *Memories of William Halsey Wood* (Philadelphia, ca. 1937), pp. 26–35. Of the sixty-seven entries (nine competitors were officially invited), four finalists were selected. Whereas the designs were roughly equally divided between the Gothic and Romanesque styles, the finalists were two Romanesque designs from Heins & LaFarge and Potter & Robinson, both of New York, one Gothic from Huff & Buck, also of New York, and a bold and extraordinarily suave design by William Halsey Wood, "Jerusalem the Golden," drawing inspiration from both Gothic and Romanesque and anticipating the future path of Goodhue in his move toward modernism.

69. Cathedral of Saint John the Divine, *Comparative designs for the Cathedral of St. John the Divine, New York* (Boston, n. d.), collected designs 1889–91; Richard Oliver, Bertram Grosvenor Goodhue (New York & Cambridge, MA, 1985), passim. Ralph Adams Cram had left his first architectural association with Rotch and Tilden, a local Boston firm, to submit a design on his own. He had formed a partnership with Charles Wentworth. Goodhue would join them by 1890.

70. Ralph Adams Cram, "Preface," in Wood, *Memories*, pp. 9–13.

71. Douglass Shand-Tucci, *Boston Bohemia 1881–1900*, vol. 1 (Ralph Adams Cram: Life & Architecture) (Amherst, MA, in press). Henry Vaughan, who had introduced Cram to the current English design of the 1880s, would never be a publicist as Cram became, maintaining a private practice for the balance of his life. Enhanced by the move of Bertram Goodhue to join Cram in 1890, bringing his dazzling delineation talents to the mission, the Boston Gothic movement coalesced around Cram at a time when the decorative arts were rising through the Museum of Fine Arts and other active Boston art circles. The market, means, and leadership for America's Gothic Quest were at hand in a broad way that had never obtained for Pugin.

72. Montgomery Schuyler, "The New St. Thomas' Church, New York" (1891), reprint in H. William Jordy and Ralph Coe, eds., *American Architecture and Other Writings by Montgomery Schuyler* (Cambridge, MA, 1961), pp. 598–604.

73. James McLachlan, *American Boarding Schools: A Historical Study* (New York, 1970), passim. See also Morgan, *The Almighty Wall*, pp. 89–116.

74. Pugin, *True Principles*, pp. 62–63.

75. Stanton, *Pugin*, pp. 151–66.

76. John Ruskin, *The Seven Lamps of Architecture* (New York, 1961), passim.

77. A. C. Pugin, *Gothische Ornamente*, passim.

78. Wright, *Some Notable Altars*, p. 330. Finished in 1894 with paintings by Clayton and Bell of London, the reredos was given in honor of the eldest son of Cornelius Vanderbilt and displayed an elaborate iconography with statues carved by Kirchmayer, and Gothic lambrequins by Irving and Casson of Boston. The altarpiece at Saint Paul's marks the point at which importation of decorative arts becomes optional rather than an exclusive requirement.

79. J. Mordaunt Crook, *William Burges and the High Victorian Dream* (Chicago, 1981), passim.

80. Paul Venable Turner, *Campus. An American Planning Tradition* (New York & Cambridge, MA, 1984, 1990), pp. 215–47.

Catalogue of the Exhibition

Paul Atterbury
with Malcolm A. C. Hay, Roderick O'Donnell, and Clive Wainwright

Gothic Background and the Development of Pugin's Design Principles

Ecclesiastical Work

The Palace of Westminster

Domestic Designs

The Mediaeval Court of the Great Exhibition of 1851

The catalogue is arranged to follow the organization of the exhibition. The first part highlights Pugin's early years and his growing passion for the integrity of medieval architecture and design, a passion articulated in *Contrasts* and other books. A convert to Roman Catholicism, Pugin devoted his great talents to reviving the rich liturgy of the Catholic Church in the Middle Ages. He created many remarkable vessels and vestments for liturgical use, a selection of which are included in part two. Pugin's work at the Palace of Westminster, the most important design commission in Britain's history, comprises the third part of the catalogue. The vast range of his contributions to domestic interiors, from hardware to tableware, is examined in part four. The catalogue and exhibition close with Pugin's final consuming project: The Mediaeval Court at the Great Exhibition of the Works of Industry of Many Nations, held at London's Crystal Palace in 1851. It was here and in the many publications spawned by the Great Exhibition that the public on a large scale saw and appreciated Pugin and his work; its impact can still be felt today.

Editor's note: The dimensions of object are given with height before width before depth. The references are cited in shortened form; full citations will be found in the bibliography, where a key to abbreviations is also given.

1. Portrait of A. W. N. Pugin (1812–1852)
1845
John Rogers Herbert (1810–1890)
Oil on canvas; 35⅜ x 27½ in.
(90 x 70 cm)
Carved gilt wood frame designed by
A. W. N. Pugin
Inscription: "JRH [in monogram] erbert / 1845"
Palace of Westminster, London

J. R. Herbert exhibited this portrait at the Royal Academy (no. 423) in 1845, the year in which he was elected Royal Academician. A close friend of Pugin, he became a Catholic as a result of Pugin's influence and often visited him at Ramsgate. Pugin was unwilling to give up any time to sit for a portrait, but Herbert eventually bargained for a mere twenty minutes (Wedgwood, ed., "Pugin in his Home," p. 191).

Pugin is shown dressed in an all-enveloping black garment; his lack of interest in clothes is well known

(Ferrey, *Recollections*, p. 35). The background to the portrait is a green velvet curtain on which is painted "Augustus Welby de Pugin" on a scroll beneath the Pugin coat of arms which features his emblem, the martlet, a mythological bird used in heraldry. Because it has no feet, the martlet never rests, a quality that must have appealed to Pugin. The bird and the Pugin monogram also feature in relief on the frame, along with the painted "En Avant" motto.

The design on the curtain, which is closely based on Italian fifteenth-century textiles, has a strong ogee stem that terminates in a large pineapple motif. It seems likely that this was a joint venture of 1845 by Pugin and J. G. Crace, who called it "Gothic Tapestry" (RIBA, Crace papers, PUG 1/43). The pattern was subsequently adapted and used widely as a wallpaper at the Houses of Parliament beginning in the 1850s. According to Pugin's biographer, Benjamin Ferrey (*Recollections*, p. 63), the pocket compasses shown in the portrait are the ones given to Pugin in 1830 by Gillespie Graham who befriended the young Pugin in Edinburgh and persuaded him to become an architect. Pugin designed the splendid frame which was made by Crace. There are two drawings for it in the Victoria & Albert Museum (Pugin Catalogue nos. 581, 582) and two letters to Crace that mention it (RIBA, Crace papers, PUG 2/12, 13).

This is the best-known portrait of Pugin and has been engraved and frequently illustrated and exhibited. Other portraits of him include several that show him as a child. One may have been painted by his uncle, while another, by A. J. Oliver, was shown in the Royal Academy in 1819. A set of silhouettes shows him with his parents and his aunt (see chap. 2, fig. 2-11). There is also a portrait of him in his early twenties (issued much later as a lithograph), now in the collection of the National Portrait Gallery, London. On a few occasions Pugin, following the medieval tradition, included a self-portrait in stained glass window designs, with typical examples to be seen in the chapel at The Grange, Ramsgate (fig. 1a), at the Convent of Mercy, Nottingham, and in Saint Wilfrid's Church, Cotton. The rucumbent figure of Pugin on his tomb is a good likeness, as is the image of him carved in relief on the base of the Albert Memorial. One photograph of Pugin (a daguerreotype, ca. early 1840s, now lost) is known through a posthumous copy made in the 1850s by a Ramsgate photographer (see chap. 2, fig. 2-3).

Herbert was well known for his paintings of religious subjects and executed several mural paintings at the Houses of Parliament. He worked extensively within the Pugin circle, producing portraits of the Birmingham metalworker, John Hardman Senior, and Bishop Thomas Walsh, among others. He also painted the side panels for the chapel altar at Saint Mary's College, Oscott. After Pugin's death, Herbert had a serious dispute with Pugin's son Edward; he was by no means the only one to fall foul of Edward's erratic and demanding personality.

2. **Portrait of Jane Pugin (née Knill) (1827–1909)**
1859
G. A. [George Augustus] Freezor (active 1861–1879)
Oil on canvas; 36 x 28 in. (90.0 x 71.0 cm)
Carved gilt wood frame designed by A. W. N. Pugin
Inscription: "G F [in monogram] rezzor / 1859"
Collection, Mrs. J. Sherliker and Mrs. J. E. Franklin

Pugin married for the third time in June 1848, writing to a friend on his wedding day: "I am married, I have got a first-rate Gothic woman at last" (quoted in Atterbury and Wainwright, eds., *Pugin*, p. 5). His wife, Jane Knill, is shown wearing some of the jewelry that Pugin designed for their wedding. She also wears a memorial brooch which has a central container for hair. It is probably the one supplied by John Hardman to Pugin's son Edward in October 1852, a month after Pugin's death, and presumably given to her by her stepson (Shirley Bury, "Jewellery," in Atterbury and Wainwright, eds., *Pugin*, p. 169).

This portrait must always have been intended as a mate to Herbert's portrait of Pugin (cat. no. 1). The pattern in the background matches the earlier painting, with a red velvet curtain on which appears the Knill coat of arms with "Jane de Pugin" below. The frames are identical, except for the addition of the Knill arms and mottoes. It is possible that Pugin had both frames made by Crace in 1845, when he was a widower, knowing that he would one day remarry. It is difficult to understand why this companion portrait was not painted during his lifetime, but Pugin clearly disliked personal display. Both paintings hung in The Grange until the 1890s, perhaps later; this one is still owned by Pugin descendants.

Pugin's first wife, Anne Garnet, died in childbirth in 1832 at age eighteen. His second wife, Louisa Burton (fig. 2a), whom he married in 1833, died in 1844, having borne him five children. His third wife, the youngest daughter of Thomas Knill of Tiptree Hall, Essex, had two children and outlived her husband by fifty-seven years. There are drawings and photographs (see cat. fig. 131a) and a carved representation of her, with her children, on Pugin's tomb chest.

Fig. 1a. Stained-glass self-portrait by A. W. N. Pugin, created for his private chapel at The Grange, Ramsgate, Kent, 1844.

Fig. 2a. Watercolor sketch of Louisa Burton, ca. 1844, attributed to Pugin, who designed the gilded and painted wooden frame. (Private collection)

226

3. Tribuna at Strawberry Hill

1774–1780
Edward Edwards (1738–1806)
Watercolor on paper; 22½ x 19 in.
(57.2 x 48.3 cm)
The Lewis Walpole Library,
Yale University

This drawing shows the Tribuna at Strawberry Hill, a little quatrefoil-shaped room designed by Horace Walpole and John Chute and completed in 1764. Notable for its vaulting and lavish tracery, adapted from the west window at York Minster, the room housed much of Walpole's collection, including his miniatures which were kept in a cabinet specially made for them. According to Walpole this decorative room had "all the air of a Gothic chapel" (quoted in Aldrich, *Gothic Revival*).

Fig. 3a. *The Gallery at Strawberry Hill*, by Edward Edwards; watercolor on paper, 1781. (The Lewis Walpole Library, Yale University)

4. Strawberry Hill Chair

1755

Horace Walpole (1717–1797) and
Richard Bentley (1708–1782)
Ebonized beechwood, modern
upholstery; 52⅜ x 23¾ x 21¼ in.
(133.0 x 60.3 x 54.0 cm)
Made for the Great Parlour at
Strawberry Hill
The Lewis Walpole Library, Yale
University

Horace Walpole's Strawberry Hill,
a decorative extravaganza near the
Thames, west of London, established the fashion for Gothic in
eighteenth-century England. Walpole and his friend Richard Bentley
shared a passion for the Gothic
style and were among the first to
approach it with a degree of historical and archaeological interest.
Strawberry Hill was designed as a

major Gothic setting for Walpole's
huge collection and library, and all
the fittings of the house were
planned accordingly.

This chair is from a set of eight,
originally with rush seats, supplied
in September 1755 at a cost of £30.
Walpole wrote of the chairs in his
*Description of the Villa at Straw-
berry Hill*, published in 1784: "The
chairs are black, of a Gothic pat-

tern." The ebonized beech used for them was a cheap substitute that nonetheless gave a suitably Tudor Gothic appearance. Their backs were based on medieval window tracery, apparently an idea originating with Walpole himself. En suite with the chairs for the Great Parlour were an ebonized side table with a top made of Sicilian jasper and a pair of mirrors, all crafted by the celebrated cabinetmaker William Hallett. The design of this furniture established a new standard of archaeological accuracy for the Gothic Revival. Walpole had already equipped the Holbein Chamber at Strawberry Hill with actual ebony furniture, bought at the instigation of the architect William Kent who believed it to have belonged to that infamous Tudor prelate, Cardinal Wolsey.

The chairs established a style for decorative Gothic furniture that remained fashionable for over a hundred years, completely replacing the early Georgian form with its perfunctory Gothic detailing. At Strawberry Hill the Great Parlour (fig. 4a) still exists, complete with Bentley's remarkable chimneypiece, but the chairs were sold at the auction of the contents of the house in 1842.

Fig. 4a. *The Great Parlour at Strawberry Hill*, John Carter; watercolor, 1788. In this view the chairs are in situ. (The Lewis Walpole Library, Yale University)

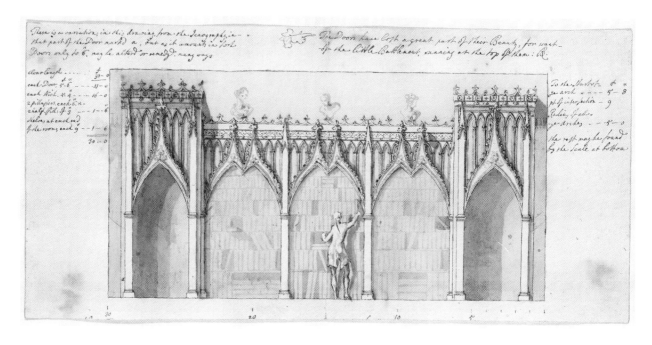

5. Designs for Strawberry Hill: Chimneypiece for Refectory; Gothic bench; Library
1760
Richard Bentley (1708–1782)
Watercolor on paper; a. 6⅜ x 9⅝ in. (16.2 x 24.5 cm); b. 9 x 8 in. (22.9 x 20.3 cm); c. 12 x 5⅝ in. (30.5 x 14.3 cm)
The Lewis Walpole Library, Yale University

These three designs, typical of Richard Bentley's work for Strawberry Hill, are for the chimneypiece in the Refectory, a garden bench, and library bookcase. The library drawing is annotated with instructions and dimensions; it is initialed "RB." The designs clearly relate the decorative Gothic style developed by Walpole and Bentley for Strawberry Hill. It depended largely on medieval architectural and sculp-tural forms. This archaeological approach to Gothic was considered revolutionary at the time, although the resulting designs were later to be strongly rejected by Pugin for their dishonest use of sources.

230

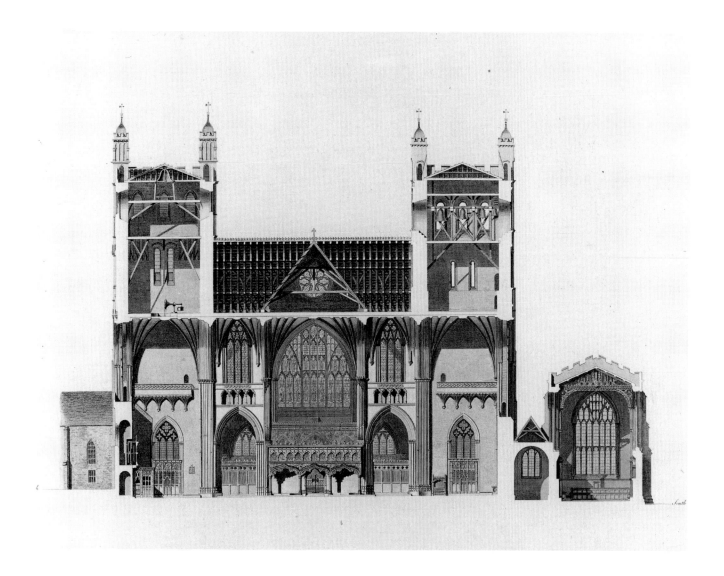

6. Exeter Cathedral

1797
James Basire after John Carter
(1748–1817)
Engraving; 19⅝ x 26⅜ in. (50.0 x
67.0 cm)
Collection, Rosemary Hill

John Carter produced a series of
publications that pioneered the
archaeological approach to the
study of Britain's surviving medieval structures. This engraving appeared in one of his monumental
books, *Plans, Elevations, Sections
and Specimens of the Architecture*
*and Ornaments of the Cathedral
Church at Exeter* (plate 6). Carter,
an architect, scholar, and antiquary,
was a major influence on both
Auguste Charles Pugin and his
son. A. C. Pugin's own volumes
of measured drawings of medieval
buildings were directly inspired
by Carter's achievement. Young
A. W. N. Pugin, working closely
with his father, must have come
across Carter at an early age. Certainly, no other architect of the
earlier generation had so profound
an impact on the development of
A. W. N. Pugin's polemical views
and writings, and on his analytical
approach to medieval art and
architecture.

From 1798 until his death in
1817, Carter wrote a series of articles for *The Gentleman's Magazine*
entitled "Pursuits of Architectural
Innovation." In these, he attacked
the destructive "restoration" work
then being carried out on many
medieval buildings by various
architects, notably James Wyatt.
Pugin was to follow the same line
of argument in his book, *Contrasts,
or a Parallel between the Noble
Edifices of the Middle Ages and
Corresponding Buildings Showing
the Present Decay of Taste*, and was
often outspoken in his criticism of
Wyatt. Pugin and Carter were also
linked through their Catholicism
and their work in the theater.

7. Pier Table

1806
Sir John Soane (1753–1837)
Ebonized mahogany, ivory; 36¼ x
55⅞ x 17⅛ in. (92.0 x 142.0 x
43.5 cm)
Made for the Gothic library at
Stowe
The Board of Trustees of the
Victoria and Albert Museum,
London
Inv. no. W32-1972

Sir John Soane was commissioned to design the library at Stowe, a celebrated eighteenth-century house in Buckinghamshire, built in the classical idiom. Soane chose the Gothic style for this commission as suitable for the Marquis of Buckingham's collection of medieval manuscripts, designing two pier tables, an octagonal table, and armchairs. The furniture was ebonized so that, like the furniture at Strawberry Hill, it would relate to real ebony pieces, in this case turned ebony chairs then thought to be of Tudor origin but actually imported from the East Indies. The use of ivory enrichments was also inspired by the East Indies. The inspiration for the decorative motifs and for the shallow fan vaulting on the library ceiling came from Henry VII's chapel at Westminster Abbey, probably the most famous Tudor Gothic interior. The library still exists at Stowe, but the furniture was dispersed at the auction of 1848 that followed Buckingham's bankruptcy.

8. View of Fonthill Abbey
1813–14
Francis Danby (ca. 1818–1886)
Watercolor; 9¼ x 12⅝ in. (23.5 x 32 cm)
Private collection

The vast Gothic mansion known as Fonthill Abbey was built for William Beckford to house his celebrated collection of art. At the time, it was the largest and most archaeologically correct example of Gothic Revival architecture ever seen, with a central tower over 280 feet high. The Fonthill estate near Salisbury in Wiltshire had been inherited by Beckford from his father, along with a huge Palladian house and a fortune made from estates in the West Indies. Beckford demolished his father's house and set to work to replace it with a Gothic Revival abbey designed by James Wyatt, the most fashionable architect of the day and best known for his Gothic additions to Windsor Castle. The project began in 1796 and, although it was never fully completed, was to influence a whole generation of later nineteenth-century buildings, including the Palace of Westminster.

After Wyatt's death in 1813, his nephew Jeffry Wyatville took over the work at both Fonthill and Windsor. In the late 1820s Pugin was to work with Wyatville at Windsor, but he wrote later of his hatred for the man and his uncle, and for their insubstantial and dishonest Gothic architecture. "All that is vile, cunning and rascally is included in the term Wyatt . . . Mr Wyatt, this monster of architectural depravity" (Ferrey, *Recollections*, pp. 80, 85). Pugin was delighted when Wyatt's tower at Fonthill collapsed, noting: "1825 Dec 21 The tower of Fonthill Abbey fell with a tremendous crash at 1/2 past 3PM" (notes for an unfinished autobiography, Victoria & Albert Museum, London, L.5204-1969). Beckford had sold the abbey along with most of his collection in 1822, and after the tower collapsed it was abandoned as a ruin.

9. The Entrance Hall at Abbotsford

ca. 1830
Artist unknown
Watercolor; 14¾ x 19⅛ in. (36.5 x
48.5 cm)
Private collection

Abbotsford, near Melrose on the
banks of the Tweed River, was
among the most famous houses in
the world in the early nineteenth
century. It was built for Sir Walter
Scott from designs by several architects and was paid for by the royal-
ties from his poems and novels.
Architecturally its style was known
as "Old Scotch" which later became the more familiar designation,
Scottish Baronial. As such, it was to
have a lasting influence in Europe
and America throughout the nineteenth century.

The house was packed with
Scott's collection, which included
many objects with important historical associations, such as Napoleon's
blotter and Rob Roy's sword and
gun. Many leading political and
literary figures came to the house—
Washington Irving wrote a full description of his stay there ("Abbotsford," in *The Crayon Miscellany*
[New York, 1835])—and in this
painting Scott is shown coming out
of his study perhaps to greet a visitor. Several of Scott's novels were
adapted for the stage, and Pugin
was to design the sets for the London production of *Kenilworth*.

10. Chair

ca. 1827
A. W. N. Pugin
Maker: Morel & Seddon, London
Rosewood, gilt bronze, upholstery;
39½ x 23 x 22 in. (100.3 x 58.4 x
55.9 cm)
Made for Windsor Castle in about
1827; reproduced by gracious per-
mission of The Royal Collection©
Her Majesty Queen Elizabeth II.

This elaborate chair is typical of the
wide range of furniture designed by
the young Pugin in the late 1820s.
His work was destined for the
splendid Gothic Revival interiors
created by architect Jeffry Wyatville
for George IV at Windsor Castle.
Pugin's designs for furniture and
metalwork showed his sure grasp of
contemporary taste, developed during the years he had spent at his
father's side. Some of this furniture
was in oak, following medieval
precedent, but the majority of the
Windsor pieces were made from
rosewood and mahogany which

were then fashionable. To modern
eyes these richly decorated pieces
with their meritorious use of Gothic
ornament appear typical of the
early nineteenth century, but their
originality set them apart from the
conventional Gothic Revival styles
of the time. They were widely influential not only in Britain, but in
France and Germany as well. In
later years, Pugin was very critical
of his early work. In his book, *True*

235

Principles of Pointed or Christian Architecture (1843), he included an "Illustration of the extravagant style of Modern Gothic Furniture and Decoration" as an example of dishonest Gothic, writing "everything is crocketed with angular pro- jections, sharp ornaments and turreted extremities. . . . I have perpetrated many of these enormities in furniture, designed some years ago for Windsor . . . although the parts were correct and exceedingly well executed, collectively they appeared a complete burlesque of pointed design." Apart from the large sideboard, destroyed in the 1992 fire, much of Pugin's furniture remains in the State Rooms at the castle. (This chair is not in the exhibition.)

Fig. 10a. Table designed by Pugin; made by Morel & Seddon for Windsor Castle; rosewood, gilt, and gilt bronze mounts, ca. 1827. (Reproduced by gracious permission of The Royal Collection© Her Majesty Queen Elizabeth II)

Fig. 10b. The Banqueting Hall at Windsor Castle, from *Views of the Interior and Exterior of Windsor Castle*, by Joseph Nash, published in 1848. Tables designed by Pugin can be seen on the right.

11. Design for Sideboard for Windsor Castle

1827
A. W. N. Pugin
Pen and ink, watercolor; 8¾ x
16¾ in. (22.2 x 42.6 cm)
Inscription: "First design for
sideboard" (in pencil on mount in
Wyatville's hand); "No.187:
Dining Room" (in another hand)
The Board of Trustees of the
Victoria and Albert Museum,
London
Inv. no. E787-1970

Pugin's work at Windsor Castle is well documented. The commission to furnish the new apartments was given to the London company, Morel & Seddon, and they asked for help from A. C. Pugin, probably on the strength of his Gothic furniture designs published in Rudolph Ackermann's *Repository of the Arts*. Pugin in turn passed the work on to his son, who noted, "1827. June 26 went to design and make working drawings for the Gothic furniture of Windsor Castle at £1.1s per day for the following rooms: the long gallery, the coffee room, the vestibule anti [sic] room, halls grand staircase, octagon room in the Brunswick tower and the Great Dining Room" (notes for an unfinished autobiography, Victoria & Albert Museum, London, L.5204-1969). The elder Pugin was clearly confident of his son's abilities, and their styles were quite similar at this time.

Several of Pugin's meticulously prepared watercolors for Windsor survive in the collections of the Victoria & Albert Museum and the Royal Library. From these and other evidence it is possible to establish that Pugin designed the sideboard (cat. no. 11), tables, chairs, benches, window seats, firescreens, and a series of standing candelabra (cat. no. 12) in gilded cast iron, made for the dining room and gallery. Morel & Seddon followed the design closely in making the rosewood and gilded sideboard, the largest of the Windsor pieces. It survived at Windsor until the 1992 fire, when it was destroyed. Eight of the dining room candelabra and forty-six of the simpler "gallery" version (right) were made by William and George Perry, but none are known today.

**12. Designs for Standing
Candelabra for Windsor Castle**
1827
A. W. N. Pugin
Pencil, pen and ink, watercolor;
11 x 16⅝ in. (28 x 42.2 cm)
Inscription: "Candelabra for the
dining room"; "Candelabra for the
gallery"; (both inscriptions
endorsed) "GR" [monogram of
George IV]; "Insc." (on mount);
"Dining room; gallery"; "40"
The Board of Trustees of the
Victoria and Albert Museum,
London
Inv. no. E788-1970

Fig. 12a. Candlestick and sanctuary
lamp designs, drawn by Pugin in 1846
for the Hardman & Co. catalogue, are
in marked contrast to his early work.

238

13. The Coronation Cup

Assay, 1826–27
A. W. N. Pugin
Maker: John Bridge, Rundell,
Bridge and Rundell
Silver-gilt, jewels, enamel;
H. 11 in. (28 cm); diam. 4⅛ in.
(10.5 cm)
Marks: town and maker's; date
letter 1826–27
The Royal Collection© Her
Majesty Queen Elizabeth II
Inv. no. 3D 12747

This remarkable cup was designed by the fifteen-year-old Pugin, the result of a chance meeting with an employee of Rundell, Bridge & Rundell, a prestigious London goldsmith firm (Ferrey, *Recollections*, p. 51). The meeting occurred in the Print Room of the British Museum, where Pugin was studying the works of Albrecht Dürer. Pugin had a profound admiration for Dürer and owned a selection of his engravings. The design of this cup shows that even as a young man Pugin was determined to use medi-

eval source material in a suitable and historically correct manner. The cup, with its decoration emblematic of the links between Britain and the House of Hanover, may well have been a royal commission. It is clearly a domestic piece and perhaps was displayed on the sideboard that Pugin designed for Windsor Castle a year later.

14. Design for a Chalice

1827
A. W. N. Pugin
Pen and red ink, yellow and blue washes; 19⅛ x 18½ in. (48.5 x 46.5 cm)
Inscription: "A. Pugin Junr. Invent et fecit 1827"; "J. G. Bridge" (verso)
The Board of Trustees of the Victoria and Albert Museum, London
Inv. no. E751-1925

This drawing is one from a group of designs for altar plate signed by Pugin, and countersigned by John Gawler Bridge. The set was to have been made by Rundell, Bridge & Rundell, the Royal goldsmiths, for George IV, probably for use in the Chapel of Saint George, but it was never made. It comprised this chalice, a standing paten, flagon, alms dish, and altar candlestick, all distinguished by their use of detailed medieval forms. They show the same meticulous concern for detail with carefully applied washes of color, a style that characterizes the young Pugin and is quite unlike the rapid and fluid technique he developed later in his life. According to his biographer Benjamin Ferrey (*Recollections*, p. 52), the young Pugin carried out a number of designs for Rundell, Bridge & Rundell, but apart from the Coronation Cup (cat. no. 13) none is known today.

240

15. Office at Store Street

1821

A. C. Pugin (1769–1832), with possible additions by A. W. N. Pugin

Pen and ink; 7⅞ x 11 in. (20 x 28 cm)

Inscription: "Office at Store Street A Pugin 1821" (on verso)

Collection, The Family of the late Michael Pugin Purcell (1926–1993)

In 1819 the Pugin family moved into a large terrace house in Store Street, Bloomsbury. Their previous house, in Keppel Street nearby, had established the Pugins at the heart of the artistic and literary milieu in that part of London. This finely detailed drawing shows the top floor studio/office that was built into the roof space and well lit by large windows. It was used by A. C. Pugin and the pupils, including his son, who attended his drawing school. These pupils, or rather apprentices, learned their craft by producing drawings and illustrations for A. C. Pugin's books. The strong sense of perspective gives the drawing the look of an exercise in architectural rendering. A. C. Pugin was skilled at architectural drafting and his son was adept at drawing figures, but there is no evidence to say what each contributed to this drawing.

The Pugins left Store Street in 1823, moving to a larger house, but for the same rent, in nearby Great Russell Street.

16. Ceremony of the Homage, Coronation of George IV,
July 19, 1821, Westminster Abbey, London
A. C. Pugin (1769–1832) and James Stephanoff
Pencil and watercolor; 14 x 19 in. (35.5 x 48.2 cm)
The Board of Trustees of the Victoria and Albert Museum, London
Inv. no. 55-1878

Well known as an architectural draftsman and designer, A. C. Pugin was a prolific artist, whose friends included fellow artists such as Thomas Rowlandson and John Nash. Pugin was interested in and frequently drew architecture in Britain and in Europe, especially details, and was skilled at capturing the effects of light. Both qualities are noticeable in this watercolor, which is one of a pair illustrating the coronation of George IV. As was often the case, Pugin was responsible for the composition and architecture while another artist, in this case James Stephanoff, drew the figures. The two watercolors were issued as acquatints in 1824, published by Sir George Nayler.

17. La Rotonde, Passage Colbert, Paris

Benjamin Ferrey (1810–1880)
Watercolor; 5⅛ x 6⅞ in. (13 x
17.6 cm)
Private collection

During the late 1820s A. C. Pugin and his wife Catherine, with whom he ran a small drawing academy, took their pupils to Paris on several occasions to make preliminary drawings for a forthcoming book, *Paris and Its Environs, Displayed in a series of picturesque views.* This collection was published in two volumes by C. Heath in 1829 and 1830, with engravings based on watercolors by Pugin and his pupils and credited accordingly. It was an appropriate project for students whose training emphasized architectural and topographical work. A number of the surviving watercolors are studies of the same subject, and it is likely that Pugin sometimes asked several pupils to draw their own versions of a particular view and then selected the best for the final engraving.

The Pugins and their pupils made frequent drawing visits to sites of interest in Britain and France. Among the pupils were his son A. W. N. Pugin (see cat. no. 18), T. T. Bury, Joseph Nash, and Benjamin Ferrey, the artist who made this painting. The view, taken from a similar drawing by Joseph Nash, was engraved and published in the first volume of *Paris and Its Environs* (fig. 17a). Ferrey, a close friend of the young Pugin, was later to become his biographer.

Fig. 17a. "La Rotonde, Passage Colbert," engraving based on a watercolor by Joseph Nash. From *Paris and Its Environs*, vol. 1 (London, 1829).

Fig. 17a

18. Le Petit Trianon, Paris (not shown)
ca. 1828
A. W. N. Pugin
Watercolor; 16⅞ x 15 in. (43 x 38 cm), framed
Private collection

The engraving shown here, by T. T. Bury, is based on Pugin's watercolor. It was published in *Paris and Its Environs* (vol. 1; London, 1829).

19. Pugin's Gothic Furniture: Title Page and Two Plates
1825 (title page), 1827
A. C. Pugin and A. W. N. Pugin
Title page: etching, aquatint, hand-colored; 10⅜ x 7½ in. (26.5 x 18.5 cm)
Private collection

The two plates are from a series of Gothic furniture designs published in *The Repository of Arts, Literature, Commerce, Manufactures, Fashions and Politics* (vol. 4, pl. 35; and vol. 10, pl. 5). This pioneering illustrated periodical was produced between 1808 and 1828 by Rudolph Ackermann who had come to London from Saxony, via Paris, in the late 1780s, bringing with him the latest in printing and publishing techniques from the Continent. He worked with A. C. Pugin on a number of projects, the most important of which was *The Microcosm of London* (1808–10); A. C. Pugin drew the architecture in many of the plates.

The Gothic furniture designs, of which these are typical examples, are likely to have been drawn by A. C. Pugin with the help of his son, who was then designing Gothic furniture for Windsor Castle. The whole set was republished in book form in 1827 under the title *Pugin's Gothic Furniture* (not to be confused with A. W. N. Pugin's book of the same title, published in 1835).

20. Examples of Gothic Architecture: Frontispiece, Volume 2

1836
A. C. Pugin and A. W. N. Pugin
Pen and red and black ink; 11 x
9⅛ in. (27.6 x 23.1 cm)
The Board of Trustees of the
Victoria and Albert Museum,
London
Inv. no. E77 (82)-1970

Examples of Gothic Architecture,
with its detailed engravings of a
wide range of medieval buildings,
was an important source book for

the Gothic Revival. There were two
volumes: the first was published in
1831, and the second, with this
frontispiece, in 1836. The text was
by E. J. Willson, a well-known antiquary and friend of the Pugins. The
engravings, by both A. C. and
A. W. N. Pugin, were based on
studies made on site by some of the
Pugins' pupils. Clearly the long production process for the book represented an important element in the
school's curriculum over several
years.

Following his father's death in
1832, A. W. N. Pugin assumed

responsibility for completing the
second volume. He drew this frontispiece to illustrate his vision of the
medieval world and wrote in the
preface: "This composition represents an artist of the fifteenth century seated in his study amidst his
books and drawings making an
architectural design. The furniture
of the room is altogether agreeable
to the fashions of the supposed
period; and the inscriptions, and
other ornaments of the border, are
also designed in a corresponding
style."

21. Eglington Tournament Jug
1840
William Ridgway, & Company,
Hanley
Stoneware; H. 11¼ in. (28.5 cm)
Private collection

The stoneware jug with embossed decoration was a characteristic Staffordshire product of the 1830s and 1840s. Made in simple molds by various Staffordshire potteries, these jugs are known in a great many forms and styles. They were issued in a range of sizes and colored finishes. To give an indication of the scale of production, one manufacturer, Minton & Company, made more than 300 jug variants between the 1830s and the 1850s. After the 1846 development of Parian porcelain, a fine, unglazed

white porcelain used predominantly for figure modeling and named after the white marble used for sculpture by the ancient Greeks, many jugs were issued in that material.

This jug celebrates the great medieval pageant organized by the thirteenth Earl of Eglington, held at his castle in April 1839. Despite appalling weather, this event was said to have done much to generate public enthusiasm for Gothic Revival.

22. Apostle Jug
1842
Charles Meigh, Hanley
Stoneware; H. 9⅞ in. (25 cm)
Private collection

There are at least two variations of this design, one (seen here) encircled by apostles in niches and the other by a choir-screen window motif. A third jug (cat. no. 23) was derived from tracery or architectural motifs. It was exactly this kind of popular decorative Gothic, with its casual abuse of sources, that so enraged Pugin. For him, the correct design source for a modern Gothic jug was an example of related medieval tableware, not an altar reredos or choir screen.

23. Gothic Jug
After 1862
G. L. Ashworth & Brothers, Hanley
Stoneware; H. 8¼ in. (21 cm)
Impressed: "A Bros, Hanley. Gothic"
Private collection

24. Jug and Goblet

ca. 1850
Zalmon Bostwick (active 1846–1852)
Silver; jug, 10⅞ x 8½ x 5⅝ in.
(27.6 x 21.6 x 14.3 cm);
goblet, 7⅞ x 3¾ in. (20.0 x 9.5 cm)
The Brooklyn Museum, Other
Restricted Income Fund
Inv. nos. 81.179.1-2

Charles Meigh's "Apostle Jug," which was first made in 1842, inspired many variants in stoneware, but it is remarkable to find the basic form and decorative style being copied in silver in the United States just a few years later. The existence of this jug underlines the thriving nature of the Staffordshire potters' export business during this period. The silver jug is not a precise replica; for one thing it lacks, presumably for reasons of cost, apostles standing in the niches. However, it is close enough to be certain that the American silversmith, Zalmon Bostwick, had a version of the Meigh stoneware jug in front of him as he worked. The accompanying goblet may be an American invention; if such goblets were ever made in Staffordshire, none seems to be known today. After the development of the electroplating process in 1840, a deposit of silver and other metals was sometimes laid onto a ceramic vessel, and experiments with this technique may have given Bostwick the original idea.

Little is known about Zalmon Bostwick. He is recorded as working in New York City beginning around 1846 until his death in 1852. He advertised himself in *The New York Mercantile Register* in 1848 and 1849 as "successor to Thompson" (presumably silversmiths A. R. or William Thompson). He is also listed in New York City directories for 1851 and 1852.

25. Portable Font and Cover
ca. 1840
Minton & Company, Stoke-on-Trent
Stoneware; H. 12⅝ in., with lid (32 cm)
Marks: "St. Mary Mag[dalene], Oxford"
Private collection

Designed for the baptism of infants who were too ill to bring to church, the portable baptismal font was a feature of Minton production from the early 1840s until the latter part of the century. There were several designs, made initially in stoneware, later in Parian porcelain, and usually based on actual medieval forms. This one is a replica of the font at the Church of Saint Mary Magdalene, Oxford. In the late 1840s a portable font designed by Pugin was added to the range.

26. Plate, Gothic Ruins Pattern
ca. 1840
Charles Meigh, Hanley
Earthenware, transfer-printed
decoration; 10 in. diam. (25.5 cm)
Private collection

Picturesque and Gothic scenes, adapted from popular engravings, were used frequently by potteries in Staffordshire and elsewhere to decorate transfer-printed table and domestic wares. Charles Meigh's "Gothic Ruins" pattern, featuring a range of identifiable buildings and views, is a well-known example. It was probably in production until the late 1840s.

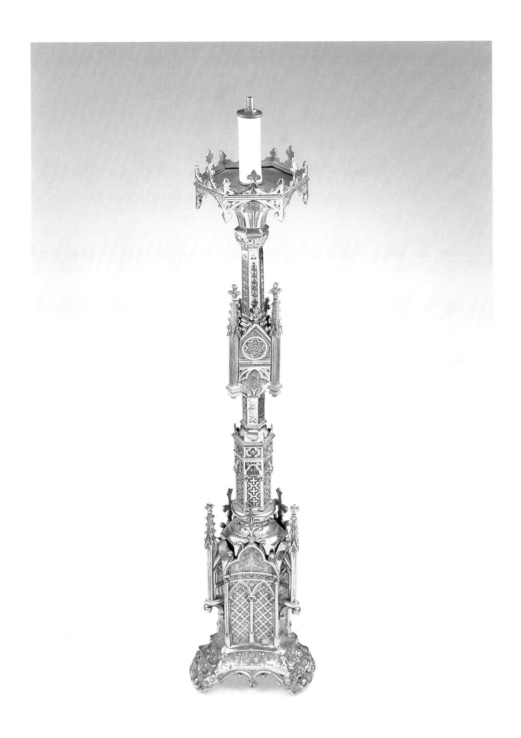

27. Candlestick

ca. 1830
Brass; H. 32 in. (81.3 cm)
Private collection

This candlestick is typical of the domestic metalwares produced during the 1830 to 1860 period. It has a broadly decorative Gothic style drawn from architectural sources and designed to reflect fashionable taste, but without any concern for historical accuracy. Candlesticks, lamps, grates, inkstands, andirons, clock and thermometer cases, footscrapers, and many other forms were produced in rich profusion by the metalworkers of Birmingham and Sheffield, but Pugin dismissed both centers in *True Principles* (1843) as "those inexhaustible mines of bad taste." He went on to say of such wares, "Neither relative scale, form, purpose, nor unity of style, is ever considered by those who design these abominations; if they only introduce a quatrefoil or an acute arch, be the outline and style of the article ever so modern and debased, it is at once denominated and sold as Gothic."

28. Mustard Pot

1837
Henry Wilkinson, Sheffield
Silver, glass; H. 3½ in. (9 cm)
Private collection

The restrained form of this mustard pot, with its frieze of simple pierced arches, echoes the decorative Gothic of the late eighteenth century, rather than the exuberance of the 1830s. Pieces in this style, whose inspiration is drawn largely from architecture and sculpture, are relatively unusual. The English silversmiths of the early nineteenth century were still steeped in the traditional language of decorative classicism.

29. Armchair

ca. 1836
A. W. N. Pugin
Carved oak, imitation leather
upholstery; 44½ x 24 x 25¼ in.
(133.0 x 61.0 x 64.0 cm)
The Board of Trustees of the
Victoria and Albert Museum,
London
Inv. no. Circ 237-1951

One of a series of chairs made for Scarisbrick Hall in Lancashire, this is a variation of a design published by Pugin in *Gothic Furniture in the Style of the 15th Century* (1835). It was based on late medieval examples illustrated in manuscripts. As such, it represents Pugin's move away from the decorative and fanciful Gothic of the Regency period toward a correct and more honest use of sources. The manufacturer is not known. It is even possible that the chairs were made in North Germany, for the Wardour Street antique dealer John Coleman Isaacs had furniture of this type made there from designs in Pugin's book and imported into England via Hamburg. Pugin was closely involved at this time with the London antique trade, buying and selling through the dealer Edward Hull, whose premises were also in Wardour Street. In 1834 Pugin designed a range of furniture for Hull, and at Pugin's suggestion, Charles Scarisbrick patronized these dealers through the late 1830s and into the 1840s.

Pugin worked for Charles Scarisbrick between 1836 and 1845, making major alterations and additions to Scarisbrick Hall, the sixteenth-century manor house which had already been extensively altered by Thomas Rickman between 1813 and 1816. Scarisbrick represented Pugin's first important architectural commission.

Fig. 29a. Scarisbrick Hall, by A. W. N. Pugin; pencil on paper, 1836. This perspective drawing shows Pugin's original concept for the entrance facade, including the clock tower that was a model for Big Ben. (RIBA, Drawings Collection)

30. Knight, Death, and the Devil

1513
Albrecht Dürer (1471–1528)
Engraving; 9½ x 7⅜ in. (24.2 x
18.7 cm)
The Board of Trustees of the
Victoria and Albert Museum,
London
Inv. no. 595.1940

Pugin was an enthusiastic collector of early printed books, mainly for their illustrations which he often used as design sources. He inherited many of the books in his library from his father, who was probably responsible for encouraging in his son a taste for early books and prints. Pugin assembled a large collection of early woodcuts, engravings, and etchings, by artists from Dürer onward. These were also valuable to him as source material. His enthusiasm for Dürer was certainly established by the age of fifteen, and this developed into a wide-ranging interest in prints. His collection included topographical works, by artists such as Hollar, Perelle, and, rather surprisingly perhaps, Canaletto. There were also images of historical, Christian, and source interest by Dürer and his followers and by French artists such as Jacques Callot. Pugin's collection of prints and books indicates the diversity of his taste, which was by no means limited to medieval material. The Baroque and the eighteenth century were well represented, despite Pugin's often outspoken rejection of those periods. He owned, for example, a complete set of Canaletto's etched views of Venice.

The three prints shown here were not actually owned by Pugin but are similar to those known to have been in his collection.

256

Tabulam hanc olim ab ANDREA MANTENIO cum penna delineatam, et nunc
Londini in Ædibus Arundelianis conservatam. Wenceslaus Hollar, *Bohem. aqua forti æri insculsit.*

31. Chalice

1640
W[Wenzel Václav] Hollar
(1607–1677)
Engraving; 18⅛ x 8¾ in. (46 x
22.3 cm)
The Board of Trustees of the
Victoria and Albert Museum,
London
Inv. no. 25086

32. Imaginary View of San Giacomo
Canaletto [Giovanni Canal]
(1697–1768, Venetian)
Etching; 5¾ x 8½ in. (14.5 x
21.7 cm)
The Board of Trustees of the
Victoria and Albert Museum,
London
Inv. no. E.23213.5

33-45. Travel Sketches

Always an enthusiastic traveler, Pugin was first taken to France on drawing and collecting expeditions by his parents when he was quite young. This established a habit that he maintained throughout his life. His diaries are scattered with references to visits to Europe, sometimes for a few days, sometimes for much longer. Even when he was at his busiest he seems to have found time for trips to the Continent. There were two reasons for the visits: firstly, to see, study, and draw buildings, sites, and objects of medieval and later periods; secondly, to collect medieval objects and architectural fragments, either for his own use or to sell in England. He filled many notebooks with sketches that proved to be invaluable sources for his work as an architect and designer.

France was always Pugin's favorite destination, thanks in part to its proximity to Ramsgate and the other Channel ports, and to its great wealth of medieval buildings. Sometimes Pugin crossed in his own boat, sometimes on the ferries that by around 1830 were offering scheduled services to ports such as Dieppe, Boulogne, Calais, and Ostend. Throughout the 1830s and 1840s he made regular visits to Rouen, Amiens, Paris, and other northern European towns such as Bruges and Antwerp, sometimes perhaps to do little more than recharge his mental batteries.

Rouen was perennially popular for its streets of timber-framed buildings, its cathedral and churches, and its museums, particularly the Musée des Antiquités. Longer tours took Pugin to other parts of France, such as the Loire Valley, and the major towns and cities of Holland, Switzerland, and Germany, where he visited, among other places, Augsburg, Bonn, Cologne, Frankfurt, Freibourg, Hamburg, Hanover, Koblenz, Mainz, Mannheim, Munich, Nuremburg, and Ulm. A particularly long and important trip took place in 1847, when he sailed for Boulogne on March 26 and did not return to England until June 16. He visited Amiens, Paris, Orleans (and other Loire towns), Bordeaux, Toulouse, Carcassonne, Montpellier, Avignon, and Marseilles, from which he sailed for Italy. In Rome he had an audience with the Pope. He toured Italy, seeing Foligno, Assisi, Perugia, Pisa, Florence, Bologna, Padua, Venice, Verona, and Milan. Returning via Switzerland, he paused at Lucerne and Basle, before traveling north through France via Besançon, Dijon, Troyes, Rheims, Laon, Saint Quentin, and Douai and finally sailing for home from Ostend. The day after his return to Ramsgate, he was hard at work in London, meeting, among others, the Earl of Shrewsbury, one of his principal clients.

Pugin continued to visit Europe until 1851, despite his failing health and other problems. His last trip seems to have been from July 15th to 31st of that year, when he was in northern France, Chartres, Sens, the Loire, and Paris returning via Belgium. Surviving drawings from this tour, for example those of medieval objects at a convent in Namur, show that at the end of his life his appetite for medieval art was undiminished.

33. Saint Gervais, Paris
1836
A. W. N. Pugin
Watercolor; 26¾ x 19⅝ in. (68 x
50 cm), framed
Private collection

Fig. 33a. Saint Gervais, interior view by
Pugin; pencil on paper, 1837.

**34. Selection of Metalwork and
Altar, Gallery, Antwerp**
1842
A. W. N. Pugin
Watercolor; 7⅝ x 6¼ in. (19.5 x
16 cm)
Inscription: [signed and dated];
"Gallery Antwerp"; "For Holy
Oils"; "A. W. Pugin" (on mat)
Osborn Collection, Beinecke
Library, Yale University
Inv. no. 95.3.3; *Catalogue of the
Drawings Collection of the Royal
Institute of British Architects,
Pugin Family*, by A. Wedgwood
[Wedgwood 112.2]

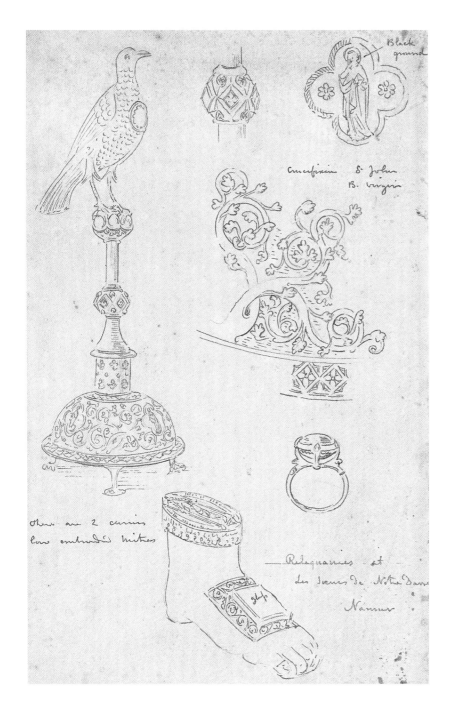

35. Selection of Metalwork including Foot Reliquary, Convent, Namur
1851
A. W. N. Pugin
Pen and ink, with pencil underdrawing; 9⅞ x 6¼ in. (25 x 16 cm)

Inscription: "Reliquariea at Les Soueur de Notre Dame Namur"; "There are 2 curious low embroidered mitres"; "A. W. Pugin" (on mat]
Osborn Collection, Beinecke Library, Yale University
Inv. no. 95.3.3; *Catalogue of the Drawings Collection of the Royal Institute of British Architects, Pugin Family*, by A. Wedgwood [Wedgwood 114]

Fig. 35a. Metalwork and other objects from the Cabinet de Mons Gevente, sketched by Pugin, 1847.

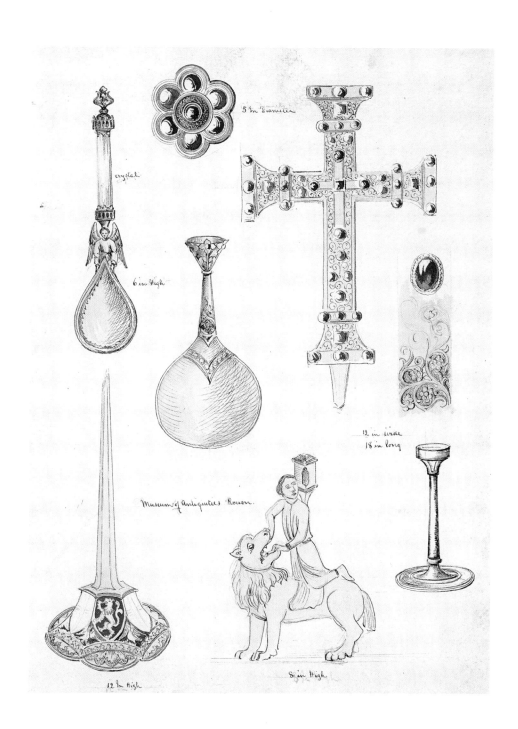

36. Medieval Metalwork at Rouen Museum of Antiquities

1836–37
A. W. N. Pugin
Pen, watercolor, and pencil; 10¼ x
8⅛ in. (26 x 20.5 cm)
Inscription: "Museum of
Antiquities Rouen"; "A. W. Pugin"
(on mat) [also dimension of drawn
objects]
Osborn Collection, Beinecke
Library, Yale University
Inv. no. 95.3.3; *Catalogue of the
Drawings Collection of the Royal
Institute of British Architects,
Pugin Family,* by A. Wedgwood
[Wedgwood 135]

263

clock. Cathedral. Beauvais A.Pugin

37. Medieval Clock in Cathedral
1847
A. W. N. Pugin
Pen and ink, pencil; 7½ x 4½ in.
(19 x 11.5 cm)
Inscription: [signed]; "Clock
Cathedral Beauváis"; "A. W.
Pugin" (on mat)
Osborn Collection, Beinecke
Library, Yale University
Inv. no. 95.3.3; *Catalogue of the
Drawings Collection of the Royal
Institute of British Architects,
Pugin Family*, by A. Wedgwood
[Wedgwood 119.3]

Fig. 37a. Pencil sketch by Pugin of the
north transept, Beauvais Cathedral,
1836.

38. Stained Glass in Saint Maclou, Rouen
1836–37
A. W. N. Pugin
Watercolor; 9 x 4 in. (23 x 10 cm)
Inscription: [signed]; "S.Maclou,

window of N. transept"; "A. W. Pugin" (on mat)
Osborn Collection, Beinecke Library, Yale University
Inv. no. 95.3.3; *Catalogue of the Drawings Collection of the Royal Institute of British Architects, Pugin Family*, by A. Wedgwood [Wedgwood 132]

Fig. 38a (top). Pulpit and nave of Evreux Cathedral, by Pugin; water-color, 1837. (Private collection)

Fig. 38b (bottom). Saint Patrice, Rouen, by Pugin; watercolor. (Private collection)

265

39. Rouen, Timber-framed Houses

1836–37
A. W. N. Pugin
Pencil; 8¼ x 5½ in. (21 x 14 cm;
31 x 23.5 cm with mat)
Inscription: "A. W. Pugin" (on
mat)
Osborn Collection, Beinecke
Library, Yale University
Inv. no. 95.3.3; *Catalogue of the
Drawings Collection of the Royal
Institute of British Architects,
Pugin Family*, by A. Wedgwood
[Wedgwood 138]

Fig. 39a. Pencil sketch by Pugin of
timber-framed houses in Blois, France,
1847.

40. Cologne, Stained glass details, Saint Ursula, North Aisle
1845
A. W. N. Pugin
Pen and ink, watercolor; 10⅝ x
7½ in. (27 x 19 cm)
Inscription: [signed and dated];
"North Aisle Dom. Cologne";
"A. W. Pugin" (on mat)
Osborn Collection, Beinecke
Library, Yale University
Inv. no. 95.3.3; *Catalogue of the*
Drawings Collection of the Royal
Institute of British Architects,
Pugin Family, by A. Wedgwood
[Wedgwood 141]

267

windows of nave.   Dom

**41. Cologne, Stained Glass and
Reliquary Figures, Saint Ursula**
1845
A. W. N. Pugin
Pen, watercolor; 10⅝ x 7½ in.
(27 x 19 cm)
Inscription: "Silver reliquaries
St. Ursula"; "Windows of Nave.
Dom"; "A. W. Pugin" (on mat)
Osborn Collection, Beinecke
Library, Yale University
Inv. no. 95.3.3; *Catalogue of the
Drawings Collection of the Royal
Institute of British Architects,
Pugin Family*, by A. Wedgwood
[Wedgwood 143]

**42. Amiens, North Transept
Facade of Cathedral**
1836
A. W. N. Pugin
Pencil; 10 x 6⅞ in. (25.5 x
17.5 cm)
Inscription: "S. Germain, Amiens";
"A. W. Pugin" (on mat)
Osborn Collection, Beinecke
Library, Yale University
Inv. no. 95.3.3; *Catalogue of the
Drawings Collection of the Royal
Institute of British Architects,
Pugin Family*, by A. Wedgwood
[Wedgwood 116]

**43. Basle, Saint Martin with
Medieval Conduit**
1845
A. W. N. Pugin
Pencil; 11 x 7⅞ in. (28 x 20 cm)
Inscription: "Basle"; "A. W.
Pugin" (on mat)
Osborn Collection, Beinecke
Library, Yale University
Inv. no. 95.3.3; *Catalogue of the
Drawings Collection of the Royal
Institute of British Architects,
Pugin Family*, by A. Wedgwood
[Wedgwood 159]

44. Cologne, Saint Martin and Another Church
1846
A. W. N. Pugin
Pen; 8¼ x 5⅜ in. (21 x 13.5 cm)
Inscription: "A. W. Pugin" (on mat)
Osborn Collection, Beinecke Library, Yale University
Inv. no. 95.3.3; *Catalogue of the Drawings Collection of the Royal Institute of British Architects, Pugin Family*, by A. Wedgwood [Wedgwood 144]

45. Drawing of Boat at Honfleur

1836
A. W. N. Pugin
Pencil
4⅞ x 6½ in. (12.5 x 16.5 cm)
Inscription: "Honfleur";
"A. W. Pugin" (on mat)
Osborn Collection, Beinecke
Library, Yale University
Inv. no. 95.3.3; *Catalogue of the
Drawings Collection of the Royal
Institute of British Architects,
Pugin Family*, by A. Wedgwood
[Wedgwood 126]

In this pencil sketch, an English lugger, which probably sailed from Ramsgate or Deal on the Kent coast, is beached at low tide at Honfleur, on the northern coast of France. It is tempting to think that Pugin may have crossed from England in this vessel. A devoted sailor, Pugin is reported to have said, "there is nothing worth living for but Christian architecture and a boat" (quoted in Atterbury and Wainwright, eds., *Pugin*, p. 8). He had owned boats at least since 1831 and frequently sailed from Ramsgate to London or across the English Channel on his own craft. In 1849, in partnership with his friend and benefactor the Reverend Alfred Luck, he bought the Deal lugger, *The Caroline*, a substantial vessel with a crew. He used it to cross the Channel with ease, transporting antiquities and architectural fragments from Europe. He also engaged in rescues and wrecking operations for ships in distress on the Goodwin Sands, a notoriously dangerous stretch of water off the Kent coast. The area was clearly visible from the tower of his Ramsgate house. When he acquired the *Caroline* he wrote to a friend: "I have got a boat fit for any work. She is just 6 inches longer than my studio, 40 feet 6 inches, and will carry 36 tons I shall have a red cross painted on the foresail" (quoted in Atterbury and Wainwright, eds., *Pugin*, p. 10).

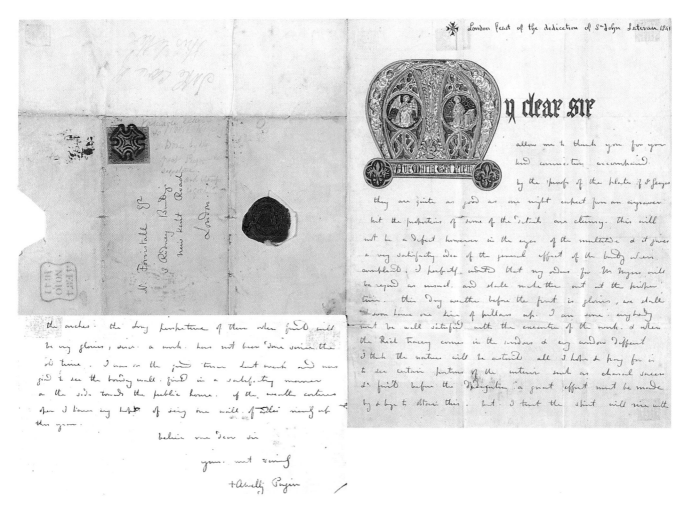

46. Illuminated Letter

1841
A. W. N. Pugin
Pen and watercolor
Saint George's Cathedral,
Southwark

Pugin's habit of illuminating his letters with elaborate initials and other decorations was established quite early in his life and reflects his almost romantic approach to medievalism. Examples are known from the 1830s, when he was living at Saint Marie's Grange and in regular correspondence with his friend William Osmond, an antiquary and scholar. A fine example sent to Osmond is illustrated in Ferrey's biography of Pugin, *Recollections* (facing p. 77). Other examples include letters to J. R. Bloxam, fellow of Magdalen College, Oxford, and to J. F. Russell, a member of the Cambridge Camden Society (illustrated in Atterbury and Wainwright, *Pugin*, eds., p. 107).

A feature of Pugin's illuminated letters was that they were not reserved for his close friends and supporters. Many, like this one, were sent to acquaintances and often were a prelude to a letter of relative unimportance. Michael Forristalm, the recipient of this letter, was the secretary of the committee of seventeen who superintended the construction of Saint George's Cathedral, Southwark. After this dramatic opening, the letter is really nothing more than a progress report. Its content reflects Pugin's hopes for the building at this early stage of its construction. He writes, "the long perspective of these [arches] will be very glorious . . . such a work has not been seen since the old times."

273

47. Casket

France [?], ca. 15th century, with
later additions
Wrought iron; 5¾ x 5¼ x 20⅜ in.
(14.6 x 13.4 x 51.8 cm)
The Board of Trustees of the
Victoria and Albert Museum,
London
Inv. no. 1235.1853

This French-made casket, from
Pugin's own collection, is typical of
the medieval antiquities he acquired
on his many visits to Europe. Its

solid and relatively simple form and
finish probably made it a useful
model for Pugin's wrought iron
work. It would originally have been
brightly painted, and small traces of
the polychrome finish still survive.
It was bought for £5 at the sale of
Pugin's collection in 1853 by the
Museum of Manufactures, the pre-
cursor of the Victoria & Albert
Museum, and was one of the first
pieces of medieval metalwork to
enter that collection.

274

48. Knocker

France [?], ca. 15th century
Wrought iron; 15½ x 5 in. (39.4 x
12.7 cm)
The Board of Trustees of the
Victoria and Albert Museum,
London
Inv. no. 1221.1853

Bought by the Museum of Manufacture, London, from the Pugin
sale in 1853 for £14, this knocker
was much admired at the time by

Gottfried Semper, a celebrated Prussian writer, scholar, and designer.
He was a close associate of the
museum, which would evolve into
the Victoria & Albert Museum.
He believed—wrongly as it turned
out—that the knocker was an early
example of cast iron. It was heavily
altered and restored early in the
nineteenth century, but it is not
known whether this work was completed before or after Pugin
acquired the piece.

49. Perfume Burner

France, ca. 15th century
Wrought iron; 14¼ x 14¼ in.
(35.5 x 35.5 cm)
Roman Catholic Archdiocese of
Birmingham, England

This singular object, with its unusually detailed architectural form,
was inherited by Pugin from his
father, who had acquired it from
N. X. Willemin, a renowned French
artist, antiquary, and collector. It
is illustrated, along with other
Pugin-owned objects, in Willemin's
*Monuments Francais Inedits pour
servir a l'Histoire des Arts depuis
le VIeme siecle jusqu'au commemce-
ment du XVIIeme* (plate 215). Published in installments between 1806
and 1839, this was one of Pugin's
most important sourcebooks.

Although Willemin believed this
object to be a rechaud (brazier), a
detailed examination undertaken
recently has proven it to be a per-
fume burner. Because the form and
decoration, including functional
doors and a drawbridge, are
entirely architectural, it is likely
that this was made for secular use.
The wrought iron has traces of the
original polychrome finish. As no
other medieval object quite like this
is known, it is not possible to do
more than speculate about its date
and origin. There is one parallel in
form, though not in detail: the celebrated twelfth-century censer styled
as a Byzantine church that is in the
Basilico San Marco, Venice.

50. Encaustic Tiles

France, ca. 14th century
Earthenware, colored clay inlay;
4⅝ in. square (11.5 cm) each tile;
29½ in. long (75 cm) overall size
Roman Catholic Archdiocese of
Birmingham, England

These tiles, displayed in their original wooden box, were acquired by Pugin from the Ducal Palace in Caen in Normandy on one of his many visits to northern France. They formed part of a large collection of medieval and later objects assembled by Pugin for Saint Mary's College, Oscott, where they would be used for teaching purposes and design sources. Saint Mary's was a large new seminary north of Birmingham that was in the process of development when Pugin was introduced to it in 1837

by the Earl of Shrewsbury. He was soon given the responsibility for the completion of the college buildings and their contents. Oscott remains today the major depository of objects associated with the early phase of Pugin's life as an architect and designer. An important component was Pugin's collection of woodcarvings, metalwork, textiles, tiles, and other medieval material, generally referred to at the time as "Pugin's things." They were displayed in a special exhibition room at the college.

Pugin and his lectures on medieval art and architecture, based on the collection, were such a regular feature of Oscott life that he was given the title of Professor of Ecclesiastical Architecture and Antiquities at Saint Mary's. His association with Oscott continued for the rest of his life, and he remained a familiar figure in the college chapel, corridors, teaching rooms, and refectory. When Dr. Kerril Amherst, later Bishop of Northampton, was a student, he kept a diary and recorded his impressions of Pugin: ". . . we used

to hear Pugin's loud voice as he gave directions, sounding through the corridors, or his ringing laugh when he was struck by some ridiculous idea. He was then quite a young man, not more than two or three and twenty, beardless, with long, thick, straight black hair, an eye that took in everything, and with genius and enthusiasm in every line of his face and play of his features. He was rather below the ordinary stature, and of a thick set figure, and the style of his dress inclined to that of a dissenting minister of those days, combined with a touch of the sailor. A wide-skirted black dress coat, loose trousers, shapeless shoes tied anyhow, a low-crowned battered hat, and a black silk handkerchief thrown negligently round his neck was his usual attire" (Thompson, "History of Oscott," pp. 63–84).

51. Dish

Deruta, Italy, ca. 1520
Maiolica or tin-glazed
earthenware, enameled; diam.
16½ in. (41.9 cm)
Painted decoration depicting the
Incredulity of Saint Thomas
Inscription: "TOMA QUI ME
VEDISTI ET CREDISTI" [Thomas
who saw me and believed]
The Board of Trustees of the
Victoria and Albert Museum,
London
Inv. no. 3036–1853

Maiolica is probably the quintessential decorative art form of the Renaissance and, as such, might have had a somewhat limited appeal to as devoted a medievalist as Pugin. In fact, the impact of the Renaissance upon Pugin was considerable. He designed wallpapers and textiles based on samples of early Italian fabrics, and some of his ceramics, notably the stove tiles designed for Minton & Company and shown at the Mediaeval Court in the Great Exhibition of 1851, indicate a familiarity both with maiolica in general and with the works of the Florentine Della Robbia family in particular.

Pugin's taste as a collector was wide ranging, encompassing objects of different periods, materials, and styles. His interests in maiolica, and the French Palissy wares of the same period, were highly developed. He was a pioneer collector of such wares and owned many examples of maiolica, including this dish, with its painted scene depicting the Incredulity of Saint Thomas. The dish was bought by the Museum of Manufactures (a forerunner of the Victoria & Albert) from the Pugin sale in 1853. It was one of the first pieces of this type of pottery to be acquired by the museum. The British Museum also bought maiolica from Pugin's collection.

52. Panel

English, ca. 16th century
Oak; 17⅜ x 13 in. (44 x 33 cm)
Roman Catholic Archdiocese of
Birmingham, England

According to an old label at Saint
Mary's College, Oscott, this panel
came from an ancient building in
the city of Salisbury in Wiltshire
where Pugin lived in the mid-1830s.

It was not far from the site on
which he built his first house, Saint
Marie's Grange, in 1835. At the
time, there were still medieval and
Tudor timber-framed buildings surviving in Salisbury, and it is possible
that this panel came from one of
them. In 1835 Pugin was involved
in the restoration of the fifteenth-
century Salisbury house of John
Halle, converting it into china
showrooms for a Mr. Payne. (Today, part of this work survives as
the foyer to a cinema.)

The Oscott label, possibly an old
inventory label, also shows that the
panel was formerly in Pugin's collection, part of which made its way
to Oscott College, to be used for

teaching purposes when Pugin was
Professor of Ecclesiastical and
Architectural Antiquities. Pugin
assembled a large collection of
examples of early carved woodwork and frequently incorporated
such pieces into his interior design
schemes, notably at Scarisbrick
Hall and Taymouth Castle. Judging
by the Tudor-style hat worn by the
triple Janus figure, the panel is
probably of sixteenth-century
origin.

279

53. Cabinet Door Panel

French, ca. 15th century
Oak, iron lockplate and hinges;
20 x 12 in. (50.8 x 30.5 cm)
The Board of Trustees of the
Victoria and Albert Museum,
London
Inv. no. 8207.1863

In the 1840s, while working on designs for the Palace of Westminster, Pugin collected examples of carved medieval woodwork and plaster casts of architectural details to use in teaching the wood and stone carvers who had been engaged for the project. For many years these pieces were stored in a hut at the Thames Bank Workshops in Westminster. In 1863 the London Board of Works donated them to the South Kensington Museum (a forerunner of the Victoria & Albert). Most of the hundred or so woodcarvings, of which this is one, survive, but the plaster casts, which numbered in the thousands, have been lost.

The combination of Pugin's teaching skills and the availability of these examples of medieval craftsmanship encouraged the nineteenth-century carvers to produce the remarkable work in wood and stone that still adorns almost every part of the palace. The cabinetmakers working on the furniture and fittings for the palace were similarly inspired.

It is unusual that this example is in its original condition, complete with its ironwork. Ancient fragments were all too often incorporated into so-called medieval furniture by early nineteenth-century restorers and antique dealers.

54. Madonna

1850
John Hardman Powell (1827–1895)
Oil on [metal]; 14¼ x 14¼ in. (35.7 x 35.7 cm), framed
Private collection

This copy of an Old Master painting is by John Hardman Powell, Pugin's assistant who in 1850 married Pugin's eldest daughter Anne, the only child of Pugin's marriage to Anne Garnet. It shows a detail of a painting that Pugin bought at auction in 1839 under the title, "The Madonna and Saint John, by Filippo Lippi." It had formerly been owned by Charles Aders, an important collector of early Old Master paintings. Pugin's own collection of paintings was extensive, including some very fine works on wood-panels by early Flemish and Italian masters. Two were attributed to Albrecht Dürer, and others were by or attributed to such artists as Domenichino and Jan Mostaert. One, a late-fifteenth-century Flemish triptych, a Descent from the Cross, is now in the collection of the Barber Institute, Birmingham, England, but the present whereabouts of the majority of Pugin's paintings, including this one, are not known. It remained in the Pugin family until 1960 when it was sold by Sotheby's as a Jacopo Sellaio to an Italain dealer but has since disappeared.

55. Vestments (from left): Cope, Chasuble, Dalmatic
ca. 1841
A. W. N. Pugin
Maker: Lonsdale and Tyler, London
Red silk and gold fabric
Roman Catholic Archdiocese of Birmingham, England

Pugin's desire to take the Catholic liturgy back to its medieval roots was not confined to its architectural setting but covered every aspect, including sacred vestments. He had strong views on what was correct and included a whole series of designs in his book, *The Glossary of Ecclesiastical Ornament*, published in 1844. He favored the full and heavy Gothic cut for vestments and was particularly dismissive of the various modern forms of the

Fig. 55a. *Bishop Thomas Walsh*, by John Rogers Herbert. Walsh, the president of Oscott College, is wearing a set of vestments, including a bishop's mitre, designed by Pugin. (Saint Mary's College, Oscott)

chasuble, such as the rectangular Roman style and the French, or fiddleback cut, popular because of its lightness and convenience. He described the latter as "the front resembling the body of a wasp, the back a board" (*The Glossary*, p. 63). When modern vestments were used at the 1838 opening of the Church of Saint Marie, Derby, which he designed, he and the Earl of Shrewsbury, one of his most important clients, left the service in disgust.

Pugin's concern was not just for style but also for the materials used. He rejected expensive silks from Lyons, France, and intricate laces "procured from that vitiated mass of taste the modern French school" and designed a whole new range of woven and embroidered linens, silks, velvets, and braids that would

be suitable for all types of vestments, including bishop's mitres. Many were based on surviving examples of medieval and Renaissance fabrics that he had found on his travels.

The Earl of Shrewsbury commissioned a number of sets of vestments, including a rich cloth-of-gold set (fig. 55d) for the consecration of the chapel at Oscott College in 1838. Even greater care was taken for the consecration of Saint Chad's Cathedral, Birmingham, in 1841; Shrewsbury commissioned from Pugin at least two sets of vestments for High Mass. One, this red and gold set, is still complete with its massive cope and cope hood bearing the Shrewsbury arms, its "correctly" styled chasuble, dalmatic, stole, and burse (the holder

Figs. 55b and 55c. Embroidery (*details*) designed by Pugin for alb hems.

for the corporal cloth for the altar or the chalice veil). The set was probably first worn during the lengthy ceremonies in June 1841 marking the installation of the relics of Saint Chad and the cathedral's consecration. It was made by Lonsdale & Tyler, theatrical costume makers of Covent Garden, London, perhaps a legacy of Pugin's work as a theater designer. Beginning in 1842 he gave this kind of work to John Hardman's sister whose workshop in Birmingham was known as Mistress Powell and Daughters.

Fig. 55d. Chasuble in cloth-of-gold, from a set of vestments designed by Pugin and made for Saint Mary's College, Oscott, ca. 1838.

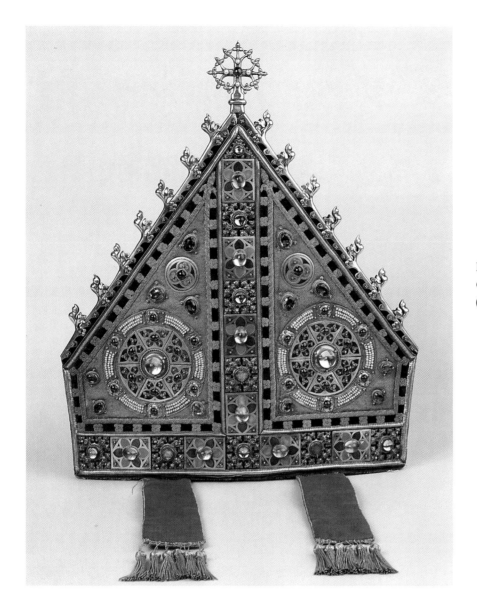

Fig. 56a. Designs for mitres, from *The Glossary of Ecclesiastical Ornament* (London, 1844).

56. Bishop's Mitre

1830
A. W. N. Pugin
Maker: John Hardman &
Company, Birmingham
Red velvet with applied cloth-of-
silver and cloth-of-gold, jewels,
brass crocketing; 13¾ x 13⅜ in.
(35 x 34 cm)
Westminster Cathedral, London

Pugin designed a series of mitres, the traditional headgear and an important liturgical and heraldic symbol of the bishop's office. Three were associated with Saint Chad's, Birmingham, and they are prominent in contemporary portraits of bishops such as that of Thomas Walsh (see fig. 55a).

This mitre was made for Bishop Nicholas Wiseman, who was a fervent Pugin supporter; it was commissioned by the Reverend Daniel Henry Haigh to celebrate his own ordination by Wiseman and the opening of Saint George's Cathedral, Southwark, on July 4, 1848. The Hardman daybook records the mitre on June 30, 1830, "Re Dr Haigh, Erdington, for Dr Wiseman. A precious mitre etc. £65: case £1 12s" (Hardman Archives, Birmingham). Wiseman, who became coadjutor to the vicar apostolic in London the same month, probably wore it on that occasion. Wiseman went on to become the first Archbishop of Westminster in September 1850 and was elevated to cardinal. As the mitre

was his personal possession, he took it with him to Westminster.

With its rich embroidery and jeweling and its decorative brass crocketing, this is one of the most splendid of Pugin's mitres. Its form and decoration show the level of sophistication that the Hardman workshop and its outworkers had attained by 1848. Pugin included designs for similar mitres in *The Glossary of Ecclesiastical Ornament*, taking care to revive a medieval form (fig. 56a).

57. Chalice

Assay, 1837–38
A. W. N. Pugin
Maker: Thomlinson and Davis,
Birmingham
Engraved silver-gilt; 10¼ x 7¼ in.
(25.5 x 14.5 cm)
Marks: town and makers' marks;
date letter for 1837–38
Roman Catholic Archdiocese of
Birmingham, England

According to tradition, this is the first chalice ever made from a design by Pugin. It was one of two commissioned for the consecration of the chapel at Saint Mary's College, Oscott, in 1838; Pugin himself is reputed to have engraved the simple crucifix on its stem the evening before the service. It is a simple design, following medieval precedents with a pedestal base, a shaft divided by a knob, and a generous calix, or bowl, with some decoration in relief. Many medieval and later chalices survived in England at that time, and Pugin had certainly seen others on the Continent, giving him a wide repertory of examples as sources. Pugin drew church metalwork for his "Ideal Scheme, The Chest," but a greater and more practical range was published in 1836 in his book, *Designs for Gold and Silversmiths* (fig. 57a). Later chalices show Pugin's increasing confidence with the form; they tend to be larger and more decorative, with extensive use of engraving, jeweling, and enameling.

As indispensable sacred vessels for the celebration of Mass, the chalice and its accompanying paten (in this case, missing), used for the service of the consecrated wine, had, by church law, to be made of precious metals. Silver or silver gilt were most commonly used.

Prior to Pugin's long association with John Hardman, which started in 1838, he seems to have used various silversmiths for his metalwork. George Frederick Pinnell of London, for example, made plate to Pugin designs for Oscott around the same time that this chalice was made by Thomlinson and Davis, a Birmingham firm.

Fig. 57a. Design for a chalice and ciborium, pen and ink, 1835. This was drawn by Pugin for *Designs for Gold and Silversmiths*, published in 1836. (Trustees of the Victoria & Albert Museum)

58. Contrasts, or a Parallel between the Noble Edifices of the Middle Ages and Corresponding Buildings Showing the Present Decay of Taste
1836
A. W. N. Pugin
Publisher: A. W. N. Pugin, London
Binding by A. W. N. Pugin: velvet, brass; 11⅜ x 9 x ¾ in. (28.5 x 23 x 2 cm)
Private collection

Contrasts is Pugin's most famous book. It has a brilliantly polemical text matched by engravings that made clear in no uncertain terms the right and wrong ways to design a wide range of buildings, both ecclesiastical and secular. It is a broadside against Neoclassicism, Rome, and the styles associated with Protestantism and the Reformation. It heralds the revival of the true Catholic styles of the Middle Ages. The book, which Pugin published at his own expense, did much to establish his reputation as a militant, outspoken supporter of modern Catholicism. It also made him many enemies within the establishment of the church. In letters to his

friend E. J. Willson, in September and October 1836, he wrote, "There is a vast deal of rage excited among certain parties by the publication of this work and I am a marked man here in Salisbury," and again, "the fact is the sale of the work has far exceeded my expectations, and the rage of the church party increases with its success" (quoted in Stanton, *Pugin*).

There were two editions of *Contrasts*, the first in 1836 and the second, with some additional plates, in 1841. The copy seen here is the first edition; it has a dedication to Pope

Gregory XVI on the title page, but it is not known when, or from whom, he received it. The library at the English College in Rome has a copy of Pugin's *True Principles* (1841), similarly dedicated to Pope Gregory. Pugin himself did not visit Rome until 1847, and, although he had an audience at the Vatican with Pope Gregory's successor, Pius IX, his book must have been in the Vatican library well before that date.

Pugin designed special bindings, usually velvet with brass mounts made by John Hardman, for a number of books, including missals, for ceremonial use in churches and colleges, and for members of his family.

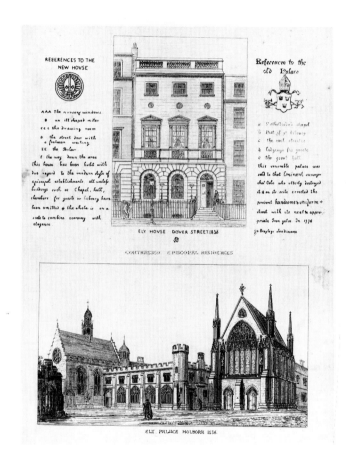

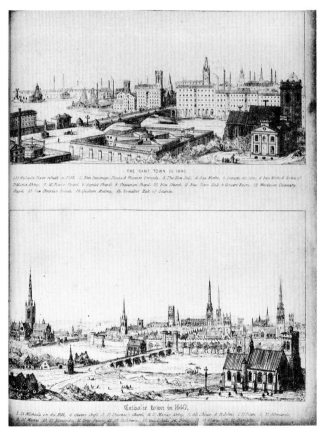

Fig. 58a. "Contrasted Episcopal Residences," from the first edition of *Contrasts* (1836).

Fig. 58b. "Contrasted Towns," from the second edition of *Contrasts* (1841).

59. Covered Flagon and Basin

Assay, 1837–38
A. W. N. Pugin
Maker: George Frederick Pinnell,
London
Engraved silver; flagon, H. 12¼ in.
(31 cm); basin, diam. 13¾ in.
(34.5 cm)
Marks: town and maker's marks;
date letter for 1837–38
Roman Catholic Archdiocese of
Birmingham, England

The design of the fittings, furnishings, and plate for Saint Mary's College, Oscott, represented an important challenge for Pugin. It was his first opportunity to develop a coordinated range of church objects on this scale. The designs for both wood and metalwork were revolutionary, breaking with the traditions of both early nineteenth-century Gothic Revival furniture and conventional church plate.

In form the flagon and basin are simple, with a carefully contrived balance between plain and decorated areas echoing the medieval models that Pugin would have used. He illustrated similar objects in his book, *Designs for Gold and Silversmiths*, published by Rudolph Ackermann in 1836. The basin is rounded, with a central depression to hold the flagon, and its lobed rim has engraved decoration. The flagon is a classic shape with rounded belly, narrow neck, and strongly defined handle. A flagon and basin were used for ceremonial hand-washing at a pontifical High Mass, a sufficiently rare occasion explaining the excellent condition of these two pieces today.

Pugin's fees for metalwork for Oscott College, including "the jug and basin for the bishop," came to £188 9s 6d. These and other items at Oscott were made by the London-based silversmith, George Frederick Pinnell; the work at Oscott represents Pinnell's only known association with Pugin.

Fig. 59a. Covered flagon and basin in silver plate, designed by Pugin and made by Hardman for Saint Augustine's, Ramsgate, in about 1849. (Private collection)

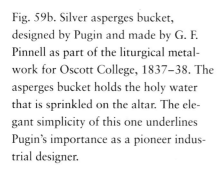

Fig. 59b. Silver asperges bucket, designed by Pugin and made by G. F. Pinnell as part of the liturgical metalwork for Oscott College, 1837–38. The asperges bucket holds the holy water that is sprinkled on the altar. The elegant simplicity of this one underlines Pugin's importance as a pioneer industrial designer.

60. Censer, or Thurible

Assay, 1847–48
A. W. N. Pugin
Maker: John Hardman &
Company, Birmingham
Silver; 5⅛ x 5½ in. (13 x 14 cm)
Marks: town and maker's marks;
date letter for 1847–48
Erdington Abbey, Birmingham

Daniel Henry Haigh, an antiquary and friend of Pugin, was ordained a priest at Saint Mary's College, Oscott, in April 1848. The same year Haigh, a generous benefactor, commissioned the building and equipping of the Church of Saints Thomas and Edmund of Canterbury at Erdington, north of Birmingham and not far from Oscott. The architect was Charles Hansom, but Pugin designed the stained

Fig. 60a. "Church Furniture Revived at Birmingham"; engraving by Pugin from *An Apology* (1843). One of the two censers resting on the floor is similar to the one shown here. A pyx sits on the shelf, left, beside a crucifix and ciborium.

glass, metalwork, and vestments. Unlike some of Pugin's other patrons, Haigh was happy to spend his money on fine things, and the metalwork at Erdington is among the best ever created by the Pugin–Hardman partnership. This is one of two censers of "Tower shape with elaborate pierced work and richly engraved etc" dispatched by Hardman on April 10, 1847 "at a cost of £32 5 0 each" (Hardman Archive, Birmingham).

The censer, or thurible, is used for the burning of incense, a symbol of prayer dating back to the Old Testament. The incense is burned over charcoal, kept alight by an acolyte, called the thurifer, who swings the censer. Examples of medieval censers were known in Pugin's time, and he probably based the distinctive architectural form of this example on medieval German models. It is a clever design, with the pierced openings and traceries in the towers allowing the passage of the fumes of the incense. Pugin used it, or versions of it, several times. A similar censer, along with other metalwork designs by him such as the pyx (cat. no. 61), is included in an illustration (fig. 60a) in his book, *An Apology for the Revival of Christian Architecture in England*, published in 1843. It is also shown in *The Glossary of Ecclesiastical Ornament* (1844).

61. Pyx

Assay, 1851–52
A. W. N. Pugin
Maker: John Hardman &
Company, Birmingham
Silver, enamel; diam. 6½ in.
(16.5 cm)
Marks: town and maker's marks;
date letter for 1851–52
Saint George's Cathedral,
Southwark

A pyx is one of the sacred vessels that were part of the traditional Catholic liturgy which Pugin was determined to restore. The pyx represented the survival of the medieval practice of church plate being kissed by the priest and congregation during the Pax Vobiscum of the Mass. In the Tridentine liturgy only the bishop and a single prominent lay worshiper participated in this ritual.

This pyx is modeled on surviving medieval examples, one of which was then in Pugin's collection of antiquities at Saint Mary's College, Oscott, and had been illustrated by him in his *Glossary of Ecclesiastical Ornament*. It is embellished with relief, engraved, and pierced decoration and an enameled head of

Christ. In the quatrefoil on the base is a bishop's mitre and the monogram "TG," for Thomas Grant, first Bishop of Southwark. The front is inscribed "Agnus Dei qui tollis peccata mundi, dona nobis pacem" (Lamb of God who takes away the sins of the world, grant us peace). The pyx was presented to Saint George's Cathedral, Southwark, by John and Elizabeth Knill who were related to Pugin's third wife, Jane, and were prominent members of the congregation.

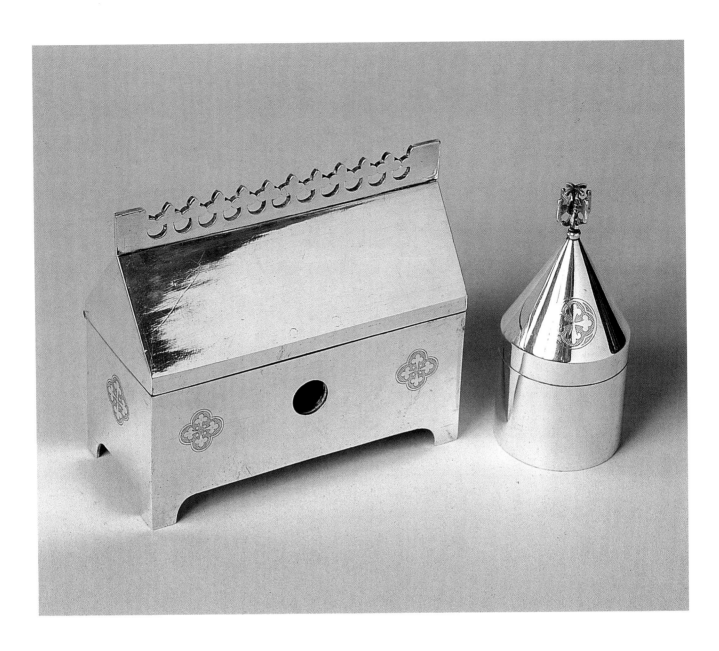

62. Chrismatory, or Ointment Box
   ca. 1846
   A. W. N. Pugin
   Maker: probably John Hardman
   & Company, Birmingham
   Engraved silver plate; left, 4¾ x
   5⅛ in. (12 x 13 cm); chrismatory,
   right, is not in the exhibition.
   Roman Catholic Archdiocese of
   Birmingham, England

A chrismatory holds the oil consecrated once a year by the bishop for
the ritual annointing at the sacra-
ments of baptism and extreme
unction, the sacrament of the sick.
These examples were made for the
Church of Saint Giles, Cheadle,
Staffordshire, which was the greatest architectural achievement of

Pugin and his patron, the Earl of
Shrewsbury. Commissioned in 1839
and designed in 1840, the church
was one of Pugin's primary concerns until its consecration on
September 1, 1846.

An ambitious structure, lavishly
finished, almost regardless of cost,
Saint Giles's represents the crowning achievement of Pugin's career as
a church builder and the fulfillment
of his dream of modern Christian
architecture. The exterior is built of
local red sandstone. It is marked by
a soaring spire and rich sculptural
decoration carved by Thomas
Roddis, a member of the Sutton
Coldfield firm of stonemasons who
worked for Pugin at Oscott College, Saint Augustine's, and Scaris-

brick, as well as Saint Giles's. The
interior is a glorious explosion of
polychromy, bringing to life the
frontispiece of Pugin's *Glossary of
Ecclesiastical Ornament* in a complex program of color and pattern.
Every vertical surface is colored—
by wall painting and stenciling,
tiling, stained glass—in a proliferation of formalized pattern. The
floors are covered with Minton's
encaustic tiles.

The richness of the decoration
is balanced by the church's fittings,
with splendid woodwork and
metalwork designed by Pugin for a
church that was always close to his
heart. On September 29, 1841 he
wrote to the Earl of Shrewsbury,
"I feel truly grateful to your lord-

ship for had it not been for you I should never have had the opportunity of doing a really good thing. Cheadle is my great comfort, at length one good building. I am sure your lordship will be delighted: it is the real thing" (Victoria & Albert, Shrewsbury letters). More than any other building, with the possible exception of the Palace of Westminster, Saint Giles's represents the complete expression of Pugin's revived Gothic style in a fully integrated blend of architecture and interior design.

The metalwork for the church, both architectural and liturgical, was made by Hardman & Company. Fittings continued to arrive almost to the day of consecration. The Hardman daybook, now in the Birmingham Reference Library, records the dispatch on August 4, 1846 of the two chrismatories shown: "The Right Honble Lord Shrewsbury for Cheadle, Alton Towers . . . A G(erman) S(ilver) Plated Chrismatory, with 2 Silver Bottles engraved £5 12s 0: a do- do- simple do with silver £2.0.0" (Hardman Archive, Birmingham, no. 77).

With their simple architectural form and minimal decoration, these chrismatories are among Pugin's most strikingly simple metalwork designs. Their geometry underlines his importance as a revolutionary designer. Pugin was aware, as usual, of medieval models but these objects show clearly how he used medieval sources for inspiration, not for mere copying or re-creation.

Fig. 62a. The interior of the Church of Saint Giles, Cheadle, completed in 1846.

Fig. 62b. The Blessed Sacrament Chapel, Saint Giles's, Cheadle, a brilliant example of Pugin's polychromy in wall painting, tiling, and stained glass.

Fig. 62c. Detail, wall painting in the Blessed Sacrament Chapel, Saint Giles's, Cheadle

Fig. 62d. Corona lucis (chandelier) and wall painting in the chancel, Saint Giles's, Cheadle.

Fig. 62a

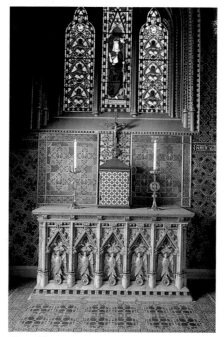

Fig. 62b

Fig. 62c

Fig. 62d

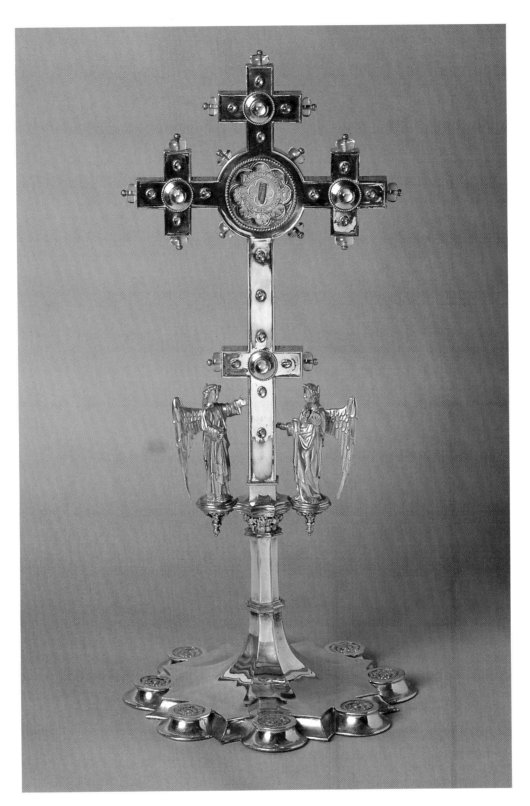

63. Reliquary Cross

ca. 1848

A. W. N. Pugin

Maker: probably John Hardman
& Company, Birmingham

Silver, parcel-gilt, jewels; 24 x
11 in. (61 x 28 cm)

Erdington Abbey, Birmingham

This reliquary holds a purported
piece of the True Cross in its central
lunette. The relic determined the
complex nature of its design. It is in
the form of a cross, with angel supports above a lobed base. The end
of each arm forms a Jerusalem
cross, which is partly an iconographic and partly a heraldic reference to the site of the Crucifixion,
the legend of the finding of the True
Cross by the Empress Helena, and
even the emblems of Saint Chad,
the patron saint of the Birmingham
diocese. The generosity of Daniel
Henry Haigh, the patron of Saints
Thomas and Edmund of Canterbury in Erdington, ensured that
this church was equipped with
some of the most splendid metalwork ever created by the Pugin–
Hardman partnership, typified by
this reliquary.

64. Altar Cross
1846
A. W. N. Pugin
Maker: John Hardman &
Company, Birmingham
Silver, brass, enamel, jewels;
24 x 12 in. (61 x 30.5 cm)
Roman Catholic Archdiocese of
Birmingham, England

At least three altar crosses of different designs were supplied to Saint Giles's, Cheadle, and this is probably the "richly gilt engraved and enamel'd cross and figure for ladye chapel £26" dispatched by Hardman on August 22, 1846 (Hardman Archive, Birmingham). Pugin's altar crosses tend to follow a standard pattern, with a stylized brass figure held on a floriated cross and supported on a flared or lobed base. Some are taller, made to stand behind, but be visible above, the tabernacle. This example was to stand directly on the altar. The cross has a central halo with quatrefoil lobes, set with gems and having trefoil terminations. The light blue enamel ground, an unusual choice of color for Pugin, has liturgical and heraldic associations with the Virgin Mary.

Pugin avoided realism in his altar crosses, relying on symbolism and his sense of design to give the object the necessary impact. He only used realistic crucifix figures on his rood screens, where Christ's body is usually shown in agony and painted in realistic colors.

Fig. 64a. Altar and processional crosses, designed by Pugin, from a Hardman & Company catalogue, 1846. (Minton Museum, Stoke-on-Trent)

Fig. 64b. Altar cross of silver-plated brass with rich enamel decoration and bearing the crest of Pugin's friend, the Reverend Alfred Luck. This is from a set, with matching candlesticks, made for Saint Augustine's Church, Ramsgate, and shown in the Mediaeval Court at the Great Exhibition of 1851. (Private collection)

Fig. 64a

Fig. 64b

65. Monstrance

ca. 1846
A. W. N. Pugin
Maker: John Hardman &
Company, Birmingham
Engraved gilt brass, jewels; 19¼ x
9 in. (49 x 23 cm)
Roman Catholic Archdiocese of
Birmingham, England

A monstrance is for the Exposition (exhibition) and Benediction (blessing) of the Blessed Sacrament. Holding the monstrance by the shaft and displaying the Host, the priest blesses the congregation. The revival of such liturgies in early nineteenth-century Britain, following the Catholic Emancipation Act of 1829, created a great demand for new church plate, including the monstrance. Pugin used two basic forms, both drawn from medieval

models. One was this sunburst type, a fifteenth-century style he had included in his 1832 "Ideal Scheme, The Chest" (fig. 65a), and the other was a Gothic type, a complex architectural form based more on reliquaries than on monstrances.

This sunburst monstrance was dispatched by Hardman to Cheadle on August 16, 1846 and described as "a Richly gilt Monstrance, Sun Pattern, Engraved & Set with Stones. £21 10s" (Hardman Archive, Birmingham). It was donated by the Earl of Shrewsbury who between 1845 and 1847 paid Hardman £1400 for metalwork. To make the most of his investment Shrewsbury insisted generally on plated base metal rather than precious metal. The electroplating process had been patented by Elkington & Company, a Birmingham firm, in 1840 and was used extensively by Hardman for Pugin-designed metalwork during the 1840s. At the time plated wares were sometimes referred to as "German Silver." The process presumably fulfilled Pugin's view that "Any modern invention which conduces to comfort, cleanliness, or durability, should be adopted by the consistent architects."

Fig. 65a. Monstrance in 15th-century style, drawn by Pugin and included in his "Ideal Scheme, The Chest," completed in 1832. (Trustees of the Victoria & Albert Museum)

Fig. 65b. Monstrance in gilded brass, designed by Pugin and made by Hardman for Saint Augustine's church, Ramsgate. This was exhibited at the Mediaeval Court at the Great Exhibition of 1851. (Saint Augustine's, Ramsgate)

Expositor of the Holy Sacrament. Gold set with jewels.

Fig. 65a

Fig. 65b

66. Reliquary

ca. 1850
A. W. N. Pugin
Maker: John Hardman &
Company, Birmingham
Engraved gilt brass, enamel,
jewels; H. 28⅜ in. (72 cm)
Saint George's Cathedral,
Southwark

Through contemporary descriptions and illustrations, Pugin was well aware of the great variety of reliquaries that had existed during the Middle Ages. He knew of the importance attached to them by pious Catholics who collected relics as objects of devotion. Many medieval reliquaries were designed to be portable and these were stored usually in special cupboards, side chapels, or sacristies. The most important relics were displayed on the high altar during major liturgical services.

For Pugin the reliquary had an equal significance. He was fascinated by accounts of those that had been destroyed during the Reformation. In his pamphlet, *Some Remarks on the Articles which have Recently Appeared in 'The Rambler' Relative to Ecclesiastical Architecture and Decoration*, published in 1850, he wrote, "by the help of the histories of the devout and painful Dugdale I replenished, in imagination, the empty sacristies of York and Lincoln with a costly array of precious vessels and reliquaries." He also designed many actual reliquaries. An important wooden one was incorporated in the reredos of the high altar at Saint Chad's Cathedral, Birmingham, in 1841.

The example seen here, described by Hardman as a "tabernacle reliquary" for three minute relics of Saint Thomas à Becket, the Archbishop of Canterbury who had been murdered there in 1174, was ordered in December 1849 by the Reverend the Honourable George Talbot at a cost of £120. It was designed to mark the primatial status of the new Cathedral of Saint George, Southwark. Talbot, an eminence grise of the new English Roman Catholic church, was only an occasional visitor to Southwark, being based in Rome. He publicized his gift in the Catholic press via an article in *The Tablet* (1848, p. 529), describing it and referring to Pugin's beautiful drawings.

The architectural form of the reliquary is distinctive. Its center, the box holding the relics in a central glass spectacle, is richly enameled with adoring angels and scenes from the saint's life and martyrdom. Above the box is a towerlike structure with a figure of the saint in a niche, all supported by flying buttresses. It is made of electroplated gilt brass, enriched with engraving, piercing, modeling in relief, cabouchon crystals and precious stones, and enameling. Reliquaries in this style were made in large quantities from the 1850s in Belgium, where Pugin's reputation was held in high regard.

67. Crowns, for Virgin and Child
Assay, 1848–49
A. W. N. Pugin
Maker: John Hardman & Company, Birmingham
Silver, rock crystal, garnet; larger, 4¼ x 5⅞ in. (10.5 x 14.5 cm); smaller, 4 x 3⅞ in. (10 x 9.5 cm)
Marks: town and maker's marks; date letter for 1848–49
Roman Catholic Archdiocese of Birmingham, England

The ceremonial crowning of statues, a pious practice that began in the Middle Ages and continued into the Baroque period and beyond on the Continent, was revived in England in the 1830s for certain feasts, and for the month of May devotions. Pugin himself followed this revived practice, designing crowns for statues at his own church, Saint Augustine's, Ramsgate. Indeed, Pugin encouraged a British revival of the public veneration of statues, first at Saint Chad's, then at Oscott and Ramsgate. It was a new practice for most British Catholics.

The Oscott crowns, probably made for the statue of the Virgin and Child above the entrance door to the college chapel, may have been supplied after Pugin's death. The larger crown, set with rock crystals, cost £9 and the smaller one, set with garnets, £6.

68. Morse, or Cope Clasp

ca. 1841
A. W. N. Pugin
Maker: John Hardman &
Company, Birmingham
Gilt brass, enamel; diam. 4¾ in.
(12 cm)
Roman Catholic Archdiocese of
Birmingham, England

Copes were cloaks worn for processions, for parts of the Mass, and at vespers. Their voluminous form required a secure clasp, called a morse, at the front. Pugin made the most of the morse, turning it into a large jeweled brooch often made from precious metal and enriched with modeling, engraving, and enameling. This example, of gilded brass, was probably given to Saint Chad's Cathedral, Birmingham, by the Earl of Shrewsbury to accompany the set of vestments (see cat. no. 55) that he presented for the consecration of the cathedral in 1841. Although incomplete, this morse is a fine example of Pugin's use of heraldic decoration and demonstrates his skill with flat pattern. It carries the Shrewsbury arms, a lion rampant supported by two Talbot hounds. The reverse is enameled with a crucifixion scene. The decorative potential of the Shrewsbury emblems was often exploited by Pugin, notably on the west doors of Saint Giles's, Cheadle, probably his most dramatic use of heraldry.

Fig. 68a. *John Talbot, 16th Earl of Shrewsbury*, artist unknown; oil on board. This portrait shows the Earl of Shrewsbury in medieval dress, with a view of the chapel at Alton Towers through the window. It is part of the reredos Pugin designed for the chapel.

Fig. 68b. The heraldic west doors at Saint Giles's Church, Cheadle, Staffordshire.

69. Chalice

Assay, 1847–48
A. W. N. Pugin
Maker: John Hardman &
Company, Birmingham
Engraved parcel-gilt, enamel,
jewels; H. 9⅞ in. (24.5 cm)
Marks: town and maker's mark;
date letter for 1847–48; arms of
Saint George
Saint George's Cathedral,
Southwark

Unlike many Pugin churches, Saint George's Cathedral, Southwark, had a notably long building period, from 1840 to 1848, when it was finally opened by Bishop Nicholas Wiseman. It was particularly well equipped with altars, fittings, and metalwork. The Hardman day-books show that most of the plate was made from precious metal, and there is a long list of donors, including: George Myers, the cathedral's builder; the Knill family; the Reverend Daniel Henry Haigh of Erdington; Ernest Scott; and Dr. Thomas Doyle.

This chalice, in a relatively simple style, was commissioned by Mrs. Petre as part of the fittings of a chantry built in the cathedral in 1848 in memory of her husband, the Honorable Edward Petre. The bowl carries the inscription, "Calicem salutaris accipiam et nomen Domini invocabo" (Receive the cup of salvation and I will call upon the name of the Lord). The stem and knob are decorated, and the flared base has enameled shields, two carrying the Petre coat of arms and a third with a floriated cross and symbols of the Passion. The total cost of the chantry and its fittings was £529.

Fig. 69a. Detail of a stained glass window, by Pugin; pen and ink, ca. 1846. Chalices and other metalwork forms were often used as decorative features for stained glass and wall painting. (City of Birmingham Museum & Art Gallery)

Fig. 69b. The Petre Chantry in Saint George's Cathedral, Southwark, for which the chalice was made.

Fig. 69c. Saint George's Cathedral, Southwark, London, by Pugin; pencil on paper, 1841. This original scheme of 1841 was considered far too ambitious, and the actual building, which was never completed, was quite different. It was largely destroyed by bombing in 1942. (Saint George's Cathedral, Southwark)

Fig. 69d. Interior of the Lady Chapel at Saint George's Cathedral, Southwark, watercolor possibly by Father Alfred White, 1854. Contemporary views of Pugin's interiors are very rare, and this example, although by an amateur artist, shows the richness and color of Pugin's original scheme which was painted by John Earley working for Hardman & Company and carried out between 1845 and 1849.

Fig. 69a

Fig. 69b

Fig. 69c

Fig. 69d

70. Model Chalice

ca. 1846–49
A. W. N. Pugin
Maker: John Hardman &
Company, Birmingham
Gilt base metal, enamel,
semiprecious stones; cast and
engraved decoration; H. 10¼ in.
(26 cm)
The Art Institute of Chicago
Bessie Bennett Fund, 1981.640

By the late 1840s, many of Pugin's
metalwork designs for Hardman &
Company had been formalized to
the point where they could be
included in Hardman's illustrated
catalogues. Indeed from the mid-
1840s Pugin drew illustrations for

these catalogues, which were
printed by lithography. The more
popular items, notably candlesticks,
crosses, and chalices, were to some
extent standardized. Clients needing to see more than the catalogue
illustration could examine actual
examples in the Hardman showrooms, or at various exhibition
displays.

It is possible that this chalice,
which is the only known example
of a Hardman model metalwork,
was made as a showroom sample,
probably one of a number of such
pieces kept on display in Birmingham to encourage orders for liturgical metalware. Stylistically, the
chalice belongs to the late 1840s.

The complex base and the rich
array of decorative techniques used
on it suggest a late date and link it
to chalices made for Erdington
Abbey (see cat. no. 72) and for the
Medieval Court of 1851 (see cat.
no. 143). The inspiration for the
design may have been the Hollar
engraving of a chalice (see cat.
no. 31). This engraving was in
Pugin's collection and he referred
to it often, although there are also
links between this model and late-
fifteenth-century Italian chalices.
It is also possible that this chalice
was displayed at the Birmingham
Exhibition of 1849, a forerunner
of the Great Exhibition of 1851.

71. Chalice

Assay, ca. 1850
A. W. N. Pugin
Maker: John Hardman &
Company, Birmingham
Parcel-gilt, enamel, jewels; 7 x
4 in. (17.8 x 10.2 cm)
Marks: town and maker's marks;
no date letter
Roman Catholic Archdiocese of
Birmingham, England

This elaborate and richly decorated chalice represents the full development of Pugin's metalwork style. It has a flared bowl in parcel gilding, with an engraved inscription, and the calix, shaft, and knob are all densely decorated in relief with hexfoils enclosing cabouchon jewels. The flared foot carries an enameled coat of arms, probably of the church's patrons, the Gandolfi and Hornyold families.

The Church of Our Lady and Saint Alphonsus, Blackmore Park, was completed in 1846 to the designs of Charles Hansom. Pugin was responsible for the fittings, whose lavishness was due to the generosity of J. V. Gandolfi. His name occurs often in the Hardman daybooks beginning in 1846, but there is no direct reference to this chalice. It may therefore be later than 1849. Pugin drawings for this type of chalice, designed for Hardman to use and adapt as necessary, are in the Drawings Collection of the Royal Institute of British Architects, London.

72. Chalice

Assay, 1849–50
A. W. N. Pugin
Maker: John Hardman &
Company, Birmingham
Silver, parcel-gilt, enamel, jewels;
H. 10⅜ in. (26.5 cm); base,
W. 7⅛ in. (18 cm), bowl diam.,
5⅛ in. (13 cm)
Marks: town and maker's marks;
date letter for 1849–50
Erdington Abbey, Birmingham

The scale and splendor of this chalice reflect the generosity of the Reverend Daniel Henry Haigh, the most lavish patron of Pugin–Hardman metalwork. The chalice is decorated in a highly complex manner with engraving, modeling in relief, jeweling, and enamels. The stem is flared and the pierced plinth is set with jeweled enamel medallions. In scale and decorative detail this is close to a chalice in Westminster Cathedral, ordered by Nicholas Wiseman, the future cardinal, in 1848. As Haigh gave the Wiseman mitre to Westminster, he may also have donated the chalice. Chalices were usually made in pairs by Hardman, and there is a possibility that Haigh kept this one for himself, for use at Erdington Abbey, and sent the other to Westminster. There is an even larger, more florid version of the design at Saint George's Cathedral, Southwark, dated 1867. The Hardman company continued to manufacture church metalwork to Pugin designs long after his death, sometimes adapting them to suit the needs of particular clients, and the designs remained in the Hardman catalogues at least until the end of the century.

73. Flagon

1869–70

Maker: John Hardman &
Company, Birmingham
Silver, glass; H. 10¾ in. (27.3 cm)
The Carnegie Museum of Art
Museum Purchase: Gift of James
H. Beal, Herbert DuPuy, Mrs. B. F.
Jones III, Mrs. Virginia Hays
Osburn, Mr. and Mrs. George
Magee Wyckoff, Mr. and Mrs.
Frederick L. Cook in memory of
Mr. and Mrs. George Magee
Myckoff, Mr. and Mrs. Barry
Duffee Jr., and Mr. and Mrs.
George M. Wyckoff, Jr., by
exchange
Inv. no. 94.113

Flagons for ecclesiastical and for
secular use made from metal-
mounted glass are known to have
been designed by Pugin, although
few seem to have survived. The
starting point was probably the
silver-mounted glass or crystal cruet
sets designed by Pugin beginning
around 1838. Well-known examples of larger flagons, inspired by
medieval models, are in churches
in Kent and Staffordshire. Monstrances in traditional fifteenth-
century styles, with a circular
crystal or glass core, a form revived
by Pugin and Hardman, were
related. The full development of

this flagon form, however, took
place after Pugin's death, initially
by his son Edward working with
Hardman and then by Hardman
who established the form as a regular part of production, offering it in
both clear and colored glass.

Although broadly Puginian in
form, this piece has many features
that reveal its late date, including
the tall neck and globular body
shape, the richly floriated band of
engraving, thin handle, and heavy
naturalism of the mounts.

74. Pair of Altar Candlesticks, from a Set of Six
ca. 1846
A. W. N. Pugin
Maker: John Hardman &
Company, Birmingham
Engraved gilt brass; H. 19¼ in.
(49 cm)
Roman Catholic Archdiocese of
Birmingham, England

Pugin's candlesticks are the most varied, inventive, and prolific of his metalwork designs. Early examples are to be seen at Saint Chad's Cathedral and Saint Mary's College, Oscott, the latter set dating from 1838. From then on, candlesticks were made both as standard designs, available from the Hardman catalogue, and to special order. The many types of candlesticks had different functions, both practical and symbolic. Tall sets of six were for the high altar and were lit only at High Mass or vespers. Shorter pairs were for Low Mass or for use in the side chapels. So-called elevation sticks were lit during the central part of the Mass. Processional sets had long handles and, some-times, an enclosed carrier for the candle. Catalogues also refer to "benediction branches."

This pair of candlesticks is from the high altar set of six designed for Saint Giles's, Cheadle, and probably delivered to the church by Hard-man on August 22, 1846 with a matching altar cross. The distinc-tive feature of the design is the flat roundel set into the stem, engraved with "Christi crux est lux mea" (Christ's cross is my light). Other elements are the swelling knob with engraved jewellike mounts and the flared foot with a pierced plinth.

75. Pair of Altar Candlesticks, from Set of Six (one shown)
ca. 1848
A. W. N. Pugin
Maker: John Hardman &
Company, Birmingham
Brass; 19⅜ x 7⅛ in. (49 x 18 cm)
Roman Catholic Archdiocese of
Birmingham, England

According to the Hardman day-book these candlesticks, part of a set of six for "J V Gandolfi Esq," were dispatched on "June 27 (1846) no 928 47s each, £14 2s" (Hardman Archive, Birmingham). The reference number, 928, indicates that this is a standard design, probably available in different sizes. Strikingly architectural in form, with a heavy base supported by crouching lions, these are excellent examples of the high-quality brass-work associated with the Hardman firm.

76. Pair of Altar Candlesticks
ca. 1846
A. W. N. Pugin
Maker: John Hardman &
Company, Birmingham
Brass; 18½ x 9⅞ in. (47 x 25 cm)
Roman Catholic Archdiocese of
Birmingham, England

The lighting of Pugin churches was
achieved primarily by means of
large standing candelabra and
hanging coronas (circular chandeliers). Occasionally, as at Saint
George's Cathedral, Southwark,
gas lighting was used. Sets of smaller candlesticks, on the main altar
and in the side chapels, were therefore symbolic, part of the consciously theatrical effect of the
revived Catholic liturgy. The dramatic lighting effects used for the
evening service at the 1846 consecration of Saint Giles's, Cheadle,
was remarked upon by John
Cardinal Newman and by the
French Gothic Revivalist A. N.
Didron.

These candlesticks have prickets
for five candles and were made not
for the celebration of the Mass, but
for special services such as Benediction or the Exposition of the Blessed
Sacrament when a multiplicity of
candles was required. The design—
with its gallery, trefoils, fleur-de-lis
brackets, flared octagonal base, and
crouching lion's feet—is complex
and untypical; it does not appear to
be recorded in the Hardman daybooks.

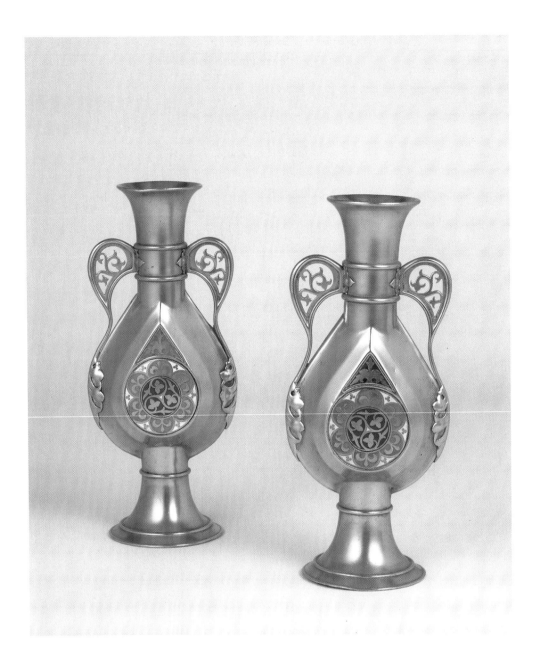

77. Pair of Altar Vases

ca. 1850
A. W. N. Pugin
Maker: John Hardman &
Company, Birmingham
Gilt brass, enamel; 9⅞ x 4¾ x
3½ in. (25 x 12 x 9 cm)
Private collection

Pugin criticized altars overloaded
with flowers but produced a number of designs for altar vases, most
of which were included in the
Hardman catalogues over a long
period. These vases, with their
slight Moorish echoes of the Al-
hambra in Granada in the pierced
handles, are a well-known design

Fig. 77a. "Ecclesiastical Vessels,"
engraving from *Art-Journal Illustrated
Catalogue* (1851). Among this selection
of Pugin-designed metalwork made by
Hardman & Company is another type
of altar vase, as well as candlesticks
made for The Grange and a crystal jug
(see cat. no. 141).

that may have been used by Pugin
himself in his private chapel at The
Grange, Ramsgate. Examples are
known with a clear family provenance linking them to the house.
Very typical of Pugin are the floral
details at the base of the handles.
The colors and iconography of the
enamel plaque attached to the front
of the vase refer to Christ and the
Virgin Mary. Another style of altar
vase can be seen in the illustration
of metalwork by Hardman (fig. 77a)
which appeared in the *Art-Journal
Illustrated Catalogue* that was published in conjunction with the Great
Exhibition of 1851.

78. Altar Vase

ca. 1835
A. W. N. Pugin
Maker: Derby Porcelain Works,
Derby; Robert Bloor period
(ca. 1811–48)
Hand-painted porcelain; 9¼ in.
(23.5 cm)
Marks: [circular red mark with
central crown]
Private collection

There are no known records relating to this design or Pugin's possible association with the Robert Bloor factory at Derby. Pugin's first church, Saint Marie's, Derby (fig. 78a), was completed in 1838, and the link may date to then. Pugin had not yet met Herbert Minton, and so his major involvement in the ceramic industry of Stoke-on-Trent was still in the future. The earliest Minton–Pugin productions date from about 1842, but nothing resembling this vase can be found in the Minton shape books. Another indication of its early date is the hand-painted decoration. Wares in this style designed by Pugin for Minton generally have printed decoration in the Collins & Reynolds color printing technique patented in 1848. There are other indications of Pugin's early interest in ceramics; for example he may have designed encaustic floor tiles in the late 1830s for Walter Chamberlain, a partner in the Worcester Porcelain Company.

Fig. 78a. Saint Marie's, Derby, 1838; etching by Pugin.

313

Figs. 79a and 79b. Minton encaustic tiles designed by Pugin for the Hospital of Saint John, Alton, Staffordshire.

79. Encaustic Tiles

ca. 1843–56
A. W. N. Pugin and E. W. Pugin
Maker: Minton & Company,
Stoke-on-Trent
Earthenware, colored clay inlay;
each tile, 4½ in. square (11.5 cm)
The Birkenhead Collection

Pugin's first meeting with Herbert Minton was in the latter part of 1840 and the two men seem to have quickly developed a close business and personal relationship. Minton had already established a strong interest in the revival of

encaustic, or inlaid, floor tiles in the medieval style, and this expanded rapidly with Pugin's encouragement. In 1842 the Minton firm published their first tile catalogue, *Early English Tile Patterns*, of which these are examples. Pugin's early designs such as these were based on medieval models, made largely for restoration projects. Also in 1842 Pugin used his first Minton tiles, in the floor of Saint Winefred, his little church in Shepshed, Leicestershire. After this the partnership, and the tile business, went from strength to strength. Minton floor tiling de-

signed by Pugin featured in many buildings, for example: the Palace of Westminster (see cat. no. 90); the Church of Saint Giles, Cheadle; the Hospital of Saint John, Alton, Staffordshire (figs. 79a, 79b); Saint Mary, West Tofts, Norfolk; and Saint Augustine's, Ramsgate. After Pugin's death, tile designs for Minton were maintained by Pugin's son, Edward, and others, freely adapting from Pugin designs published in his *Glossary of Ecclesiastical Ornament* and *Floriated Ornament*.

+ Altar of the blessed virgin

80. Design for the Altar at Saint Chad's Cathedral, Birmingham
1839
A. W. N. Pugin
Pen and ink over pencil; 13 x 8¼ in. (33 x 21.2 cm)
Inscription: "Altar of the blessed virgin"; "AW Pugin" [in monogram]; "1839"
The Board of Trustees of the Victoria and Albert Museum, London
Inv. No. E77(28). 1970

This detailed drawing for the altar and reredos in the Lady Chapel, Saint Chad's Cathedral, Birmingham, shows Pugin's clear dependence upon fifteenth-century European sources during this early period. The design was not realized; a different one was used, a drawing for which is in the Drawings Collection of the Royal Institute of British Architects, London.

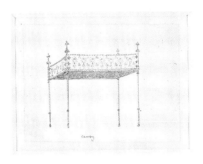

81. Selection of Designs for The Glossary of Ecclesiastical Ornament and Costume
1844
A. W. N. Pugin
Publisher: A. W. N. Pugin, London
Pen and ink, pencil; Group 1: 22⅝ x 16⅝ x 1 in. (57.5 x 42.3 x 2.3 cm), framed together; Group 2 (not shown): 22⅝ x 16⅝ x 1 in. (57.5 x 42.3 x 2.3 cm), framed together
The Board of Trustees of the Victoria and Albert Museum, London
Inv. nos. E77(64), E77(66), E77(69), E77(70), E77(72), E77(73), E77(75–79).1970

Pugin started working on the drawings for *The Glossary of Ecclesiastical Ornament and Costume* late in 1842, and it was published in 1844. *The Glossary* is his most splendid book. Its remarkable chromolithographed plates were printed in London by Henry Maguire in a range of strong colors and gold. Along with Owen Jones's *Grammar of Ornament*, Pugin's book set the standard for design source books in the nineteenth century. For Pugin, of course, it was more than that. In a richly decorative way it represented his total commitment to the revived medieval style and to his particular blend of faith and design. The book is in two parts. Firstly, there is the text by the Reverend Bernard Smith, illustrated with wood engravings by O. Jewitt from drawings by Pugin, of the kind shown here. This is an alphabetical glossary of the liturgy and the equipment associated with it. Secondly, there are the color plates, covering vestments, alphabets, crosses, borders, patterns, holy monograms, emblems, and much else, based largely on historical sources but freely developed for the newly revived faith. Altogether it is a striking and scholarly book, well received by contemporary critics. The published price was £6.6s, and there were two subsequent reprints, in 1846 and 1868.

Figs. 81a, 81b, 81c. Plates from *The Glossary of Ecclesiastical Ornament and Costume*: designs for crosses; designs for cope orphreys (ornamental borders); patterns for powderings (stencils).

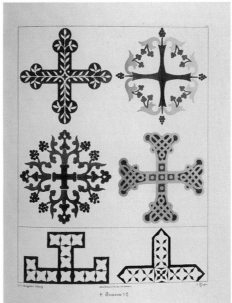

Fig. 81a

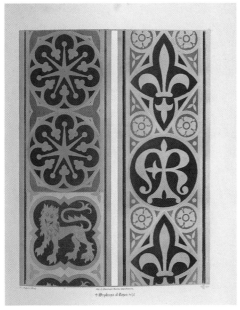

Fig. 81b

Fig. 81c

Refectory interior

82. Drawings and Designs for Saint Cuthbert's College, Ushaw

ca. 1844 and ca. 1851
A. W. N. Pugin
Pen and ink on paper; refectory,
12 x 9⅜ in. (30.5 x 23.9 cm);
window, 20¾ x 16½ in. (52.7 x
41.9 cm); chapels, 17¼ x 12 in.
(43.9 x 30.5 cm) and 18¾ x
12¾ in. (47.6 x 32.4 cm)
Private collection
Inv. nos. AWP6, AWP7, AWP12,
AWP10

Saint Cuthbert's College, Ushaw, County Durham, was the Roman Catholic seminary for England's Northern District. It had been founded in 1794 by refugee students and teachers from Douai College. In 1804 it moved to its present site and the earliest buildings are formally Neoclassical. Monsignor Charles Newsham became president of Ushaw in 1837 and encouraged Pugin to became involved in the college's develop-

ment. Pugin first visited Ushaw in 1840, and this was to be the start of a long association that continued until his death. His major contributions were the original chapel, library, and refectory, along with their fittings. The drawings and designs shown here include Pugin's original scheme for the interior of the refectory, a design for a large five-light stained glass window, and architectural plans for a cloister chapel.

318

Stained-glass window design

The drawing for the refectory, signed by Pugin but not dated, has a strong sense of perspective and is executed in a rapid but precise style. It was probably one in a series drawn by Pugin to suggest how the college should be remodeled in suitably medieval style. It shows the refectory looking west, with benches and tables for the students, a high table for the professors, windows, and the pulpit, all of which Pugin would have designed.

The long mullion and transom windows and the wide span of the ceiling supported by trusses rising from wall plates and struts suggest that his model was probably a monastic refectory. The refectory at Ushaw was rebuilt along these lines in about 1844–46. On October 23, 1846 Hardman charged £29 for painting the refectory ceiling; on December 8, 1846, £102 for eleven heraldry and bordered windows; and in March, £64 for "Wainscot-

ting canopy, door, . . . fireplaces and texts" (Hardman Archives, Birmingham, Hardman 34). A broadly similar refectory was designed by Pugin for Saint Patrick's College, Maynooth, Ireland.

The stained-glass window design was for the east window in Saint Joseph's, or Servant's Chapel, Ushaw, and was probably drawn to a Pugin design in about 1851, representing a stage in the design process. The narrative program tells

Chapel designs

the life of Saint Joseph under rich architectural canopies. It is typical of the style developed by Hardman and Pugin in the last years of Pugin's life. The cult of Saint Joseph as the spouse of the Virgin was a post-medieval development, and Pugin had to defend his use of such post-

Reformation, and therefore non-medieval, concepts in *The Tablet*, a Catholic journal. The chapel was completed by E. W. Pugin in 1854.

Pugin designed two schemes for the new chapel at Ushaw, the second of which was built between 1844 and 1848. Later, in about

1851, he prepared designs for additional side chapels to be built onto the adjacent cloister. These detailed drawings, signed and dated 1851, represent an intermediate stage of what became the Relic or Holy Family chapel. Drawn with great economy and assurance, and with

Chapel designs

a wealth of accurate detail, these show that Pugin was perfectly capable of producing final contract drawings suitable to allow the builder to price the work. Unfamiliar details, such as the feet of the trusses, the ceiling ribs, and the dada and piscina moldings are shown; other details, such as the window tracery, are vaguer. Myers (the builder) would have referred to the large stock of Pugin drawings that he held. The altar and its tall reredos labeled "pictures" was for a painting of the Holy Family by the Nazarene artist, Rhoden. Unfortunately, not many of Pugin's architectural plans of this quality seem to have survived.

83. House of Commons Chair
ca. 1850
A. W. N. Pugin
Carved oak, green leather
upholstery; 35 x 17¾ x 18 in.
(88.9 x 45.1 x 45.7 cm)
Palace of Westminster, London
Inv. no. POW2714

A letter from Pugin to J. G. Crace
around November 1850 instructs
Crace to make a prototype of "a
Pattern Chair" to show architect
Charles Barry (Wedgwood, *Cata-
logue of the Architectural Drawings*

[1985], no. 481). The letter includes
a sketch of the chair, with details of
the chamfering on the leg, the
crowned portcullis, and the brass
nail. Some details, such as finials
indicated on the uprights and an
additional stretcher at the front,
were not used for the final version
of what became the standard chair
for the House of Commons. Pugin's
original source for these chairs
would have been the common
backstools of the sixteenth and
seventeenth centuries, usually with
turned legs, a form he had already

employed elsewhere. In this chair,
he gothicized the form with the
use of chamfering (Wainwright,
"Furniture," in Atterbury and
Wainwright, eds., *Pugin*).

During a recent cataloguing of
all historic furniture in the Parlia-
mentary estate, one chair of this
type was found stamped "Crace."
It is crudely carved and somewhat
heavier than most other examples
surviving from the nineteenth century. It is possible that it is the prototype made up to show Barry.
Alternatively it may have been
submitted with a contract bid as
an example of the firm's work,
although it is unclear whether
Crace ever made any furniture for
the palace. No examples of marked
furniture in the Gothic Revival style
made by the firm have previously
been identified. One other chair has
been found with a Crace mark, of a
less common type, which seems to
have provided public seating in
committee rooms.

Fig. 83a. The House of Lords chair;
design by A. W. N. Pugin; carved oak,
with red leather upholstery, ca. 1847.
(Palace of Westminster, London, Inv.
no. POW2830)

Pugin's letter to Crace suggests that the original intention was to use the chair in the House of Commons lobbies. It was, however, made in large numbers, first by the Gillow firm in 1851; examples also survive marked "Holland & Sons" which had been suppliers to the old palace and other government offices. These two firms supplied most of the contract furniture after this date. The chair's deployment was extended to include Commons refreshment rooms, libraries, committee rooms, offices, and even the reporters' room, according to contemporary inventories and visual evidence.

The seat was usually deep buttoned, and a twisted gimp bound the chair edges, through which the gilt brass bunhead nails were pinned. The shaped handhold in the back was a normal feature, which has generally survived. The chair has continued to be made by various firms (including Waring & Gillow) into present times with little variation in the dimensions, but the alteration of the raked back leg into a curve was seemingly made before the end of the nineteenth century and is the form which is more commonly produced now.

Green is the traditional color of the House of Commons and was used as the principal furnishing color throughout the Commons areas of the new palace. The crowned portcullis is a royal badge (originally used by the Beaufort family) which has come to be accepted as the symbol of both houses of Parliament. Barry and Pugin made widespread use of it in the decoration of the building interior and its furnishings and fittings (House of Commons factsheet 12).

A version of this chair in red was made as the standard chair for the House of Lords (fig. 83a). It is lighter and more elaborate, with roll-molded column-form legs. Red,

Fig. 83b. The Palace of Westminster, looking east from the Victoria tower, 1897. (Sir Benjamin Stone MP, Birmingham Reference Library)

Fig. 83c. The Prime Minister's Room, ca. 1903. (Farmer Collection, House of Lords Record Office)

the traditional color of the House of Lords, is also a royal color; its use in the lords' chamber is appropriate for a backdrop to where monarch and peers meet. The original design also had a handhold in the back and some examples survive with brass castors on the two front legs only, recessed into the square sectioned foot. Marked examples were made by Holland & Sons; these are smaller and the back foot of other marked examples is of an attenuated raked form. Responsible for the House of Lords

library, completed in 1856, Holland compiled an official inventory in 1855 of all furnishings and fittings throughout the palace and won the contract to furnish the new House of Lords offices in 1856 and the Speaker's Room in the House of Commons in 1858 (Wainwright, "Furniture," in Port, ed., *Houses of Parliament*).

84. House of Lords X-Frame Chair
ca. 1847
A. W. N. Pugin
Maker: John Webb, New Bond
Street, London
Carved mahogany, with leather
upholstery; 39½ x 17¾ x 17½ in.
(100.3 x 45.1 x 45.7 cm)
Made for the Prince's Chamber,
House of Lords
Palace of Westminster, London
Inv. no. POW290

John Webb of Bond Street was an important dealer of antique furniture; high-quality reproduction furniture was also made in his workshop. He supplied the most important pieces to the House of Lords in the late 1840s, including sixteen of these chairs, two bracket clocks, and two octagonal tables with elaborate substructures for the lobby outside the House of Lords Chamber, originally known as the Victoria Lobby and renamed the Princes' Chamber by the early

1850s. Both this room and the chamber, where Webb supplied the royal throne, the two chairs of state, and the clerk's table, were completed for the initiation of the House of Lords in April 1847. Webb's involvement appears to have ceased after 1851 when he failed to submit a bid for work along with Gillow and Holland & Sons (Wainwright, "Furniture," in Port, ed., *Houses of Parliament*).

The Illustrated London News of May 1, 1847 described the chairs as being upholstered with "Russia leather of a red colour," which is "secured by brass nails of Gothic pattern and form. Tudor roses are stamped on the leather and gilded." On January 8, 1847 Hardman supplied Webb with "A Brass Rose die to stamp leather," and between January 12 and 19, seven gross (1,008) "Richly Gilt chair nails, New Pattern" (quoted in Wainwright, "Furniture," in Port, ed., *Houses of Parliament*). These elaborately lobed or berry-headed gilt-brass nails still survive on the chairs of state and the royal throne, but they are no longer used on the House of Lords X-frame chairs. Instead, the chairs are pinned with a modern version of the bunhead nails used on the standard chairs of the House of Lords and House of Commons.

The X-frame chair is very close to a design published in Amsterdam in 1642 by Crispin de Passe II (Wainwright, "Furniture," in Atterbury and Wainwright, eds., *Pugin*). Although it is not certain that Pugin knew this particular source, the form was used in other sixteenth- and seventeenth-century pattern books and possibly known through Continental survivals. Another set of these chairs was made by Holland & Sons for the speaker's state dining room in 1859, but the carving lacks the quality produced by Webb's workshop.

85. Chair of State

1847
A. W. N. Pugin
Maker: John Webb, New Bond
Street, London
Carved and gilt mahogany, velvet
upholstery; 43½ x 25¼ x 21¼ in.
(110.5 x 64.1 x 54 cm)
Palace of Westminster, London
Inv. no. POW3609

This state chair was made for
Prince Albert for the ceremony officially opening the House of Lords
in April 1847. It was located to the
right and one step lower than the
throne on the dais under the canopy of state in the House of Lords
chamber. The left side was occupied
by the chair for the Prince of Wales,
exactly alike, except for the "W"
monogram on the stretcher and the
embroidered badge of the Heir
Apparent on the crimson silk velvet
back, which has survived intact.
Prince Albert's chair was originally
embroidered with his arms. Both
chairs, like the royal throne, were
made by John Webb of Bond Street.
Although the final form of the
canopy, as accepted by Charles
Barry, was very different from
Pugin's earliest designs, a drawing
of 1844 (which includes the throne
and one chair) was made much as
he conceived it (Wedgwood, "The
New Palace of Westminster," in
Atterbury and Wainwright, eds.,
Pugin, fig. 426).

A document in the papers of
Holland & Sons describes refurbishment carried out in the chamber and robing room for the state
opening of Parliament on February
19, 1901 and refers to "Taking off
embroidered back of State / Chair
for use of His Royal Highness The /
Duke of Cornwall and York and
supplying / and fitting new back
and embroidered with Royal Ducal
Coronet" (Alexandra Wedgwood,
personal communication).

86. Notice Stand

ca. 1851
Designed by A. W. N. Pugin
Oak; 75 x 30¼ x 30¼ in. (190.5 x
76.8 x 76.8 cm)
Palace of Westminster, London
Inv. no. POW298

The first known contract drawing, dated October 28, 1853, shows a "Stand for business papers" for the vote office. The 1855 Holland & Sons inventory reveals that a comparatively small number of these "notice stands" were in use but those that were in service could be found in key areas such as the committee corridor or the corridors and lobbies leading to the House of Commons Chamber. They occupy similar positions and are used for the same function today. No example has been found with the brattishing intact.

87. Bracket Clock

ca. 1851
A. W. N. Pugin
Case Maker: John Webb, New
Bond Street, London. Movements:
Vulliamy. Works: [Dutton]. Dial
plates and hands: J. Hardman &
Company.
Carved oak, enameled dial; 48¾ x
24⅜ in. (121.9 x 60.9 cm)
Palace of Westminster, London
Inv. no. POW3374

Like the furniture, the finest bracket clocks for the new palace were made specifically for the Prince's Chamber and the House of Lords Chamber in April 1847 before the opening of the Houses of Lords. After 1847 attention shifted to furnishing the less elaborate interiors that were essential to the everyday business of Parliament. In August 1851 Mr. Dutton of 146 Fleet Street wrote to the Commission of Works to confirm an order for twenty clocks for lobbies and corridors, libraries, and refreshment rooms in both houses (PRO, Works, 11/8/9). Also in the Public Record Office are contract drawings dated December 28, 1851 for "N. P. W. [New Palace of Westminster] Clock cases," which show three similar clocks. The drawing (8th Contract, no. 568) specifies the supply of twenty clocks in total. Mr. Dutton probably supplied the works for these cases, and Hardman the engraved and silvered dial plates and hands, which are virtually identical to those of brass lantern clock, made around 1851

(Atterbury and Wainwright, eds., *Pugin*, fig. 416).

Three basic types of clock were made, and greater numbers survive than the twenty specified in this contract. The final form of the three is also somewhat different from this one, with the injunctions "Sic Omnia" or "Tempus Fugit" being carved in Gothic script on the front of the larger versions. The smaller clocks, such as this one,

differed in the decorative carving used on the side panels. They are inscribed simply, "Sic Omnia." Some have had their faces replaced and many have lost the delicate brattishing, an ornamental feature taken from medieval furniture, notably fitted bookcases and cupboards, overmantel mirrors, firescreens, and notice stands.

88. Standing Desk

ca. 1850
Designed by A. W. N. Pugin
Maker of escutcheon and mounts:
J. Hardman & Company
Oak, iron escutcheon; 46 x 36½ x
22¾ in. (116.8 x 92.7 x 57.8 cm)
Palace of Westminster, London
Inv. no. POW288

A small number of standing desks
survive in the Palace of Westminster. This and one other known
example are of the highest quality.
Documents in the Public Record
Office from 1851 describe some of
the planning and specifications for
furnishing the new House of Commons. In August 1851 four "Standing writing tables" were required,
and it was noted that existing specimens could be seen in the Peers
Library. An unstipulated number
of "Standing Desks" were also
wanted, following a prototype in
the west corridor, House of Peers
(probably a division lobby). Two
standing desks are seen in the
central lobby, in an 1897 photograph by Sir Benjamin Stone MP,
but these are of a much plainer
type and have not survived in the
building.

The lavish iron escutcheon, like
all metal mounts for furniture, was
designed by Pugin and made by
Hardman & Company. The iron
was coated with a thin layer of tin
to prevent rusting, which gave it an
appearance that deliberately emulated medieval examples. The furniture mounts were mostly supplied
directly to the Thames Banks Workshops where they were fixed (*A
Report by the Victoria & Albert
Museum concerning the Furniture
in the House of Lords*, 1974).

89. Desk Calendar

ca. 1851
A. W. N. Pugin
Maker: John Hardman &
Company, Birmingham
Silvered brass; 18 x 7¼ x 5¾ in.
(45.7 x 18.4 x 14.6 cm)
Palace of Westminster, London

The Holland & Sons inventory of 1855 describes "A plated Stand for the days of the month on square open work Stand" in the Speaker's Library, House of Commons. This desk calendar is one of only a few made, whereas a number of plated stationery racks, ink bottle stands, and pen trays were made for this and the original three adjoining House of Commons libraries, where they survive in situ. Hardman & Company were responsible for the manufacture of metalwork throughout the new palace, ranging in scope from individual and complex brass light fittings to simple but decorative metal mounts for furniture.

Pugin's designs for metalwork are mostly based on historic survivals of ecclesiastical metalwork, which here he has secularized. The form of the desk calendar is derived from a monstrance, the sacred vessel used for the Exposition of the Eucharist.

Fig. 90a. The 12-inch central tile in the Peers Lobby incorporates the "VR" initials, a motif much used in the scheme.

Fig. 90b. Encaustic tile border, *detail*, Saint Stephen's Hall, designed by Pugin; made by Minton & Company, ca. 1851. This design, incorporating the royal arms, reflects the complexity of the later tiles.

90. Encaustic Tiles, Palace of Westminster

ca. 1846–52
A. W. N. Pugin
Maker: Minton & Company, Stoke-on-Trent
Earthenware, colored clay inlay; mostly 4½ in. (11.5 cm) square; up to 9¼ in. (23 cm) square
Palace of Westminster, London

The floor tiling scheme for the new Palace of Westminster was the greatest creation of the Minton–Pugin partnership. In its rich and colorful diversity it represented their artistic and technical mastery of the revived encaustic process. The bulk of the tiling was carried out between 1847 and 1852, and it is notable that there was a progressive improvement in both the quality of the tiles and complexities of the designs. In the beginning there was a predominance of two-color tiles in conventional Gothic patterns, like those designed by Pugin for various ecclesiastical flooring schemes beginning in 1842. Soon afterward colors were added to the basic browns and buffs, initially blue and white and later green and black. With the increase in colors there came a far more adventurous, and technically demanding, range of designs that included lettering and elements from heraldry. Elaborate tiled pavements were designed for the major public areas such as the Peers Lobby, the Royal Gallery, Saint Stephen's Hall, and the central lobby. Simpler schemes were created for corridors.

The work, probably the largest tiling scheme then ever undertaken in the world, represented a major commission for Minton who rose to the challenge in accustomed style. Despite an inevitable dependence on handcraftsmanship in an industry that was still only partially mechanized, the technical quality of the tiles is superb, even if there was a certain amount of variation in the colors. Almost 150 years later, the large majority of the original floors are still in place. Minton also produced glazed wall and hearth tiles for the palace, the former printed in rich colors by the Collins & Reynolds process.

The dominance of Minton in the tile industry at this time is underlined by the other major commissions carried out by the firm. At about the same time as the Palace of Westminster contract, Minton & Company was also tiling the massive floors of Saint George's Hall, Liverpool, and Osborne House, Queen Victoria's palace on the Isle of White. Later they tiled the Senate House in Melbourne, Australia, and the Capitol in Washington, D.C. The styles for these commissions were classical and Renaissance in inspiration, and so it is only in the tiling for the Palace of Westminster, along with the church schemes, that Pugin was able to explore the decorative richness of the Gothic style.

The tiles here indicate the diversity of patterns by Pugin for the palace. Included are examples made specifically for primary areas such as the Peers' Lobby as well as ones for more general use. The selection only hints at the astonishing complexity of the designs on the actual floors. Most tiles are the standard 6-inch square, but there were also triangles, circles, large squares, and other shapes.

Fig. 90c. Minton encaustic tiles designed by Pugin for the Peers Lobby, made by Minton & Company, ca. 1847.

Fig. 90d. Encaustic tile border, *detail*, Central Lobby, designed by Pugin; made by Minton & Company, ca. 1851. Scottish emblems are featured, along with the complex shapes and styles that characterize the later tiles.

91. Design for Throne and Canopy
ca. 1846
A. W. N. Pugin
pencil; 16¾ x 14⅜ in. (42.7 x
36.5 cm) unframed; 24 x 20 x
1 in. (61 x 50.8 x 2.3 cm) framed
Inscription: [with scale and three
measurements]
The Board of Trustees of the
Victoria and Albert Museum,
London
Inv. no. 657-1908

Fig. 91a. The House of Lords in 1897,
looking toward the throne and canopy
and showing the original arrangement
with the throne between the two con-
sort's chairs. The final version of the
candelabra can also be seen. (Sir
Benjamin Stone MP, Birmingham
Reference Library)

This outline sketch of the throne
and canopy, a complex setting that
occupied Pugin over a long period
of time, shows in detail a design for
the flanking candelabra. These were
originally planned as gasoliers and
were then extensively redrawn as
candelabra, and completed in 1847.

92. Design for Ceiling Panel, House of Lords
A. W. N. Pugin
Pencil, red, green, blue, brown, and yellow washes; 21⅛ x 19½ in.
(53.7 x 49.5 cm)
Inscription: [colors indicated by initials and words]
The Board of Trustees of the Victoria and Albert Museum, London
Inv. no. D943.1908

This detailed watercolor of the pattern to be painted onto square ceiling panels indicates both the colors and foliate design with its oak-leaf border. The panels were painted to this design and have never been altered.

93. Cartoon for Stained Glass, Palace of Westminster

ca. 1847
A.W.N. Pugin
Pencil, black chalk, watercolor;
91⅜ x 22 in. (232 x 56 cm)
Inscription: "Ruby"; "Blue"
The Board of Trustees of the
Victoria and Albert Museum,
London
Inv. no. D731.1908

Pugin's scheme for the stained-glass windows in the House of Lords Chamber featured English and Scottish monarchs and their consorts, from William I to Victoria. This full-size cartoon of early 1847 shows King Edward I under an architectural canopy. It is typical of the rather formal designs produced by Pugin for this scheme. A trial window was made by Hardman and installed by April 1847. However, the main sequence of windows was made by Ballantine & Allan, of Edinburgh and completed by September 1850. The windows were destroyed by bombing during the Second World War, and today only one from the sequence, William I, survives.

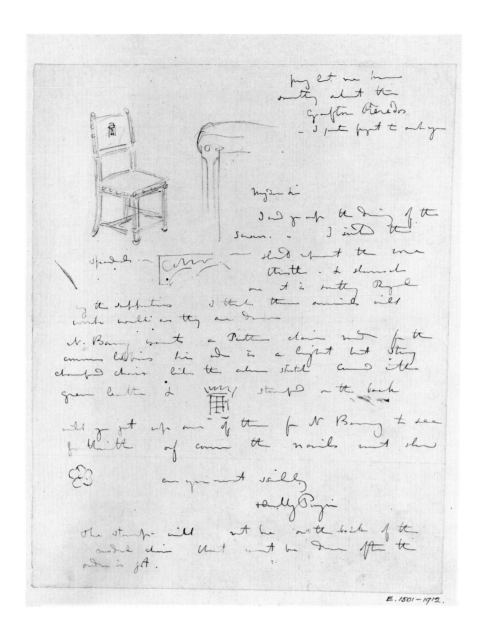

E. 1501-1912.

94. Letter with Design for House of Commons Chair

ca. 1850
A. W. N. Pugin
Pencil and pen and ink on blue notepaper; 9⅞ x 8 in. (25 x 20.2 cm)
The Board of Trustees of the Victoria and Albert Museum, London
MNE1501-1912

This letter from Pugin to J. G. Crace, probably written at the end of 1850, includes the first sketch design for what was to become the standard chair for the Palace of Westminster. It was made in large quantities from 1851 in two forms, one for the House of Commons and the other for the House of Lords. The letter indicates that the original idea probably came from Charles Barry. Pugin later sent Crace further designs for the chairs, but it is remarkable how similar the actual chairs are to this first sketch. The letter in its entirety reads:

My dear Sir/I send you up a drawing of the/screen I intend the/spandrels [slight sketch] should represent the rose/thistle and shamrock/as it is something Royal/by the supporters. I think these animals will/work well as they are drawn./Mr. Barry wants a Pattern Chair made for the/Commons lobbies. His idea is a light but strong/chamfered chair like the above sketch covered with/green leather, and [sketch of a crowned portcullis] stamped on the back/Will you get up one of them to Mr. Barry to see/forthwith. Of course the nails must show/[sketch of standard large domed-headed nail used on all the chairs in the building]. Ever yours and most sincerely/s. A.Welby Pugin/The stamp will not be on the back of the/model chair. That must be done after the/order is got./Pray let me know/something about the/Grafton Reredos/-I quite forgot to ask you.

335

95. Design for Wallpaper/Tiles

A. W. N. Pugin
Pencil, yellow wash and red, green,
blue, brown, and pink body-color;
29 x 21⅜ in. (73.5 x 54.5 cm)
Inscription: "Green 1/Pink 2/
White 3/Blue 4/ Red 5/ Brown 6"
The Board of Trustees of the
Victoria and Albert Museum,
London
Inv. no. D741.1908

This powerful pattern with its lion
passant in a diamond and the "VR"
initials linked by foliate scrolls reflects Pugin's love of heraldry. The
inspiration may have come from
fifteenth-century wall painting in
Salisbury, Wiltshire. The design was
used for a flock wallpaper for the
Palace of Westminster and was also
considered for tiles to be made by
Minton. However, no tiles are
known at Westminster in this style,
and so they may well not have been
produced.

96. Design for Wallpaper
A. W. N. Pugin
Green, black, and maroon body-colors on red-tinted paper; 24⅛ x 21 in. (61.3 x 53.3 cm)
The Board of Trustees of the Victoria and Albert Museum, London
Inv. no. D 718.1908

The dense and richly colored design, from a series of trefoil and ogee patterns in various colorings, was probably intended for the Palace of Westminster. It is unlikely, however, that this ever went into production, but it is an interesting reflection of Pugin's dogmatic, but well-balanced use of color and flat pattern, as well as his complete rejection of any hint of false perspective.

97. Designs for Wallpaper, the Palace of Westminster
ca. 1851
A. W. N. Pugin
Pencil and blue, red, brown, yellow, green, and pink washes; 24⅜ x 20⅞ in. (62 x 53 cm)
The Board of Trustees of The Victoria and Albert Museum, London
D.733-1908

In 1851 Charles Barry had the idea of developing a series of wallpapers for Westminster that featured badges and heraldry and echoed the history of the building. This design is from watercolor sketches drawn by Pugin for Crace to show the possible development of the theme. With its strong ogee panels, its initials for Richard II contained by seed pods, and its chained white deer, traditional heraldic symbols, it is a powerful and decorative design. Some of these designs may have been manufactured, but in general Barry's heraldic and historical approach to the wallpapers was not adopted. A version of the design was adapted for tiles, used in the lobby between Westminster Hall and the members' entrance.

338

Domestic Designs

The Grange, Ramsgate, Kent

Pugin designed The Grange, Ramsgate, for his own use in 1843. The house was completed the following year. Built from brick with stone dressings, it represented a deceptively simple development of his well-established enthusiasm for Jacobean and vernacular styles. Set high on a cliff to the west of Ramsgate, the house was distinquished by its well-organized and appropriate plan, its stair tower with a lookout post on the top, and its consciously domestic and asymmetrical appearance, elements that determined the subsequent development of small-scale domestic architecture in Victorian Britain. It is difficult today to understand the revolution that the house represented when it was first built, simply because its form and style have since become so familiar. All the principal rooms face the sea, while on the northern side there is a kitchen wing overlooking the entrance courtyard and a detached studio, or cartoon room, where stained-glass designs were drawn. At its heart is a staircase hall, a favorite Pugin feature.

Pugin designed the house for his growing family but its completion coincided with the death of Louisa, his second wife. By the time he drew this watercolor, which he exhibited at the Royal Academy in 1849, he was married to Jane Knill, and the armorial panel includes their conjoined emblems. The painting shows the openness of the original site, which has since been completely altered by roads and later development. The close relationship between the house, church, and monastery is a complete integration that represents the full expression of Pugin's faith.

From 1844 until his death Pugin struggled to finish Saint Augustine's, hindered by pressure of work, shortage of money, and failing health. Built from flint and inspired by local medieval churches, it became a highly individual structure in which Pugin obeyed all his True Principles. It cost him nearly £15,000, and it was in use by 1850 but without the bell tower and spire, which were never completed. Many of its fittings were shown in the Mediaeval Court at the Great Exhibition in 1851. Designed also as a family chapel and chantry, the burial vault was first used in 1852, to receive the body of its creator. The cloister and the monastic buildings were largely built by Pugin's son Edward, who was also responsible for the design of his father's tomb chest and life-size effigy.

Pugin's wife Jane outlived him by fifty-seven years, remaining at The Grange for the rest of her life. With eight children and over thirty grandchildren Pugin had plenty of descendants, and the Pugin family owned the house until the late 1920s.

98. **Aerial View of The Grange and St. Augustine's, Ramsgate, with Interior Details**
1841–49
A. W. N. Pugin
Watercolor; 56¼ x 44⅛ in. (143 x 112 cm), framed
Shown at the Royal Academy Exhibition
Private collection

99. View of Chapel, The Grange, Ramsgate

1849

A. W. N. Pugin

Watercolor; 9¼ x 5½ in. (23.5 x 14 cm)

Inscription: "A. W. Pugin" (on mat)

Osborn Collection, Beinecke Library, Yale University

Inv. no. 95.3.3, *Catalogue of the Drawings Collection of the Royal Institute of British Architects, Pugin Family*, by A. Wedgwood [Wedgwood 60.2]

This is one of two watercolors by Pugin of the interior of The Grange. It gives the view into the chapel, while the other shows the back staircase outside the chapel. A private chapel was always an essential domestic feature for Pugin, even before he became a Roman Catholic. There was one at Saint Marie's Grange, his first essay into domestic architecture. The chapel at The Grange, Ramsgate, was fully equipped with specially designed metalwork and furniture, and its interior was colorfully painted. The most striking feature, which still survives, is the stained glass incorporating portraits of Pugin, his second wife Louisa, and four of his children (Anne, Agnes, Cuthbert, and Edward).

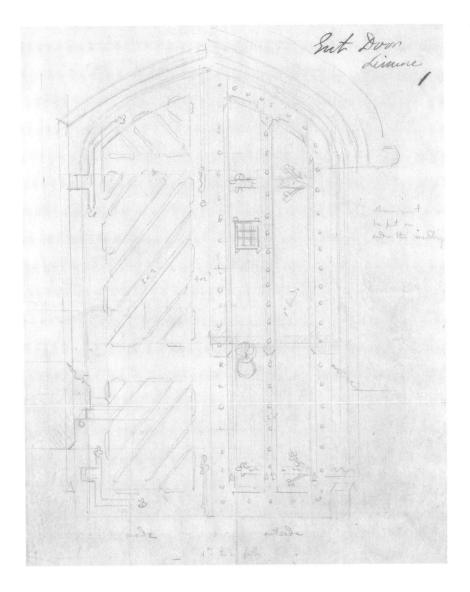

This is a very characteristic Pugin door design in its use of structuralism and strongly revealed metalwork. Pugin had a considerable interest in medieval woodwork and made extensive use of his studies of surviving examples in his designs for timber roofs, doors, lych-gates, and furniture. The actual door, which still survives at Lismore Castle in Ireland, was made exactly to this drawing.

Crace & Company, who had already worked for the Duke of Devonshire at Chatsworth, were commissioned to decorate parts of Lismore Castle in 1850. The castle had been extensively gothicized in 1811, and Crace and Pugin had to work within this existing framework. Despite that limitation, they created some spectacular interiors, particularly the banqueting hall, dining room, and small drawing room. Pugin contributed furniture and woodwork, metalwork, including a magnificent chandelier, wallpapers, and wall and ceiling painting schemes, carpets, a fireplace, stained glass, and a crozier case.

100. Design for Door, Lismore

ca. 1850
A. W. N. Pugin
Pencil on writing paper; 9⅞ x
8 in. (25 x 20.2 cm)
Inscription: "Inside, Outside"
with notes and measurements;
"Ent.Door/Lismore." (in pen and
ink in J. G. Crace's hand)
The Board of Trustees of the
Victoria and Albert Museum,
London
Inv. no. E1495-1912

Fig. 100a. The restored banqueting hall at Lismore Castle today. The richly patterned polychromy, chandelier, and elaborately carved fireplace, shown in the Great Exhibition of 1851, are typical products of Pugin's last great period of creativity, when he worked for J. G. Crace as an interior decorator.

101. Interior Design, Leighton Hall

A. W. N. Pugin
Pen and ink over pencil outline;
9⅝ x 16¾ in. (24.3 x 42.5 cm)
Inscription: "Leighton Hall/
A.W.Pugin" (on old drawing
mount); "Door" with measure-
ments; "curtains behind doors;
like the town hall centres [?]";
and a scale
The Board of Trustees of the
Victoria and Albert Museum,
London
Inv. no. E1524-1912

Drawn by Pugin for Crace &
Company around 1851, this is one
of a series of designs for Leighton

Hall, near Welshpool. As a group
they reveal much about Pugin's
working methods and his relationship with Crace. Leighton Hall was
built in 1850 to the designs of
W. H. Gee for John Naylor, a successful Liverpool banker, and Crace
was commissioned to decorate the
interior. It is clear that Crace supplied Pugin with the dimensions
and architectural details of the
rooms, from which Pugin prepared
fully detailed schemes.

The designs underline the importance of Pugin's work as an interior
designer, and show the freedom he
enjoyed when detached from the
pressures of architectural concerns.

They demonstrate his approach to
interior design during the last phase
of his life and reveal his particular
way of integrating the styles of the
past with the needs of the present.
Doorcases, fireplaces, and ceiling
and wall decoration are particularly
characteristic. Crace seems to have
followed Pugin's designs in broad
terms but altered them in detail presumably to suit the needs of the
client. The elements that survive at
Leighton—the doorcases, fireplaces
and overmantles, encaustic and
printed Minton tiles, and painted
ceiling panels—are enough to indicate the splendor of the original
scheme.

Fig. 101a. Painted ceiling panel,
Leighton Hall, Wales; designed by
Pugin, ca. 1850.

343

102. Design for Fireplace, Eastnor

A. W. N. Pugin
Pencil on blue notepaper; 9⅞ x
7⅞ in. (25 x 20 cm)
Inscription: "for Eastnor
Castle/Drawing Room"
The Board of Trustees of the
Victoria and Albert Museum,
London
Inv. no. 1529-1912

Fig. 102a. The fireplace in the drawing
room at Eastnor Castle.

Eastnor Castle, a towering Gothic Revival fortress on the Welsh borders, had been designed early in the nineteenth century by Sir Robert Smirke, the architect of the British Museum. In 1849 Crace & Company were commissioned to redecorate the drawing room in the contemporary Gothic style. As usual in these late domestic schemes, Crace turned to Pugin, who designed a magnificent room, adding paneling and painting to the walls and color to Smirke's vaulted ceiling. There was a strong element of heraldry in typical Puginian style, with much use of the initial "S" (for the Somers family) and suitable heraldic emblems, such as the white deer. The center of the room was conceived by Pugin as a monumental carved stone fireplace, for which he made this preliminary drawing in about 1849. Above the fireplace and reaching to the ceiling was a complex painted family tree, illustrating the families of the Earl and Countess Somers.

Pugin also designed a grand chandelier, elaborate brass door furniture and gilded brass andirons made by Hardman, printed tiles by Minton, and a suite of walnut furniture with rich marquetry decoration. Today, the drawing room at Eastnor survives much as Crace and Pugin left it, and as a result it is the most impressive extant Pugin interior scheme.

103. Design for Wallpaper, Scarisbrick Hall

1847
A. W. N. Pugin
Pencil, red and green washes on yellow-tinted ground; 28⅜ x 21 in. (72 x 53.5 cm)
The Board of Trustees of the Victoria and Albert Museum, London
Inv. no. 769.1908

Pugin's only visit to Italy was in 1847, and he seems to have been particularly stimulated by what he saw. After his return his flat pattern designs reflect the growing influence of the medieval and Renaissance textiles he had seen in Florence, Lucca, Venice, and elsewhere. This wallpaper design, for example, was taken from a fifteenth-century velvet brocade. It was one of a group sent to J. G. Crace by Pugin in November 1847, and in an accompanying letter he referred to its sources (RIBA, Crace papers). Made for general use, the wallpaper was patented by Crace on May 19, 1848. Printed in various rich color schemes, it was also offered in a flock finish. It became known, probably after Pugin's death, as the Scarisbrick pattern. A red-and-gold version was used there in the Red Drawing Room, but the exact date of its installation is not known. Pugin's son Edward worked extensively at Scarisbrick in the 1860s.

Fig. 103a. Another wallpaper, with heraldic devices, designed by Pugin for Henry Sharples's house, Oswoldcroft, near Liverpool, ca. 1846.

345

104. Design for Wallpaper/Chintz
A. W. N. Pugin
Pencil and red, yellow, green, and
blue washes; 41½ x 21⅛ in.
(105.5 x 53.5 cm)
Inscription: "Original colouring,
New colouring"; "Chintz and
Paper"; "AW Pugin [in mono-
gram] 1850"
The Board of Trustees of the
Victoria and Albert Museum,
London
Inv. no. D794.1908

Drawn for Crace & Company and
signed by Pugin and dated 1850,
this colorful design in heraldic style
is one of several patterns that feature birds and animals, inspired by
fourteenth-century Italian silks. It is
one of the many wallpapers and
textiles that Pugin designed after his
1847 visit to Italy. It is not known
where he intended to use this design
or whether it was put into production; the Crace family suggested it
was for the Palace of Westminster
(RIBA, Crace papers).

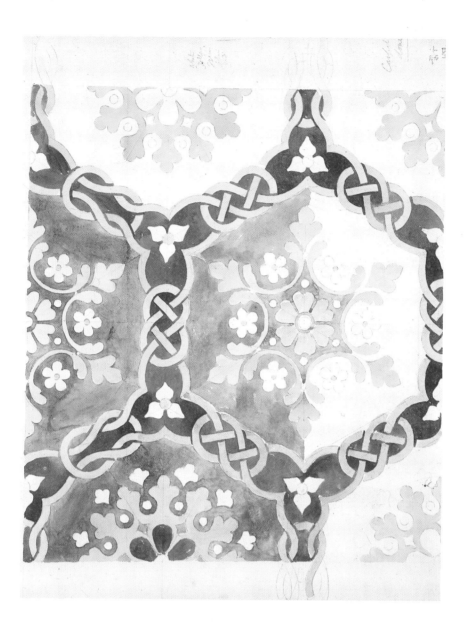

105. Design for Carpet
1850
A. W. N. Pugin
Pencil and red, blue, green, and
yellow washes; 17 x 20⅞ in.
(43.3 x 53 cm)
Inscription: "Carpet done"; "AW
Pugin [in monogram] 1850"
The Board of Trustees of the
Victoria and Albert Museum,
London
Inv. no. D1086.1908

Although original examples of
Pugin's carpets are rare today, it is
clear that they were an important
part of his design output. This pattern was drawn for Crace & Company and is signed by Pugin and
dated 1850. It is not known where
they intended to use it, but an
actual carpet does appear to have
been made from the design. A number of carpet designs, including this
one, were remade in the 1970s for
use in the Palace of Westminster.

The large collection of Pugin
design material given by the Crace
family to the Victoria & Albert
Museum in 1908 and 1912 includes
drawings for carpets for the Palace

of Westminster, for church use, for
Lismore Castle, Leighton Hall, and
other specific locations, as well as
for general use. Beginning in 1847
Crace & Company registered Pugin
carpet designs, and these can be
traced via the Public Record Office,
Kew, West London. Some designs
continued to be used, and occasionally adapted, by Crace after Pugin's
death.

347

106. Design for Stencil Alphabet
A. W. N. Pugin
Pencil with red wash; 12¼ x
19½ in. (31.2 x 49.5 cm)
Inscription: "Watts Drawing
Room" and with title; "AWP
[in monogram]"
The Board of Trustees of the
Victoria and Albert Museum,
London
Inv. no. D903-1908

Drawn by Pugin for Crace &
Company around 1851, this alphabet was designed for use at Abney

Hall, Cheshire, which was Pugin's
last major interior design scheme.
Pugin had a considerable interest in
typography, developed probably in
the early 1830s when he began to
design his own books. He created
alphabets in various Gothic, or
Blackletter, forms for use in typography, inscriptions, and interior
design. Some are included in *The
Glossary of Ecclesiastical Ornament* (1844).

Abney Hall, Cheshire, was built
in 1847 and acquired by James
Watts, a Manchester merchant, in
1849. Watts initiated a major rede-

velopment program for the house,
probably inspired by a visit to the
Mediaeval Court at the Great Exhibition in 1851. He subsequently
commissioned Crace & Company.
Pugin started work on the Abney
scheme at the end of 1851. Despite
illness and exhaustion, he was
able to design much of the house's
interior and some of its fittings
before his final collapse in February
1852. Work at Abney continued
until 1857, but Crace extensively
altered or adapted Pugin's designs
after his death.

348

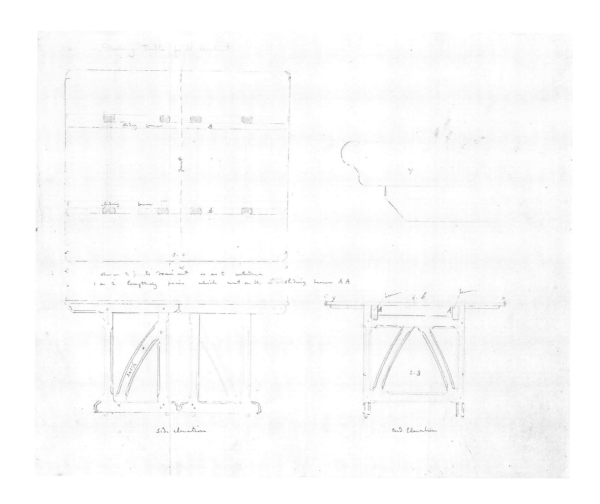

107. Designs for J. R. Herbert Table

1850
A.W.N. Pugin
Pen and ink over pencil, brown wash; 9⅞ x 12¼ in. (25 x 31 cm)
Inscription: "Dining Table for Mr. Herbert; These 2 parts draw out so as to introduce /1 or 2 lengthening pieces which rest on the sliding beams AA"; and with parts labeled and measurements.
The Board of Trustees of the Victoria and Albert Museum, London
Inv. no. 1536.1912

This is a Pugin structural table of the kind he had pioneered in his range of furniture for Saint Mary's College, Oscott, in 1838. The dining table was for his friend the painter, John Rogers Herbert. It was to be made by Crace & Company, and in a letter to Crace in April 1850, Pugin writes, "it can hardly bee [sic] too plain" (RIBA, Crace papers).

108. Design for Chairs

1849
A. W. N. Pugin
Pencil, pen & ink; 19⅞ x 12¾ in.
(50.5 x 32.5 cm)
Inscription: "The legs / and Rails
/ may sometimes / be turned /
instead of champered; plan of /
turned rails; stuffed back;
stuffing; carved back; 2 sorts of
back; cane seat"; "AW Pugin [in
monogram]" / "1849"
The Board of Trustees of the
Victoria and Albert Museum,
London
MNE1577-1912

Fig. 108a. Chair and table in Pugin
style, made by Crace & Company for
Lismore Castle, ca. 1853.

This drawing of three relatively
simple chairs was probably sent by
Pugin to J. G. Crace on November
24, 1849. In the accompanying
letter Pugin stresses his belief in the
need to make simple furniture for
the domestic market, a recurring
theme in the Pugin–Crace correspondence and one that Crace
tended to ignore. "I send you the
3 plain chairs we were talking
about. . . . It is very important to
have some simple chairs, nothing
more required, nothing more difficult to get at present" (RIBA, Crace
papers, MSS Pug 619). Of the three
chairs shown, one has an X-frame,
a favorite Pugin form based on
medieval and Renaissance models
and first developed for Scarisbrick
Hall in the 1830s (see cat. no. 29).
It was subsequently used extensively, for example at Eastnor
Castle and the Palace of Westminster. In fact, this chair appears to be
a simplified version of the Palace of
Westminster X-frame chair (see cat.
no. 84).

The other two designs are more
conventional, although the shaped
padded back is unusual for Pugin.
The variations in finish and decorative detail included in the drawing
are indicative of the Crace–Pugin
working relationship, with Pugin
supplying Crace with a number of
designs to use as he saw fit. It was
from drawings such as this one that
Crace was able to create a range of
Pugin-style furniture, even long
after Pugin's death. Typical are the
simple bedroom chairs made for
Lismore Castle.

109. Design for Octagonal table
ca. 1850
A. W. N. Pugin
Pen and ink over pencil, brown
wash; 19½ x 12 in. (49.5 x
30.6 cm)
Inscription: "Octagon table;
brace 1/4 size; brace real size; a
model to be sent for this; these
are terminated with angle / piece /
and pinned / from the top";
stamped "John G. Crace & Son /
Wigmore St.W."
The Board of Trustees of the
Victoria and Albert Museum,
London
MNE1614-1912

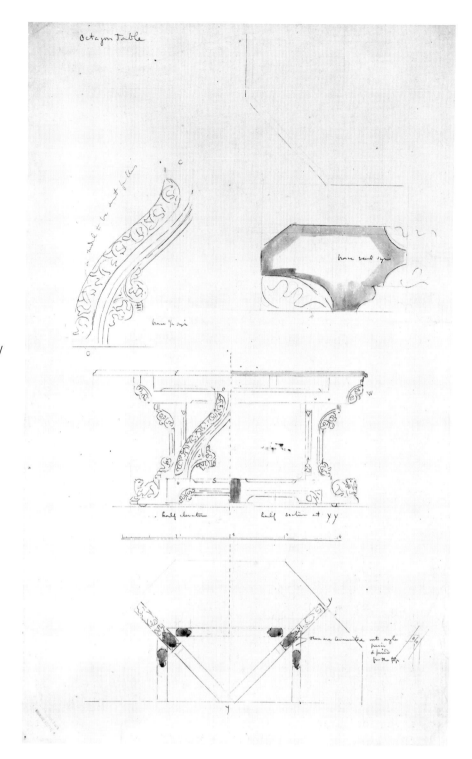

This design represents a variation
of the octagonal table, one of
Pugin's most characteristic and
impressive furniture forms. It shows
how Pugin adapted and decorated
his structuralist principles to suit
the needs of Crace's wealthy and
traditionally minded clients while
retaining the basic integrity of the
design. It also reflects Pugin's ability
to produce rapidly, and with great
fluency, a design that makes sense
in constructional terms and is in
effect a working drawing. Octagonal tables, generally in walnut and
with fine marquetry decoration,
were made for the Palace of Westminster, Eastnor Castle, and, later,
Abney Hall. An example was also
exhibited in the Mediaeval Court in
1851, but it is not known for
whom it was made.

110. Structural Table

ca. 1838 or later
A. W. N. Pugin
Oak; 29⅞ x 39⅜ x 22 in. (100 x
76 x 56 cm)
Roman Catholic Archdiocese of
Birmingham, England

The inspiration for Pugin's best-known furniture form, the structural table, came from timber-framed buildings and other architectural woodwork of the Middle Ages. The form itself was an invention, for no genuine medieval tables were known to Pugin and he had turned to the next-best source. He may first have used it at Saint Marie's Grange, but the earliest pieces that can be firmly dated are the tables he designed for Saint Mary's College, Oscott, in 1838. There is a remarkable range, from little side tables in pine for the students' rooms to massive oak refectory tables over fifteen feet long, all linked by their revealed structure, minimal ornament, and strong functionalism.

Pugin continued to design structural tables for the rest of his life, for both ecclesiastical and secular settings. Many convents, monasteries, colleges, and churches were equipped with them, and in some cases they are still in use. Most were designed to be freestanding, but there are versions to go against a wall and others with flaps. There is a great degree of variation in the structural details and supports, showing how much Pugin enjoyed playing with the basic form. Toward the end of his life he designed a version that could be made to be packed flat in component form for easy assembly at home, a reflection of his eagerness to make modern Gothic a genuinely universal style. While these hopes were not fulfilled, the structural style became a part of the design language of the latter part of the nineteenth century.

111. Hall Chair

ca. 1840
A. W. N. Pugin
Oak; 37⅜ x 15¾ x 17¾ in. (95 x 40 x 45 cm)
Made by Pugin for his own use
Marks: painted Pugin emblem
Private collection

Several of these hall chairs are known, with and without the Pugin martlet-bird device, and all with Pugin family provenances. Both the martlet and the "En Avant" motto are carried on his worktable which is known for certain to have been made for Saint Marie's Grange. It seems possible therefore that the hall chairs were originally made for Saint Marie's in 1835 and later used at The Grange, Ramsgate, where they remained after Pugin's death.

They may have been made by Edward Hull, along with other chairs in the house. The design is a witty Gothicizing of the standard Georgian hall chair, which in turn was derived from the Sgabelli chair, an Italian Renaissance design. Pugin has combined the traditional form with a medieval backstool. The chair demonstrates perhaps the earliest use of Pugin's tusked-tenon joint, the hallmark of all his later structural furniture. A stool with this construction was illustrated in his *Gothic Furniture*, also published in 1835.

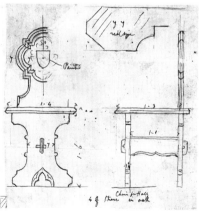

Fig. 111a. Pugin's design for the hall chair for The Grange. (Myers Family Trust)

353

112. Side Table

ca. 1851
A. W. N. Pugin
Maker: John Gregory Crace
(1809–1889)
Walnut with marquetry
decoration, brass rail; 31½ x
29½ x 18½ in. (80 x 75 x 47 cm)
James Hervey-Bathurst, Eastnor
Castle

Pugin's involvement in the redecoration of the Grand Salon, or
drawing room, at Eastnor Castle
by Crace & Company is well documented by letters (RIBA, Crace
papers) and designs (Victoria &
Albert Museum and elsewhere). A
major component in the room is the
suite of specially designed walnut
furniture with marquetry decoration, which includes an octagonal
table and set of velvet-upholstered
chairs, a library desk, bookcase,
pair of pole-screens, and this side
table. Taken together the suite
exemplifies the high-quality furniture that Crace encouraged Pugin
to design, perhaps against his better
judgment, for the domestic interior
design schemes of the late 1840s
and early 1850s.

Elegant and delicate, yet reflecting Pugin's design principles, the
side table was probably commissioned by Lady Harriet Wegg-
Prosser as a wedding present for
her sister-in-law, Virginia Prattle,
whose marriage to Earl Somers
took place on 2nd October 1850. It
carries her initials in the marquetry.
The metalwork was by Hardman.
Letters from Pugin to both Crace
and Hardman show that the table
was not completed in time for the
ceremony, and there are three designs by Pugin showing alternative
constructional and decorative
details.

Fig. 112a. A marquetry panel (*detail*) on the bookcase designed by Pugin for the drawing room at Eastnor Castle.

Fig. 112b. Painted ceiling and chandelier in the drawing room at Eastnor Castle, with the original 1810 vaulting by Sir Robert Smirke, decorated by Crace and Pugin in 1851.

Fig. 112c. Door furniture (*detail*), designed by Pugin for Eastnor Castle.

113. Plate

ca. 1851
A. W. N. Pugin
Maker: Minton & Company,
Stoke-on-Trent
Porcelain, color-printed
decoration; diam. 8⅝ in.
(21.9 cm)
Motto: "Souveigne Vous de
Moy" (Remember Me)
The Board of Trustees of the
Victoria and Albert Museum,
London
Inv. no. 460.1852

On March 14, 1848 F. M. W. Collins and Alfred Reynolds patented a new method of color printing onto ceramics, using the transfer process with oil-based inks and stone or metal plates. This technique, developed from the Baxter woodblock color-printing process for books, and commonly known as block-printing or New Press, was in use at the Minton factory by 1849. With his known enthusiasm for the new color-printing processes then in widespread use in the publishing industry, Pugin is likely to have watched the development of the Collins and Reynolds process with considerable interest, fully aware of its potential for the mechanical printing of flat pattern in strong colors. It was first used on tiles for the Palace of Westminster, but in the Minton archive there are watercolor designs drawn by Pugin between 1850 and 1851 for tablewares using Collins and Reynolds printed patterns. Some of these were for his own use at The Grange.

This particular design, for which there is a matching watercolor, was shown in the Mediaeval Court at the Great Exhibition in 1851, and the plate itself was bought by the museum from the exhibition.

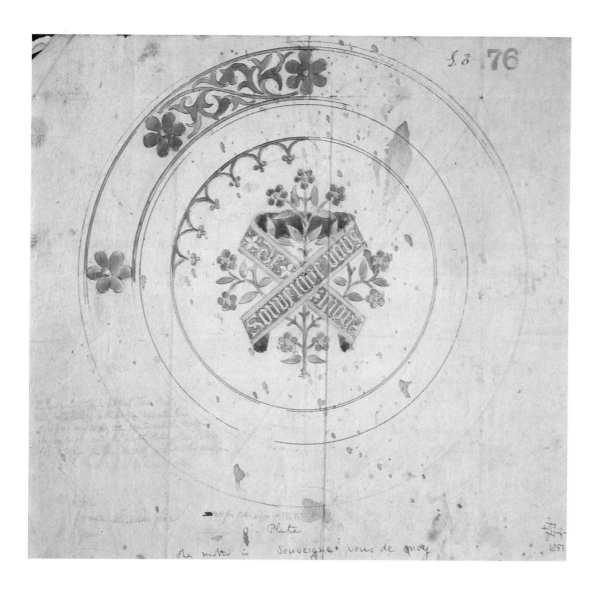

114. Design for Plate

ca. 1851
A. W. N. Pugin
Maker: Minton & Company,
Stoke-on-Trent
Pencil and watercolor; 12¼ x
10⅞ in. (30.5 x 27.5 cm)
Minton Museum, Royal Doulton
Plc

Pugin's association with Herbert
Minton, a relationship that for
ten years was based as much on
friendship as on business, is not
well documented and so tends to
be overshadowed by Pugin's relationships with Hardman and Crace.
None of the letters that passed
between Pugin and Minton have
survived, but one or two are
quoted by Benjamin Ferrey in his
biography of Pugin (*Recollections*
[London, 1861]). They indicate the
depth of friendship that existed.

Herbert Minton's pottery in
Stoke-on-Trent had been founded
by his father in 1793. By the late
1830s it was well on the way to
becoming Britain's leading ceramic
manufacturer, with interests in
many branches of ceramics and a
burgeoning export trade. During
the 1830s Herbert Minton had
become interested in encaustic tiles,

and by the time of his first meeting
with Pugin toward the end of 1840
he had mastered this complex technique. It is likely that Minton's tiles,
which blend medieval inspiration
and modern technology, appealed
to Pugin and brought the two men
together. By 1842 the Minton pottery was producing encaustic tiles
designed by Pugin. For the next ten
years the two men seemed to have
worked closely together. Pugin's
inventive exploration of the encaustic process culminated in a series

of designs for the Palace of Westminster. Minton tiles were used in most of Pugin's architectural commissions, and Pugin's tile designs remained in production at the pottery long after his death.

Pugin went on to design a wide range of wares for Minton, including bread plates, tablewares, a luncheon tray, washstand set, jardinière and stand, a portable font, Renaissance-style ewer and basin, garden seats, door furniture, and, possibly, Parian figures. Beginning in 1848 he became involved in the application of the new Collins and Reynolds color-printing process on both domestic wares and tiles. The culmination of the Pugin–Minton relationship was their collaboration on the Mediaeval Court at the Great Exhibition of 1851. Because Herbert Minton was one of the exhibition's original sponsors and had invested £10,000 in the project, his products, including those designed by Pugin, were well displayed.

The only documentary record today of this long association is a group of Pugin's designs for tiles, domestic wares, and doorplates, which are preserved in the archives of the Minton Museum in Stoke-on-Trent. These all date from around 1849 to 1851 and are unusual for the high quality of their detail and finish. Outline designs for encaustic tiles and tiling plans are found in other collections.

Fig. 114a. Pugin's watercolor design for color-printed plate borders, ca. 1851. (Minton Museum, Royal Doulton)

Fig. 114b. Pugin's watercolor design for a color-printed plate. The actual plate, made by Minton, was shown at the Great Exhibition of 1851. (Minton Museum, Royal Doulton)

Fig. 114a

Fig. 114b

115. Designs for Flagon and Plate
ca. 1850
A. W. N. Pugin
Maker: Minton & Company,
Stoke-on-Trent
Pen; 12⅝ x 6¾ in. (32 x 17 cm)
Minton Museum, Royal Doulton
Plc

It is not known whether these
designs, which are obviously related
to metalwork, were put into production. The form is close to a ewer
and stand that was based on Renaissance models and is in the
Minton shape books where the
records of their designs are kept.
This flagon and plate were made
with majolica glazes and shown in
the Great Exhibition of 1851.

116. Three Designs for Doorplates
ca. 1850
A. W. N. Pugin
Maker: Minton & Company,
Stoke-on-Trent
Pencil and watercolor; each
12¼ x 4⅜ in. (30.5 x 11 cm)
Minton Museum, Royal Doulton
Plc

Designs in the Minton archives for
doorplates suggest an additional
use for the Collins and Reynolds
color-printing process. No examples are known today, but it is possible that these were designed for
the Palace of Westminster and were
never put into production. Minton
manufactured door furniture
throughout the nineteenth century.

117. Gothic Tableware

ca. 1844, 1857
A. W. N. Pugin
Maker: Minton & Company,
Stoke-on-Trent
Earthenware, transfer-printed
and hand-colored decoration;
tureen, L. 11½ in. (29.2 cm); tea
plate, diam. 7 in. (17.8 cm); jug,
H. 3¼ in. (8.3 cm); teacup,
H. 2¼ in. (57 cm)
Private collections

The first fruit of the Pugin–Minton partnership in the domestic field was this tableware. Its origins are, unfortunately, rather unclear. Examples of the service bearing the coat of arms of Magdalen College, Oxford, where Pugin was working in 1844, suggest that it may have first been designed for use there. However, no documentary evidence exists to support this, nor is there anything in the Minton archives to indicate when it was first made. The decoration is printed by the conventional transfer process from engraved copper plates, with additional hand-coloring, and so the design must predate the development of the Collins and Reynolds color-printing process of 1848,

which Pugin used for the production of all subsequent tableware designs.

For Minton this was clearly a very successful design. It was applied to a wide range of dinnerware and teaware and occurs on some rather un-Puginian neo-Rococo shapes typical of the 1840s. In later Minton pattern books it is referred to as "Pugin's Gothic." It was still being made, presumably for schools and seminaries, as recently as 1924.

118. Motto Bread Plate

ca. 1850
A. W. N. Pugin,
Maker: Minton & Company,
Stoke-on-Trent
Earthenware, colored-clay inlaid
decoration; diam. 13 in. (33 cm)
Philadelphia Museum of Art:
Purchased with Funds given in
memory of Sophie E. Pennebaker
and with the Elizabeth Wandell
Smith Fund
Inv. no. 1993-14-1

The "Waste Not Want Not" plate,
the best-known of the two bread
plates that Pugin designed for
Minton, is probably the most familiar of all his designs in any material. It is broadly acknowledged to
be one of the key icons of the
Victorian Gothic Revival. There
were a number of attempts by
Pugin and Minton to adapt the
encaustic tile process for domestic
wares, but this is the only one that
was truly successful. First produced
in 1849, and shown that year at the
Birmingham Exhibition, where its
critical reception was mixed, the
bread plate achieved its success in
the Mediaeval Court at the Great
Exhibition in 1851, where it was on
sale to the public. It was made in
three versions, in three- and six-
color encaustics and in earthenware
with majolica glazes.

119. Two Motto Plates (one shown)
ca. 1852
A. W. N. Pugin
Maker: Minton & Company,
Stoke-on-Trent
Earthenware, color-printed motto
decoration; diam. 10¼ in.
(26 cm)
Minton Museum, Royal Doulton
Plc (red-green version); private
collection (green-gold version)

Recorded in the Minton factory
records as the "Motto Dinner
Service," this is Pugin's most
famous tableware range. It has
always been attributed to him, even
though there are neither drawings
nor documentary evidence to confirm this. Its particular combination

Fig. 119a. Motto Tureen designed by
Pugin; made by Minton & Company;
earthenware, color-printed decoration,
1856. The motto here reads, "Welcome
is the best cheer. The cheerfulness of the
guests makes the feast" (on the tureen),
and "A most indispensible quality
of a cook is punctuality: it should also
be that of the guests" (on the dish).
(Collection, P. D. Rose / H. A.
Gallichan)

of color-printed Gothic decoration
and moralizing proverbs seems
entirely in the spirit of Pugin.
Among the many proverbs were:
"Without wood the fire goeth out
and without a tale bearer the strife
ceaseth"; "A Merry Heart doeth
good like medicine but a broken
spirit drieth the bones"; and "It is a
good tongue that says no ill and a
better heart that thinks none."

Motto Ware was popular and
continued to be made by Minton
through the 1850s and probably
later. A new version, with different
mottoes and on bone china, was
introduced by Minton in 1994.

120. Jardinière and Stand
  ca. 1850
  A. W. N. Pugin
  Maker: Minton & Company,
  Stoke-on-Trent
  Earthenware, color-printed
  decoration; H. 9 in. (22.9 cm)
  Private collection

This square-form jardinière is a
standard Minton shape. Only the
decoration can be attributed to
Pugin. A number of different
designs are known, all printed by
the Collins and Reynolds process.
Their strong colors and dramatic
patterning make these jardinières
and stands among the most striking
and successful of the wares decorated with the new color-printing
technique. They demonstrate
Pugin's ability to make the most of
new technologies in the industrial
field.

121. Garden Seat

ca. 1848–50
A. W. N. Pugin
Maker: Minton & Company,
Stoke-on-Trent
Polychromed glazed earthenware;
18⅞ x 14⅝ in. (47.9 x 37.2 cm)
Detroit Institute of Art
Founders Society Purchase,
Joseph M. DeGrimme Memorial
Fund; Estate of W. Hawkins
Ferrey, by exchange, Inv. no.
1994.6

Shape number 329 in the Minton factory shape book is titled "Pugin's Garden Seat," and the accompanying drawing, dating from about 1849, shows this hexagonal waisted form. This was also known as the "Gothic Garden Seat," a name derived from the formal decoration, also designed by Pugin, that was applied in a number of color schemes. Garden seats, based mostly on Chinese models, were made at Minton's from as early as 1824 and maybe earlier. More than forty different styles are recorded in

the factory shape and estimate books. Most were made between the 1840s and the 1860s, decorated with the colorful majolica glazes.

122. Pair of Heraldic Andirons

ca. 1850
A. W. N. Pugin
Maker: John Hardman &
Company, Birmingham
Brass, polished steel; 31½ x 29½ x
12 in. (80 x 75 x 47 cm)
The Birkenhead Collection

A design element much favored by Pugin was the large carved stone fireplace. He designed small-scale ones for Saint Marie's Grange, and this established a pattern he would follow in his later work. Grand examples, generally made by George Myers, were created for: the Bishop's House, Birmingham; Bilton Grange; The Grange, Ramsgate; Eastnor Castle; Horsted Place, subsequently installed in Lismore Castle; and many other domestic or secular interiors, notably the Palace of Westminster.

To match the fireplaces Pugin designed a splendid range of grates and andirons, or firedogs, which made the most of his fascination with heraldry. His first pair, made from cast iron in a robust architectural style, were probably for Saint Marie's Grange and inspired by an early sixteenth-century model. Later examples, such as those made for Bilton Grange and Eastnor Castle, feature heraldic animals in iron and brass. In 1845 Pugin visited Adare Manor in Limerick, Ireland, the seat of Windham Henry, second Earl of Dunraven, and during the next two years he designed furniture and fittings for the house, including these armorial andirons in steel and brass.

Fig. 122a. Pair of iron and brass andirons made for Adare Manor, Ireland. The ravens are a rebus for the Earl of Dunraven, Adare's owner.

123. Domestic Candlesticks
ca. 1842
A. W. N. Pugin
Maker: John Hardman &
Company, Birmingham
Silver plate, enamel; H. 19½ in.
(48.5 cm), diam. 7½ in. (18.6 cm)
Private collection

Domestic metalwork designed by
Pugin is far less common than
ecclesiastical objects. Among the
earliest known today are these
richly decorative candlesticks, made
for Henry R. Bagshawe, a friend of
Nicholas Cardinal Wiseman. The
Hardman daybook for 1842 has
several references to work for
Bagshawe, but these candlesticks
are the only pieces known today
from these commissions (Hardman
Archives, Birmingham).

124. Pair of Candlesticks
ca. 1844
A. W. N. Pugin
Maker: John Hardman &
Company, Birmingham
Engraved gilt-brass; H. 13⅜ in.
(35 cm), diam. 6¾ in. (17 cm),
base
Inscription: "Christi Crux est
Mea Lux" (Christ's cross is my
light); "en Avant" (Forward);
[Pugin's coat of arms]
The Board of Trustees of the
Victoria and Albert Museum,
London
Inv. no. M35 & A-1972

Some of the metalwork designed by
Pugin for his own house, The
Grange, Ramsgate, has been preserved by various descendants. At
least two pairs of these candlesticks
are known, probably made by
Hardman & Company in about
1848. The distinctive design features a central pierced roundel,
engraved with Pugin's coat of arms
supported by Knill lions from his
wife's coat of arms, and Pugin's
"En Avant" motto. A pair of these
candlesticks was shown in the
Mediaeval Court at the Great
Exhibition in 1851 and can be seen
in the group of Hardman metalwork illustrated in the *Art-Journal
Catalogue* (fig. 77a).

125. Dish

Assay, 1847–48
A. W. N. Pugin
Maker: John Hardman &
Company, Birmingham
Parcel-gilt, enamel; diam. 16⅛ in.
(41 cm)
Inscription: "Henry Benson
Esquire from his grateful friend
A W Pugin March XXVI AD
MDCCCXLVIII"
Marks: town and maker's marks;
date letter for 1847–48
The Board of Trustees of the
Victoria and Albert Museum,
London
Inv. no. M23-1972

This magnificent piece, whose form
is that of a traditional alms dish,
was designed by Pugin for his
friend Henry Benson as a token of
gratitude and is inscribed accordingly. Benson was Pugin's neighbor
at Ramsgate, and his wife was the
aunt of Helen Lumsdaine, to whom
Pugin was briefly engaged in the
early part of 1848. When the
engagement was broken off, in
response to pressure from the
Lumsdaine family, Benson tried to
intercede on Pugin's behalf, but to
no avail. A Pugin alms dish of a
similar design was shown in the
Mediaeval Court at the Great
Exhibition in 1851, and examples
in brass are known.

126. Tazza

ca. 1846
A. W. N. Pugin
Maker: John Hardman &
Company, Birmingham
Silver plate; H. 5⅞ in. (15 cm),
diam. 9 in. (22.5 cm)
Made for The Grange, Ramsgate
Collection, The Family of the late
Michael Pugin Purcell (1926–93)

One of the few examples of Pugin
domestic metalwork that has no
ecclesiastical source or even an
identifiable medieval model, this
tazza is one of four known to survive today among Pugin's descen-

Fig. 126a. Pair of silver-plated storage
canisters, made for The Grange and
bearing Pugin's crest. These are rare
examples of ordinary domestic wares
designed by Pugin for his own use.
(Private collection)

dants. There were originally eight,
and a letter from Pugin to Hardman (now in a private collection)
refers to their design and manufacture. Pugin explains to Hardman
that he has no dessert service but
does not want one in china "as it
would be expensive & in a very
short time it will be all smashed."
He goes on to say that for everyday
use "form is everything I have made
them of a grand shape quite plain
easily made & easily cleaned what
can I do better" (HLRO, microfilm
no.36). The tazza is an interesting
example of Pugin's work as a practical industrial designer and shows
a concern for function.

127. Flagon

Assay, 1849–50
A. W. N. Pugin
Maker: John Hardman &
Company, Birmingham
Silver; H. 11 in. (28 cm), diam.
5⅞ in. (15 cm)
Marks: town and maker's marks,
and date letter for 1849–50
The Birkenhead Collection

The fluted hexagonal form, flared
neck and handle, rounded cover,
and delicately applied trefoils at the
base of the handle distinguish this
flagon from similar ecclesiastical
designs. It is not known for whom
this was made.

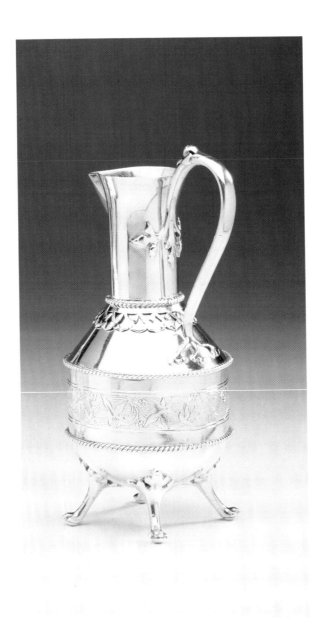

128. Cream Jug
Assay, 1851–52
A. W. N. Pugin
Maker: John Hardman &
Company, Birmingham
Embossed silver; H. 6¼ in.
(16 cm), diam. 3 in. (7.5 cm)
Marks: town and maker's marks;
date letter for 1851–52
Private collection

This was probably made for S. L.
Somers Cocks, a relative of the
family that had previously em-
ployed J. G. Crace and Pugin at
Eastnor Castle. Cocks was soon to
build Treverbyn Vean, a remarkable
Gothic Revival house in Devon.
The architect was William Burges,
but the furniture and fittings were
Puginian in style and were made for
Burges by Crace. In many ways the
house represented the link between
Pugin and the next generation of
Gothic Revival architects and
designers.

The shape of this jug is more
advanced than Pugin's other metalwork. It shows that, at the very end
of his life, he was developing his
ideas and pioneering a style of
Reformed Gothic that in the hands
of the next generation—G. E.
Street, William Butterfield, William
Burges, and ultimately Christopher
Dresser—was to result in some of
the most significant designs of the
nineteenth century.

Several interesting pieces of
Hardman metalwork made for
Treverbyn Vean survive, and their
date letters indicate that Cocks continued to use the Birmingham company after Pugin's death. These
later pieces are likely to have been
designed by John Hardman Powell,
Pugin's son-in-law.

129, 130. Watercolor Designs for Floriated Ornament

ca. 1848
A. W. N. Pugin
Watercolor; 12¼ x 9½ in. (30.5 x 23.6 cm)
Private collection

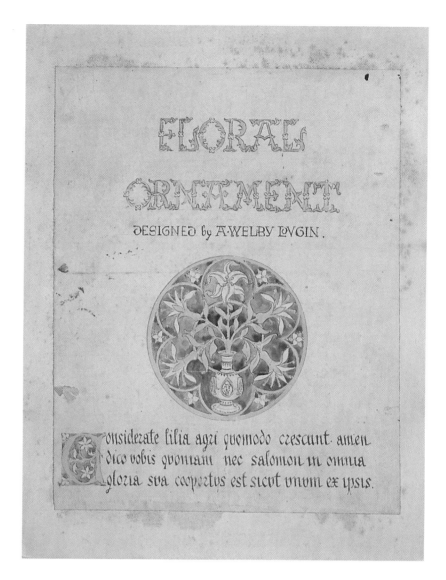

Floriated Ornament, published by Pugin in 1849, was his last major book. It was a very effective weapon in his campaign to popularize the Gothic style. There are thirty-one chromolithographed plates that illustrate the practical design application of identifiable botanical specimens. Pugin's inspiration was a late sixteenth-century German botanical book, *Tabernae Montanus Eicones Plantarum*, a copy of which he had in his own library. It is clear from his correspondence that Pugin was planning the book over a long period. In a letter to his friend J. R. Herbert, he wrote, "I am now preparing a work on vegetable and floral ornament, in which, by disposing natural leaves and flowers in geometrical forms, the most exquisite combinations are produced, and of precisely the same character as those found in the illuminations—stained glass, incised plates, &c., of the thirteenth and fourteenth centuries" (*The Builder*, August 1845).

In its published form, *Floriated Ornament* is a practical design manual, underlining the natural inspiration for all forms of medieval art and architecture, and showing how such inspiration could be seen as the root of all modern design. As such, it anticipates the work of designers such as Christopher Dresser and William Morris.

Fig. 129a. Title page, *Floriated Ornament* (London, 1849).

A group of the original watercolor designs for *Floriated Ornament* survives. They were probably drawn by John Hardman Powell from Pugin sketches (now lost), in some cases with annotations by Pugin who had strong views about the colors. The watercolor for the title page (cat. no. 129) shows the lily-vase motif, but this was considerably altered for the printed version (fig. 129a). The same is true for the original drawing for plate 28 (cat. no. 130) and the published version (fig. 130a).

Floriated Ornament was reissued in 1875 and a modern facsimile was published in 1994.

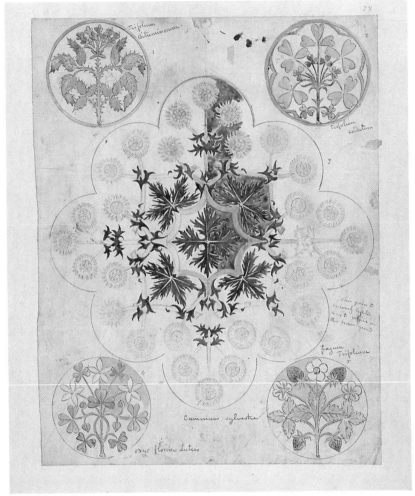

130. Watercolor design for
Floriated Ornament
(plate 28).

Fig. 130a. Plate 28, *Floriated Ornament* (London, 1849).

**131. Elements of a Parure
(Headband, Brooch,
Necklace, and Pendant Cross)**
1848
A. W. N. Pugin
Maker: John Hardman &
Company, Birmingham
Gold, jewels, enamel; headband,
L. 6⅛ in. (15.6 cm); brooch, 2⅛ x
2½ in. (5.4 x 6.4 cm); necklace
chain L. 21⅛ in. (53.7 cm), cross
2¾ x 1⅞ in. (7 x 4.8 cm)
The Board of Trustees of the
Victoria and Albert Museum,
London
Inv. no. M10, M20, M21-1962

Pugin made a point of designing
jewelry for his wives and children.
He may have designed a parure for
Louisa, his second wife, but nothing survives today except a small
gold cross and chain, delicately
decorated with enamel and enriched with rubies and pearls. The
Hardman daybooks show that it
was completed in December 1843

Fig. 131a. Jane Knill Pugin, ca. 1870s,
photographed wearing a pectoral cross
and other jewelry designed by Pugin.
(Private collection)

375

at a cost of £47 15s. A few months later Louisa was dead, and Pugin seems to have kept the cross and chain.

Far more significant is this parure, which survives in an incomplete state. It was designed originally by Pugin as a present for Helen Lumsdaine, to whom he was briefly engaged during the early part of 1848, and the final cost was over £237. When the engagement was finally, and irrevocably, broken, Pugin kept the parure, and when in July the same year he became engaged to Jane Knill, he sent it back to Hardman to be adapted, incorporating within it the cross and chain that had originally belonged to Louisa. He then presented the parure to Jane as a wedding present. It was subsequently displayed in the Mediaeval Court at the Great Exhibition in 1851, where it was apparently admired by Queen Victoria. Jane Pugin wears the parure in the formal portrait painted in 1859 (see cat. no. 2). An illustration of the full parure (fig. 131b) in Matthew Digby Wyatt's souvenir book of the exhibition, *The Industrial Arts of the XIX Century*, hints at Pugin's skill as a jewelry designer. His work is significant in breaking with the classical traditions and attitudes characteristic of the jewelry business of his time.

Fig. 131b. The parure designed by Pugin for Jane Knill; chromolithograph from Matthew Digby Wyatt, *The Industrial Arts of the XIX Century, from the Great Exhibition of 1851* (London, 1853).

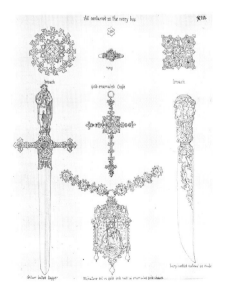

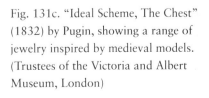

Fig. 131c. "Ideal Scheme, The Chest" (1832) by Pugin, showing a range of jewelry inspired by medieval models. (Trustees of the Victoria and Albert Museum, London)

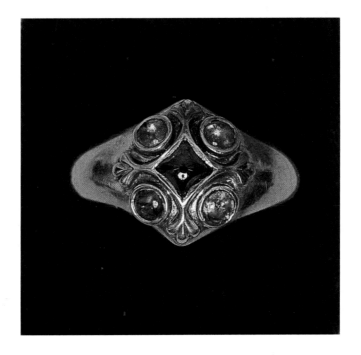

132. Episcopal Ring

ca. 1838
A. W. N. Pugin
Maker: John Hardman &
Company, Birmingham
Gold, jewels
Roman Catholic Archdiocese of
Birmingham, England

Pugin's earliest practical jewelry
designs were ecclesiastical and
included episcopal rings and pectoral crosses for the bishops associated with Pugin's early church
building and collegiate commissions, Nicholas Wiseman, Thomas
Walsh, and Robert William Willson, brother of Edward T. Willson.
Pugin was inspired by medieval and
Renaissance models from which he
developed his preference for the
combination of gold and colored

Fig. 132a. Portrait of Nicholas Cardinal
Wiseman (*detail*), by J. R. Herbert,
showing a pectoral cross designed by
Pugin.

enamel, mounted with pearls and
cabouchon stones. He regarded cut
stones and gems as dishonest. In a
February 1848 letter to Hardman
he wrote, "I want gold like my old
ring yellow gold-rich looking gold-
precious looking gold like all the
old work . . . a jewell ought to look
so rich as if you could eat it"
(quoted in Stanton, *Pugin* [1971]).

   This ring, typical in its simple
use of cabouchon emeralds and
rubies and its gold setting, was
designed by Pugin for Bishop
Thomas Walsh, who probably wore
it at the consecration ceremonies
for the chapel at Saint Mary's
College, Oscott, and Saint Chad's
Cathedral, Birmingham. More spectacular were the pectoral crosses.
None of these are known to have
survived but they can be seen in the
series of formal portraits of bishops
painted by J. R. Herbert at Oscott
(fig. 132a, and see fig. 55b). Simple
crosses are known to have been
designed by Pugin for large-scale
production in silver or brass.

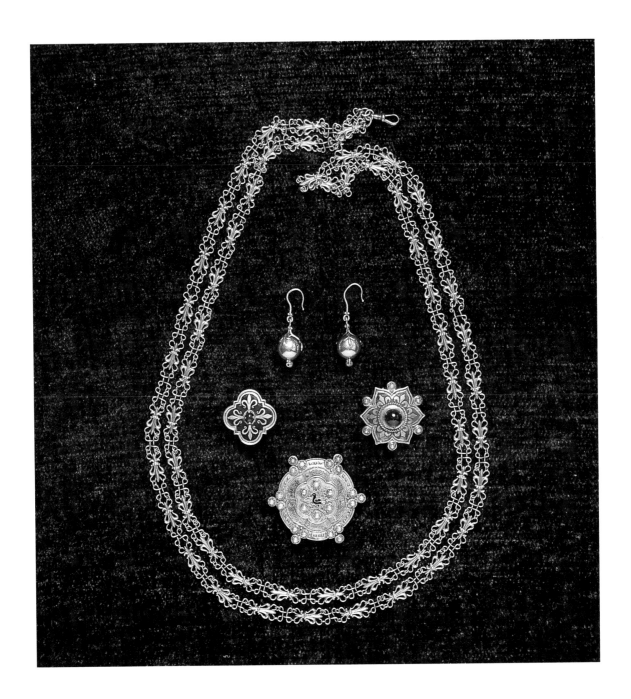

**133. Chain Necklace, Pendant
Earrings, and Brooches**
1850
A. W. N. Pugin
Maker: John Hardman &
Company, Birmingham
Gold, pearls, jewels, enamel;
necklace, L. 55⅞ in. (142 cm);
earrings, L. 1⅝ in. (4.2 cm);
brooches, diam. 2 in. (5 cm),
1½ in. (3.5 cm), 1⅛ in. (2.8 cm)
Private collections

The delicate gold chain with its
linked trefoil motif and the simple
gold earrings with the single pearl
drop were designed by Pugin for his
daughter Anne, perhaps at the time
of her marriage to John Hardman
Powell in 1850. Their style reflects
Pugin's ability, despite his frequent
complaints in his letters to Hardman, to work within the limitations
of contemporary Birmingham
workshop practice.

The three brooches may also
have been designed by Pugin for
his daughter Anne. Each piece is
personal and underlines the fact

that the creation of jewelry for his
family was one of Pugin's few ex-
travagances. In two of the brooches
he uses characteristic gold and blue
enamel, enriched with pearls and
cabouchon rubies, in styles that
echo the jewelry of the medieval
period. Pugin used famous models,
such as the so-called William-of-
Wykeham piece in New College,
Oxford. The third brooch, with its
decorated gold ground, clusters of
pearls, and martlet bird in black
enamel, is more unusual, its design
emphasizing the family link.

134. Brooch

1850
A. W. N. Pugin
Maker: John Hardman &
Company, Birmingham
Gold, jewels, enamel; diam.
1⅝ in. (4 cm)
Made for A. W. N. Pugin's wife
Jane
Collection, Mrs. J. E. Franklin

This brooch has always been in the Pugin family, and tradition has it that Pugin gave it to his wife Jane some time after their marriage. In the portrait of Jane (see cat. no. 2), she is wearing a similar brooch as a pendant around her neck. Pugin had a substantial private account with Hardman which he used largely for jewelry for his family. While he was often critical of Hardman workmanship he was prepared to spend large sums. Several pieces of jewelry ordered for Jane are recorded in the Hardman daybooks. The gold mount of the brooch is delicately pierced and modeled, and the central cabouchon ruby with its flanking groups of pearls reflects Pugin's lasting fascination with both the techniques and styles of jewelry of the Middle Ages and Renaissance.

135, 136. Bracelet and Brooch

1859 (bracelet); 1883 (brooch)
Bracelet: John Hardman Powell
(1827–1895), after A. W. N.
Pugin; brooch: A. W. N. Pugin
Maker: John Hardman &
Company, Birmingham
Bracelet: gold, jewels, enamel;
7¼ x 1¼ in. (18.4 x 3.2 cm);
brooch: gold, enamel, pearls;
1¾ x 1¾ in. (4.5 x 4.5 cm)
Private Collection, via Wartski,
London

A feature of Pugin jewelry designs
is the repetitive use of certain decorative motifs. A bracelet in the
parure made for Jane Knill includes
a gold and enamel quatrefoil, enriched with jewels. This is known

to exist as a single brooch and
appears again in this bracelet,
designed in 1859 by John Hardman
Powell for his wife, Anne, Pugin's
eldest daughter. By the 1850s
Powell was completely familiar
with Pugin's design language and
was able to use it to great effect
while imposing his own style in the
lightness of the design and the variation in the quatrefoils.

Pugin's jewelry remained popular
for several decades in the nineteenth century, making it easy to
overlook the revolutionary nature
of the designs. Pugin pioneered the
revival of medieval and Tudor
forms and decorative techniques,
creating in the process a distinctive
style. As in other forms of metal-

work, the Pugin style became quite
recognizable and remained popular
long after his death. This was partly
due to his immediate successors—
his son Edward and son-in-law
John Hardman Powell—but some
of his most familiar design motifs
achieved a wider currency. Typical
was the lily-vase motif first drawn
by Pugin for the title page of his
last book, *Floriated Ornament*,
published in 1849 (see cat. no.
129). This exists on Minton color-
printed tiles of the 1850s and is
seen here in the form of a brooch,
whose late date indicates the lasting
popularity of the Pugin style.

The Mediaeval Court at the Great Exhibition of 1851

The Great Exhibition of the Works of Industry of All Nations, also known as the Great Exhibition of 1851, is particularly well documented, thanks in part to the new technologies available at the time. The construction of Joseph Paxton's Crystal Palace and the exhibition itself were extensively photographed; many of the exhibits were depicted in engravings in the *Art-Journal Illustrated Catalogue*, and similar publications. However, the most important records are the great books of chromolithographed plates that illustrate views of the exhibition and details of the objects on display. *Dickinson's Views of the Great Exhibition*, with its color lithographs by L. Haghe, includes the best image of the Mediaeval Court (fig. 137a, above), a most valuable image clear enough to allow many of the objects to be identified. Another Haghe lithograph gives a view of the Pugin objects displayed by George Myers and includes a range of predominantly architectural material in wood and stone, a surprising amount of which is still known today.

Fig. 137a. The Mediaeval Court, from *Dickinson's Views of the Great Exhibition*; chromolithograph by L. Haghe (London, 1851).

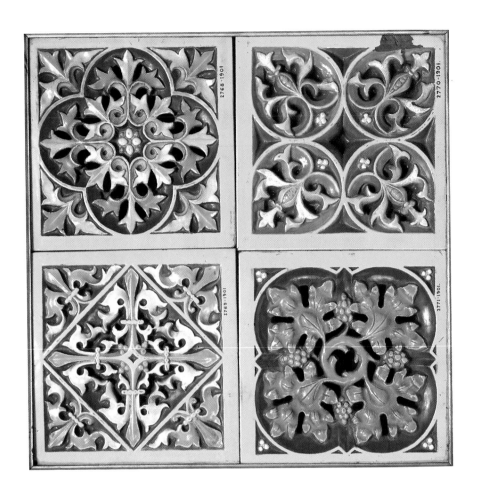

137. Framed Set of Stove Tiles
ca. 1851
A. W. N. Pugin
Maker: Minton & Company,
Stoke-on-Trent
Buff-colored earthenware molded
in relief and pierced, majolica
glazes; 8¾ in. square (22.2 sq.
cm), each tile
Made for the Great Stove
The Board of Trustees of the
Victoria and Albert Museum,
London
Inv. no. 2768-2771.1901

138. Design for a Stove Tile

ca. 1850
A. W. N. Pugin
Maker: Minton & Company,
Stoke-on-Trent
Pencil and watercolor; 19⅜ x 12¼
in. (49 x 30.5 cm)
Minton Museum, Royal Doulton
Plc

One of the most dramatic features of Pugin's Mediaeval Court at the Great Exhibition of 1851 was the huge stove, based on early German models. This was made for Alton Towers, but presumably the design could also be used in cathedrals and large churches. The metalwork was by Hardman and the tiles that covered it—large, heavily molded and pierced, and covered with rich majolica glazes—were made by Minton. Curiously, this appears to be Pugin's only use of the colored majolica glazes developed in about 1850 by Leon Arnoux, Minton's French art director. Examples were shown for the first time at the Great Exhibition. None of the Pugin-designed stoves are known today, but a number of the tiles survive.

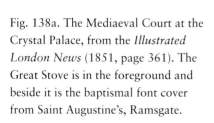

Fig. 138a. The Mediaeval Court at the Crystal Palace, from the *Illustrated London News* (1851, page 361). The Great Stove is in the foreground and beside it is the baptismal font cover from Saint Augustine's, Ramsgate.

Stove in the Medieval Style

139. **Plates from The Industrial
Arts of the XIX Century, from
the Great Exhibition of 1851**
1853
Matthew Digby Wyatt; prepared
by F. Bedford; printed by Day &
Son, London.
Chromolithographs; each plate,
12¾ x 17½ in. (32.5 x 44.5 cm),
horizontal; 17½ x 12¾ in.
(44.5 x 32.5 cm), vertical
Subjects: Stove in the Medieval
Style; Carpet in the Medieval
Style; Altar and Reredos; Jewelry
in the Medieval Style (see cat.
fig. 131b); Cabinet in Oak with
Brass Panels (see cat. fig. 144a)
Private collection

PLATE 142.

ALTAR AND REREDOS DESIGNED BY THE LATE A.W. PUGIN,
CARVED IN STONE BY MYERS OF LONDON, AND FITTED-UP
BY HARDMAN OF BIRMINGHAM.

LONDON, PRINTED AND PUBLISHED FEBY 1ST 1853 BY DAY & SON, LITHOGRAPHERS TO THE QUEEN

M. DIGBY WYATT, DIREXT.

F. BEDFORD LITH

Altar and Reredos

The best images of individual pieces designed by Pugin and shown in the Mediaeval Court are the lithographed plates in Matthew Digby Wyatt's *The Industrial Arts of the XIX Century, from the Great Exhibition of 1851*, which was published in 1853. A selection of these are shown here. There are Pugin designs for at least four stoves on the scale of the Great Stove, all featuring colorful tile cladding. They may have been produced and installed in other buildings, but none are known today. The carpet is a useful indication of Pugin's work in this field, as actual examples are very rare today. The altar and reredos (now in Saint David's, Pantasaph, North Wales), which was made by George Myers, underlines Pugin's competent handling of carved stone.

Carpet in the Medieval Style

140. Jardinière

ca. 1850–51
A. W. N. Pugin
Maker: Minton & Company,
Stoke-on-Trent; and John
Hardman & Company,
Birmingham
Earthenware tiles, color-printed
decoration; gilt cast-iron frame;
11¾ x 10 in. (29.9 x 25.4 cm)
The Board of Trustees of the
Victoria and Albert Museum,
London
Inv. no. 926-1852

Clearly visible in the left foreground of Dickinson's plate of the
Mediaeval Court (see fig. 137a)
are two square metal-framed
jardinières, decorated with colorful
Gothic designs. This jardinière is
one of those and, along with the
other one (fig. 140a), it was bought
directly from the Great Exhibition
by the forerunner of the Victoria &

Albert Museum. The museum, or
rather its predecessor, bought extensively from the Great Exhibition
and particular attention was paid
by the purchasing committee to
Pugin's Mediaeval Court.

Fig. 140a. The second jardinière exhibited at the Great Exhibition; designed
by Pugin and made by Minton &
Company. (Trustees of the Victoria &
Albert Museum)

The jardinières are composed of
large Minton tiles, color-printed by
the Collins and Reynolds process,
and mounted into a gilded cast-iron
frame made by Hardman. The two
jardinières are quite different, in
size, decoration of the tiles, and
detailing of the frame. It is apparent
from the inside of both jardinières
that the tiles, standard ones from
the Minton range, were cut rather
crudely to fit the frame, making it
possible that the jardinières in the
Mediaeval Court were made
rapidly as prototypes for a range
that was never developed. Other
than these two pieces, no examples
of the design are known. It is likely
that Minton decided to concentrate
on the version that was made
entirely in ceramic and already in
production (see cat. no. 120).

141. Crystal Jug
ca. 1851
A. W. N. Pugin
Maker: John Hardman &
Company, Birmingham
Silver, silver-gilt [or base metal],
lead crystal; H. 6 in. (15.2 cm)
Private collection

The combination of crystal with
silver, silver-gilt, or base metal was
one that Pugin used frequently,
drawing upon the many well-
known medieval precedents. This
jug, which is traditional in form
and may be from a cruet set, was
shown in the Mediaeval Court at
the Great Exhibition in 1851. It is
included in the group of Hardman
metalwork illustrated in the *Art-
Journal Catalogue* (see fig. 77a).

142. Chalice

A. W. N. Pugin
Parcel-gilt, enamel, jewels;
H. 9 in. (22.9 cm), diam. 6 in.
(15.3 cm)
Inscription: "Calicem Salutaris
Accipiam et Nomen Domini
Invocabo"
The Board of Trustees of the
Victoria and Albert Museum,
London
Inv. no. 1328.1851

Among the pieces purchased from the Great Exhibition of 1851 by the Museum of Manufacture, forerunner of the Victoria & Albert Museum, were four important pieces of metalwork: two candelabra and two chalices, all made by Hardman. The chalices, one of which is shown here, are both in Pugin's rather elaborate and ambitious late style. They are made of silver with parcel gilding and enriched with enamels and jeweling.

The brass candelabrum was designed for the House of Lords and bought by the museum as an example of Pugin's work for that major interior design scheme.

143. Candelabrum

ca. 1846
A. W. N. Pugin
Maker: John Hardman &
Company, Birmingham
Brass, crystal; H. 28 in.
(71.2 cm), W. 18 in. (45.8 cm)
Made for the House of Lords
The Board of Trustees of the
Victoria and Albert Museum,
London
Inv. no. 2740-1851

144. Cabinet

ca. 1846
A. W. N. Pugin
Maker: George Myers (1804-
1875)
Painted and carved oak, brass
mounts; 90⅜ x 59⅝ x 23⅞ in.
(229.5 x 151.5 x 60.5 cm)
The Birkenhead Collection

Designed by Pugin for his own use
at The Grange, Ramsgate, this cabinet is among the most splendid of
his known domestic pieces. He had
no need to compromise to accommodate a client or the restrictions
of a limited budget. The cabinet
captures the full splendor of the late
medieval court cupboards, on
which its design was based. It even
fulfilled the functions of its ancient
prototype by acting as a serving
and storage cupboard in Pugin's

own dining room. The pierced
foliage of the upper doors allowed
the air to circulate around the
bread, cheese, and fruit stored in
the cupboard between meals. The
carving of the oak is of the highest
quality, a reflection of George
Myers's excellent craftsmanship.
Indeed, Myers included cabinets in
his display at the Mediaeval Court
at the Great Exhibition in 1851
(fig. 144a). The metalwork, by

Hardman, is also of excellent quality. Despite its elaborate decoration, the cabinet maintains Pugin's principles: revealed construction, control of ornament, and overall integrity. On the lower doors, for example, the richly carved ornament is contained within the structural members.

The cabinet was made after the death of Pugin's second wife, Louisa, and before his third marriage. The emblazoned heraldic shields carry, therefore, only his initials, the Welby arms of his mother, and the Pugin arms. Pugin designed one or two other cabinets in this style, but without this degree of decoration. One known today was made at about the same date by George Myers for Henry Sharples house, Oswaldcroft, near Liverpool.

Fig. 144a. Cabinet in Oak with Brass Panels; chromolithograph from Matthew Digby Wyatt's *Industrial Arts of the XIX Century, from the Great Exhibition of 1851* (London, 1853).

Bibliography

Archival material relating to Pugin, his colleagues and clients, may be found in the following collections among others:

The Beinecke Rare Book and Manuscript Library, Yale University

Birmingham Public Reference Library, Birmingham, England (Hardman Archives—Hardman & Company daybooks and Hardman–Pugin correspondence)

HLRO, House of Lords Record Office (Hardman–Pugin correspondence)

The Metropolitan Museum of Art, New York

Magdalen College Archives, Oxford, England (Bloxam–Pugin correspondence)

Minton Archive, Minton Museum, Stoke-on-Trent (Pugin designs)

PRO, Public Record Office, Kew, West London (Commission of Works, papers relating to Pugin's work at the Palace of Westminster)

RIBA, Royal Institute of British Architects (Library, Crace–Pugin correspondence; Drawings Collection)

Saint Mary's College, Oscott

Ushaw College, Durham

Victoria and Albert Museum, London (Pugin diaries, letters, drawings; Earl of Shrewsbury–Pugin correspondence; Crace Archive).

For transcriptions of Pugin's diaries and correspondence, see below, Wedgwood 1977 and idem 1985.

Actes du Colloque International Viollet-le-Duc, Paris 1980. Paris: Nouvelles Editions Latines, 1982.

Aldrich, Megan. *Gothic Revival.* London: Phaidon Press, 1994.

——. "Gothic Architecture Illustrated: The Drawings of Thomas Rickman in New York." *Antiquaries Journal* 65 (1985), pp. 427–33.

Alexander, Boyd. *Life at Fonthill, 1807–1822.* London: R. Hart Davis, 1957.

Altholz, Joseph. *The Liberal Catholic Movement in England.* Montreal; London: Burns & Oates, 1962.

"Architect P. W. Ford, 33 School Street." In *Leading Manufacturers and Merchants of the City of Boston.* Boston, 1885.

Atterbury, Paul, and Clive Wainwright, eds. *Pugin: A Gothic Passion.* New Haven; London: Yale University Press, 1994.

Auzas, Pierre-Marie. *Eugène Viollet-le-Duc, 1814–1879.* Paris: Caisse Nationale des Monuments Historiques et des Sites, 1979.

Beck, G. A., ed. *The English Catholics, 1850–1950.* London: Burns & Oates, 1950.

Belcher, Margaret. *A. W. N. Pugin: An Annotated Critical Bibliography.* London; New York: Mansell Publishing Co., 1987.

Bellaigue, Geoffrey de, and Patricia Kirkham. "George IV and the Furnishing of Windsor Castle." *Furniture History* (1972), pp. 1–34.

Bellenger, Dominic Aidan. *The French Exiled Clergy in the British Isles after 1879.* Bath, Eng.: Downside Abbey, 1986.

Bercé, Françoise. *Les Premiers Travaux de la Commission des Monuments Historiques, 1837–1848.* Paris: A. & J. Picard, 1979.

Bergdoll, Barry. Introduction to *The Foundations of Architecture: Selections from the Dictionnaire Raissoné of Viollet-le-Duc,* New York: Braziller, 1990.

——. *Karl Friedrich Schinkel: An Architecture for Prussia.* New York: Rizzoli, 1994.

——. *Léon Vaudoyer: Historicism in the Age of Industry.* New York: The Architectural History Foundation, 1994.

Bleiler, E. F., ed. *Three Gothic Novels.* New York: Dover Books, 1966.

Bonnet, Jean-Claude, ed. *La Carmagnole des Muses, L'homme de letters et l'artiste dans la Révolution.* Paris; Armand Colin, 1988.

Borger, Hugo, ed. *Der Kölner Dom im Jahrhundert seiner Vollendung.* Exhib. cat. 2 vols. Cologne, Historischen Museen, 1980.

Börsch-Supan, Eva. *Berliner Baukunst nach Schinkel, 1840–1870.* Munich: Prestel, 1977.

Bossaglia, Rossana, ed. *Il Neogotico nel XIX e XX secolo.* vol. 1. Milan: Mazzotta, 1989.

Bossy, John. *The English Catholic Community, 1570–1850.* London: Cambridge University Press, 1975–76.

Brady, W. Mazière. *Annals of the Catholic Hierarchy*. New York: Oxford University Press, 1883.

Bressani, Martin. "Notes on Viollet-le-Duc's Philosophy of History: Dialectics and Technology." *Journal of the Society of Archiectural Historians* 48 (1989), pp. 327–50.

Brisac, Catherine, and Jean-Michel Léniaud. "Adolphe-Napoléon Didron ou les media au service de l'art chrétien." *Revue de l'Art* 77 (1987), pp. 33–42.

Britton, John. *The Architectural Antiquities of Great Britain*. London, 1827.

Brooks, Chris, and Andrew Saint, eds. *The Victorian Church Architecture and Society*. Manchester: Manchester University Press; New York: St. Martin's Press, 1995.

Bullen, J. B. *The Myth of the Renaissance in Nineteenth Century Writing*. Oxford, Eng.,: Clarendon Press, 1994.

Bunting, Bainbridge. *Houses of Boston's Back Bay*. Cambridge, MA: Harvard University Press, 1967.

— and Margaret Henderson Floyd. *Harvard: An Architectural History*. Cambridge, MA: Harvard University Press, 1985.

Byrne, John F. *The Glories of Mary in Boston. A Memorial History of the Church of Our Lady of Perpetual Help, 1871–1921*. Roxbury, MA: Mission Church Press, 1921.

— et al. *History of the Catholic Church in the New England States*. Boston: Hurd & Everts Co., 1899.

Carlyle, Thomas. *Past and Present*. Edited by Richard Altick. New York: New York University Press, 1977.

Chadwick, W. O. *The Victorian Church*. London; New York: Oxford University Press, 1966–70.

Chapman, Ronald. *Father Faber*. London; Westminster [MD]: Newman Press, [1961].

Chard, Chloe, ed. *The Romance of the Forest*. Oxford, Eng.: Oxford University Press, 1986.

Charton, Edouard. *Patria*. Paris, 1846.

Chinnici, J. P. *The English Catholic Enlightenment, John Lingard and the Csalpine Movement, 1870–1850*. Shepherdstown, WV: Patmos Press, 1980.

Choay, Françoise. *L'Allégoire du Patrimoine*. Paris: Seuil, 1992.

Christiansen, Rupert. *Romantic Affinities*. London: The Bodley Head, 1988.

Clark, Kenneth. *The Gothic Revival: An Essay in the History of Taste*. 3rd ed. London: John Murray, 1962.

Cleven, Jean van, ed., *Neogotiek in Belge*. Ghent: Lanoo, 1994.

Clifford, Ann. "John Evans (1847–1923) and Architectural Sculpture in Boston." Masters thesis. Tufts University, Medford, MA, 1992.

Cobbett, William. *A History of the Protestant Reformation in England and Ireland*. Dublin: Balto, 1826.

Cole, Henry, Richard Redgrave, and Owen Jones. *Department of Practical Art: A Catalogue of the Ornamental Art Selected from the Exhibition of the Works of Industry of all Nations in 1851 and Purchased by the Government*. London, 1852.

Colling, James Kellaway. *Art Foliage, for Sculpture and Decoration; with an Analysis of Geometric Form, and Studies from Nature, of Buds, Leaves, Flowers, and Fruit*. London: [published by the author], 1865.

Collard, Frances. *Regency Furniture*. Woodbridge, Eng.: Antique Collectors' Club, 1985.

Colvin, Howard. *A Biographical Dictionary of British Architects, 1600–1840*. London; New York: Facts On File, 1978.

Comparative Designs for the Cathedral of St. John the Divine: Collected Designs, 1889–1891. Boston: Heliotype Printing Co., ca. 1891.

Connolly, S. *Priests and People in pre-Famine Ireland, 1780–1845*. Dublin: Gill and Macmillian; New York: St. Martin's Press, 1982.

Corish, Patrick J., ed. *A History of Irish Catholocism*. Dublin: Gill, 1967.

—. *Maynooth College 1795–1995*. Dublin: Gill and Macmillan, 1994.

Cospéric, Annie. *Blois, la forme d'une ville, étude topographique et monumentale*. Paris: Cahiers de l'Inventaire, 1994.

Countess of Dunraven. *Memorials of Adare*. Oxford, Eng.: [printed for private circulation by Messrs. Parker], 1865.

Crook, J. Mordaunt. *William Burges and the High Victorian Dream*. Chicago: University of Chicago Press, 1981.

Csorba, László, József Sisa, and Zoltán Szalay. *The Hungarian Parliament*. Budapest: Kit Képzömüvészeti Kiadó, 1993.

Curran, Kathleen. "The German Rundbogenstil and Reflections on the American Round-arched Style." *Journal of the Society of Architectural Historians* 47 (December 1988), pp. 351–73.

Dessain, C. S., ed. *Letter and Diaries of J. H. Newman*. London; New York: T. Nelson, 1961–68.

Didron, A. N. "Une cathédrale au concours." *Annales Archéologiques* 16 (1856). Paris: Bureau des Annales Archéologiques, 1844–81.

Dixon, Roger, and Stefan Muthesius. *Victorian Architecture*. 2nd ed. London: Thames and Hudson, 1985.

Downing, A. J. *The Architecture of Country Houses*. 1850. Reprint. New York: Dover Publications, 1969.

——. *A Treatise on the Theory and Practice of Landscape Gardening.* Henry Winthrop Sargent, Supplement to Sixth Edition. New York: A. O. Moore & Co., 1859.

Drüeke, Eberhrd. *Der Maximianstil, Zum Stilbergriff der Architektur im 19. Jahrhundert.* Mittenwald: Mäander, 1981.

Duffy, Eamon. *Challoner and His Church: A Catholic Bishop in Georgian England.* London: Darton, Longman & Todd, 1981.

Eastlake, Charles. *A History of the Gothic Revival.* 1872. Reprint. Foreword and text by J. M. Crook. Leicester, Eng.: Leicester University Press, 1971; Deposit, NY: American Life Foundation, 1975.

Escoffier, Maurice. *Le Mouvement Romantique 1788–1850: essai de bibliographie synchronique et méthodique.* Paris: Maison du Bibliophile, 1934.

Ferrey, Benjamin. *Recollections of A. W. N Pugin and his father Augustus Pugin.* 1861. Reprint. Appendix by E. Sheridan Purcell; introduction and index by Clive and Jane Wainwright. London: Scolar Press, 1978.

Flood, W. H. Grattan. *History of Enniscorthy and its vicinity.* Enniscorthy, Ireland, 1889.

——. *History of the Diocese of Ferns.* Waterford, Ireland: Donwey, 1916.

Floyd, Margaret Henderson. "A Terra-Cotta Cornerstone for Copley Square: Museum of Fine Arts, Boston, by Sturgis and Brigham (1870–1876)." *Journal of the Society of Architectural Historians* 34 (December 1973): 83–103.

Foster, R. F. *Modern Ireland 1600–1972.* London: Penguin Books, 1989 [ca. 1988].

Fothergill, Brian. *Nicholas Wiseman.* London: Faber and Faber, 1963.

Frankl, Paul. *The Gothic: Literary Sources and Interpretation through Eight Centuries.* Princeton: Princeton University Press, 1960.

Friedrich von Schmidt (1825–1891), Ein gothischer Rationalist. Exhib. cat. Vienna: Historisches Museum der Stadt, 1991.

Garnett, J., and Matthew, C., eds. *Revival and Religion Since 1700.* London: The Hambledon Press, 1993.

The Georgian Group. *A Gothick Symposium.* London: The Georgian Group, 1983.

Germann, George. *Gothic Revival in Europe and Britain: Sources, Influences and Ideas.* Translated by Gerald Onn. London: Lund Humphries; Cambridge, MA: MIT Press, 1972.

Gilley, Sheridan. "The Roman Catholic Mission to the London Irish, 1840–1860." *Recusant History* 10 (1969), pp. 123–45.

Gilman, Arthur Delavan. "Architecture in the United States." *North American Review* 58 (April 1844), pp. 436–80.

Goodhart-Rendel, H. S. *English Architecture Since the Regency: An Interpretation.* 1953. Reprint. Foreword by Alan Powers. London: Constable, 1988.

Gwynn, Denis. *Lord Shrewsbury, Pugin, and the Catholic Revival.* London: Hollis and Carter, 1946.

Hahn, August. *Der Maximilianstil in München, Programm und Verwirklichung.* Munich: Heinz Moos Verlag, 1982.

Hersey, G. L. *High Victorian Gothic: A Study in Associationism.* Baltimore: Johns Hopkins University Press, 1972.

Hill, Rosemary. "Bankers, Bawds and Beau Monde." *Country Life* (November 3, 1994), pp. 64–67.

Hitchcock, H.-R. *Early Victorian Architecture in Britain.* 1954. 2 vols. Reprint. New York: Da Capo Press, 1972.

Hobsbawn, Eric J. *The Age of Revolution 1789–1848.* London: Weidenfeld & Nicolson, 1962.

Holmes, Derek. *More Roman than Rome: English Catholicism in the Nineteenth Century.* London: Burns & Oates, 1978.

—— and Bernard Bickers. *A Short History of the Catholic Church.* London: Burns & Oates, 1992.

Honour, Hugh. *Romanticism.* Harmondsworth, Eng.: Penguin Books, 1979.

House of Commons. *Detailed Account of Expenditure of the Sum of £30,000 granted for the putting of Maynooth College in repair: total amount of the grant, 1846–1850.* London: House of Commons, 1851.

Hunt, John Dixon. *William Kent: Landscape Garden Designer.* London, 1987.

In what style should we build?: the German debate on architectural style. Introduction and translation by Wolfgang Hermann. Santa Monica: The Getty Center for the History of Art and the Humanities, 1992.

Jones, Stephen. Introduction to *Ackermann's Regency Furniture and Interiors.* Marlborough, Eng.: Crowood Press, 1984.

Jordy, William H., and Ralph Coe, eds. *American Architecture and Other Writings by Montgomery Schuyler.* Cambridge, MA: Harvard University Press, 1961.

—— and Christopher P. Monkhouse, eds. *Buildings on Paper: Rhode Island Architectural Drawings 1825–1945.* Providence: Brown University, Rhode Island Historical Society, and the Rhode Island School of Design, 1982.

Ker, Ian. *John Henry Newman.* Oxford, Eng.: Clarendon Press, 1988.

Koch, Georg Friedrich. "Karl Friedrich Schinkel und die Architektur des Mittelalters." *Zeitschrift für Kunstgeschichte* 29 (1966), pp. 177–222.

——. "Schinkels architektonische Entwürfe im gotischen Stil 1810–1815." *Zeitschrift für Kunstgeschichte* 32 (1969), pp. 262–316.

Krim, Arthur J. "Francis Peabody and Gothic Salem." *Peabody Essex Museum Collections* 130, no. 1 (January 1994), pp. 18–35.

Kugler, Franz. *Vorlesung über die Systeme des Kirchenbaues, gehalten am 4. März 1843 im wissenschaftlichen Verein zu Berlin von F. Kugler.* 2nd ed. Berlin: Ernst & Korn, 1852.

Lafever, Minard. *The Modern Builder's Guide.* Reprint. New York: Dover Publications, 1969.

Lamb, Martha J. *The Homes of America.* New York: D. Appleton, 1879.

Larkin, Emmet. "Economic Growth, Capital Investment and the Roman Catholic Church in Nineteenth-century Ireland." *American Historical Review* 82 (1969), pp. 852–884.

Larson, Leslie. "Boston Churches Designed by Patrick Charles Keely (1816–1896)." Tour Notes. National Trust for Historic Preservation, Boston, October 26, 1994.

Laroche, Claude. *Paul Abadie, architecte, 1812–1884.* Paris: Réunion des Musées Nationaux, 1988.

Lassus, Jean-Baptiste. "De l'Art et Archéologie," *Annales Archéologiques* 2 (1845). Paris: Bureau des Annales Archéologiques, 1844–81.

——. *Réaction de l'Académie des Beaux-Arts contre l'art gothique.* Paris, 1846.

Lenoir, Albert, and Léon Vaudoyer. "Etudes de l'Architecture en France." *Magasin Pittoresque* 12 (1844).

Léon, Paul. *La Vie des Monuments Français.* Paris: A. & J. Picard, 1951.

Leniaud, Jean Michel. *Jean Baptiste Lassus (1807–1857) ou le temps retrouvé des cathédrales.* Paris; Geneva: Arts et Métiers Graphiques, 1980.

——. *L'Administration des cultes pendant la période concordataire.* Paris: Nouvelles Editions latines, ca. 1988.

——. *Les Cathédral au XIXe siècle.* Paris: Economica, 1993.

Lewis, Michael. *The Politics of the German Gothic Revival: Auguste Reichensperger.* New York: The Architectural History Foundation, 1993.

Lewis, W. S. "The Genesis of Strawberry Hill." *Metropolitan Museum Studies* 5 (1934–36), pp. 57–92.

Loudon, J. C. *An Encyclopaedia of Cottage, Farm and Villa Architecture.* New York: R. Worthington, 1833.

Loyer, François, and Hélène Guéné. *L'Eglise, l'Etat et les Architects, Rennes, 1870–1940.* Paris: Norma, 1995.

Macaulay, James. *The Gothic Revival, 1745–1845.* Glasgow: Blackie and Sons, 1975.

Macleod, Robert. *Style and Society.* London: Routledge, 1971.

Maeyer, Jan de. *Sint-Lucasscholen en de neogotiek 162–1914* Belgium: Universitaire Pers Leuven, 1988.

Marrinan, Michael. *Painting Politics for Louis Philippe.* New Haven: Yale University Press, 1988.

Mathew, David. *Catholicism in England, 1535–1935.* London / New York: Longman, Green and Co., 1936.

McCarthy, J. J. *Suggestions on the arrangements and characteristics of Parish churches.* Dublin, 1851.

McCarthy, Michael. *The Origins of the Gothic Revival.* New Haven; London: Yale University Press, 1987.

McLachlan, James. *American Boarding Schools: A Historical Study.* New York: Scribner, 1970.

Meara, David. *Victorian Memorial Brasses.* Boston; London: Routledge and K. Paul, 1983.

——. *A. W. N. Pugin and the Revival of Memorial Brasses.* London / New York: Mansell, 1991.

Mews, Stuart, ed. *Modern Religious Rebels.* London: Epworth Press, 1993.

Middleton, Robin. "Viollet-le-Ducksy?" *Architectural Design* 49 (1970), pp. 67–68.

——. "Viollet le Duc's influence in nineteenth-century England." *Art History* 4, no. 2 (1981), p. 206.

——. "The Rationalist Interpretations of Léonce Reynaud and Viollet-le-Duc," *AA Files* 11 (1986), pp. 29–48.

——, ed. *The Beaux-Arts and Nineteenth-Century French Architecture.* London; Cambridge, MA: MIT Press, 1982.

—— and David Watkin. *Neoclassical and Nineteenth Century Architecture.* New York: Rizzoli, 1987.

Morgan, William. *The Almighty Wall: The Architecture of Henry Vaughan.* New York; Cambridge, MA: The Architectural History Foundation and MIT Press, 1983.

Mozley, Anne, ed. *Letters of the Revd. J. B. Mozley, D. D.* London: Longmans, Green, 1885.

Muthesius, Stefan. *The High Victorian Movement in Architecture.* London: Routledge and Degan Paul, 1972.

Newman, John. *The Buildings of England: North East and East Kent.* Harmondsworth, Eng.: Penguin Books Ltd., 1976.

Newman, John Henry. *Sermons Preached on Various Occasions.* London, 1857.

Nora, Pierre, ed. *Les Lieux de Mémoire: La Nation*. Paris: Gallimard, 1986.

Norman, Charles. *A new Parallel of the Orders of architecture, according to the Greeks and Romans, and modern architects. With original plates drawn and engraved by Charles Normand. With the Text translated and two additional plates by Augustus Pugin*. London, 1829.

Norman, Edward. *The English Catholic Church in the Nineteenth Century*. Oxford, Eng.: Clarendon Press, 1984.

O'Caoimh, Tomas. "Killarney Cathedral." *Irish Heritage Series* 66 (Dublin, 1990).

O'Connell, Lauren M. "A Rational, National Architecture: Viollet-le-Duc's Modest Proposal for Russia." *Journal of the Society of Architectural Historians* 52 (1993), pp. 436–52.

O'Donnell, Roderick. "Catholic church architecture in Great Britain and Ireland." Ph.D. thesis. Cambridge University, 1983.

——. "A Note of Baroque Splendour: New-Classical Catholic Churches in Dublin." *Country Life* 169 (May 1981), pp. 1288–89.

——. "Roman Reflections on the Liffey: Classical Catholic Churches in Victorian Dublin." *Country Life* 176 (July 1984), pp. 52–53.

Oliver, Richard. *Bertram Grosvenor Goodhue*. New York and Cambridge, MA: The Architectural History Foundation and MIT Press, 1985.

The Parish of the Advent in the City of Boston. A History of One Hundred Years, 1844–1944. Boston: Parish of the Advent, 1944.

Patrick, J. "Newman, Pugin, & Gothic." *Victorian Studies* (Winter 1981).

Pawley, Margaret. *Faith and Family: The Life and Circle of Ambrose Phillipps de Lisle*. Norwich, Eng.: Canterbury Press, 1993.

Pearlman, Jonathan N. "The Architecture of George Minot Dexter: Link from Bulfinch to the Back Bay." Honors Thesis. Medford, MA: Tufts University, 1980. Contains listing of drawings in the George M. Dexter Collection, Boston Athenaeum, Boston, MA.

Peck, Amelia, ed. *Alexander Jackson Davis, American Architect 1803–1892*. Exhib. cat. New York: Metropolitan Museum of New York and Rizzoli Books, 1992.

Perry, William Stevens. *The History of the American Episcopal Church, 1587–1883*. 2 vols. Boston: James R. Osgood & Co., 1885.

Pevsner, Nikolaus. *The Buildings of England: Buckinghamshire* 2nd ed. by Elizabeth Williamson. Harmondsworth, Eng.: Penguin Books Ltd., 1994.

Pierson, William H. *American Buildings and Their Architects. Technology and the Picturesque, the Corporate and the Early Gothic Styles*. Garden City, NY: Doubleday & Company, Inc., 1978.

——. "Richard Upjohn and the American Rundbogenstil." *Winterthur Portfolio* 21 (Winter 1986), pp. 223–42.

Plunkett, Count. "James Cavanah Murphy." *The Irish Builder and Engineer* 51 (May 15, 1909), pp. 295–97.

Pons, Jacques. "Félix-Jacques Duban: Architecte du gouvernement 1797–1870." Thesis. École Nationale des Chartres, France, 1985.

Port, M. H., ed. *The Houses of Parliament*. New Haven; London: Yale University Press, 1976.

Pugin, Auguste Charles. *Pugin's Gothic Ornament*. 1828–31. Reprint. New York: Dover Publications, 1987.

——. *Gothische Ornamente. Einzelheiten der Berühmtesten Baudenkmäler Des Mittelalters in Frankreich und England. Aufgenommen und gezeichnet von A. Pugin, Architekt*. Berlin; New York: Bruno Hessling, ca. 1897.

Pugin, Augustus Welby Northmore. *Contrasts, or a Parallel between the Noble Edifices of the Middle Ages and Corresponding Buildings Showing the Present Decay of Taste*. London: [A. W. N. Pugin], 1836.

——. *An Apology for a Work Entitled Contrasts: Being a Defence of the Assertions Advanced in That Publication Against the Various Attacks Lately Made Upon It*. Birmingham, England: [A. W. N. Pugin], 1837.

——. "West Front of Rouen Cathedral." *The London and Dublin Orthodox Journal of Useful Knowledge* 6 (February 17, 1838), p. 97.

——. "Lectures on Ecclesiastical Architecture, delivered to the students of St Mary's College at Oscott, by A. W. Pugin, Professor of Ecclesiastical Antiquities in that College. Lecture the Third." *Catholic Magazine* 3 (1839), p. 18.

——. *The True Principles of Pointed or Christian Architecture: set forth in two lectures delivered at St Marie's Oscott*. 1841. Reprint. New York: St. Martin's Press, 1973.

——. *An Apology for the Revival of Christian Architecture in England*. London, 1843.

——. *The Present State of Ecclesiastical Architecture in England*. London, 1843.

——. *The Glossary of Ecclesiastical Ornament and Costume*. London: [A. W. N. Pugin], 1844.

——. *Floriated Ornament*. London: H. G. Bohn, 1849.

——. *Les Vrais Principes de l'Architecture Ogivale ou Chrétienne, avec des remarques sur leur renaissance au temps actuel.* Bruges: T. H. King, 1850.

——. ["Notes for an unfinished autobiography."] Manuscript. Inventory no. L.5204-1969. London: Victoria & Albert Museum, n.d.

Pugin, Edward Welby. *Who was the Architect of the Houses of Parliament?* London, 1867.

Purcell, E. S. *Life and Letters of Ambrose Phillipps de Lisle.* London, 1900.

Réau, Louis. *Histoire du Vandalisme: les monuments detruits de l'art français.* 1958. Reprint. Paris: R. Lafont, 1994.

Reilly, A. J. *Fr. John Murphy Famine Priest.* Dublin: Clonmore and Reynolds, ca. 1963.

A Report by the Victoria & Albert Museum concerning the Furniture in the House of Lords. London: Victoria & Albert Museum, 1974.

Reynolds, John S. "Alfred Reynolds and the Block Process." *Journal of the Tiles & Architectural Ceramics Society* 5 (1994), pp. 20–26.

Richardson, Douglas Scott. *Gothic Revival Architecture in Ireland.* 2 vols. New York: Garland Publishing Co., 1983.

Rickman, Thomas. *An Attempt to Discriminate the Styles of English Architecture.* 4th ed. London, 1835.

Robinson, John Martin. *The Wyatts: An Architectural Dynasty.* Oxford, Eng.: Oxford University Press, 1979.

Robson-Scott, W. D. *The Literary Background of the Gothic Revival in Germany.* Oxford, Eng.: Clarendon Press, 1965.

Rowan, Alistair, ed. *North West Ulster.* The Buildings of Ireland. Harmondsworth, Eng.; New York: Penguin Books Ltd., 1977.

——. *North Leinster.* The Buildings of Ireland. Harmondsworth, Eng.; New York: Penguin Books Ltd., 1992.

Ruskin, John. *The Poetry of Architecture.* London, 1839.

[——]. "Samuel Prout." *The Art Journal* 11 (1849), p. 77.

——. *The Stones of Venice.* 3 vols. London: Smith, Elder, 1851–53.

Rutter, John. *Delineations of Fonthill and Its Abbey.* London, 1823.

Saint, Andrew. *Richard Norman Shaw.* London; New Haven: Yale University Press, 1976.

Schorske, Carl E. *Fin-de-Siècle Vienna, Politics and Culture.* New York: Random House, 1981.

Semper, Gottfried. *The Four Elements of Architecture.* Translated by Mallgrave and Herrmann. Cambridge, Eng.; New York: Cambridge University Press, 1989.

Shand-Tucci, Douglass. *Boston Bohemia 1881–1900.* Ralph Adams Cram: Life & Architecture, vol. 1. Amherst, MA: University of Massachusetts Press, 1995.

——. *Church Building in Boston.* Boston: Dorchester Savings Bank, 1974.

Sheehy, Jeanne. *J. J. McCarthy and the Irish Gothic Revival.* Belfast, Ireland: UAHS, 1977.

Sisa, József. "Steindl, Schulek und Schulcz—Drei ungarische Schüler des Wiener Dombaumeisters Friedrich von Schmidt." *Mitteilungen der Gesellschaft für Vergleichende Kunstforschung in Wien* 37 (Sept. 1985), pp. 1–8.

Smith, R. J. *The Gothic Bequest: Medieval Institutions in British Thought, 1688–1863.* Cambridge, Eng.; New York: Cambridge University Place, 1987.

Southey, Robert. *Sir Thomas More.* London: J. Murray, 1829.

Spencer-Silver, Patricia. *Pugin's Builder: The Life and Work of George Myers.* Hull, Eng.: Hull University Press, 1993.

Stanton, Phoebe. *The Gothic Revival and American Church Architecture.* Baltimore: Johns Hopkins Press, 1968.

——. *Pugin.* London: Thames and Hudson, 1971.

Steegman, John. *Victorian Taste.* London: T. Nelson, 1970.

Steiner, Frances H. *French Iron Architecture* Ann Arbor, MI: UMI Research Press, 1984.

Street, G. E. "On the revival of the ancient style of domestic architecture." *The Ecclesiologist* 14 (1853), p. 76.

Sturgis, John Hubbard. "Sketch of the Church of the Advent, Boston." *American Architect and Building News* 1 (May 27, 1876).

Sullivan, James S., ed. *A Graphic, Historical, and Pictorial Account of the Catholic Church of New England Archdiocese of Boston.* Boston; Portland: Illustrated Publishing Co., 1895.

Summerson, John. *Georgian London: An Architectursal Study.* Rev. ed. London; Baltimore: Penguin Books Ltd., 1962.

Thackeray, William Makepeace. *The Irish Sketchbook of 1842.* 1873 ed. London: Chapman & Hall, 1843.

Thomas, Lately. *A Pride of Lions: The Astor Orphans, The Chanler Chronicle.* New York: William Morrow & Company, Inc., 1971.

Thompson, J. H. "History of Oscott College." *The Oscottian* 2 (1931).

Thompson, Paul. *William Butterfield.* London: Routledge and K. Paul, 1971.

Trappes-Lomax, Michael. *Pugin: A Mediaeval Victorian.* London: Sheed and Ward, 1932.

Turner, Paul Venable. *Campus. An American Planning Tradition.* New York; Cambridge, MA: The Architectural History Foundation and MIT Press: 1984, 1990.

Upjohn, Everard M. *Richard Upjohn. Architect and Churchman.* New York: Da Capo Press, 1968.

Vandame, Chanoine H. *Iconographie de la Basilique Notre-Dame de la Treille à Lille.* Lille, 1906.

Viollet-le-Duc, Eugène-Emmanuel. "Un mot sur l'architecture en 1852." *Revue Générale de l'Architecture de l'Architecture* 10 (1852), pp. 371–79.

——. *Dictionnaire raisonné de l'architecture française du XIe au XVIe siècle.* 10 vols. Paris: B. Bance [etc.], 1854–68.

——. *L'Art russe: ses origines, ses éléments constitutifs, son apogée, son avenir.* Paris, 1877.

Viollet-le-Duc. Paris: Réunion des musées nationaux, 1980,

Vardy, John. *Some Designs of Mr Inigo Jones and Mr William Kent.* London, 1744.

Wainwright, Clive. "A. W. N. Pugin's Early Furniture." *The Connoisseur* 191 (1976), pp. 3–11.

——. *The Romantic Interior: The British Collector at Home, 1750–1850.* New Haven and London: Yale University Press, 1989.

——. "Some Nineteenth Century American Furniture in the Collection of the Victoria & Albert Museum." *Nineteenth Century* 11, nos. 1–2 (1992).

——. "Principles true and false: Pugin and the foundation of the Museum of Manufactures." *The Burlington Magazine* 136, no. 1095 (1994), pp. 357–364.

Wallis, G. *Recent Progress in Design as applied to Manufacture.* London, 1856.

Waquet, Françoise. *Les fêtes royales sous la restauration ou l'ancien regime retrouvé.* Paris: Arts et Metiers Graphiques, 1981.

Ward, Bernard. *The Sequel to Catholic Emanicipation.* London and New York: Longmans, Green and Co., 1915.

Ward, Wilfred. *William George Ward and the Catholic Revival.* London; New York: Longmans, Green and Co., 1893.

Wedgwood, Alexandra. *The Buildings of England: London 2, South.* Harmondsworth, Eng.: Penguin Books Ltd., 1983.

——. *Catalogue of the Royal Institute of British Architects Drawings Collection: The Pugin Family.* London: RIBA, 1977.

——. *Catalogue of the Architectural Drawings in the Victoria and Albert Museum: A. W. N. Pugin and the Pugin Family.* London: Victoria & Albert Museum, 1985.

——, ed. "Pugin in his Home: A Memoir by J. H. Powell." *Architectural History* 31 (1988), pp. 171–201.

Williams, Jeremy. *A Companion Guide to Architecture in Ireland, 1837–1921.* Dublin: Irish Academic Press, 1994.

Wilson, Michael I. *William Kent: Architect, Designer, Painter, Gardener, 1685–1748.* Boston; London: Routledge & K. Paul, 1984.

Wilton-Ely, John. "The Genesis and Evolution of Fonthill Abbey." *Architectural History* 23 (1980), pp. 40–51.

Winsor, Justin, ed. *The Memorial History of Boston.* 4 vols. Boston: James R. Osgood & Co., 1881.

Wiseman, Nicholas. *The Religious and Social Position of Catholics in England.* London, 1864.

Wood, Florence. *Memories of William Halsey Wood.* Philadelphia: [Mrs. William Halsey Wood], c. 1937.

Wright, John. *Some Notable Altars in the Church of England and the American Episcopal Church.* New York: Macmillan Company, 1908.

Zaitzevsky, Cynthia. *Frederick Law Olmsted and the Boston Park System.* Cambridge, MA: Harvard University Press, Belknap Press, 1982.

Zanten, David van. *Building Paris.* Cambridge, Eng.; New York: Cambridge University Press, 1994.

Index

Photocredits

Photographs of objects in the exhibition were taken by Graham Miller, with the exception of those listed below. Other photographs were provided by the photographic department of the Victoria & Albert Museum and by other institutions and private collections who have kindly granted permission to reproduce them herein.

Archives, Roman Catholic Archdiocese of Boston: fig. 10-7.
Inge Altena: cat. nos. 34-45.
Dirk Bakker, The Detroit Institute of Arts: cat. no. 121.
Beaver Photography: 2-13, 8-14, cat. fig. 111a.
H. Blairman: cat. nos. 77, 128.
Bridgman Art Library: fig. 1-2 (Giraudon), 1-4, 1-7.
A. C. Cooper Ltd.: cat. no. 13.
M. H. Floyd: fig. 10-13.
George Garbutt: cat. nos. 1, 2, 83-90; cat. figs. 83c.
Robert Hashimoto: cat. no. 70.
Haslam & Whiteway: cat. nos. 123, 127, 141.
Richard Holt: cat. nos. 6, 46, 56, 117, 119, 134-136; cat. figs. 69d, 144a.
Carl Kaufman: cat. nos. 21, 23, 25, 26, 27, 28, 78; cat. fig. 22a.
A. F. Kersting: fig. 1-2.
Calder Loth: fig. 10-3.
Graham Miller: figs. 2-14, 6-3, 6-4, 6-5, 6-8, 6-17, 7-12, 9-15–9-18, 9-22, cat. figs. 55b, 65b, 108a.
National Monuments Record, Royal Commission on the Historical Monuments of England: figs. 1-3, 1-14, 6-2, 6-6, 6-11, 6-12, 6-15, 6-19, 6-20, 6-21, 6-22, 9-12, 9-13.
National Monuments Record of Scotland, Royal Commission on the Ancient and Historical Monuments of Scotland: fig. 9-9.
J. N. Pearlman: figs. 10-1, 10-11, 10-14, 10-16.
Royal Institute of British Architects: cat. fig. 29a.
William K. Sacco: figs. 1-5, 1-6, cat. nos. 3, 4, 5; cat. figs. 3a, 4a.
Society for the Preservation of New England Antiquities: fig. 10-5.